Affective Narratology

Frontiers of Narrative

SERIES EDITOR

David Herman *Ohio State University*

Affective
Narratology

The Emotional Structure of Stories

PATRICK COLM HOGAN

University of Nebraska Press | Lincoln and London

Parts of the introduction and chapter 1, "The Brain
in Love," were originally published as "The Brain in
Love: A Case Study in Cognitive Neuroscience and
Literary Theory" in *Journal of Literary Theory* 1.2
(2007): 339–55. An earlier version of part of the intro-
duction appeared as "A Passion for Plot: Prolegomena
to Affective Narratology" in *symplokē* 18.1–2 (2011).
Parts of chapters 3 and 4 were originally published as
"Narrative Universals, National Sacrifice, and *Dou E
Yuan*" in *Ex/Change* 12 (2005): 18–25.

Library of Congress Cataloging-in-Publication Data
Hogan, Patrick Colm.
Affective narratology : the emotional structure
of stories / Patrick Colm Hogan.
p.   cm.—(Frontiers of narrative)
Includes bibliographical references and index.
ISBN 978-0-8032-3002-6 (cloth: alk. paper)
1. Discourse analysis, Narrative. 2. Emotions in
literature. 3. Narration (Rhetoric). I. Title.
P302.7.H64 2011
808'.036—dc22
2011015514

Set in Minion Pro by Bob Reitz.
Designed by A. Shahan.

For my teachers, including Sister James Louise, Miss Phelan, Mrs. Larsen, Mr. Schmertz, Father Ralph, Brother James, Joe Kramer, John Craig, Pat Conley, Mr. Azzara, Father Renner, Father Ong, Dan Dahlstrom, Jim Friedman, Joseph Demartini, James Degnan, Northrop Frye, Marshall McLuhan, Donald Davidson, Jim McCawley, Murray Schwartz, Irving Massey, and Norman Holland.

Contents

Acknowledgments

An earlier version of the discussion of *The Injustice Done to Tou Ngo* was published as "Narrative Universals, National Sacrifice, and *Dou E Yuan*" in *Ex/Change* (Hong Kong) 12 (2005): 18–25. I am grateful to the editor, Zhang Longxi, for very helpful comments and suggestions on an earlier draft of that essay. Parts of the introduction and chapter 1 appeared previously in "The Brain in Love: A Case Study in Cognitive Neuroscience and Literary Theory," *Journal of Literary Theory* 1.2 (2007): 339–55. An earlier version of part of the introduction appeared as "A Passion for Plot: Prolegomena to Affective Narratology" in *symplokē* 18.1–2 (2011).

Ellen Litman kindly checked some passages in the Russian of *Anna Karenina*. Lalita Pandit helped greatly with difficult points in the Urdu of *Meenaxi* and the Sanskrit of *Abhijñānaśākuntalam*. David Conrad provided invaluable assistance on the Son-Jara epic, giving me access to unpublished parts of Condé's version (in Conrad's own translation) and patiently answering my questions about difficult parts of Condé's text. I am very grateful to all three. I am also grateful to three readers for the University of Nebraska Press and to David Herman, who read the two different versions of the manuscript with great care and provided very helpful comments. Finally, I wish to thank Kristen Elias Rowley of the University of Nebraska Press for her careful handling of the manuscript, as well as Ann Baker, my production editor, and Lona Dearmont, who copyedited the manuscript.

Introduction
A Passion for Plot

Human beings have a passion for plots. Stories are shared in every society, in every age, and in every social context, from intimate personal interactions to impersonal social gatherings. This passion for plots is bound up with the passion of plots, the ways in which stories manifest feelings on the part of authors and characters, as well as the passion from plots, the ways stories provoke feelings in readers or listeners. Less obviously, but no less importantly, the structure of stories and even the definition of the constituents of stories are inseparable from passion as well. The goal of this book is to explore this last aspect of passion and plots—the ways in which, so to speak, emotions make stories.

Over the last two decades, there has been an enormous increase in attention to emotion as a crucial aspect of human thought and action. This attention has spanned a range of disciplines, prominently including the fields gathered together under the rubric of *cognitive science*—thus parts of psychology, neuroscience, philosophy, anthropology, and so on. Narratology has perhaps been the area of literary study most closely connected with cognitive science. However, current research on emotion has had only limited impact on narrative theory. Of course, everyone recognizes that emotion is important in stories, and theorists of narrative usually have some place for emotion in their work. However, narratological treatments of emotion have on the whole been relatively undeveloped, at least in comparison with other aspects of narrative theory.

Given recent advances in research on emotion, it seems clear that any theory of narrative would benefit from a more fully elaborated treatment of emotion based on this research. In the following pages, however, I develop a stronger claim. Specifically, my contention is that story structures are fundamentally shaped and oriented by our emotion systems. Of course, other neurocognitive systems play a role in the production and reception of narrative—perceptual systems, long-term and working memory systems, language systems. But in the view developed here, the distinctive aspects of stories are to a great extent the product of emotion systems.

The point holds most obviously for goals that define the large trajectories of action in stories. That may seem straightforward. But in fact it is not intuitively obvious just what emotion systems there are and just how they generate goals, in combination or separately. For example, it may seem that the system for sexual desire readily generates narratives.[1] Narratives based on purely sexual goal pursuit—romantic love without attachment—do occur cross-culturally. But they are impoverished in development, thus rarer than one might anticipate, for specifiable emotional reasons (as we discuss in chapter 4). As this suggests, emotion systems govern not only goals but also the ways in which stories are developed, what sorts of things protagonists do or encounter, how trajectories of goal pursuit are initiated, what counts as a resolution, and so on. In consequence, emotion systems define the standard features of all stories, as well as cross-culturally recurring clusters of features in universal genres (romantic, heroic, and so on). Beyond—or perhaps below—these larger structures, the determination of story organization by emotion systems goes all the way down to the level of events and incidents, pervading the way in which we make causal attributions. Far from being straightforward, this is highly counterintuitive, given our usual folk theories of emotion. As all this indicates, in order to formulate a systematic theoretical account of stories, we need to turn first of all to affective neuroscience and related fields of study.

Before going on, it is valuable to get a preliminary sense of what is involved in emotion—what emotion is, how it operates, and so on. I therefore briefly sketch an outline of emotion, anticipating the fuller development found in chapter 1. I then turn to the place of emotion in narrative theory, in order to present some context for the present work. After this, I outline the chapter structure of the book. In the course of the following chapters, I often consider ideology as an important factor in both emotion and narrative. In order to orient the reader somewhat with respect to this aspect, I conclude this introduction with some comments on ideology.

Some Preliminary Notes on Emotion

The most basic elements of an emotional experience are the following. First, there are eliciting conditions. These are the situations, occurrences, and properties to which we are sensitive in emotional experience and that serve to activate emotion systems. Second, there are expressive outcomes. These are the manifestations of an emotion that mark the subject as experiencing an emotion. They range from vocalizations (e.g., sobs) to facial gestures (e.g., smiles) to postural changes to perspiration. A third component of emotion is actional response or what one does in reaction to the situation. This action may be undertaken to maintain a desirable situation or to alter an aversive situation. For example, when faced with a threatening stranger, I might look for an escape route and begin to run away. A fourth component is the phenomenological tone, or just what the emotion feels like. This is important in part because it motivates us to sustain or change the situation by making us experience the situation as desirable or aversive. The phenomenological tone is often understood as the subjective experience of a further component, physiological outcomes, such as increases in respiration.[2] (We might isolate other components as well. However, these will suffice for present purposes.)

A remarkable fact about expressive outcomes is that they are also eliciting conditions for emotion. Depending upon the nature of the emotion and its orientation, an emotional expression may affect us in a parallel or a complementary way. If I am out on a dark night in the woods and my companion gasps in fear, I will feel fear—a parallel emotion triggered by my companion's emotion expression. When I meet a stranger in a dark alley and he looks at me with anger, I am also likely to feel fear, but in this case the fear will be a complementary emotion triggered by the expression of anger. Our emotional response to emotional expressions appears to be largely innate. Indeed, it is arguable that we do not need to posit much else in the way of innate emotional triggers. Our emotional sensitivity to the emotional expressions of others serves to guide us in just what we should fear, what should make us happy, and so on. For example, for some time it was thought that fear of snakes is innate in monkeys. In fact, it may be that it is not innate per se. Rather, the fear of snakes is in effect acquired by monkeys when at a young age they experience their mother's fear of snakes (see Damasio *Looking* 47). It may still be that there is an innate fear-related sensitivity to snakes, making this fear particularly easy to acquire. But whether or not it is sufficient, the experience of someone else's fear expression seems to be necessary in this case.

As this suggests, the eliciting conditions for emotion bear, first of all, on innate feature sensitivities or triggers—perhaps most importantly, other people's expressions of emotion. Thus, faces expressing fear tend to make us fearful. More generally, there are genetic instructions that, through complex interactions with one another and the environment, produce emotion systems. In part, the genetic instructions lead to the formation of feature sensitivities, thus emotion triggers. However, there are variables here. First, there are genetic instructions that require certain sorts of experience to generate feature sensitivities and genetic instructions that do not.[3] The experientially unconstrained genetic instructions define our (genetically specified) emotion triggers. (I have already mentioned sensitivity to emotion expressions. For other examples, see Lewis "Emergence" 266–67.)

These genetically specified sensitivities are very complex, and despite their genetic fixity, may be manifest in diverse ways. For example, I suspect that our emotional response to facial beauty is genetically fixed as a graded match between a prototype and an experience. (This is a technical way of putting the fact that we find the most beautiful facial features to be, roughly, the most statistically average features [see Langlois and Roggman].) However, the prototype is not genetically fixed—only the process for generating the prototype is fixed. Specifically, it is generated by weighted averaging over experiences. Thus the experience of different faces (in, say, Kenya and Norway) will produce different prototypes, thus different emotion manifestations, despite the genetic fixity of the trigger.

Among triggers that are not fully genetically specified—thus among triggers that require some specific sorts of experience—another parameter enters. This leads to a further division in types of feature sensitivity. We may refer to this as a division between developmentally specified or "critical period" triggers and episodic triggers.

It is well established that genetic instructions leave certain specifications open to experience. These instructions often bear on particular points in development. There is "experience-dependent plasticity in . . . cortical connections, functional architecture, and receptive field properties." These "continue to be refined" through "experience-dependent regulation for a limited period . . . known as the *critical period*" (Gilbert 598). For example, there is a critical period for language acquisition in early childhood. One does not acquire language in the same way or with the same ease and fluency if the learning takes place after this period. The point is not confined to language. As Jenkins notes, "It is clear that, quite apart from language, the development of systems for memory, perception, and attention all must have their own innate programs and developmental windows [thus, critical periods] under genetic control" (Jenkins 219). For example, we find similar phenomena in the projection of facial neurons first to the cerebellum, then to the thalamus, then to somatosensory cortex, with a critical period at each stage of projection (see O'Leary, Ruff, and Dyck). This suggests that critical periods are a matter of patterned activities in newly maturing or, more generally, what might be called "experience enabled" systems. In other words, a particular system develops to a point where it can be affected by relevant sorts of experience. The initial phase of its operation defines the critical period. In the case of language, for example, the various component systems that subserve language must develop to a certain state before, say, syntactic processing may begin. At this point, early experiences may serve to limit further developments. In a Chomskyan framework, for example, experiences would set parameters sequentially, beginning with parameters determining very broad relations between morphology and syntax (see Baker).

It seems clear that the same general point holds for certain aspects of emotion. Thus it is probably the case that there are early maturational periods in which particular experiences specify certain eliciting conditions for emotion (thus emotion triggers) or define aspects of expressive or actional outcomes. For example, early childhood experiences—including the experience of "display of disgust in others" (Rozin, Haidt, and McCauley "Disgust" [2000], 646)—may be critical for the development of disgust. Moreover, considerable research in attachment theory indicates that there is a critical period for the development of trust (see, for example, Schore and citations).

Finally, what I have just referred to as "episodic" triggers form *emotional memories*. Emotional memories, like skills memories—such as how to ride a bicycle—are "implicit" memories. Thus, when activated they do not lead us to think about some representational content. When we activate the skill of riding a bicycle, we do not represent to ourselves the processes by which one rides a bicycle. Rather, we just ride the bicycle. Similarly, when an emotional memory is activated, we may or may not think of the event with which it is associated. Rather, we feel the emotion.

Triggers of each sort are found in all emotion systems. I say "emotion systems" because we do not have just one. Rather, we have different systems for different emotions. As Panksepp put the point, "There is no single 'motivational' circuit in the brain, and there is no unitary 'emotional' circuit there either" ("Emotions" 137). In connection with this, I follow LeDoux in rejecting the idea of a limbic system as anything other than a sort of shorthand for the various brain regions that figure importantly in distinct emotion systems. Of course, the various emotion systems are not entirely unrelated—quite the contrary. As Panksepp puts it, "each basic emotional system of the brain . . . interacts with other systems" ("Emotions" 138). The interactions are complex and consequential. But the systems remain at least partially autonomous. Specifically, there are two ways in which emotion systems interact—through mutual enhancement and through mutual inhibition. As to the former, two emotion systems may simultaneously draw our attentional focus to the same features of our environment (e.g., in certain cases of fear and disgust) or they may both produce the same physiological responses (e.g., increased heart rate). Similarly, they may reinforce one another in action tendencies or neurochemistry, as when sexual desire and attachment are related through oxytocin, which fosters physical contact (see Hatfield and Rapson 659).

It is perhaps more common for emotion systems to inhibit one another. Emotions typically direct our attentional focus differently. Specifically, emotion systems orient us toward feature types and configurations related to their particular genetic or mnemonic sensitivities. They also direct our attention to aspects of the environment and our own bodies that bear on their particular actional outcomes. For example, both fear and anger may direct our attention to someone's face. But fear, unlike anger, will also draw our attention to aspects of the environment that are occluded (e.g., dark places) and to enclosed areas that prevent escape. As this suggests, emotions commonly differ not only in attentional focus for actional outcomes but in actional outcomes themselves. One broad division here is between emotions that lead to approach (such as anger) and emotions that lead to withdrawal (such as fear). The arousal of one will tend to inhibit the arousal of the other. The same point holds across emotions of approach, which themselves may be somewhat crudely divided into emotions of pulling or embracing (such as attachment or affection) and emotions of pushing or repelling (such as anger). There are also inhibitions in phenomenological tone and physiological expression, as in the case of hunger and disgust.

We have just noted several particular emotion systems. This leads to the question of precisely what emotion systems there are. There is disagreement on this topic. An incomplete but relatively uncontroversial list would include fear, anger, attachment, disgust, hunger, and lust.

Up to this point I have been stressing biological factors. For instance, I take it that the number and general characteristics of emotion systems are biologically fixed. However, the underdetermination of emotion systems by genetic instructions allows for—indeed necessitates—the introduction of both developmental and social analysis. Consider social analysis. The impact of social factors is important not only in relation to higher cortical modifications of emotional response (e.g., in small differences in constraints on expressive outcomes, such as the ease with which one laughs in public). There may be cultural patterns even at the level of critical period phenomena. It seems very unlikely that there will be anything like uniformity in emotional response within any society. However, it is certainly possible that one society will differ from another in the percentages of people with, say, one or another type of attachment pattern.

Perhaps most significantly, social operations enter not only into the specification of emotion itself but also into the ideologies that intensify and particularize our representations of emotion, including those in literary narrative. Interestingly, these social factors need not manifest cultural differences. At least in their general outline, social ideologies may substantially converge due to general principles of group dynamics. For example, social ideologies contribute significantly to the idealization of romantic love. Consider a standard plot sequence that involves the chaste damsel being abducted by the villain and saved by her true love—a staple of romantic storytelling from the Sanskrit *Rāmāyaṇa* to Hollywood westerns. This is not only an idealization of romantic love. It is a particular idealization that stresses the dependency of the damsel, the martial protection given by the husband-to-be, and the dangers posed by other men. I take it that the social function of this is transparent. Indeed, generally, the endings of romantic plots not only bring the lovers together in romantic union; they bring the lovers together in a socially sanctioned marriage. Thus such plots almost invariably co-opt the idealized union of the couple into a stable social order—specifically, a heteronormative order, as queer theorists would rightly emphasize. I take it that none of this is determined by the neurobiology of emotion. On the contrary, in fact, such narratives work against the instabilities of emotion—for example, in identifying romantic union with marriage, which in practice restricts the possibilities for the dissolution of that union. Indeed, more generally, we might expect dominant ideology to focus with some frequency on unstable junctures in human motivational systems—when those junctures have social functions (e.g., when they bear on the regulation of sexuality).

Emotion and Stories

In the following chapters, I argue that an account of emotion along these lines provides a framework for both describing and explaining detailed patterns in story structure that recur across traditions of literature and orature.

More exactly, in examining narratives of verbal art, we may have several different concerns. Most obviously, we may have a *hermeneutic* interest, an interest in interpreting the *particularity* of the work. But we may equally have an interest in *commonality across works*. Moreover, the two enterprises are not unrelated. One aspect of the particularity of a given work is precisely the way it specifies a general pattern. For example, part of our understanding of and response to *Hamlet* is connected with our understanding of revenge plots and the way *Hamlet* both fits into the revenge category and deviates from its standard routines. Thus our isolation of patterns in stories is significant not only in itself, but also in its interpretive implications.

But, of course, the isolation of such patterns is no easy thing. First of all, there are countless ways in which we might group works together and countless ways in which we might isolate properties shared by works. Moreover, there are different principles we might use to select the works we are grouping. For example, we might narrow our selection to works by women in a particular literary movement in a particular decade or we might expand it to works across traditions and historical periods that have had success among readers. A wide range of such selection principles is valuable. However, there is an asymmetrical relation here. If we look only at a small selection of works, we really do not know how to understand the particularity of that group—unless we know the broader patterns that recur across such groups. For example, critics who focus only on Sanskrit drama are likely to be struck by the pattern of people falling in love, then being separated and reunited. But this is not a distinctive pattern in Sanskrit drama. It is pervasive in the literature of the world. It may appear with greater frequency in Sanskrit drama—but that too is determinable only by reference to cross-cultural and transhistorical patterns.

Thus the particularity of an individual work is at least in certain respects comprehensible only by reference to the ways in which it relates to a more general pattern. That pattern itself may be very narrowly defined—for example, in terms of a literary movement. But the same point reapplies to the literary movement. It too can be understood (in part) only in relation to broader patterns. This is the reason why one fundamental task in a general narratology would be the isolation of patterns that recur across works in different traditions and different historical periods. This provides a basis for understanding the various sorts of particularity that are important for historical or hermeneutic study.

But even cross-cultural patterns are not as easy to sort out as one might think. Not all recurring patterns have the same significance or the same consequences. Indeed, if we are faced only with the literary works, we may not be able to tell how we should group such properties together. As with data in any area, we need preliminary theoretical hypotheses to give an initial shape to the data, to guide us in looking for patterns, or in expanding on patterns that we have already recognized.

One contention of the following pages is that recent work in affective science provides just that framework. However, this is not a mere mechanical application of affective science. It is a use of affective science that is inseparable from the social and political dynamics that serve to develop our emotional responses—sometimes in convergent ways, sometimes not.

This, then, is the initial project of this book—understanding the fundamental, universal properties of narrative within the explanatory framework of affective science. However, there is a second goal as well. As a student of literature, my own interests are as much oriented toward particular interpretation as toward general theorization. Having isolated these broad affective and narrative patterns, it is valuable to consider how they are instantiated in individual works. In other words, it is important to consider the ways in which these patterns have hermeneutic consequences. Here, too, affective science is crucial. Just as emotion is at the root of the narrative patterns, it underlies the development of recurring properties into unique stories. An author's elaboration of a prototype into a singular plot and a reader's response to that plot (in part as an instance of the prototype) are inseparable from the emotion systems that guide the prototype initially. In this way, the emotional dynamics of recurring story patterns are not only of broad explanatory importance but of particular, interpretive significance as well.

Emotion and Narratology

Needless to say, I am not the first person to have seen a link between story structure and emotion. The theory of story structure begins in the West with Aristotle's *Poetics*, which stresses the emotional force of such recurring story elements as recognition and reversal. Indeed, for Aristotle, story structure is fundamentally guided by the generation and catharsis of emotions, particularly fear and pity. Similar concerns may be found in other traditions as well. Thus the early Sanskrit theorists such as Bharatamuni and Dhanaṃjaya stressed the emotional operation of literature and the organization of stories by reference to (emotionally driven and emotionally consequential) goal seeking.

A broader range of theorists have stressed that stories must operate to sustain some interest from a reader or auditor. For example, William Labov has influentially outlined the ways in which oral narratives involve structural elements, such as evaluation or the ordering of events in terms of "tellability," that bear on audience engagement. This is entirely valid. But it is clearly different from an exploration of the ways in which emotion systems shape stories and story constituents. First, the structural elements in Labov's account are partially a matter of discourse or the manner in which story events are presented, rather than the story structure itself. Second, when they do bear on the story proper, they touch on emotion only in a general way.

Moreover, in treating stories and emotions, most of these writers have not drawn on recent research coming out of cognitive science and neuroscience, sometimes termed "affective science." That does not at all invalidate their work. But it does make it different from the project of this book. For example, writers such as James Phelan have focused on the rhetorical appeals of narratives. This contributes importantly to our understanding of the structure and function of stories. But it can rely on relatively commonsense ideas about emotion. It does not need to draw on the technical research of the last decade or so. Like Labov's work, Phelan's writings make their compelling points without the need for reference to specific, neurologically defined emotion systems, technical distinctions between innate and critical period sensitivities, differences among expressive outcomes, actional outcomes, attentional orientations, and so forth.

Conversely, many authors who have drawn on recent cognitive research have largely ignored emotion. David Bordwell's pathbreaking *Narration in the Fiction Film* and his erudite work of metatheory, *Making Meaning*, bring his profound knowledge of cognitive research to bear on film. But these and other works of his do not engage with the emotion research that has been part of the "cognitive revolution." Similarly, Marisa Bortolussi and Peter Dixon's psychonarratology focuses on language ("psychonarratology" is parallel to "psycholinguistics" in this way). As they put it, "in psychonarratology we attempt to draw together the insights and analytical tools of narratology and related branches of literary studies together with empirical techniques used to investigate cognitive processes found in *discourse processing*" (33, emphasis added). This is extremely valuable work. It does not in any way diminish the value of that work to say that it has a different project from that of the present book, or to say that the project of an affective approach to story structure is important.

One early exception to this general trend was Ed Tan. Tan is deeply familiar with current research on emotion. He was one of the pioneers in bringing this research into the study of narrative. Specifically, he has explored the ways in which interest is sustained in films. But even this is not really an analysis of emotion and story structure. First, interest is perhaps more appropriately categorized as an adjunct to the activation of emotion systems, rather than an emotion itself. For example, romantic love, anger, fear, jealousy, and shame all involve interest. That seems to suggest that interest is not a psychological system parallel with romantic love, anger, fear, jealousy, and shame. Moreover, Tan's focus on narratives is only partially a matter of story structure, and that at a very general level. Specifically, Tan is concerned with the ways in which readers generate possible outcomes for narrative sequences, form preferences for some of those outcomes over others, and tacitly calculate probabilities for the likelihood of those outcomes. Tan is undoubtedly correct in isolating these processes and relating them to our engagement with film (and noncinematic narrative). But there are necessarily issues that his book cannot address. The relation of emotion systems to recurring story patterns is one of those issues.

Tan is particularly concerned with characters and with readers. This is a recurring pattern among writers who have drawn on research in affective science. For example, Alan Palmer has treated the centrality of emotion in readers' understanding of "fictional minds." Palmer makes some particularly illuminating comments on the bearing of stylistic devices on the report and representation of emotion in characters. This is important and consequential work but has only marginal consequences for our understanding of recurring patterns in story structure.

The most thoroughgoing and rigorous treatment of character, audience, and emotion available to date may be chapter 13 of Jens Eder's *Die Figur im Film*. Drawing on a broad range of current research, Eder argues for a multilevel approach to understanding character and audience emotion which seeks to incorporate different accounts of emotion. One may wonder whether or not he has fully succeeded in reconciling these accounts. But the treatment is learned and illuminating. Here too, however, the task is not the study of story structure.

Palmer himself points toward the relatively limited treatment of emotion in narratology when he explains that "a good deal of work has been done within narrative theory on fictional consciousness"; however, "very little has been done specifically on the emotions" (115), despite the close relation between the two. We see both the relation and the disproportionate emphasis on consciousness in, for example, the recent *Cambridge Companion to Narrative* (edited by David Herman)—a lucid, highly informative, scholarly volume that is representative of the best current theoretical approaches to narrative. The substantive treatment of emotion in this three-hundred-page book amounts to one page in David Herman's essay on "Cognition, Emotion, and Consciousness." This page draws a distinction between "naturalist" and "social constructionist" approaches to emotion. It goes on to note the importance of understanding character emotions for understanding a story. Herman observes in particular that "what the characters say and do can be sorted into classes of behaviors in which one is likely to engage when motivated by happiness, resentment, fear, sadness, etc." ("Cognition" 255). The comments on character motivation are unexceptionable. But it should be clear that this hardly goes beyond common sense—unlike Herman's nuanced discussion of consciousness. In any case, they tell us very little about recurring patterns of story structure—as one would expect, since that was not Herman's aim.

Finally, the distinction between social constructionist and naturalist, though common, is perhaps too great a simplification. For example, Herman characterizes my view as "an account of emotions as innate" (259n.18). Here is my summary from the book he cites: "Emotions are much more malleable than we are inclined to believe. They are formed from biologically given proto-emotions. . . . These proto-emotions are specified by socially functional practices and ideas that affect eliciting conditions, phenomenological tone, and actional/expressive outcomes. These specifications are, in part, culturally distinctive. But universals are not confined to biology. Social specifications are to a great extent universal as well" (263). In other words, there is not only divergence but convergence across cultures as well—due to principles of group dynamics, the likelihood of resolving similar environmental problems in similar ways, the tendency for more successful patterns in childrearing to be socially reproduced, and so forth.[4] An account of this sort simply does not fit into either slot in a dichotomy of naturalist and social constructionist.

Herman develops these ideas further in "Storytelling and the Sciences of Mind." There he discusses "emotionology," which is to say, "the collective emotional standards of a culture" (322). He goes on to discuss emotion in performance aspects of oral storytelling, such as prosody. He does turn to events but only to discuss what he calls "actions that are . . . conventionally linked with the emotion of fear." These include "running away from a threatening agent . . . screaming and feeling unable to breathe" (324), thus what emotion researchers would call actional, expressive, and physiological outcomes. One might wonder what leads Herman to think that, say, running away from a threat is conventional. It certainly is not a conventional link in real life. First, people all over the world do it all the time and evidently do so spontaneously. Second, withdrawal in the face of aversive stimuli is a response that occurs in a range of species. Given this, it seems unlikely that we could see it as conventional in literature. Of course, we can flee or fight or freeze when faced with threat. If it turned out that, in a given tradition, characters always and only flee (never fighting or freezing), then we may have a sort of convention. But Herman does not seem to be making that argument. In any case, Herman does to some extent set out to treat the relation between emotion and story structure. But his analysis really only suggests that if a character has a certain emotion, then he or she is likely to exhibit the actional, expressive, and physiological outcomes associated with that emotion.

Peter Stockwell is another cognitivist who has turned to emotion recently. In "Texture and Identification," Stockwell explores the ways in which Kipling's poem "If" creates a "textual emotional impact" (145). He maps out "subworlds" in the text that involve hypotheticals (as one would expect from the title of the poem). He sets out the content of each of the subworlds and their dependencies on one another. For example, the lines "If you can keep your head when all about you / Are losing theirs" (145) create a "primary subworld conditional" of "keeping your head" (149). After leading us through numerous subworlds of this sort, he notes that readers are likely to identify themselves with the "you" of the poem, "either because the qualities being placed conditionally on 'you' are attractive to You, or because You as a reader are so anxious to resolve the conditional" (150). It seems much more likely that this is the result of the sorts of alignment discussed by Murray Smith or the various partial simulations treated by Berys Gaut. Moreover, the emotion of the poem seems to have more to do with the father-son acceptance theme as discussed by Ed Tan and Nico Frijda ("Being accepted as a son or a man by a father . . . is a theme that makes male viewers cry in the cinema" [57]). In any case, it seems clear that Stockwell is not treating story structure, but an aspect of reader response.

Suzanne Keen is another author who has taken up emotion research to discuss narratives. Indeed, Keen has studied recent writings on emotion both broadly and deeply. She brings this knowledge to bear in insightful discussions of the empathic appeal of novels to readers, the issue of whether those appeals have actual effects in the real world, the empathic intentions of authors, and other theoretical and historical topics. Her book is a model of its kind. But, while it deals with emotion and with stories, it has little to say about the ways in which emotions actually shape repeated patterns of story structure.

Other recent work on emotion and narrative has tended to focus on reader response in a more strictly empirical or experimental way. This is understandable, since perhaps the most salient manifestation of emotion in narrative experience is in reader (or audience) response. Indeed, beyond authorial "inspiration," that is the only place where real emotional events occur. Empirical studies by writers such as Keith Oatley have been extremely important in demonstrating the effects of reader dispositions (e.g., emotional memories) on response to stories (see his "Emotions") and in showing the value of experience with narratives for developing human emotional response and understanding—specifically, for expanding emotional intelligence ("Communications"). This is not unrelated to the study of story structure, though the relations are usually limited and indirect in this research.

On the other hand, there is some research in this area that does begin to treat story structure more directly. Probably the best case is David Miall's exploration of subnarrative or "episode" units in stories. Miall's research on this topic contributes valuably to the initial stages of an examination of emotion and story structure. However, it does so as part of a different project—fundamentally, a project in reader response, not a project in either emotion theory or the isolation and explanation of story organization. (I consider Miall's analysis of emotion and episodes in chapter 1.)

In sum, there has been extremely valuable work treating emotion and narrative. However, very little of that work has drawn on contemporary affective science to describe or to explain recurring story structures. The little work that has addressed these topics at all has tended to do so indirectly or as an adjunct to treatments of character and/or reader response.

We may identify at least three reasons for this relative neglect of emotion and story structure. First, modern narrative theory has tended to draw on linguistic models, which largely ignore emotion. Second, the explanatory (and even descriptive) problems with early treatments of story patterns have tended to make the topic less appealing to recent researchers. Third, literary theory generally has been far more influenced by psychoanalysis than by cognitive science or neuroscience. As a result, approaches to story structure that might have incorporated emotion have often been framed in terms of a (somewhat problematic) psychoanalytic conception of desire or pleasure.[5] Since this is not a history of narratology, I cannot consider these in detail, but I should make a few brief remarks on each.

The standard narrative of narrative theory distinguishes between "classical" and "postclassical" narratology. Postclassical narratologists (such as those discussed above) have certainly begun to draw on affective science in certain respects. Nonetheless, many fundamentals of narratology were set out in the founding works of classical narratology, which were often Structuralist in orientation. Many main figures of classical narratology—Genette, Greimas, Barthes, Todorov—were setting out to use Saussurean linguistics to understand narrative structure. Though this work was enormously valuable, it was embedded in linguistic theories that had nothing to say about emotion. In and of itself, this is not necessarily a problem. However, it tended to orient research programs in narratology toward issues and explanations that had little to do with emotion.

Consider, for example, the study of time in narratology. I argue in chapter 1 that narrative time is fundamentally organized by emotion. For example, our isolation of something as an event and our attribution of a cause to that event are both crucially a function of emotional response, even if other systems are necessarily involved as well. However, as Brian Richardson points out, "The starting-point for most theories of time in narrative is Genette's account of the categories of order, duration, and frequency" ("Drama and Narrative" 147). In keeping with the prevalent linguistic model, this division is closely related to distinctions of tense (thus order) and aspect (thus duration and repetition). This is not at all to diminish Genette's insights. His three categories certainly correspond to real properties of narrative. However, they are not the only ways in which we might understand narrative time. Nor, as I will argue, are they the most important.

Again, the second main reason for the relative lack of work on emotion and patterns in story structure concerns problems with prior studies of the latter. The research on recurring story patterns has a long history, which I cannot cover in a brief introduction. Indeed, Aristotle's abstraction of reversal and recognition could be understood as an isolation of one such recurring pattern. In North America, the isolation of such patterns is most often associated with writers such as Northrop Frye. Frye did very significant work in describing recurrent narrative structures. Indeed, he is an important precursor for the present study. However, his organization of the data and formulation of patterns is notoriously messy, as Todorov has shown (see *The Fantastic* 8–21). Moreover, he has almost no explanatory framework for his findings.

The point applies not only to Frye but to other narrative theorists. Since Frye has been so thoroughly treated by Todorov, we might briefly consider Scholes and Kellogg instead. Scholes and Kellogg seek to organize their account of plot structures by reference to "the annual cycle of vegetative life" (220). As Frye also noticed, there are some parallels between literary structure and seasons. Scholes and Kellogg see these parallels as mediated by rituals (220). It is not entirely implausible to think that at least some sorts of literature have a historical relation with ritual. But it is not clear why new stories would continue to manifest the structures they do, once storytelling becomes disconnected from ritual. Indeed, it is not even clear that ritual came before stories—or that it even could come before stories, since rituals themselves involve stories. A more plausible account would be something along the following lines. Insofar as there are parallels among verbal art, ritual, and ideas about the seasons, these all derive from underlying emotion systems in their interaction with the environment and with other neurocognitive systems such as long-term and working memory. Moreover, verbal art, ritual, cosmology, agriculture, and other discourses and practices interact with one another in various ways at different times and in different social circumstances. That interaction is facilitated by the shared emotional (and cognitive) substrate.

Finally, we have the effects of psychoanalysis. Here, too, constraints of space prevent a systematic overview, but we may consider one illustrative case. The most influential psychoanalytic narratologist is probably Peter Brooks. Brooks articulates an account of plot as an active structuring of experience driven by desire. At a general level, Brooks is no doubt correct. We begin to engage in something like emplotment as soon as we are faced with human agents engaged in activities that we consider significant. In keeping with this, Brooks is right to emphasize that this engagement is an ongoing process, not a fixed product. Moreover, this account of plot leads Brooks to insightful and illuminating interpretations of individual literary works.

But this is not an account of plot in terms of complex, multiple, well-studied emotion systems. Drawing on psychoanalytic theory, Brooks sometimes speaks as if desire is predominantly sexual, or rather, libidinal (thus sexual in origin if not in manifestation). At other times, he takes up Freud's much broader concept of Eros. At other times, "desire" seems to refer to any sort of motivation whatsoever.

The problems with the third usage are obvious. It is trivial to say that we—authors, readers, characters—act on the basis of motivation. For Brooks's interpretive purposes, further analysis of motivation systems may not be necessary. But without that further analysis, his treatment of motivation will tend to remain at a pretheoretical, intuitive level.

The problem with the notion of Eros is different. There is simply no reason to believe that there is a neural system corresponding to this putative drive. In other words, there is no reason to believe that there is such a thing as Eros in Freud's sense. Of course, some systems—most obviously, sexual desire and attachment—share characteristics with Freud's idea of Eros. But they remain distinct systems with their own particular conditions, outcomes, and so forth. Moreover, there is no reason to believe that the features abstracted in the idea of Eros have narrative or other consequences. Finally, even if they had such consequences, we would need to understand those consequences in terms of the emotion systems, not in terms of a relatively arbitrary abstraction from them.

This leaves the sexual use. The advantage of the sexual use of the term "desire" is that there is a sexual motivation system. There are two disadvantages to this usage. First, it is not at all clear that the sexual system plays a fundamental and distinctive role in narrative structure generally. As we will see, there are some features (e.g., goal generation) that are common across a number of emotion systems and that bear on narrative organization. There are other features that are distinctive of particular emotion systems. These have consequences in particular narratives or in genre patterns. The sexual system appears predominant in only one minor genre (as we discuss in chapter 4). In short, one cannot explain very much about narrative by confining oneself to sexual desire. Second, the current understanding of sexual desire is rather different from Freud's understanding. For example, a great deal of Freud's work on early parent-child relations would now be seen as bearing on attachment (a separate system) rather than sexuality. Moreover, the Lacanian formulation of desire in relation to metonymy and the place of castration in the psychoanalytic account—both of which are important to Brooks's analysis—seem improbable (to say the least) in light of more recent research.

From Incidents to Genres

Again, it is the task of this book to explore the relation between emotion and recurring story structures and components. In order to do this, it begins with the smallest units of stories—which, it argues, are also the smallest units of emotional response: incidents. Thus chapter 1 explores incidents and the way these are built up through causal attribution into events and episodes. At each step, the key systems defining these structures are emotional. This chapter also sets out a fuller account of emotion, synthesizing the two main approaches to emotion in cognitive science—appraisal theory and what we may refer to as "perception theory."[6] This synthetic account then provides a basis for the analyses of the following chapters.

Chapter 2 moves beyond episodes and takes up the issue of just what constitutes a story. It examines the basic conditions that distinguish the beginnings and endings of stories and the nature of story development. Here, too, the governing, explanatory principles are emotional. This chapter also revisits the distinction between story and discourse, addressing some criticisms of the distinction and the relevance of the distinction to the understanding of narrative and emotion. In connection with this, it treats the place of cultural knowledge in the construal of stories from discourses. (The integration of cultural knowledge with cross-cultural cognitive and emotive patterns is an important concern of subsequent chapters.) Finally, this chapter considers the more encompassing level of the literary work, discussing what makes a multistory movie or a novel into a single work rather than a collection.

Chapter 3 turns from the broad structure of stories to the main cross-cultural types of stories.[7] Thus it moves to a level of greater particularity in story patterns. *The Mind and Its Stories* argues that there are three predominant story prototypes that recur across cultures—heroic, romantic, and sacrificial. In addition, it argues that these prototypes derive from particular emotion systems. For example, the romantic prototype appears to derive primarily from an integration of the system for attachment with that for sexual desire. Chapter 3 reviews and refines that analysis. This chapter particularly develops the relation between these genres and one element of culture—ideology—a relation only hinted at in previous work.

If this account of the main prototypical genres is correct, it makes certain rough predictions about other sorts of patterns we should find in stories. For example, if these genres derive from the combination of distinct emotional components, we would expect those components to operate separately also, perhaps generating further genres. Thus, if the romantic plot derives from an integration of sexual and attachment systems, then we might expect at least some literary narratives to derive from those systems in isolation from one another. Of course, the combination of emotion systems commonly increases the motivational force of the resulting goals. Moreover, the goals of individual systems in isolation may not be as conducive to the full development of emotionally effective stories (e.g., when sexual goals are isolated from attachment goals, the resulting stories have some serious limitations, as we discuss in chapter 4). For these reasons, the genres derived from the isolated emotion systems—such as attachment and sexual desire—may not be as ubiquitous or enduring as the main prototypical genres. Nonetheless, we would expect to find works of each sort (e.g., attachment-based works and sexuality-based works) recurring in different cultures and in different time periods. Chapter 4 explores several such "minor genres," as I call them. Specifically, it takes up stories of attachment, sexuality, and crime, the last in both impersonal investigation and personal revenge variants.

One striking aspect of these minor genres is that, at least in their canonical forms, they are often highly ambivalent. This ambivalence has consequences for our understanding of the major genres as well, for these also show ambivalence, if less frequently. Indeed, the minor genres may lead us to wonder if ambivalence is, so to speak, the default case for narrative and thus if the relative lack of ambivalence in the major genres is the result of ideological constraint.

The Mind and Its Stories isolates a broad set of data to support claims about cross-cultural narrative patterns. However, literary study has historically—and rightly, in my view—been particularly concerned with and devoted to the interpretation of individual works. One question readers have had about my previous analyses is whether these analyses have interpretive consequences, whether they help us to understand individual stories more fully. Of course, a generalization about narrative structure may be valuable in many ways. Most obviously, it may tell us something about the human mind or about human society. In this way, the worth of a narrative theory does not rise or fall with its applicability in interpretation. However, the analysis of story structure in relation to emotion systems, and in particular the isolation of cross-cultural patterns in narrative, is in fact very consequential for interpretation. For this reason, I concentrate for the most part on a relatively small number of individual works in the following pages, seeking to draw out the interpretive implications of the theoretical abstractions.

Two main criteria guided the choice of stories. The first is cultural and historical diversity. My claims concern cross-cultural and transhistorical patterns. Even when seeking to interpret individual works, it is important to represent a broad range of traditions and periods. Thus I include some treatment of Indian (i.e., South Asian), Middle Eastern, Chinese, Japanese, Native American, sub-Saharan African, and European works, ranging in time from Homer to the contemporary Indian filmmaker M. F. Husain. In connection with this, I also seek diversity of media, from oral to chirographic to typographic to post-typographic.

The second criterion is, roughly, stature. One trend in contemporary narratology is to focus on the small, everyday stories we tell one another (e.g., in response to such questions as "How was your day?"). This is extremely important. It is a form of narratological investigation that should be pursued extensively, for it is likely to tell us a great deal about human interactions and daily life. However, these stories are ephemeral and context-bound. Other stories fascinate people at different times and places. These are my concern—stories that are at least canonical and, in many cases, are widely accepted as paradigmatic of literary excellence in their respective traditions. I hope it goes without saying that these stories too tell us a great deal about the human mind and human society, precisely because their impact is not contingent on personal acquaintance with or interest in the teller or the circumstances immediately surrounding the tale.

Chapter 1, then, focuses particularly on Tolstoy's *Anna Karenina*. *Anna Karenina* is not only widely recognized as one of the greatest novels ever written, but it also figures prominently in Keith Oatley's pathbreaking treatment of narrative and emotion. I chose it in part to establish continuity with Oatley's important work. I take up Tolstoy's novel also because it is so insistently concerned with exploring emotion. Indeed, it scrutinizes the close interrelations between cognition, particularly social cognition, and emotion. For example, Vladimir Alexandrov argues persuasively that "understanding is intertwined with love in *Anna Karenina*" (235)—one very striking way in which social cognition and emotion are inseparable in this novel. Needless to say, the novel is also famously effective in producing emotion (as Alexandrov notes, "Were it not for Tolstoy's remarkable ability to engage us emotionally, *Anna Karenina* would not be the great work it is" [9–10]).

Chapter 2 shifts from modern Russia, first to ancient North Africa, then to Renaissance England, then to postmodern India. Specifically, it examines a story from Middle Kingdom Egypt in connection with general story structure. It then turns to *King Lear* to illustrate the ways in which a work, with its integration of stories, differs from a collection. Finally, narratologists sometimes claim that postmodern works radically challenge any account of narrative structure based on non-postmodern texts. I therefore take up a postmodern work, in this case one from India— M. F. Husain's film *Meenaxi*—to further examine the general organization of story structure and the nature of a work. The treatment of these narratives obviously allows the application of the theory to different literary traditions, different modes of presentation (prose, drama, film), and different contexts of orality and literacy.

Chapter 3 considers the three main, prototypical genres, treating one or two works in depth for each genre. It first takes up a sacrificial narrative by the most important dramatist of Yüan dynasty China—Guan Hanqing's *Dou E yuan*. In discussing this work, I am particularly concerned to locate it within its historical and political context, stressing its development of nationalist ideology. I do this in part to demonstrate that the exploration of universal prototypes is not at all incompatible with the interpretation of historical particulars. The treatment of heroic tragicomedy considers the widely retold West African oral narrative *Epic of Son-Jara*. Since this story is available in different versions, we can compare and contrast the ideological particularities of different tellings. In this case, I focus on the version by Djanka Tassey Condé, paying particular attention to gender ideology. The heroic plot often includes a peculiar "afterword," what may be called an "epilogue of suffering." This afterword frequently involves the development of a complete, if brief story, subsequent to the main heroic plot. To treat this, I consider the ending of another African oral narrative, *The Mwindo Epic*, as told by Shé-Kárisi Rureke, "the only great performer of the Mwindo epic alive in Nyanga country in the mid-fifties" (Biebuyck and Mateene 17). This epic is particularly valuable for studying cross-cultural patterns as well as cultural particularization, for, as Biebuyck explains, "In general, the Western influence on the Nyanga finds no expression in the epics" (42). This story is, I argue, largely if implicitly critical of the statist and militarist ideologies that are standard in heroic narratives.

Finally, chapter 3 takes up the romantic plot. In general, romantic plots tend to be less ideologically conservative than heroic or sacrificial plots. This chapter examines the paradigmatic work of Sanskrit dramatic literature, *Abhijñānaśākuntalam*. This work allows us to consider some further nuances of ideological analysis. Note that an ideology comprises not only a set of ideas or beliefs but—perhaps even more crucially—a set of feelings or motivations as well. Thus ideological analysis—in narrative or elsewhere—is inseparable from a treatment of emotion. The overt ideology of Kālidāsa's play is fairly conservative and patriarchal. However, when placed in the context of Sanskrit literary tradition, we can recognize that the story is highly allusive—and its allusions are ideologically consequential. Indeed, *Abhijñānaśākuntalam* is in many ways a response to Vālmīki's *Rāmāyaṇa*, a text of central importance in the formation of Hindu gender ideology. In this context, the gender ideology of *Abhijñānaśākuntalam* may be recognized as at least complex and ambivalent, including elements that are quite strongly antipatriarchal.

Having not previously isolated minor genres, in chapter 4 I include a broader range of reference than earlier chapters. The purpose of this is to suggest some of the historical and geographical scope of the genres. On the other hand, I try to give at least some interpretive detail for one or two works of each sort. In the case of the attachment narrative, this chapter makes reference to stories from the Bible and the great Sanskrit epic, the *Mahābhārata*; the Japanese Nō dramas *Kagekiyo* and *Yoroboshi*; the Chinese drama *The Story of the Circle of Chalk*; *King Lear*; *The Odyssey*; and other works—with a longer discussion of Alain Robbe-Grillet's *Dans le Labyrinthe*. For the sexual plot, it takes up stories from the *Mahābhārata* and the *Kalevala*, the ancient Sumerian story of Enlil and Ninlil, sequences from Lady Murasaki's *The Tale of Genji*, Terence's *Mother-in-Law*, the Don Juan story (particularly Tirso's version), and other works—with more extended attention to Goethe's *Faust*. It considers the revenge plot and the criminal investigation plot under the same general category, as they are closely related to one another. This section refers to Chikamatsu's *The Drum of the Waves of Horikawa*, Zeami's *Atsumori*, the massively popular Japanese *Chūshingura*, *The Changeling*, *The Spanish Tragedy*, the Mayan *Rabinal Achi*, the medieval Chinese *Flower of the Back Courtyard*, *Oedipus the King*, Kafka's *The Trial*, and other works—with somewhat greater attention to *Hamlet* and the *Oresteia*.

The four chapters comprising the main body of the book are concerned with the ways in which our emotion systems affect and explain our stories. The afterword turns briefly to the converse issue—the ways in which our stories affect and explain our emotions. A full treatment of this topic would obviously require a separate book. However, it is important at least to suggest some of the ways in which most or all aspects of our emotions—eliciting conditions, actional outcomes, and so on—may be affected by stories. Indeed, stories may even be a necessary part of the development of our emotional lives. Again, we are born with emotional (or proto-emotional) propensities. But those propensities are realized and inflected by experience. It may be that stories are a key part of that realization and inflection. If so, the point only reveals once again the profound interconnection of emotions and stories.

A Note on Ideology

Since ideology is a recurring concern in the following chapters, it is useful to preface those chapters with a preliminary indication of just what I have in mind when speaking of ideology. First of all, I follow Raymond Geuss and others in distinguishing a descriptive and a pejorative sense of the term. The descriptive sense is found in such phrases as "the ideology of our party." It refers to a guiding set of ideas. As a first approximation, we might say that "ideology" in the pejorative sense refers to a guiding set of ideas that support some sort of injustice, oppression, or exploitation. In folk psychological terms, we could say that ideology is fundamentally a complex of goals and beliefs that are functional in relation to some social hierarchy. Specifically, ideology serves to maintain an unjust or non-meritocratic hierarchy through false beliefs and skewed aspirations. Thus patriarchal ideology comprises (false) beliefs about differences in the capacities of men and women and a differential cultivation of aspirations in men and women (e.g., women may be less likely to aspire to being engineers). These differences serve to maintain a political and economic hierarchy based on sex.[8]

A slightly fuller account extends from beliefs and goals to problematics, which is to say, sets of possible beliefs or goals. For the most part, ideology does not operate by forcing everyone to believe exactly the same things and to adopt the same goals. Rather, dominant ideology (i.e., the set of ideas that functions to maintain the currently dominant social hierarchy) cultivates a range of beliefs and goals that people will take to encompass all the reasonable options. For example, Democratic and Republican views on treating the financial crisis that began in 2008 are basically variants of mainstream capitalist economics, with slight differences in the degree to which there should be constraints on finance capital, but with consensus on the function of government as supportive of private wealth. There is no consideration of policies that aim primarily at democratizing the economy. Dominant political ideology in the United States does not require that we all accept either Democratic or Republican policies. However, it does foster a common view that these policies represent the left- and right-wing poles of reasonable opinion. Thus they define a problematic.

Still more precisely, I would say that there is a wide range of cognitive and affective structures that lead us to act (or to refrain from action) in such a way as to support the continuation of current unjust hierarchies in the distribution of goods and services and current unjust constraints on liberty. Following classical Marxist theory (see, for example, Althusser), we may divide these structures into two groups—coercion and ideology. Coercion may result from threats of physical force or confinement (most obviously, police action) or from economic factors (e.g., fear of losing one's job) or from more diffuse social factors (e.g., fear of ostracism or simple unpopularity). Relating these threats to possible actions usually involves some sort of inferential process. Thus we could say that coercion typically operates through self-conscious awareness of threat. Ideology is the much larger set of unself-conscious ways of thinking about the world—spontaneously selecting and organizing information from the world and responding emotionally to it—that fosters unreflective complicity with social hierarchies.

For example, our minds appear to operate significantly through prototypes or, roughly, average cases of given categories. The averaging in these cases proceeds over a wide range of sources, including fiction. Moreover, it is biased toward high salience. In other words, some instances of a category—prominently, instances of a category that are emotionally intense—count much more than other instances. Moreover, our minds spontaneously organize the social world in terms of in-group/out-group divisions. The general tendency appears to be innate, or acquired very early, though precisely what constitutes such a division varies socially and even contextually. When prototypes are applied to out-groups, they commonly yield stereotypes. Violence against out-groups, such as national enemies, may be facilitated by these cognitive and affective tendencies, which often inhibit empathy. Obviously, in-group/out-group prototypes are not the only cognitive and affective factors in ideology. Since this is not a book on the theory of ideology, I cannot go into a wide range of such factors.[9] However, this example illustrates the general point.

Nonetheless, here one might ask—just how does this cognitive/affective account relate to the previous account in terms of false or unjustified belief or sets of beliefs and overly narrow aspirations? The cognitive/affective structures do not seem to be the same as beliefs and goals, nor do they seem open to the same evaluative criteria (e.g., a prototype does not seem to be true or false in the way a belief is true or false). To make matters worse, we may act on the basis of prototypes—for example, racist stereotypes—even when we do not hold racist beliefs. A more accurate account of my criteria for ideology would be as follows. The cognitive and motivational processes that produce an action are usually too complex to be represented simply in terms of beliefs and goals. However, were they formulated in terms of beliefs and goals, we would find those beliefs to be false, unjustified, or part of overly narrow problematics, and we would find the goals to be overly narrow. In other words, the demarcation criteria for ideology (in the pejorative sense) apply not to cognitive and affective processes per se, but to their functional equivalents in beliefs, sets of beliefs, and aspirations.

While there are some connections between this approach and some of the more influential Marxist theories of ideology, it should be clear that that there are quite significant differences as well. For example, my fundamental unit of analysis is not a social class but the individual mind. Thus the sources of ideology are not classes per se. Rather, the sources of ideology are all the things that contribute to the formation of prototypes, emotional memories, critical-period experiences, and other cognitive and affective contents that bear on social hierarchies. Indeed, speaking of a particular ideology (e.g., "capitalist ideology") is always an abstraction of common features from diverse individual cognitive and affective operations.

Thus, I agree with Macherey that "a historical period does not spontaneously produce a single, monolithic ideology, but a series of ideologies determined by the total relation of forces." But I cannot agree that "each ideology is shaped by the pressures upon the class which generates it" (128). Classes, in my account, cannot generate ideologies. Rather, individuals come to form different complexes of ideological prototypes, attitudes, and so forth, that never entirely overlap. Of course, it is important that the individual ideologies are not, so to speak, equidistant from one another. By their nature, social networks link some sets of people more closely than others. Thus we would expect people with more connections to one another to be more similar to one another in prototypes, critical-period experiences, and so on, and thus more similar to one another in ideology. In other words, we would expect the networks to form clusters. Moreover, here as elsewhere, there may be convergent development of unconnected individuals. For example, there may be ways in which peasants develop certain emotional propensities due simply to the conditions of peasant life. Thus we may, in certain conditions, refer (somewhat loosely) to class ideologies, taking up the common features of individual responses. But we may also refer to regional, religious, familial, or other ideologies.

Moreover, the abstracted ideologies and the groups that they benefit or harm cannot be conceived of as having a "dialectical" relation with one another in the classical Marxist sense. There are not two broad tendencies that confront one another as antitheses, yielding an historical synthesis, with its own antithesis, and so on. Rather, there are only the usual small causes bearing on individuals and the patterns produced by these small causes due to the complex and always changing networks in which the individuals find themselves.[10] Of course, it may sometimes happen that these patterns approximate some dual relation, and it may sometimes be useful to simplify complex social relations by referring to dialectic. But that is always a simplification. Moreover, it is a theoretically opaque simplification since the notion of dialectic is an extra type of (indeed, a supernatural type of) causality in effect imposed upon the smaller, local, natural causes.

In sum, ideology operates through the cognitive and affective structures and processes of the human mind, embedded in diverse networks. A set of ideas—for example, a story in a novel—may foster actions by its effects on inferential and motivational systems. Those actions may in turn be translated into justificatory criteria involving beliefs and goals. In order for these ideas to constitute ideology (in the pejorative sense), they must satisfy two criteria. The first criterion is that those beliefs should be either implausible or too narrow in range (i.e., too narrow in their problematic). Alternatively, the goals should be overly limited in terms of human flourishing (as Nussbaum would put it [see *Upheavals* 4]). The second criterion is that the actions should also serve the function of preserving unjust hierarchies in the distribution of goods and services or unjust constraints on freedoms. This account allows for reference to class ideology only as a simplification of certain network configurations. It does not allow references to a non-natural, "dialectical" explanatory or causal pattern, except as a simplifying metaphor.

1 Before Stories
Emotional Time and Anna Karenina

Emotional Geography and Emotional History

Anna Karenina begins with a rift in a family.[1] Dolly Oblonsky has discovered that her husband has been having an affair. One morning, a few days after the initial quarrel, Stiva Oblonsky, the husband, wakes up alone in his study. For a moment, he does not remember the rift, or even his own precise location in the home. For a moment he is content, tacitly imagining his ordinary life, his ordinary bed. But then he remembers. "All the details" come rushing back, but they are not uniform. He particularly recalls "the first moment when, on coming back cheerful and satisfied" he "saw her . . . holding the unlucky note that had revealed everything" (2).[2] He goes on to reflect on the entire "event," feeling particular torment over the "silly smile" with which he greeted his wife's reproaches and the way, seeing this, "Dolly shuddered as though in physical pain" (3). He begins to feel "despair," unable to answer the question "What is there to do?"

In *Being and Time*, Martin Heidegger draws a valuable distinction between the uniform, objective time of clocks and the subjective temporality of human experience; this is parallel with a distinction between the objective space of maps and the subjective spatiality of human activity.[3] The opening of *Anna Karenina* brings home this distinction sharply. Spatiality is perhaps the more obvious here. In themselves, rooms are simply organizations of space. Objectively, Stiva's location is just a matter of a physical body located at a particular point relative to other physical bodies. But the spatial experience of Stiva is quite different from this. Stiva understands his location by contrast with where he should be, where he would like to be, where he would be if everything were right. Jean-Paul Sartre refers to this experience as *nothingness*. Stiva's location is not only a matter of where he is, but equally of where he is not.

My first contention here is that spatiality, the "existential" experience of location, is fundamentally an emotional experience. As my characterization of Stiva's place already suggests, nothingness—the judgment of where one is not but should be or should have been—is first of all a function of what one feels about locations. In this case, there are two aspects to the feeling. The first is not precisely emotion per se, but rather forms the baseline from which emotions arise. This is normalcy. More often than not, emotions are a response to changes in what is routine, habitual, expected. We anticipate normalcy unreflectively. When our anticipations are violated, attentional focus is triggered (see, for example, Frijda 272–73, 318, and 386) and a sort of pre-emotional arousal occurs, an arousal that often prepares for a particular emotion (see, for instance, Simpson et al. 692). It is just when Stiva puts down his feet toward the expected slippers and reaches out toward the expected robe, the moment when he finds the nothingness where the slippers and the robe should be, that his attention is focused. In this case, the focus is recollective; it is a matter of memory—and that increased attention carries in its train the entire sequence of happenings that pushed this body from his wife's bed to the couch in the study.

This leads to the second aspect of feeling that bears on our experience of space. Our experience of the world is not uniform. It is focused on particular areas. The center toward which we tend, and against which we experience all other places, is home. I am not simply referring here to the building we call "home," as when we "go home" at the end of the day. Rather, I am referring to the location that, paradigmatically, both is home (in the sense of the origin and end point of journeys) and, so to speak, "feels like home." Thus it is a point of cognitive orientation ("Where is the restaurant?" "About a five-minute drive from your home") and a point of emotional ease and security. The idea is not merely phenomenological. There are neurobiological reasons for "place attachment," as it is called. Indeed, the same subcortical structures appear to be involved in place attachment as in attachment to persons, leading the affective neuroscientist Jaak Panksepp to suggest that perhaps "the ancient mechanisms of place attachment provided a neural impetus for the emergence of social attachments" (407n.93).

Deviation from normalcy or removal from home may have different valences. But leaving home and normalcy is always a matter of risk—specifically, emotional risk. That is what attentional focus responds to—risk, both threats and opportunities. Because leaving home and normalcy involves risk, it involves emotion as well, at least potentially. Conversely, being at home and surrounded by what is routine involves the avoidance of risk. This too can give rise to emotion, if risk is expected or has recently been eluded.

In short, the spatiality of human being-in-the-world (to use the Heideggerian idiom) is a sort of *emotional geography* that develops out of fundamental human propensities toward organizing the world along two fundamental axes: normalcy and attachment.

Similar points may be made about the temporality of our being-in-the-world. It too is organized—or, more precisely, encoded—emotionally. Encoding is the process whereby we select, segment (or "chunk"), and give preliminary structure to our experience. There are many different ways in which we encode aspects of our experience. These depend on current interests, expectations, contextual relations (e.g., figure/ground relations in perception), and so forth. Moreover, there are different levels of encoding. Most basically, there is the perceptual encoding that gives us our sensory experience of the world. This is a function of the sensitivity of sensory neurons (e.g., visual neurons, with their sensitivities to colors or particular orientations of lines), processes such as lateral inhibition (in which neurons surrounding a highly activated neuron are inhibited; this results in, for instance, the sharpening of lines in vision), and so on. There are also higher levels of selection, segmentation, and structuration. Some of these are self-conscious. In those self-conscious cases, we may refer to the processes as "construal" or, even more broadly, "interpretation." Though only partially recognized by theorists of emotion, it seems that our emotional encoding of experience also occurs repeatedly and at different levels. For example, there is a very basic level of emotional encoding that is bound up with perceptual encoding. Joseph LeDoux has argued that there are two perceptual streams, one of which goes directly to subcortical emotion systems, while the other goes to cortical areas. Thus a potentially threatening movement in our vicinity might activate a circuit connected to the amygdala, thereby generating fear. At the same time, a more informationally rich encoding of that experience may be sent to cortical areas, which may then inhibit or enhance the amygdala response. Put differently, in the "low road" (as LeDoux calls it), particular sorts of motion and proximity (commonly in relation to expectation) are selected by our sensory systems and given a tentative structure in relation to fear. At this fundamental level, emotional encoding is directly part of perceptual encoding.

But again, that is only the initial level. The development of emotional experiences involves repeated encodings. Consider again Stiva's conflict with Dolly. As Stiva recalls this highly emotional experience (or sequence of experiences), a few components stand out sharply. The first is the image of Dolly with the letter, "looking at him with an expression of horror, despair, and fury" (2). What is striking here is that this immediately divides the experience into an almost atemporal focus and a broader periphery. The focal moment is in some way the key experience. It is the point that defines the emotion, or that crystallizes it. There is of course a larger event here. Dolly presumably moves and speaks; so does Stiva. The occurrences that constitute the event involve change. But this key moment is compressed, almost frozen. There is at least one other compressed, emotionally crucial moment as well—Stiva's "silly smile" (3). Here, too, there must have been many occurrences surrounding the smile. But Stiva seems almost fixated on this one act, which he deeply regrets. In short, the temporal landscape here is uneven, and the unevenness is emotional. Some of the occurrences that constitute this sequence—itself forming a sort of whole or episode—are highly salient and consequential; others are downplayed.

It is worth considering just what gives these particular moments their importance or, more precisely, what leads to this particular encoding of this sequence. Here, then, is the episode as Stiva recalls it. Stiva is return-ing home from the theater. His mood is "cheerful" and he carries "a huge pear for his wife." He looks for her, sees her "in the bedroom holding the unlucky note" (2). She asks him, "What is this? This?" (3). He responds with his smile. Her reaction follows. It is difficult to say how long this sequence took. There is a "torrent" of words that may have lasted ten seconds or ten minutes. Either way, the entire matter is reduced to the key emotional moments isolated above. We may refer to these moments as "incidents." Incidents, as I am using the term, are the focal points of emotional response, the minimal units of emotional temporality. More-over, they seem to operate through something akin to lateral inhibition. Specifically, the isolation of an incident appears to reduce the saliency of surrounding occurrences. (I use "occurrence" as a neutral term, indiffer-ent as to duration, structure, etc.) In this way, incidents stand out more sharply from the sequence of occurrences than is warranted by the occurrences themselves. Finally, incidents serve as the nuclei of "events." An "event," as I am using the term, is the next level of temporal segmentation, encompassing a cause and response to an incident. Events themselves compose episodes. An "episode" in this sense is a series of events that begins and ends in temporary normalcy. Above the episode, we have stories. A story begins and ends in permanent normalcy.

To understand the segmentation of incidents here, and particularly its emotional nature, it is helpful to establish the context for Stiva's meeting with his wife. One important aspect of emotional response is that our experience of emotion does not operate on an absolute scale. It is in part a function of the gradient of change from one moment to the next. To some extent, this is a matter of our prior mood. But it also crucially involves our expectations, including—perhaps most importantly—our tacit anticipations. In keeping with this, Tolstoy informs us about Stiva's positive mood. Moreover, he suggests that Stiva anticipated enhancing his cheerfulness by presenting the pear to his wife and receiving a warm response from her. The oral, sensual nature of this particular gift also suggests that he envisioned at least a playful physical response from her. (Contrast, say, the gift of a book or theater tickets.) This is not to say that we should envision Stiva as self-consciously thinking out all this. Rather, insofar as we imagine Stiva as a full person, we must imagine him as having a series of implicit anticipations. Given all this, we may begin to understand the isolation of this particular incident. When Stiva sees Dolly holding the incriminating letter, he sees a face filled with "horror, despair, and fury" (2). This hostility directed at Stiva provides perhaps the most striking contrast with his own mood and, more significantly, his tacit anticipation of Dolly's response to the pear.

But why does Stiva (or Tolstoy) isolate just these aspects of the scene—Dolly's expression and the letter itself? As noted in the introduction, certain features of the world and of our own bodily experience are encoded almost immediately as emotion triggers. In some cases, this is due to innate sensitivities—perhaps most crucially, innate sensitivities to the *expressive outcomes* of emotion. The point holds with particular force for attachment figures. Attachment enhances the likelihood of emotional contagion—as suggested by the case of monkeys acquiring fear of snakes from their mothers.

Thus it is no accident that Stiva experiences a particular emotional spike in connection with the facial, emotion expression of his wife, an attachment figure (on spikes in an emotion experience, see Greg Smith "Local"). Note that in this case the response is partially complementary and partially parallel. Stiva feels "despair" in parallel with her "despair" (2, 3). But he feels fear and shame in the face of her "fury" and "horror" (2). No less importantly, Stiva remarks on her posture and movement. These too are emotionally expressive. He had tacitly imagined her "bustling about" in the sort of motion that would fit with his own "cheerful" mood. He is faced, instead, with her "sitting motionless" (2), thus in an attitude in keeping with her despair—the one parallel emotion that he experiences (2, 3).

So, the first incident of this episode segments a moment of sharp emotional change, due to a sharp change in expectations, a change triggered by emotional expressions from an attachment figure. It is becoming clear why so much else in the larger occurrence fades into obscurity. However, we are still left with one unexplained detail—why the letter?

There are several reasons why the letter is important. I address only one. When we experience an emotional spike, our cognitive response is partially automatic. Crucially, we shift our attentional focus. But just what do we shift our attentional focus to? It is relatively simple—causes, or possible causes. Almost immediately upon experiencing an emotion, we begin to attribute a cause. More precisely, we narrow our attentional focus to candidate causes, attributing a cause very quickly. This is crucial because causal attribution is a necessary prerequisite for any actional outcome. Put very crudely, if I am afraid, I need to know what I am afraid of in order to run away in the right direction. It may seem that this is just obvious. We just know directly what causes our emotion. Indeed, it may seem that we would not even have the emotion if we were unable to attribute a cause. But in fact our causal attributions are highly fallible. Later in the novel, Tolstoy makes the point that "sometimes [Anna] had no idea of what it was that she was afraid of and what she wanted. Whether she was afraid of what had happened, and wanted that, or of what was going to happen, and wanted that, or just what it was that she wanted, she had no idea" (345). Research suggests that Anna's state is far less remarkable than it might seem. The condition is unusual only in the fact that Anna recognizes that she does not know the cause of her fear or of her desire. We never directly know these causes. We must always infer them. Most often, however, we do not realize that we have to do this. We *think* that we know. As Frijda explains, "One knows, generally, that one has an emotion; one does not always know why, and what exactly makes one have it; and if one does know, it is a construction, a hypothesis, like those one makes about the emotions of someone else" (464). Moreover, even when "correct," our causal attributions are only partial. I may feel sad for many reasons. But I will be inclined to isolate only one or two—the most obvious or salient ones but not necessarily the most significant ones (see Clore and Ortony 27; Zajonc 48; and Damasio, *Looking* 75). Of course, we usually do get our causal attributions roughly right. Moreover, our simplifications and inferences based on normalcy are usually reasonable. I am going along in the usual way, then receive a letter explaining that I made a mistake in my income tax return, and rather than receiving a $392 refund, I actually owe $4,723. Later in the day, I feel unhappy. I attribute it not to the ordinary things that occur every day but to this unusual and unexpected occurrence. Nonetheless, even in cases such as this, our causal attributions remain simplifying inferences.

One important, simplifying aspect of our automatic and immediate causal attribution is that we tend to stop with the most proximate cause. We may elaborate on the causal sequence subsequently and self-consciously. But we tend not to do this spontaneously. The one clear and consistent exception to this is the case of emotions that result from other people's emotional expressions. We may refer to these as "expression-triggered emotions." In those cases, it is crucial that we attribute a cause, not only to our emotions but to the emotions of the other person as well. If my friend shouts in fear, it is his shout that causes my fear. But I do not want to run away from his shout or from him. Rather, I want to run away from, say, the bear he has spotted.

Here we may return to the letter. The letter figures importantly because it is the salient object for causal attribution. Its salience is enhanced by Stiva's expectation of handing Dolly the pear, an expectation that would draw his attention to anything she is holding, and of course by her following question, with its demonstrative repetition ("What is this? This?"), presumably accompanied by appropriate movement. Indeed, the question itself is included in Stiva's recollection primarily because it converges with Stiva's attentional focus on the letter as the cause of Dolly's emotion.

But, of course, this cause does not in itself give the crucial information about the direction of Dolly's emotion. Thus we need to add a further sort of inference here. In expression-triggered emotions, we need to isolate the *target* of the other person's feeling as well as the cause. The two are often the same, but they need not be. We commonly isolate the target of an emotion by isolating the target of a trajectory of motion, a look, a verbal address. In the case we have been considering, the emotional target is of course Stiva, for Dolly was "looking at him" with her "expression of horror, despair, and fury" (2). This target isolation also makes Stiva salient for himself. Indeed, recognizing oneself as the target of someone else's attention regularly makes one self-conscious, makes one aware of oneself as an object. This self-awareness may have different foci. For example, it may be a matter of physical beauty, status markers (as in dress), or racial group. Most importantly for our purposes, it may be a matter of one's own emotional expressions, particularly in a context where emotional expressions are already salient, as here. In keeping with this, the second incident in this episode is Stiva's experience of his own facial gesture, his "silly smile" (3).

Before going on to this, however, we need to return to the hierarchical organization of temporality. The treatment of causal attribution begins to move us from the incident (Dolly motionless in the chair with the expression of horror, despair, and fury) to the encompassing event. As briefly indicated above, the event includes the proximate cause and what we might call the "situational response," the immediate actional outcome. Consider a paradigmatic scenario for fear. A predator appears unexpectedly within my field of vision. I feel fear—attributing this (accurately) to the presence of the predator. Since this is a highly aversive situation, my unreflective response is to try to alter it. Since it is fear in particular, my response is to try to run away. I look around for a path that will take me away from the predator. The situation for Stiva is similar though more complex. It is highly aversive. Thus his spontaneous impulse is to change the situation or his relation to it. This general response is particularized by the specific emotions involved—the shame, despair, and fear or anxiety. The difficulty for Stiva is that this combination of emotional responses does not point toward any clear actional outcome.

Shame counsels concealment. Shame is bound up with our acute sense that we are the target of other people's aversion, particularly disgust, physical or moral.[4] Our immediate response to this is the wish "to hide, disappear, or die" (as Lewis puts it in "Self-Conscious" 748). Note that this sense of shame further enhances Stiva's self-consciousness about himself as the target of Dolly's attention. This self-consciousness is likely to make him intensely aware of his own emotional expressions. The salience of these expressions increases the likelihood that he will isolate them in causal attribution for any subsequent incidents in Dolly's emotional response. Thus Dolly's subsequent shudder, "torrent" of words, and exit might in principle have been provoked by any number of things. Stiva's self-consciousness at this moment makes his own emotional expression—in this case, the facial gesture—highly salient for him, thus a likely object for causal attribution. It may, in turn, become isolated as the focus of his own intense regret, thus becoming an incident in a separate emotional event.

In any case, Stiva's experience of shame points toward an actional outcome of hiding. However, it may also point to an actional outcome of appeasement or submission. Many emotions involve more than one possible actional outcome. Typically, they are hierarchized—in fear, first try flight, but if that does not work, try to fight (or in certain cases, freeze). More generally, actional outcomes are bound up with spontaneous, rapid, unself-conscious possibility assessments. An assessment that one option is not viable shifts one's response down the hierarchy of actional alternatives. In some cases, that shift can be repeated until no options remain. Tolstoy is particularly sensitive to our experience of such complete impossibility. Thus, when Stiva first begins to recall his situation, he thinks of "his impossible position" (2). He experienced the first shift in the direction of such impossibility in relation to shame when he initially saw Dolly holding the letter, for he could not hide. This left an appeasement response as his only option. We will return to this below.

Stiva finds himself in a similar position with regard to fear or anxiety. He could of course flee the immediate situation. However, even in the short term, that would not prove much of a solution. Where would he go? He could not simply remove himself to another part of the house, since Dolly could follow. If he left the house, where would he spend the night? I do not believe that this is a matter of long-term calculations, as the preceding questions might suggest. The exclusion of flight as a possible response is much the same as would occur in cases of physical threat when all escape routes pose dangers (the predator could catch me if I go right, but there is a battlefield with landmines to left).

A subsequent response option is to fight. But that too is not possible here, in part because Dolly's "fury" has not manifest itself in physical aggression. The only possible fight would be a verbal conflict over Stiva's guilt—"making denials or excuses" (3), as Stiva puts it retrospectively. But Stiva is guilty; the letter proves it. More importantly, his own sense of shame inhibits his fight response along precisely this axis of dispute. The fight response relies on a feeling of anger being connected with the anxiety. However Stiva's sense of his own guilt inhibits this response. Stiva "couldn't manage to put on the right expression . . . now that his guilt was exposed." There were several possibilities for that "right expression." One involved "acting offended" (3), thus a form of anger, but again, that was emotionally excluded.

Freezing too is an option within the hierarchy of fear outcomes. However, it is preferential only in cases where one is not already the target of gaze, motion, and/or address from the threatening agent. None of this is the case for Stiva. On the other hand, freezing tends to occur when no other actional outcome is initiated and this partially happens with Stiva.

Finally, there is the option of appeasement. This opposes both flight and aggressive motion and thus may partially converge with freezing. Still, as in the case of shame, it is not clear that this provides a solution.

The despair felt by Stiva only compounds the problem. Despair leads to just the sort of motionlessness that Stiva sees in Dolly. It is bound up with Stiva's possibility assessments—or, more properly, impossibility assessments: "What is there to do? He said to himself in despair, without finding an answer" (3). The despair inhibits any possibilities for concealment, flight, conflict—or even much in the way of appeasement. It is most obviously compatible with submission, but submission of a very minimal sort—submission that does not really go beyond the absence of a refusal to submit.

What, then, does Stiva do? What is the actional outcome of his emotion, his response to this provoking incident, the outcome that results from the interaction of these emotion systems and situational constraints? It is his silly smile. It is a form of emotional expression that serves generally to indicate benevolence. It is a "goodhearted" smile (3). Izard and Ackerman explain that "the smile has the capacity to operate as a universally recognizable signal of readiness for friendly interaction" (258). Brody and Hall note that smiling "is socially useful in that it puts others at ease" (346). This suggests that Stiva's smile may be viewed as a sort of appeasement response. Tolstoy later makes this use of smiling explicit. Seryozha is a poor student, yet he "always conquered" his tutor with a "gay and affectionate smile" (625). Indeed, Stiva himself later has an unpleasant exchange with Karenin about Anna. In response to Karenin's anger, Stiva's face assumes "an embarrassed smile" as he says, "Forgive me then, forgive me if I've wounded you" (867). Stiva's response to Dolly is an expressive and actional outcome of the same sort.

At the same time, it is more than this. First, it is a sort of default facial expression for Stiva. It is his "usual" expression (3), by implication an expression that his face assumes when there is no strong emotional reason for it to assume any other expression—or when there are conflicting emotional pressures that are not easily resolved. Perhaps most importantly, the smile suggests Stiva's own attitude toward himself. The target of Stiva's smile is in part Dolly, suggesting his goodhearted friendliness. But the target is in part himself. Again, at this point, he is highly self-consciousness. With regard to himself, this smile suggests his sense of his own ludicrousness. He feels the smile to be "silly" because he feels himself to be silly. It may, then, be consistent with a sense of shame. Later in the novel, Tolstoy reports something of just this sort. Specifically, Levin smiles in such a way as to express the feeling that he is at once ridiculous and blameworthy: "Levin smiled at his own thoughts and shook his head at them disapprovingly; a feeling something like remorse tormented him" (581).

One obvious problem with a smile as an appeasement response is that a smile is ambiguous. Beyond a desire for reconciliation or a sense of one's own ludicrousness, it could suggest self-contentment, amusement, or mockery. Here we need to shift to Dolly's perspective. She anticipates some strongly negative emotional response on Stiva's part—perhaps remorse, perhaps anger, but certainly something clearly indicating that he finds the situation emotionally aversive. In the context of this expectation, any sign of a positive affect is, at best, disconcerting. In Dolly's case, it pushes her complex emotions in the direction of fury (rather than horror or despair). This is compounded by the fact that Stiva's smile must frustrate Dolly's desire regarding Stiva's response, not only her expectations. Specifically, her preference—based in part on attachment—would be that he is not guilty (in which case, he would respond with anger) or that, if guilty, he begs forgiveness.[5] Stiva's apparent amusement frustrates both desires—and frustration is a primary trigger for anger.

To recapitulate, we have just outlined an event. There is the emotion-provoking incident (Dolly, motionless, looking at Stiva with horror, despair, and fury), causal attribution (the letter), target isolation for the emotional expression, and expressive and actional outcomes. Stiva experiences this as an event, Tolstoy depicts it as such, and we presumably experience it as such as well.

This event is causally enchained with a second event. In this case, Stiva's expressive and actional outcome (the smile) serves as an emotion-provoking incident for Dolly. This makes Dolly angry, leading to the expressive outcome of a shudder, followed by the actional outcome of shouting and leaving the room. Dolly plays out a more ordinary sort of anger response here. She experiences something akin to "physical pain" (3) and responds with aggression—verbal rather than physical. When the aggression is complete, she leaves, flight following fight in a fairly predictable way.

Thus we have a second event. I will not consider this in great detail. However, it should be clear that the incident arises in much the same way here as in the first case and that the event forms by the same principles as well. For Dolly, Stiva's facial expression is a highly emotionally provocative violation of expectation, and if construed as mockery or even amusement, a violation of attachment-based preference as well. The target isolation is obvious (we can assume Dolly takes Stiva to be smiling at her). Finally, the actional and expressive outcomes are clear.

Dolly's departure, the end of this second event, marks an interruption in the causal sequence, if only temporarily. That is why this sequence of two events constitutes an episode. For example, that is why it makes sense for Tolstoy to end the first chapter with Stiva "in despair," thinking, "But what can I do? What is there to do? . . . without finding an answer" (3). Prior to the first incident, we have ordinary life, normalcy. After Dolly leaves, there is a sense in which that situation is restored. For example, Stiva is able to go to sleep and to wake up expecting to find his robe and slippers. He would not be able to do this if Dolly were in the room, questioning him about the letter or berating him. But at the same time, it is clear that the emotions aroused by these incidents and their encompassing events will have further expressive and actional consequences. In other words, it is clear that further events will follow in the same emotional/causal sequence. Indeed, the incident that provoked Stiva's regret has not been developed into a full event. The possibility of any satisfactory actional outcome on Stiva's part has been lost by Dolly's departure. The temporary return to normalcy marks this as a structural unit of emotional history. But it is not a *story*, because the non-normal enchainment of emotional causes initiated by the opening incident will continue.

Of course, this eventually does change. Despite Stiva's feeling at the end of chapter 1 that his situation is impossible, it is not really impossible. It is apparently impossible in the short term, but not in the long term. Again it is clear that the incidents will continue to provoke emotions, actions, and further incidents. The issue is whether there is anything that will produce an enduring normalcy—either a comic, nonaversive situation that demands no further action or a tragic situation that could never be altered. In principle, there are several possibilities here. Tolstoy offers one option in particular. It is a version of the submission or appeasement response and is named by Stiva in the course of this episode—"asking forgiveness" (3). A recurring motif in the novel is that human emotional conflict requires continual forgiveness—the guilty parties seeking forgiveness, the offended parties granting it. We are oriented toward this from the epigraph to the novel, "Vengeance is mine; I will repay, saith the Lord" (xv). Punishment should be in the hands of God alone.[6] In Tolstoy's novel, forgiveness has the highest place among possible responses to the emotional pains that result from social interaction. Indeed, forgiveness is itself an emotional response, and one that is not unrelated to attachment—as we see when Dolly forgives Stiva later on, when Levin forgives Kitty for rejecting his first proposal, and when Kitty forgives Levin for his premarital affairs. Forgiveness is what rounds out this particular episode, turns it into a story, and brings the life of Stiva and Dolly back from this rift into normalcy. The normalcy is of course not untroubled. But that normalcy, and its troubles, are no longer part of this particular story.

In sum, our experiences of both space and time are encoded non-homogeneously. The principles by which objects and occurrences are selected, the principles by which they are segmented, and the principles by which they are structured, both internally and in embedded hierarchies, are crucially (though of course not exclusively) emotional. In relation to this, our sense of normalcy, our expectations, our experience of other peoples' emotional expressions, our attachment relations with those people, and our tacit possibility assessments are of particular importance in our organization of emotional geography and, even more, emotional history. Finally, the hierarchical organization of emotional history involves almost atemporal provoking incidents, "thicker" structures of causal attribution and actional outcome (events), episodes or sequences of causally enchained events that move from normalcy through disruption to temporary normalcy, and finally, stories that conclude the sequence of episodes with enduring normalcy.

The Nature of Emotion

One thing that is striking about the embedding of occurrences is what it suggests about the relation between our emotional life and various time scales of expectation and aspiration. Incidents seem to narrow emotions to almost timeless points. Stories expand them to long-term projects, which may unfold over years or even decades. This difference in emotional encoding may be at the basis of some differing theories of emotional response. For example, in his discussion of emotion in *Anna Karenina*, Keith Oatley (*Best*) stresses Tolstoy's keen awareness of the way events interact with goals—often quite long-term goals—in the development of emotions. Oatley is right to stress this, because the interaction of events and goals is profoundly important in the novel, and in life.

Yet that sort of long-term calculation is only part of emotional history. To use the terminology introduced above, it is encoding at the level of interpretation—self-conscious, rational, projected into the future. However, what is perhaps most striking about Stiva's situation is that its emotional peaks are, for the most part, not large, rational, calculative, but small, immediate, spontaneous. The possibilities for large, interpretive plans guiding our emotional response to events has led many emotion theorists to explain emotion in terms of judgments about the relation between an occurrence or situation on the one hand, and our interests, needs, and desires on the other. At the same time, the possibilities for small, proximate occurrences to excite emotional responses has led other theorists to stress relatively mechanical and automatic processes. The former approach is commonly referred to as "the appraisal theory of emotion." The latter does not have a common name. I refer to it as "the perception theory of emotion." Both names are somewhat misleading. For example, appraisals, according to most theorists, need not be consciously undertaken, despite the apparent implication of the term. Moreover, the perception theory does not require that emotion elicitors be perceived by the senses; they may be imagined or remembered (through emotional memories, as noted in the introduction).

Appraisal theory is associated with such theorists as Nico Frijda and Keith Oatley. Perception theory is connected with writers such as Joseph LeDoux and Antonio Damasio. There is some crossover between the theories and there are some overlapping principles.[7] However, for the most part, the two theories are not readily reconciled. In terms of the preceding discussion, it seems that theorists who focus on episodes and particularly on stories are likely to view emotion in terms of appraisal. In contrast, theorists who focus on events and particularly on incidents are likely to view emotion in terms of perception.

The remainder of this chapter considers these two alternative approaches to emotion, developing a possible synthesis that brings together the benefits of each, and examining the relation of the resulting account to subnarrative temporal encoding. It begins by briefly sketching these two alternatives, stressing the perceptual account, which is fundamental for the eventual synthesis, and which I have already outlined in the introduction.

Appraisal accounts of emotion begin from the fact that we do not respond emotionally to simple perceptual facts. Rather, we respond emotionally to facts with a certain meaning or significance, facts interpreted in a certain way. Consider again the case of Stiva and Dolly. The appraisal theorist would say that Stiva cannot simply be responding to Dolly's physical appearance, with the sheet of paper in her hand. Rather, he is responding to an understanding of that appearance, a knowledge that the sheet of paper is a particular letter, an inference that she has read the contents of the letter and therefore learned of his affair.

Indeed, Stiva's response involves cognitive processes beyond even these interpretations. For example, he would have responded differently if he had been trying to find some way of informing Dolly about the affair so that he could end their marriage. Specifically, he not only interprets the situation but also relates the situation to his own concerns and interests. These concerns and interests are a function of goals—short-term and long-term goals, goals relating to different areas of life, goals bearing on maintaining or changing certain situations or conditions. Stiva is largely happy with his current life. One of his goals is to maintain the routines of this life. He has probably never formulated this goal explicitly. It is nonetheless a real goal. He goes to work, organizes his relation to his wife and children, interacts with friends and colleagues—all in such a way as to preserve the basic structure of his daily existence. He also has various subsidiary goals, ranging from having access to his wife's wealth to avoiding unpleasant conflict. When he interprets the situation, when he understands that Dolly has learned of his affair, he places the new knowledge in the context of these goals. Specifically, he judges the bearing this new situation will have on the likelihood of achieving those goals.

Appraisal is just this process of evaluating the ways in which a particular, interpreted situation affects one's ability to achieve one's goals. Broadly speaking, we may say that positive emotions reflect situations that make goal achievement more likely while negative emotions reflect situations that make goal achievement less likely. Particular positive or negative emotions reflect particular configurations of goals and facilitations or inhibitions of the achievement of those goals. For example, jealousy arises when attachment goals are threatened by a rival. Some appraisal models, such as that of Oatley, are modular. They posit distinct mental systems that govern different types of goal. These systems have specifiable relations with one another (e.g., the disgust system may inhibit the lust system) and particular orders of importance (e.g., in cases of conflict, the fear system may take preference over the hunger system—as when we see some tasty-looking berries right next to a bear and are trying to determine whether we should go for the food or run from the animal).

Returning once more to Stiva and Dolly, the appraisal account tells us that Stiva quickly and unself-consciously judges that the new situation (Dolly learning of his affair) has harmful effects on his pursuit of several goals. Most simply and obviously, it makes his goal of avoiding unpleasant conflict almost impossible, as her look of "fury" suggests that an argument is likely. Since Stiva is undoubtedly aware of laws governing divorce and of cases of divorce, he is undoubtedly aware that this change in situation raises the possibility that Dolly will divorce him. That interpretation in turn suggests that this new situation will affect Stiva's ability to maintain his current life. Put simply, the likelihood that he would be able to maintain his current life seemed virtually certain a few minutes earlier. Now his ability to fulfill that goal has been put in doubt.

In short, Stiva sees something, a physical situation. That mere configuration of objects has no emotional consequences in itself. The emotional impact of the situation on Stiva is the result of two processes. First, he must interpret the situation, giving it meaning. Second, he must evaluate the ways in which that interpreted situation impacts his ability to fulfill certain goals. The positive or negative valence of his emotional response results from the degree of impact and the value of the goals (strong inhibition of important goals is more negative; weak inhibition of trivial goals is less negative). In addition, the precise emotions are governed by the nature of the inhibition or facilitation and the nature of the goals (inhibition of attachment goals through a rival gives rise to jealousy; facilitation of such goals through a helper gives rise to gratitude).

The benefits of the appraisal account are obvious. It seems clear that we do not respond emotionally simply to physical configurations. Rather, we respond to the meaning of situations for us, thus their consequences for things we care about. Moreover, it seems clear that we do evaluate situations in light of our goals. Someone in Stiva's position would realize that he and Dolly are likely to quarrel. Someone in Stiva's position would think that she may now divorce him. Conversely, someone in Dolly's position would not have an emotional response simply to the sight of marks on a piece of paper. Rather, she would have an emotional response to an interpretation of those marks, an interpretation according to which Stiva was having sexual relations with another woman. Indeed, in light of these examples, it seems difficult to imagine how anyone could hold to a perceptual account of emotion.

But there are complications. First, we respond to certain perceptual experiences very quickly. Indeed, in at least some cases, our emotional responses appear to be governed by precisely those aspects of experience that we do *not* judge, evaluate, or appraise. Again, Joseph LeDoux has presented neurological evidence that there are two perceptual pathways that bear on fear. One pathway goes from the thalamus to the amygdala. Signals are passed quickly along this pathway and produce a very swift emotional response. The other pathway goes from the thalamus to the sensory cortex, and from there to the amygdala and elsewhere (see *Emotional* 164, 166). The standard example of this is the following. I am walking in the woods. I notice something at my feet, and with a sudden sensation of fright, I jump back, letting out a little yelp and flailing my arms awkwardly. As I look further, I realize that the thing at my feet is a wet, smooth branch of a tree. I explain to my laughing colleagues that I thought it was a snake.

The neurological processes in cases of this sort are something along the following lines. Our perceptual systems are configured in such a way as to be sensitive to certain sorts of perceptual features—for example, certain shapes, certain shape and location correlations, certain types of motion. These encoding sensitivities are connected with certain emotion systems. To put it very crudely, when my visual system detects certain features in certain areas (e.g., features that we might associate with snakes, in locations that we might connect with snakes), then it signals the amygdala. This activation gives rise to a shift in attentional focus combined with an actional outcome of avoidance. Thus I jump back and look intently at the spot where I (or my visual system) detected those features. At the same time, my visual system sends the usual visual information through the usual visual processing circuits. Depending on the proximity of the perceived threat, thus the strength of the signal to the amygdala, I may actually recognize that the thing in the grass is a stick (not a snake) before I jump. In that case, I may be able to inhibit my response before it begins or when it is only partially completed (e.g., I may jerk my body slightly to one side but not actually leap away).

There are numerous cases of this sort in *Anna Karenina*. For example, it is a cliché that, when speaking with women in certain contexts, some men have a tendency to fix their gaze rather too low. Hence the comic phrase addressed by a woman to her date—"Hey, I'm up here!" Tolstoy was aware of this dilemma, and he reports an amusing occurrence of this sort when Levin goes to visit a family that, he suspects, desires him as a groom for one of the young women. He is seated across from the woman in question. She is wearing a dress with "a particularly low, square-cut décolletage showing her white bosom." Levin "kept trying not to" look at "it" and found it "impossible . . . to think freely" (394). Here we have a case of a perceptual encoding sensitivity, in this case linked to the system for sexual arousal.

More generally, the visual system is presumably sensitive not only to potential threats, bearing on fear or anger, but also to potential opportunities, bearing on, for example, sexual desire or hunger. These systems should then operate in the usual way. Thus particular perceptions should activate relevant subcortical emotion systems along with neocortical systems. The activated emotion systems arouse and direct attentional focus. This leads to enhanced encoding of the target perceptual object or area, with further activation of the relevant emotion system. At the same time, the neocortical activation allows the possibility of inhibiting actional and expressive outcomes that derive from the activation of the emotion systems.

Returning to Levin, we see a case of just this sort. Levin's visual system is sensitive to the secondary sexual characteristics of nubile women. This sensitivity is emotional in being linked to the system of sexual desire. Elicitors or triggers of this encoding sensitivity include breasts. Once activated, the system directs attention to the elicitors, thereby increasing activation, and so on. Neocortical activity may have an inhibitory function, but this is not always successful. Thus, Levin finds his gaze drawn repeatedly to the low-cut neckline of his dinner companion's dress. He tries to avoid this, but the downward movement of his eyes is automatic— a function of the attention system. In addition, he finds that his thought patterns are directed by the perceptual saliency produced by the young woman's outfit.

Here we have not only a neat illustration of the operation of perceptual emotion triggering but also a suggestion of how appraisal or appraisal-like processes may enter into a fundamentally perceptual generation of emotion. Specifically, we see that Levin evaluates the consequences of his attention to the décolletage and seeks to suppress the actional, expressive, and attentional consequences of his emotional arousal. Moreover, Tolstoy delicately explains that Levin was having thoughts that he could not control. It does not take too much imagination to infer what sorts of thoughts Levin was having. These thoughts undoubtedly involved the elaboration of the sexual opportunity indicated by the partial exposure of the young woman's body. This is not perhaps a paradigmatic case of appraisal in the sense usually discussed by appraisal theorists. However, it does proceed along the same lines. It involves the relation of a current situation to the fulfillment of interests, even if those interests involve goals that (in this particular case) Levin might repudiate. In other words, he would not consider sexual relations with this woman to be a goal—hence his attempt to inhibit his gaze, thoughts, and so on. Nonetheless, he does have longstanding interests in sexual satisfaction, and these bear directly on his gaze, thoughts, and so forth, guiding his perception, memory, and imagination. In short, even in cases where the perceptual account applies most obviously to a focal emotion-eliciting perception, there is still a penumbra of appraisal-like thought that bears on the ways in which the emotion is sustained, enhanced, inhibited, and so forth. That appraisal-like thought continually incorporates perceptual and related emotional elements.

This partial reconciliation of perceptual and appraisal accounts begins to suggest that a longstanding debate about emotion and cognition may have been misguided. Specifically, emotion researchers have disagreed with one another over whether emotion may or may not be independent of cognition. At one level, subsequent neurological and other research has fairly clearly demonstrated that the advocates of affective independence were correct (see Zajonc for discussion; for an early essay disputing this independence, see Lazarus). Nonetheless, this debate seems mistaken at two levels. First, even the most minimal innate sensitivity involves some shaping of experience by the neurocognitive architecture, even though it does not involve elaborative cortical processing. Second, even if the emotion activation is itself perceptual, not inferential, inferences and other forms of elaborative cognitive processing are perhaps the primary means by which we experience imagined emotion triggers and emotion memories. Moreover, even in cases where an emotion begins with a perception (external or internal), it is commonly sustained by the imaginations and memories that are engaged subsequent to that perception.

More precisely, as noted in the introduction, the perception account admits three sources of emotion elicitors—innate sensitivities, critical-period experiences, and emotional memories. There are also three modalities of emotion elicitation—current perception, recollection, and imagination. Imagination operates because it is parallel to perception. For instance, the same areas of the brain become active when I imagine a cup as when I perceive a cup (see Kosslyn 295, 301, 325; Rubin 41–46, 57–59). The emotional operation of imagination is particularly important in evolutionary terms, as it extends the adaptive value of emotion beyond current situations to possible future situations. For example, imagination allows me to anticipate what might happen if I go down a dark alley late at night. The emotional effects of imagination lead me to experience apprehension in the face of that imagination and thus lead me to avoid going down the dark alley.

Imagination is particularly important for understanding temporal organization, for it operates in conjunction with current perception and memory and it involves a range of time scales. As Robert Jourdain notes, "the brain perceives by anticipation." The point applies not only to the perception of external objects but also to the experience of our own movement—"the brain makes the body move not merely by shouting commands down the corridors of the nervous system, but also by anticipating the sensations that will result from those commands" (302). Specifically, we may distinguish three degrees of anticipation, linked with functional and structural properties of neurocognitive architecture. The first are spontaneously calculated, very short-term expectations that extend only a fraction of a second into the future. These "sensorimotor projections," as we might call them, operate most obviously in connection with the relation between one's body and external objects—a baseball flying in one's direction, the trajectory of one's movement toward the water when diving into a swimming pool. These relations are "not calculated by the perceiver" but by "a perceptual system" (van Leeuwen 272). In keeping with this, research indicates that actions are initiated about a half-second before they are performed and about a fifth of a second before we become aware of them or may inhibit them (Walter 248–50).

The idea of awareness and inhibition takes us to working memory. Inputs from perceptual and long-term memory systems are integrated in working memory, which allows modification of automatic responses. Those modifications are in part the result of slightly longer-term expectations, which we may refer to as "working anticipations." Working anticipations organize experience and sensorimotor projection into slightly larger inferences and actions that extend beyond spontaneous calculations of a half-second or so. In keeping with the temporal limits of working memory (see Gathercole 20), we may tentatively fix these at about two seconds in extension. Note that by "working anticipations" I am referring specifically to working memory operations that bear on continuous activities that include an ongoing integration of sensorimotor projections. A simple case would be catching a baseball. My perceptual systems calculate the trajectory of the ball. They also calculate my own trajectory—for example, how fast I am moving toward the outfield fence. My working memory integrates this information, contributing to adjustments in my movement (e.g., to avoid tripping over a clump of dirt in the outfield). Working anticipations may also operate outside current perception in the case of vividly imagined experiences. Literature is a prominent instance of this sort, as suggested by Scarry's work.

Of course, working memory itself may project longer time scales as well. Specifically, it may draw on semantic memory to organize large, prototypical futures. Thus I may draw on my prototype for a career and expect to be hired, promoted, and then retire. These "long-term expectancies" may or may not incorporate working anticipations and sensorimotor projections. For example, I might imagine my retirement with considerable (if fragmentary) concreteness—if, say, I am writing a story. Alternatively, my view of retirement may be entirely vague, going hardly beyond the bare meaning of the word.

Appraisal accounts of emotion tend to stress what I am calling "long-term expectancies." In contrast, my perceptual account stresses sensorimotor projections and working anticipations. Indeed, by my account, long-term expectancies will usually have emotional consequences only insofar as they integrate the more concrete, short-term expectations. In any case, they will need to integrate perceptual/imaginative triggers—innate or critical-period derived—and/or emotional memories. Of course, in the context of dynamic planning, these triggers and memories would often be part of long-term imagined expectancies. Thus by the perceptual account, we would expect "appraisals" to have emotional effects, but only in cases where they incorporate perceptual contents—through perception proper, imagination, or emotional memory, often by way of embedded sensorimotor projections and working anticipations.

It is worth dwelling a bit further on the emotional operations of expectation. Expectations serve as eliciting conditions for emotion both in themselves and in their relation to actual results. As to the latter, we have different emotional responses to expected and unexpected outcomes. The point is obvious when we feel relief or disappointment, since these feelings depend entirely upon the contrast between expectation and experience. However, expectation-based effects are actually ubiquitous in our emotional experience. For example, having left her husband, Anna manages to return to the house on the occasion of her son's birthday. She makes her way into Seryozha's bedroom. After a brief meeting, she is informed that Karenin is on his way to the room. Anna's face takes on "an expression of fear and something like shame" (643). By a perception account, what is going on here is something along the following lines. Anna anticipates encountering Karenin. She tacitly imagines seeing his face, with a look of both anger and disgust. Given the imagined direction of his gaze and her more general relations with him, these inspire complementary (rather than parallel) emotions in her—thus fear (complementary to anger) and shame (complementary to disgust).

The various "perceptual" factors we have been considering combine to make it *seem* that appraisal gives rise to emotion. Appraisal makes certain sorts of imagination and recollection likely. Moreover, emotional experiences regularly give rise to appraisals or appraisal-like processes. Indeed, these processes serve to inhibit, sustain, or intensify emotional responses that would otherwise be likely to fade with the passing of the immediate triggers. In that sense, appraisal does indeed give rise to emotion. It does so indirectly, and it is not always present in emotional experience. But it is a crucial part of most emotional experiences—particularly the sorts of complex emotional experiences that pervade interpersonal relations in both literature and life. Still, it remains important to keep in mind that the appraisal itself is not the cause of emotion. It is simply an occasion for emotion-generating (or emotion-inhibiting) imagination, perception, and memory.

Anna Karenina includes many cases where appraisal processes provide the occasion for emotional response. We might now ask to what extent these fit a pure appraisal account and to what extent they are in keeping with the perceptual account, as it incorporates appraisal. Consider, for example, the early incident when a guard is run over by a train. Stiva sees "the mangled corpse." Tolstoy tells us that he had a strong emotional response, manifest in his facial expression: "Oblonsky was visibly distressed. His face was puckered up; he seemed ready to burst into tears" (76). It seems at first that Oblonsky's response must be simply to the sight of the corpse. This is somewhat peculiar. Oblonsky is exhibiting a response suggestive of grief. We might expect a disgust or fear response to the corpse of a stranger—and indeed, Tolstoy mentioned earlier that people in the crowd initially looked "frightened," a feeling that was communicated to Oblonsky before he went and saw the corpse. As it turns out, seeing the corpse itself does not constitute the crucial incident here. When Stiva is finally able to moderate his emotional response, he explains that the guard's "wife is there. . . . It's horrible to see her. . . . She flung herself on the body" (76). We now understand that Stiva's response is to this last incident and that it mirrors the grief of the widow. As if he is feeling that mere emotional contagion is an inadequate excuse for his response, he supplies a justification in the form of an appraisal, explaining that the guard was "the sole support of a huge family" (76). At this point, the contribution of pure appraisal—as opposed to perception, perceptual imagination, and emotional memory—is not clear. However, particularly given the intense emotional expression by the wife, an account of Stiva's response does not seem to require any distinct contribution of appraisal per se.

The emotional concerns of this episode continue with Anna. She is "agitated" by what Stiva tells her. It is at first difficult to say if this is due to the concrete image of the wife flinging herself on the dead body of her husband or due to an appraisal—perhaps a nonperceptual appraisal—of the family's situation. The actional outcome she recommends—giving the widow money—is certainly related to the appraisal. But that, of course, does not mean that it is motivated by pure appraisal processes. Soon after, Anna hears some passersby discussing the death. One explains that the man was "cut in two." Another says that it is the "easiest" death as it is "instantaneous" (77). While Anna had only been "agitated" before, now "her lips were trembling and . . . she was only holding back her tears with difficulty" (77). Her expression here is somewhat ambiguous. It suggests both fear and grief. It is not entirely clear why this would be the case. In appraisal terms, we do not know just what goals and assessments would bear on the recent exchange—for example, how the new information about the condition of the corpse would affect her appraisal of the widow's situation. From a perceptual perspective, the fear makes some sense, as the new information would be likely to foster an imagination of the corpse. But the apparently intensified grief seems more difficult to explain. Stiva reflects the reader's own uncertainty when he asks about the cause of Anna's emotion. Anna responds, "It's a bad omen" (77). This too is ambiguous between appraisal and perceptual construals. In purely appraisal terms, this appears to be a simple case of superstition. The sudden, tragic accident, just at the moment of her arrival, suggests to Anna that the likelihood of fulfilling important goals in her life will decrease suddenly and tragically. Perhaps this bears on particular goals. Thus perhaps it might foreshadow her own husband's death or the impoverishment of herself and her son.

But Anna's response is equally consistent with a perceptual account. In this view, the discussion by the passersby served as an externally imposed elaboration process that gave rise to concrete visualizations in her mind.

The obvious option for this concrete visualization is the one just suggested—the death of her husband. Indeed, readers unfamiliar with the course of the novel might tacitly imagine that Anna visualizes the death of her own husband and feels grief on that account. However, those familiar with the ending of the novel may suspect that, even here, Anna's grief is for herself. Her visualization was not triggered by the fact that the man was cut in two, but by the other claim, that it was the "easiest" death—thus the sort of death that one might desire for oneself. Retrospectively, we can understand how the image would occur to her. She is not, as one might at first imagine, the weeping widow in this scenario. Rather, the weeping is done by those she has left behind. She is the one for whom they are weeping. That is why, much later, on a strange railway platform, she recalls "the man who had been run over the day she first met Vronsky." That is why, at that moment, she realizes "what she [has] to do," thinking, "I'll punish him"—thus place him in the position of the bereaved widow—"and escape from everyone" (917–18). Indeed, after her suicide, Vronsky's grief, his "futile but indelible remorse" (933), crystallizes around an image parallel to that of the man cut in two by the train, "*she* . . . that is, what had been left of her . . . the mangled body, still full of recent life, stretched out shamelessly on a table before the eyes of strangers" (932–33). The incident in this early scene is, then, Anna's imagination of her own death.

In retrospect, we might reconsider Stiva's judgment regarding the bereaved family's finances. In cases such as this, appraisal may not only provide an opportunity for the elaboration of imagination, thus the enhancement or inhibition of emotional response. It might also serve as a post facto rationalization or justification for a more spontaneous, perceptual response. The idea turns up elsewhere in the novel. A nice case of this sort occurs when Karenin is contemplating a duel with Vronsky. He seems to engage in an appraisal of this course of action. There are two possibilities. He would shoot Vronsky or he would be shot by Vronsky. As to the former, he reasonably asks himself, "What would be the sense of killing a man in order to define one's own relations with a guilty wife and with one's son?" And what if he himself were shot? "There I'd be, an innocent man, victimized—killed or wounded. That's even more senseless" (335). He finds both options aversive and rejects them, thus presenting us with an apparently pure case of appraisal (if in a somewhat cooler and more fully rational form that envisioned by most appraisal theorists). But in fact, we know that Karenin had made up his mind before any of this appraising took place. Moreover, we know that his decision was based on an emotional response to a perceptual elicitor. Specifically, Tolstoy reports to us that "vividly picturing the night he would spend after the challenge and the pistol aimed at himself [Karenin] shuddered and realized that he would never do it" (335). The vivid imagination produces the emotion. The elaborate appraisal of different options follows and serves only to rationalize the prior emotion and consequent decision.

In sum, emotions require triggers in the perceptual theory sense. However, these momentary spikes of emotion are often not sustained without elaborative thought processes of the sort stressed by appraisal theorists. Specifically, we must add to the preceding perceptual account of emotion an encompassing set of appraisal-like processes—or more generally, a set of cognitive processes that *elaborate* on aspects of the emotional experience, including its object, context, history, personal associations, and so on. The elaborative processes do involve appraisal. Moreover, that appraisal is important. However, it has its consequences through the imagination of concrete conditions—thus perceptual emotion triggers, including sensorimotor projections and/or working anticipations—and through the activation of emotional memories. My contention is that this gives us a more plausible and powerful account of emotion. Moreover, it is bound up with just the sort of hierarchical structure of time that we considered at the outset of this chapter. In short, it provides a more adequate emotional theory and serves to ground a part of narrative theory—and the theory of existential temporality—in a neurocognitive theory of emotion. The remainder of this chapter first considers the relation of emotion to literature. It then returns to incidents, events, and episodes, briefly reconsidering them in relation to this account of emotion and further exploring their properties, particularly those of episodes.

Literary Feeling

Up to this point, we have been considering emotion that people experience in the real world or that we take characters to experience in fictional worlds. We have not been focusing particularly on the feelings readers or audience members experience in response to those fictional worlds. This is because there is no special emotion system for literature. To understand literary emotion, we need to understand emotion generally. Indeed, this continuity itself poses a problem. Specifically, there is a recurring issue in aesthetics as to why we respond emotionally to literature. For example, why do we cry at the depiction of suffering? We are not suffering ourselves. Moreover, we know perfectly well that the characters are not real. Thus they are not suffering either. Appraisal theorists such as Oatley suggest that we respond emotionally to literature because we mentally simulate the experiences of a character from his or her point of view (see *Best* 107–8). As his or her situation changes, we calculate the likely outcomes and the changes in that likelihood. As goal achievement becomes more likely, we become happy. When goal achievement—particularly goal achievement bearing on attachment—seems impossible, we become sorrowful. But this does not really explain fiction. It explains why we might cry when we hear a true story of someone's suffering. But it does not explain why we cry when we hear a story that is clearly fictional. One might get around this by arguing that we assume things like this happen all the time. Romeo and Juliet are not real, but there are real lovers who are separated like that. So perhaps we are weeping for them. But that seems odd. I know right now that real lovers are often separated, and I know it just as well as I know it at the end of *Romeo and Juliet*. Why is my response to that fact so different in those two situations? After all, it would seem that my appraisal of the situation of some abstract lovers being separated is the same now as at the end of Shakespeare's play.

Obviously, the perceptual account of emotion does not have this problem. The perceptual account may easily treat all the preceding facts. In the case of a live performance or film, we directly experience the actors' and actresses' facial expressions, their gestures, tone of voice, gait, posture, and so forth—all important emotion triggers. More significantly for our present purposes, our emotional response is bound up with our simulation of a character's experiences, as Oatley indicates. As Currie puts it, we "run a simulation which takes as initial conditions a perceptual state different from [our] own" (145). However, our emotional response is not a matter of the probability calculations that go along with that simulation. Rather, it is a matter of the concrete images we experience when engaging in that simulation. It is also a matter of the emotional memories that are activated during simulation—in the case of *Romeo and Juliet*, memories of romantic love, separation, and/or the death of loved ones.[8]

Clearly, our response to characters is some version of an empathic response. Hoffman points out that direct experiences of facial expressions, emotion vocalizations (such as sobs), and other perceptual factors tend to foster empathy. Verbal accounts may also inspire empathy "when the decoded message enables the observer to construct visual or auditory images of the victim (sad face, blood, cries, moans) and respond empathically to these images through the preverbal modes" ("Empathy" 442). This response may be enhanced by effortful "perspective taking" (442). This is of course precisely what the perceptual account suggests.

Crucially, in the perceptual model, the fictionality of the work is irrelevant. Again, our emotional responses are generated by the concrete imaginations and emotional memories, not by inferences as such. Thus there is no need to follow writers such as Currie who seem forced to posit "a pretend desire that the hero succeed, backed up by a pretend belief in his existence" (151). Our desire is a real desire. The idea of a belief is not well specified in terms of cognitive architecture, so it is a little harder to say anything about that. However, one sense of the term would refer to the outcome of a self-conscious inferential process—roughly, what we would say if answering a question about our beliefs. In that case, we probably have no belief of any sort in the hero's existence, pretend or otherwise. But again, positing such beliefs is necessary only for an appraisal account. It is irrelevant for a perceptual account.

Finally, a perceptual account indicates that we should respond more forcefully to more detailed and more concrete images, and less forcefully to abstract likelihoods or related evaluations. As a corollary of this, we should in general respond more intensely to sensorimotor projections and working anticipations than to long-term expectancies. This is precisely what occurs. Writers such as Elaine Scarry have discussed the exquisite sensory vivacity that great writers are able to create in our minds. That vivacity is just what we would expect in emotionally compelling works if it is concrete experience that triggers emotional response.

On the other hand, a problem remains here. The perceptual account of emotion predicts that we will have strong emotional responses to some fictions. But it faces us with the opposite issue. Why are our emotional responses in some ways so inhibited? Consider film, where the issue can be put very concretely. If a lion jumps out on the screen, why do we not run from the theater, or at least hide under our seats? One way of accounting for this is by reference to habituation. I believe that this is in fact a significant part of the explanation. However, it fails to fully connect our limited response to fiction with our limited response to imagination. Most components of an emotion play an important role in our ordinary, worldly imagination of possible situations and actions. These components most obviously include eliciting conditions (what gives rise to the emotion; in this case, that is the content of the imagination), phenomenological tone (what it feels like to have the emotion), and attentional focus. In extreme cases, they include expressive outcomes as well (such as crying or laughing), if typically in a muted form. What they do not include are the partially stereotyped actional outcomes that commonly result from emotions. Obviously, an emotion-eliciting imagination may lead us to act. But it leads to planned action, not to the spontaneous response of emotion. For example, if I imagine lions roaming in a certain part of the savanna, I avoid going there to hunt. However, I do not immediately start running, for fear of the imagined lions. The situation seems fundamentally the same as that in our experience of literature.

In the case of imagination, this is clearly not a matter of habituation. Thus it seems likely that in the case of fiction, our parallel inaction is not solely the result of habituation. Norman Holland has suggested that our involvement with literature and film is bound up with our physical immobility and our location of objects in space (see Holland "Willing" and "Where"). Though I would not follow Holland's specific analyses here, I believe that he is onto something in drawing our attention to action, inaction, and space. Specifically, the facts of imagination indicate that it is possible for us to inhibit the actional response component of an emotional episode completely or almost completely, without affecting the other emotion components. I suspect that this is connected with our location of events in space.

Standard neurocognitive architecture includes two sorts of spatial organization. One sort is objective and based in the hippocampus. This maps the relations of objects to one another, independent of one's own location. The other is egocentric and is connected most importantly with the superior parietal lobule (see Clark, Boutros, and Mendez 43). This keeps track of one's spatial relation to the rest of the world. In other words, this maps out not just the spatial relations of things on my desk but also where they are in relation to me right now. The ventral intraparietal area, which borders the superior parietal lobule, includes neurons "responsive to visual targets representing spatial reference frames (maps)." Among the "multiple reference frames" are, for example, neurons that "react to stimuli within reaching distance" (Clark, Boutros, and Mendez 46). My conjecture is that there is a critical proximity range, calculated by the superior and inferior parietal lobule and bearing on our position in the world and our activity within that position. The likelihood of actional outcomes for a given emotion is sharply increased by the location of triggering conditions within that critical range, currently or by anticipation. Take a simple example. I am up on a cliff. I see a lion below me on the plain. I feel fear. But I do not run. Indeed, I have no need to run. I probably do feel some tenseness in my muscles, resulting from the more general orienting response. But there is no actional outcome of the fear. Imagination, in my view, is basically the same sort of thing. In imagination, we typically do not integrate the emotional object (e.g., the lion) into that egocentric space of direct action, even in anticipation.

Yet this is not a full answer either. Sometimes we do integrate the emotional object in this way. Indeed, one could distinguish planning from fantasy largely on these grounds. In planning, we bring the object into the space of direct actional engagement in imagination. The point is even clearer in connection with literature, and it returns us to Oatley. Again, simulation involves imagining from the point of view of the character. That imagination must involve not only objective, hippocampal organization of space, but egocentric, parietal situatedness as well. Of course, this does not always happen in literature. But when it does occur, why do we not respond with actional outcomes?

In fact, it may be that we do respond, only in limited conditions and in a limited way. The most obvious case is the startle reflex. When something very surprising happens on-screen in a movie, I may jerk back in my seat. I may even jump up or push my feet into the ground, giving the start of a push away for flight. The same point holds in life. Imagine again that you are on a cliff overlooking a field. A lion appears. You see a fawn and, even without realizing it, adopt the spatial perspective of the fawn in imagination. The lion leaps toward the fawn. Your whole body pushes back as if to avoid the lion.

It seems likely that the limited conditions and scope of our response are a function of the speed of the reaction and the degree to which it can be inhibited. The startle reflex operates very quickly and is notoriously difficult to inhibit. Fleeing in fear allows some room for decision, thus inhibition. More exactly, there are perceptual experiences and sensorimotor projections that immediately initiate expressive outcomes or motor routines. Most large and complex motor routines (e.g., those involved in running away) are mediated by working memory processes. The motor routines involved in emotion expression (e.g., facial expressions) or attentional orientation (e.g., eye movement) are not initially mediated by working memory processes. We would expect that the components of our emotional response will differ to the extent that they are mediated by working memory. Thus we would expect both emotion expression and attentional orientation to be more subject to excitation in a film (or in reading a book) than would full-fledged actional outcomes.

We might begin to tie together the various strands of the preceding discussion in the following way. First, the spatial nature of our experience of the movie theater itself should bear at least in part on the operation of the egocentric parietal system for space. That system is the one that is crucial for sensorimotor projection. As such, we would expect a reduced (though by no means absent) sensorimotor projection component in our responses to the world depicted on the screen.[9] This would generally reduce the intensity of emotional response to a film. Second, working memory processes have greater impact on some components of emotional response, such as actional outcomes, and less on others, such as physiological arousal or attentional focus. As such, we would expect actional outcomes to be more fully inhibited than physiological arousal or attentional focus (with emotional expression falling between the two). On the other hand, there are variables here. People have different degrees of emotional sensitivity and of habituation. Moreover, different works present emotion triggers at different levels of density. Thus we might expect highly sensitive viewers with low habituation to have greater expressive and perhaps even actional outcomes, particularly when faced with a high density of emotion triggers. This is just what we seem to find. Viewers appear to be most likely to experience physiological arousal (thus the feeling tone of emotion) and to have their attention oriented by emotion triggers in films. They have somewhat more limited expressive outcomes—with a gradient that depends on the "display rules" (see, for example, Frijda 62 and citations) that govern expression of different emotions. (For example, men are expected not to cry during melodramas.)

Finally, this account suggests why some viewers of, say, *The Passion of the Christ*, left the theater moaning and trembling (as in one case I witnessed).

The preceding discussion suggests some of the problems with many treatments of reader or audience emotion. Consider, for example, Kendall Walton's influential analysis. Walton's treatment of the topic is insightful and challenging. Indeed, it anticipates the present discussion in a number of ways. However, it is based on the assumption of an appraisal account of emotion that grounds emotion in belief. But this assumption does not seem to accord well with the details of Walton's discussion. In addition, Walton's account lacks an adequately fine-grained analysis of the components of an emotion episode. Finally, Walton's account does not seem to have any explanatory consequences for the data he isolates.

More exactly, Walton wonders whether Charles, watching a movie about green slime, with "muscles tensed" and a quickened pulse, hands clutching the chair, is really feeling fear (196). Walton says that this cannot be the case because "to fear something is in part to think oneself endangered by it" (197; Walton slightly qualifies this, but the qualification is not important for our discussion). For Walton, this conclusion is bound up with the fact that "the possibility of physical interaction is disallowed" (196).

By the present account, Walton is indeed onto something. The issue of physical interaction is crucial, as is the limited emotional response. But this is not a matter of real fear versus "quasi-fear" (196). Rather, the inhibition on interaction affects specific aspects of our projections and anticipations bearing on the parietal organization of space (or, rather, spatiality, in the Heideggerian sense). The results of our different expectations have different consequences for physiological response and actional outcomes, as well as other components of emotional experience. These component responses vary predictably with the degree of working memory mediation.

These points bear on Walton's claims about Charles's beliefs as well. Walton rightly notes out that "Charles has *no* doubts about whether he is in the presence of an actual slime" (198). But this simply means that, if Charles formulates an explicit belief for himself or for someone else, then—through working memory mediation—he affirms that he is not in the presence of an actual slime. Rather than showing that Charles is not feeling fear, this suggests that emotional response is not governed by beliefs as such. Rather, some aspects of emotional response are affected by the elaborations involved in working memory processes, whereas others are not.

In sum, Walton's evidence seems to point not toward his own conclusions but toward the inadequacy of a belief-based appraisal account and the explanatory value of a perceptual account.

Incidents, Events, and Episodes Revisited

Given this account of emotion, we may now return to our division of subnarrative temporality into incidents, events, and episodes, defining them more precisely.

Incidents comprise the eliciting conditions for an emotion along with the sensorimotor projections that are activated by those conditions and, finally, the immediate physiological outcomes, phenomenological tone, attentional orientation, expressive outcomes, and emotional memory activations that result without working memory mediation.

Events involve the temporal elaboration of incidents through working memory. Specifically, they include working anticipations and causal attributions. Both are largely derived from prior sensorimotor projections and attentional orientations along with emotional and representational memories. In other words, anticipations and causal attributions are primarily a matter of what is salient in the current (real or imagined) experience. In social emotions, causal attribution commonly involves the positing of an emotional/motivational state on the part of some other agent. This is often related to emotion expression by that agent, thus part of the initial incident. However, it may also result from more effortful (working memory–based) simulation of the other person's feelings and intentions. Finally, events involve the initiation of actional outcomes, thus the activation of procedures and the modification of those procedures in relation to current conditions.

Episodes are of course a development beyond events. They are defined in part by the causal interconnection of events. However, their endpoint involves a temporary suspension of current, working anticipations and the replacement of those working anticipations by longer-term expectancies. When Stiva and Dolly are together, both continue to have working anticipations of possible actions and reactions—imminently possible incidents. However, when Dolly leaves, then both must shift to longer-term expectancies (e.g., what will occur on the following day). In addition, episodes commonly involve the elaboration of fuller explanations out of simple causal attributions (roughly, praise or blame), as found in events.

To clarify these points, we might consider a final example. One evening, expecting to be courted by both Levin and Vronsky, Kitty Shcherbatsky spends the time after dinner "imagining" these two men, sifting through her past with them, envisioning a future. At 7:30, after much mental anguish of anticipation, Levin arrives at the Shcherbatsky household. He was planning to propose to Kitty and hoping for—thus envisioning as one possibility—a positive reply. Anticipating that Levin will propose when they are alone in just a few moments, Kitty experiences the sort of complex social emotion that one expects in a novel. But what she feels is, at the same time, a version of a more basic "physical" emotion. Specifically, she experiences fear. Fear always comes from an anticipation of one's own pain. The complexity in this case derives from the fact that Kitty's pain will be empathic, a matter of feeling what Levin will feel and will undoubtedly express on his face. To make matters worse, that empathic experience of Levin's pain will be enhanced by Kitty's attachment to Levin. As Tolstoy puts it, reflecting Kitty's own imagination of the event, "she would have to hurt a man she loved" (56). The imagination of these developments forms itself into an incident in Kitty's mind, and she has the usual response, guided by the fear system: she directs her attention to various options for action. She does not do this in a slow, deliberative way, but in the way one considers alternatives when facing a threat. She settles on one of the usual protocols—flight: "I'll go away, just go away!" (56). But as she approaches the door, she hears Levin's footsteps and opts instead for a sort of confrontation, asking herself "What is there for me to be afraid of?" (56).

Levin enters and makes some preliminary comments. The two look back and forth at one another, avert their gazes, look again. Finally, Levin manages to blurt out an incoherent but nonetheless comprehensible proposal. This forms a second incident for Kitty. Kitty's immediate emotional response is one of "rapture" (57). This is not simply a response to the words of his proposal but to the context that gave those words emotional force—thus Levin's gaze, facial expression, tone of voice—and indeed to all the emotional memories of attachment these provoked in her. This rapture radically violates her anticipation—"she had not in the least expected" it (57). We may assume it is all the more forceful for that reason. But this response is as brief as the provoking incident itself. She thinks of Vronsky and says only, "It's impossible . . . Forgive me" (57, ellipsis in the original). After agreeing with the impossibility, Levin bows and turns to depart.

I suspect that most readers would agree that this constitutes a temporal unit above the level of the event. In the terms I have been using, it is an episode. But what makes it constitute an episode? To begin with, we find the usual emotional fragments—facial expression, tone of voice. We find the crystallizing incidents—most importantly, the proposal itself. We find the elaboration of the incident into an event with Kitty's projection of the underlying cause of Levin's "expression," that is, "his love," and with her own selection of an actional outcome. But this is not all that happens here. As an episode, this sequence first of all chains together related events. Kitty's imaginations of Levin and Vronsky, Levin's proposal, Kitty's reply, and Levin's response are all connected—in terms of the persons involved, their interests, their expectations. But clearly that cannot be all there is to an episode. If it were, then episodes could include almost anything, and they could be of infinite length.

We saw that events elaborate incidents in the direction of the past and in the direction of the future, thus in the direction of causes and in the direction of actional responses. This elaboration was severely limited in the case of events. Episodes expand elaboration into a more encompassing set of causal conditions and consequences. But as just noted, this is not simply a matter of extending the elaboration to other events. It is also a matter of *stopping* the causal enchaining of events.

In order to clarify episode elaboration, it is valuable to consider just what constitutes an explanation, since this elaboration is bound up with our sense of explanation. I am not referring to explanation in the sciences, though that is directly parallel, as we will see. I am referring, rather, to *existential* explanation, what counts as an explanation in our lived experience. There seem to be at least two criteria for a good existential explanation. The best explanations satisfy both. One is the reduction of the unusual to the normal, the surprising to the expected.[10] In science, a version of this desideratum is achieved by the isolation of laws. We show that an event is ordinary by showing that it follows the principles isolated by the encompassing science. As Kahneman and Miller note, we tend to ask "a why question" when faced with unexpected or surprising phenomena (148). We feel that we have received an explanation when such phenomena are reduced to patterns we routinely accept. Suppose a child sees someone eat something out of the garbage. He asks why. The man replies that he has not had any food in three days. This reduces the behavior to normalcy, expectation, pattern. Phrasing that pattern in terms of a lawlike regularity, we might say that, as hunger increases, disgust responses decrease and thus the range of things that one considers edible expands. Or, rather, the explanation does not make the new event normal. It shows that it fits with normalcy, normalcy of pattern. But it also highlights that the particular conditions in which the normalcy applies are indeed abnormal. In terms of events, this criterion suggests that chains of events requiring explanation arise out of normalcy or routine and fade back into normalcy or routine when particular conditions are no longer exceptional.

It follows from this that an episode should begin and end with routine. In the case of Levin's proposal, this is clearly the case. Levin is living his normal life. His proposal to Kitty is a striking departure from that normalcy. Had she accepted his proposal, then a series of unusual events would have followed, eventually leading to a different sort of normalcy after the wedding. As it is, his (apparent) departure after the refusal marks a return to the normalcy—the routines of daily life—that preceded the proposal. We see the same thing with the episode discussed at the outset. It too begins and ends with a sort of normalcy—if a normalcy still troubled and unstable.

One might say that the first criterion for explanation—normalcy—looks toward the past, thus what has always happened, and against which the explanandum appears strange. The second criterion turns instead toward the future. The first criterion tells us how the strange event can be understood in relation to normal patterns and abnormal conditions. The second criterion, in contrast, tells us how we can affect the event, how we can manipulate it, how we can make it normal (or otherwise change it). This "manipulability" or "controllability" criterion has two correlates in science—the repeatability of tests and the application of theories in technology. Put simply, the best existential explanation of an occurrence has two consequences. First, it leads us to feel that the occurrence, though initially surprising, should have been expected, given the particular conditions that preceded it. Second, it allows us to control that occurrence, or occurrences like it, in the future. In stories, manipulability commonly enters in character actions between the shift from and return to normalcy.

Episodes may be understood as units of existential explanation. As such, an episode begins with a shift away from normalcy, most obviously through an incident and its encompassing event. This leads to the asking of a why question, the instantiation of normal patterns in non-normal particularizing conditions, and the elaboration of means for manipulating those conditions. The episode ends when there is a return to normalcy. Such normalcy is usually temporary, as the non-normal, emotionally consequential causal sequence has only been interrupted—most often when there is no possibility for current manipulation. If normalcy is restored in a more enduring way, we have not just an episode, but a story. (We will examine this point in chapter 2.) This is what happens with Kitty's assertion that marriage with Levin is "impossible" and Levin's concurrence that "it could not have been otherwise" (57). (As this suggests, it is possible for a story to comprise only a single episode. One reader of an earlier version of this book found this claim to be confusing. I do not see why. The fact that there are one-room houses does not make the difference between rooms and houses confusing.)

This treatment of episodes, then, leads us to stories. However, before going on to stories, we might briefly consider the relation between the preceding discussion and the suggestive research done by David Miall on episodes. In a field such as literature, researchers should always be cautious about a coincidence of names. It often happens that two literary theorists use the same term for quite different concepts. There is at least some overlap between Miall's use of the term "episode" and mine. For example, Miall notes that episodes commonly have "coherence in the temporal or spatial setting or both" (120). Moreover, his research stresses the *emotional* coherence of the unit. Temporal and spatial continuity are almost necessary features of episodes in my sense. (Science fiction could produce episodes spanning different times and places through, say, time travel.) Most often, there will be a certain emotional coherence as well. On the other hand, the causal sequence of incidents and events may involve shifts in emotion—from hope to fear to grief, for example. Moreover, episodes in my sense are perhaps not so readily defined in terms of discourse length ("a number of sentences taking up half a page or a page" [120]). They also need not be marked by "a special twist . . . in the final sentence or two" (120). Again, there is some sort of interruption and temporary normalcy. But Miall is referring to something much more intense and unexpected than, say, leaving the room (as in the case of Dolly). Finally, it may be the case that an episode in my sense will involve "a thematically distinctive topic requiring a shift in the reader's understanding" (120). But that is not at all necessary, unless one takes "theme" very broadly to include any topic of relevance to the understanding of the encompassing work and one takes a "shift in the reader's understanding" to occur any time the reader receives new information. But this is not what Miall has in mind, and it would apply to subepisode events and incidents anyway.

Thus my conception of an episode and Miall's do overlap. But they are not at all the same. One important aspect of the overlap, however, is that both stress the emotional organization of the text. It may well be that Miall's division and mine are complementary. Mine is related to story— or more properly, substory—structure, while his is related to theme. In this way, it may be possible to interconnect the two ideas in productive ways—preferably with different terms to avoid confusion.

Conclusion

In sum, our experience of time is not uniform. We encode experience into hierarchized units, organizing temporality first of all by reference to emotional response. Our emotion systems respond to perceptual fragments (innate or acquired during a critical period; directly sensed or imagined) and to emotional memories. These cluster into incidents that provoke emotional spikes in emotional experiences that are, like time, not smoothly continuous but jagged. Though temporally very thin, these incidents incorporate our smallest units of expectation, sensorimotor projections, which modulate our emotional response to perceptual elicitors and clusters of such elicitors.

We elaborate emotional incidents into events by extending them in both the past and the future. The past is elaborated through causal attribution, the future by anticipations in working memory, which integrates protocols provided by the relevant emotion systems with information provided by our emotionally directed attentional focus. These anticipations have actional responses as their resolving outcome.

Beyond this, we engage in more fully elaborated explanations and appraisals. Explanations expand causal inference still further back beyond the basic causal attributions of events. Ideally, explanations locate occurrences in relation to larger, normal patterns and particular, unusual circumstances, and they indicate the ways in which such occurrences may be altered through actional response. In keeping with this, episodes emerge out of normalcy and end with a temporary return to normalcy. That temporary return to normalcy involves the (temporary) inhibition of effective actional response. Finally, appraisals expand the imagination of consequences, including actional outcomes, beyond the current situation, thus the episode proper. As we will see in the next chapter, they do this by situating episodes in larger trajectories of (emotionally driven) goal pursuit.

2   Stories and Works
From Ancient Egypt to Postmodernism

We have considered the elementary units of temporal experience (incidents), their derivation from our emotion systems, their concatenation into larger units (events), and the elaboration of these larger units into complexes (episodes). But clearly that is not the end of the story. In fact, it is not the story at all. In all these cases, we are still dealing with "substory" units. In this chapter, we need to consider three larger organizations of temporal experience—sequences, stories, and works.

We stitch together occurrences in various ways. I refer to these raveled units as "sequences." The most obvious cases occur in personal narratives. (I use "narration" and "narrative" here in a very broad sense to cover telling of anything, from components of incidents all the way up to entire works.) If my wife asks, "How was your day?," I am likely to come out with a laundry list of incidents, events, and episodes, thus a sequence—"Well, first, I ran into Smith at the bookstore—why does he seem to be everywhere? Then I lost track of time talking to Jones and was five minutes late for my class—and to make matters worse, I couldn't get the PowerPoint program to start on the computer in the classroom. I got a nice e-mail from Doe. He says 'Hi!'" In the following pages, we will not be very concerned with exploring sequences per se. However, it is important to isolate sequences in order to distinguish them from stories. Obviously, one thing stories do is incorporate incidents, events, and episodes. But stories are more than sequences. The response to my wife's question is not what we would ordinarily refer to as a story.

Of course, stories are not the only units that may be compared and contrasted with sequences. In the preceding chapter, without using a technical concept of *sequence*, we already considered the difference between episodes and mere sequences of events. There are also encompassing works, the narrative unit that links the story of Stiva and Dolly together with that of Levin and Kitty, that of Anna and Vronsky, and so on—in this case, the book *Anna Karenina*.

Works form a somewhat specialized category. The units of "incident" through "story," as discussed above, could all be understood as part of a "natural narratology" (in Monika Fludernik's phrase), which is to say, a study of all narrative as founded on the interactions of ordinary discourse. Indeed, generally, the orientation of a cognitive approach to narrative involves stressing the continuities between ordinary and specialized storytelling practices, as they are the products of the same structures and processes, in this case most importantly the same affective structures and processes. The next level of temporal organization, the work, still derives from this shared mental architecture, of course. But unlike incidents, events, episodes, and stories it may not have a precise "natural" counterpart. Nonetheless, it is obviously important in the study of verbal art. For example, if we are going to interpret an episode, we commonly feel that we need to place it not only in the context of its encompassing story but also in the context of the encompassing work. To take a simple case, the work as a whole may guide what we judge to be ironic or how we judge irony to operate, and it may do so in ways that would not be evident from any one embedded story (not to mention an episode or event) taken in isolation.

Again, a work may—indeed, often does—encompass more than one story. Moreover, it does not (in most cases) simply set two stories next to one another. If I bind *Hamlet* together with *Anna Karenina*, we would not consider that a single work. Even if I bind *Hamlet* together with *King Lear*, we would not consider it a work. In part, this is a matter of authorial intention. But it is also a matter of just how authors interrelate different parts of a work. In short, a work is no more a mere sequence of stories than a story is a mere sequence of episodes.

On the other hand, in all these cases, it is arguable that the story remains the most important unit. We tend to view incidents, events, and episodes as resolved only at the level of the story. Moreover, we tend to see the coherence and interest of the narrative work as a function of the stories it incorporates and their relations with one another. For this reason, our main focus, in this and subsequent chapters, is the story.

Sequences into Stories 1: Causal Elaborations and Emotional Relevance

It may seem at first that a story is just a sequence of episodes. But clearly this is not the case, as illustrated by the example of how my day went. It is worth considering that example again in more detail. Indeed, in order to understand what constitutes a story, we might think about how it is possible to develop this nonstory into something that is more like an "emplotment" of my day. I began my narrative by briefly recording an incident, seeing Smith (my archenemy). I then turned to a second, unrelated incident, seeing my friend Jones, then a third incident, being late for class. Since my conversation with Jones explains my being late for class, these two join together in what we might refer to as a *minimal* episode (or for reasons we consider below, we might term it a *pseudo*-episode). I added a fourth incident concerning the classroom computer. I concluded with an incident (receiving an e-mail), expanded into an episode by the addition of an elaborated actional outcome (saying "Hi!").

The episode involving the conversation with Jones and being late for class is the closest this narrative comes to a story. The obvious difference here is causal elaboration. I have two separate events—talking to Jones and being late for class—that I join causally. Our preceding analysis of the progression from incidents to events to episodes indicated that a key component of temporal expansion and embedding is causal elaboration. It is unsurprising, then, that causal relations would be important for the construction of the story unit as well. On the other hand, in this case the causal elaboration remains at the level of a single minimal episode. In fact, the narration becomes more storylike when I add "to make matters worse" and explain the fiasco with the PowerPoint presentation. Why does this seem to fit with the mini-story about being late for class in a way that it does not fit with seeing Smith?

To use a metaphor, we might say that some occurrences are "close" to one another in "story space." Thus they are more readily recruited (by speakers/authors or by listeners/readers) for emplotment. The Smith incident is narratively distant from the Jones conversation/being-late-for-class episode, while the PowerPoint fiasco is not. Why is that? There are several reasons, and they show us something important about the nature of stories—indeed, they show us that the construction of this temporal level follows from a recursive application of the same principles that yielded events from incidents and episodes from events. First, there is obvious emotional continuity. Being late for class involves frustration, embarrassment, and something like mild panic. The PowerPoint fiasco involves the same emotions. In addition, we are likely to infer a causal connection. It is quite possible that the computer simply malfunctioned that day. But it is easy to infer that the mild panic induced by my tardiness caused me to act too quickly and in a distracted way when trying to run the PowerPoint program, thus leading to mistakes. Indeed, I imagine that most people listening to my list of incidents would imagine me as being harried when entering the classroom and trying to rush with the computer. This inference to causal continuity is enhanced by the fact that there is spatial and temporal contiguity in the events. Presumably the PowerPoint fiasco followed directly upon my entering into the classroom, whereas my conversation with Jones probably did not directly follow upon my seeing Smith, nor did those events necessarily occur in the same place. Finally, and most importantly, the causal outcomes of the events are closely related. The practical effect of being late is, of course, being unable to cover as much material in class. That is the same effect produced by the PowerPoint fiasco. One also imagines that both give rise to student dissatisfaction, further enhancing my feelings of embarrassment and worry.

So, this suggests that proximity in story space is a function of several factors. One is causal relatability. Causal relatability includes such factors as spatial and temporal contiguity. Spatially and temporally distant events may cause one another. However, temporal or spatial proximity makes us more inclined to interpret events as causally related. A second factor is emotional relatability. Two events or episodes are closer, more readily combined into a story structure, if they contribute to a single emotional experience.

In short, we have something like "preference rules" here.[1] Two events or episodes are distant in story space if they are both causally and emotionally unrelated. They are closer in story space if they are causally or emotionally relatable. They are closest in story space if they are both causally and emotionally related.

I should note that emotional relatability does not necessarily mean contributing to the same emotion. It means contributing to the same emotional experience, usually as construed from some concluding point. Suppose Smith finds that he has been awarded tenure. This makes him happy. He then learns that his good friend Jones has been denied tenure. This is very distressing to him. It obviously does not make him happy. But it remains emotionally relevant. On the other hand, this is not simply a matter of qualifying Jones's emotional state. Suppose Smith finds he has gotten tenure. He is happy. In a rush of enthusiasm he trips and tears his expensive jacket. That makes him angry. This changes his emotion, but not in a way that we would consider emotionally relevant.

This last example suggests two things. First, emotional consequences and causal relatability are not sufficient for a sequence of events to be highly storylike. In keeping with the usual operation of preference rules, we may think of stories as having degrees of approximation to prototypicality. As Marie-Laure Ryan puts it, "narrative texts" define "a fuzzy set allowing variable degrees of membership, but centered on prototypical cases that everybody recognizes as stories" ("Toward" 28).[2] Thus one narrative will be highly prototypical or very storylike whereas another narrative will not. In the following pages, I often speak as if something is or is not a story. But in fact we have something much more like a gradient of "storiness." On that gradient, emotional consequence and causal relatability are not sufficient to give a narrative a high degree of prototypicality.

More exactly, we may distinguish between a series of events (without causal connections) and a chain of events (with causal links). A chain of events, even a chain of events with interrelated emotional effects, is not sufficient to produce a highly prototypical story. Consider another example. Suppose I am recounting my day. I explain that I was in a good mood, so I got up early. That allowed me to go to the coffee shop before class. Because I was in the coffee shop, I saw Smith. That reminded me of the way he had voted against me for promotion. I then ran into Jones. Because I was so upset by thinking about Smith, I talked with him about the promotion process. I became so emotionally engaged in the discussion that I lost track of time. This made me late for class, and so on. After all this, I was in such a bad mood that I couldn't do serious scholarly writing, so I decided to check my e-mail. I had a letter from Doe, where he talked about one of my favorite filmmakers and recalled a nice dinner we had together. This perked me up, so that when I drove home I was extra nice to my wife. As a result, she felt appreciated and the added energy allowed her to finish an article she had been working on—and so forth. Here we have a (causally related) chain of events. They all have emotional consequences. Moreover, parts of the sequence are storylike. But the whole is far from being a highly prototypical story. It is, as we would say, "episodic."

Conversely, in some cases, a mere series of (causally unrelated) events may contribute to a story. One can readily imagine a story that begins,

"Jones was sitting alone in the café. He knew now that it was all over with Marie. Glancing at the newspaper, he saw the headlines. More threats of war in Europe." The events are not causally related. Nor are they emotionally related (the emotion bearing on the breakup is presumably sorrow while the emotions bearing on the war are probably fear and anger). Nonetheless, depending on what follows, the headline may fit into a developing single story.

So, what else is necessary to make a sequence storylike? Let's go back and consider the case of Smith's and Jones's tenure decisions. Here is a version of that narrative: "Smith received the letter announcing that he had passed his penultimate pre-tenure review. He was overjoyed. But his mood was quickly dampened when he entered the office of Jones and saw his friend's downcast expression. 'They said no,' Jones reported, holding out the letter from the tenure committee." Okay, this is not Nobel Prize material. But it does seem to be pretty storylike. Now consider another narrative, virtually identical but slightly less storylike (i.e., slightly more "episodic"). "Smith received the letter announcing that he had passed his penultimate pre-tenure review. He was overjoyed. But his mood was quickly dampened when he entered the office of Jones and saw his downcast expression. 'The cancer is inoperable,' Jones reported." What is the difference between these two narratives? Note that in both cases the emotional response is in part a matter of direct perceptual experiences—the sight of Jones's grim face, the recognition of sadness in his voice, and so on. Part is the result of spontaneous anticipations, anticipations related to not having Jones as a colleague in the future. Moreover, in neither case is there a strict causal connection. Assuming that the number of possible tenure slots is the same as the number of people in tenure-track positions, Smith's retention has no causal bearing on Jones's nontenure. Moreover, in both cases, the emotions involved (joy and sorrow) are contradictory. We can give an initial explanation of the difference by saying that we feel two tenure-related decisions are somehow emotionally relevant to one another whereas a retention decision and cancer are not. But why would that be?

We can account for this once again by recognizing the recursive operation of a process found already at the episodic level—causal elaboration. When Smith receives his letter, we understand his happiness as the result of a number of factors. These include an elaborative appraisal of the esteem in which he is held by evaluators, the validity of their judgments, and the likelihood of his eventual tenure. (This has emotional effects through perceptual imagination and emotional memory, but for ease of exposition I leave aside the mechanics of this and talk simply in terms of appraisal.) When Smith visits Jones, however, this appraisal may be affected. Specifically, in the case of a negative tenure decision, Smith is likely to experience a conflict in the elaborative appraisal. This affects his view of the tenure committee's esteem and, more importantly, of his own likelihood of receiving tenure the following year.

Of course, not everyone will necessarily share my judgment here that the cancer version is more like two episodes, while the tenure version is more like a single story. However, I would argue that the analysis holds anyway. Specifically, my own response to the storiness of the narrative should be a function of the precise way in which I project the elaborative appraisal and other recursive processes that define the story organization. The same point should hold for everyone else. Thus, if Doe's projection of elaborative appraisal is different from mine, his sense of the storiness of a particular narrative should also be different from mine.

Beginnings and Endings

Unfortunately, however, we still have not arrived at something that we would reasonably call a "story." Or, rather, we have something that counts as a story in ordinary life but not in verbal art. In verbal art, we tend to expect stories to fill in beginnings and endings (as Aristotle emphasized). This is an overly restrictive requirement for everyday storytelling. For example, most of our ordinary stories do not have an ending yet, and we hardly want to wait until they do have an ending before we tell them. Suppose I hear from Jones that his cancer is inoperable, but I decide to follow the standards of verbal art. In consequence, I do not tell my wife anything until Jones actually dies. This would obviously be silly. In real life, we want partial stories because they present us with emotionally consequential occurrences that affect our inference and action. In contrast, suppose I was writing a novel and came to the point where the character Jones announces that he has cancer. This is clearly a newsworthy incident. But I would not adopt the standards of conversational narrative and publish the story on the grounds that the news is so important that it cannot be held back.

We might bring together the preceding observations (in this and earlier chapters) to draw the following conclusions. To have a highly prototypical story, we need occurrences that are not routine, ideally events that are emotionally significant. These events should be mutually emotionally relevant and causally integrated not only at the level of episodes but also at the level of highly elaborated appraisal. Such appraisal involves a broad range of causal relations beyond mere entailment and a range of emotional relations not confined to congruence. ("Elaboration" in a story will always be in part implicit. One task of literary interpretation is articulating those implicit elaborations.) Elaboration is not only retrospective but also prospective. In other words, any given episode should be elaboratively integrated with preceding and following episodes, with only two exceptions—the beginning and ending of the story. The beginning and the ending are the points at which we stop asking "why?" or "what then?" questions. Again, anything novel or unexpected provokes pre-emotional attention (see Frijda 272–73, 318, and 386) and leads us to ask "why?" questions (Kahneman and Miller 148). As William Labov has noted, "The end of a narrative" is connected with "precluding the question, 'and what happened then?'" In keeping with this, the beginning and the ending, are the points of transition between the unusual and the routine. Put differently, the beginning and the ending are the points that immediately follow normalcy (in the case of the beginning) or precede it (in the case of the ending).

But this already suggests two difficulties. The first concerns the beginning. Just what is it that initiates the change from normalcy? The second concerns the ending. In most prototypical literary stories, the beginning and the ending may be normal, but they are not usually identical. What is the difference between the normalcy of the beginning and the normalcy of the ending?

Needless to say, many authors have discussed the issue of story beginnings and endings. The basic principles of the discussion were laid down by Aristotle. He famously asserted that a story has a beginning, a middle, and an end. Aristotle explains that "a beginning is that which does not itself follow anything by causal necessity, but after which something else naturally is or comes to be. An end, on the contrary, is that which itself naturally follows some other thing, either by necessity, or as a rule, but has nothing following it" (8.3). The difficulty with Aristotle's account, of course, is that causal sequences simply do not work that way. Something always precedes the beginning. Something always follows the end.

Tzvetan Todorov is one of many writers who addressed this issue after Aristotle. His influential formulation runs as follows: "The minimal complete plot consists in the passage from one equilibrium to another. An 'ideal' narrative begins with a stable situation which is disturbed by some power or force. There results a state of disequilibrium; by the action of a force directed in the opposite direction, the equilibrium is re-established" (*Poetics* 111). This formulation improves on Aristotle in tacitly recognizing that there are causal precedents to beginnings and causal consequences of endings. However, it relies on a somewhat unclear metaphor that does not even hint at an explanation of story beginnings and endings. Moreover, the metaphor suggests that beginnings and endings are a matter of some objective, physical state.

As I am using the word "normalcy," it is comparable to Todorov's "equilibrium." The difference, however, is that "normalcy" is defined by emotional response, not by objective conditions. Normal is whatever does not give rise to emotion as something unusual, something provoking a "why question" and the associated activation of a motivational system.

Claude Bremond comes closer to resolving the problem when he sees the beginning of a story as occurring with "a situation that 'opens' the possibility of a behavior or an event." This is followed by "the enactment of the potentiality," which itself may involve success or failure (32, my translation). The idea of a situation opening a possibility is vague. However, Bremond's formulation has the advantage that it shifts the focus away from purely objective conditions—uncaused beginnings and causeless conclusions in Aristotle and equilibrium states in Todorov.

Along similar lines, Greimas sets out a "hierarchy of modal values" with "wanting," "knowing," and "being-able" leading to "doing" (80). The point is undoubtedly correct. Moreover, it is a matter of subjective conditions for a character's goal pursuit. But it is not clear that it has much explanatory value.

Jerome Bruner recognizes the importance of deviation from normalcy. Thus he says a story occurs "when you encounter an exception to the ordinary" (49). But I believe his full theoretical formulation of the idea is not quite right. Specifically, he writes that "the function of the story is to find an intentional state that mitigates or at least makes comprehensible a deviation from a canonical cultural pattern" (49–50). Bruner is undoubtedly correct about some cases of storytelling. But the formulation suggests that normalcy is always defined by some culturally distinctive properties, which seems overly narrow. For example, the normalcy of the heroic plots is the state of not being invaded by an enemy. It does not seem that this is culturally particular. The same point holds for the normalcy of the sacrificial plot—having food.

Nonetheless, the formulations of Bruner, Bremond, and Greimas all suggest that the beginning and ending of a story are best understood as a function of a subject's response to conditions, not of conditions themselves. The point is also suggested by Ryan's view that narrative involves "non-habitual . . . events" ("Toward" 29). Habituation is something that happens to people. It is not a property of situations in themselves.

Seeing the beginning and ending in terms of character response leads in turn to the possibility of recognizing that stories are defined, first of all, by the goals of characters and, crucially, that those goals are produced by emotional responses to situations. In the modern period, the writer who has brought out this idea most clearly is Keith Oatley. However, Oatley's magnum opus, *Best Laid Schemes*, is concerned primarily with emotion, not with narrative. Thus he does not fully develop this basic insight in connection with narrative theory, relating it to such questions as what defines a narrative beginning.

I say that Oatley is the main figure to have articulated this idea in the *modern* period, because the fundamental point was recognized by the Sanskrit theorists. For example, in the tenth-century *Daśarūpa* of Dhanaṃjaya, the "beginning" is explained as "eagerness for the obtaining of the more important result" (1.29). This "beginning" is preceded by an "Opening" which "giv[es] rise to . . . purposes and Sentiments" or emotions (1.37). The emotions engage the hero in pursuit of the "result." This result is a specification of one of "the three objects of human existence": ethical excellence, wealth/power, and sexual pleasure/romantic union (1.24). It is "the more important result" because it is differentiated from any (necessarily less important) "intermediate goal" that constitutes the "expansion" of the story (1.26, translation altered). Since Dhanaṃjaya's theory does not allow for tragedy, it characterizes the end of the story as "attainment of the result" (1.33).

Of course, Oatley and Dhanaṃjaya are hardly the only writers to have noticed that stories—or more properly, highly prototypical stories— involve an agent pursuing a goal (or in Pavel's related idiom, solving a problem). One key work here is Vladimir Propp's *Morphology of the Folktale*. After prefatory material, Propp identifies the beginning of the story either with villainy or the discovery of a lack. The conclusion comes with "punishment of the false hero or villain" and/or "wedding and accession to the throne" (154).

The difficulty with Propp's analyses is that they are based on a narrow corpus, the Russian folktale. In consequence, theorists such as Greimas have sought to generalize Propp's insights, commonly by making them more abstract. A recent extension of this approach, combining Greimas with Todorov, Bremond, and others, may be found in Emma Kafalenos's valuable study *Narrative Causalities*. Drawing on Todorov, Kafalenos abstracts Propp's idea of villainy to "destabilizing event" and his idea of discovering a lack to "reevaluation that reveals instability." She revises his dual conclusions to "success (*or* failure)" (7). In connection with this, Kafalenos states that the initial destabilizing event may be unmotivated (65), whereas "the ameliorative move" (thus the main story development of overcoming a difficulty) is more commonly "the result of motivated action" (65). This seems doubtful. In a typical romantic tragicomedy, the lovers may fall in love due to a chance meeting, but they are usually kept apart by motivated action (e.g., parental interference). Moreover, in a comedy, their final reunion—though diligently pursued by both parties—may ultimately result from an accumulation of chances.

As will become clearer in the next chapter (through our discussion of prototypes), a high level of abstraction is not always the best way to approach the definition of stories. Indeed, in some ways Propp's insights are remarkable precisely for their intermediate or prototype level of description—and their convergence with other traditions. For example, Propp's three criteria for the conclusion of a story map directly onto the three result-defining goals of life in the Sanskrit tradition. The goal of ethical excellence is represented negatively in the punishment of the villain. The goal of sexual pleasure and romantic union is represented in the wedding. Finally, the goal of wealth and power combined is represented in "accession to the throne" (154).

This convergence partially extends to Aristotle as well—also at a sort of intermediate level. Aristotle's entire development of the tragic fault is ethical in treating someone who is fundamentally good, but who errs in an ethically significant way. Of course, Aristotle is treating tragedy, not comedy, so the precise development of the punishment must be different—most obviously, it is the punishment of the hero, not of a villain. But there is nonetheless a connection. Moreover, it is difficult to forget that Aristotle's prototype for tragedy is *Oedipus the King*. In that play, Oedipus's suffering is precisely a matter of the negation of a wedding or romantic union and accession to the throne or acquisition of wealth and power. Specifically, his wife commits suicide and he is dethroned and exiled. This is just what we would expect from a tragedy following the general principles of Dhanaṃjaya or Propp.

I take it that the reason for this convergence is precisely the relation of these elements to emotion and the connection of story structure with emotion—a connection explicit in the Sanskrit tradition and in Aristotle. Moreover, I take it that the level of abstraction represented by the Sanskrit writers is roughly correct for defining genres (to which we will turn in chapter 3). On the other hand, at least some degree of abstraction is necessary when we set out an account not of a genre prototype, but of a more general story prototype.

All this begins to suggest some ways in which we may resolve the issue of beginnings and endings. First, we might in part take up Todorov's metaphor but shift it away from the stability implied in "equilibrium." Specifically, we might first extend one of Kafalenos's alternatives and say that the beginning of a story is prototypically marked by some sort of instability. More exactly, an initial condition of normalcy is likely to be *fragile* or *temporary*. Of course, this too is metaphorical. We may specify the idea in technical terms in the following way. An initial condition is fragile if it is readily open to enduring change through some incident. It is temporary if the simple passage of time will produce non-normalcy. Consider instances from two genre prototypes (which we examine in chapter 3). In heroic tragicomedy, the political structure of society is undermined through defeat in combat with an enemy. The beginning of such stories involves a normal society. But the normalcy is fragile in that it is endangered by a powerful enemy. In romantic tragicomedy, the hero and heroine fall in love. Their prior family life is normal. However, in the nature of things, the hero's and heroine's entrance into adulthood means that the normal situation at the opening will inevitably change. In other words, it is temporary. Of course, in romantic stories too, an incident precipitates the shift from normalcy to story. But it is commonly a different sort of incident than we find in heroic plots. Thus the lover and beloved may simply see one another and fall in love. This indicates a prior preparation for and receptivity to falling in love that itself signals a prior if latent change from normalcy. Since the fragility and temporariness in these cases are not encompassing, we might refer to them as *aspect* fragility and *aspect* temporariness. The situation just before the beginning is generally normal. However, there is some aspect of that situation that is fragile or temporary.

The most obvious way of treating the ending in this context is through a sort of idealization, not necessarily an idealization in general but an idealization in the relevant aspect, thus "aspect idealization." The society that is threatened by an enemy becomes ideally normal after that enemy is resoundingly defeated. The life of the romantic hero and heroine, disrupted by their separation, is normalized by enduring union. On the other hand, there is another way in which the ending can achieve normalcy. This is by eradicating the possibility of achieving aspect idealization. For example, in romantic plots, the hero and the heroine may be joined in lasting union and thus live "happily ever after." However, it might also occur that one lover dies. As a result, that union becomes impossible.

Thus the fundamental change from the normalcy of the beginning to the normalcy of the ending is that the ending does not have the aspect instability of the beginning. In comic versions of these stories, which are more common cross-culturally, that shift is produced by aspect idealization in the ending. In tragic versions, that shift is produced by foreclosing the possibility of such idealization. Of course, many stories combine the two, presenting different possibilities for stabilizing normalcy, then foreclosing some while developing others. For example, if the rightful leader of a society is displaced in heroic tragicomedy, he or she may be killed before being restored. That renders a particular idealization impossible. However, his or her child may defeat the usurper and take the leadership position, producing a different aspect idealization.

Sequences into Stories 2: Characters and Goals

This example of a story involving different people and different agents returns us to our initial difficulty—how to distinguish stories from sequences. Think back to my narrative about reading the e-mail, then treating my wife particularly well, so that she finished a particular article, and so on. We could imagine a sort of postmodernist narrative in which this occurs: someone then reads my wife's article in a journal and is inspired to become a literature professor; that person then teaches a composition course which incorporates material about African epics; a student in that course becomes excited about African epics and decides to devote herself to research on the topic; in the course of her research in Africa, she meets a young African student who is able to attend an American university because of her letter of recommendation—and so on. This could be highly emotionally engaging. But it is not very close to story prototypicality.

One might initially suggest that a story requires greater causal rigor or perhaps some larger causal connectedness. The causal elaboration of a story goes all the way up to "the causal laws that govern a literary work," to use Brian Richardson's phrase (*Unlikely Stories* 36). Richardson subdivides these laws into three types—supernatural, naturalistic, and chance. In fact, all stories involve naturalistic causality. Many involve some form of supernatural causality as well, ranging from localized magic to global providence. But it is not clear that all such forms of supernatural causality are identical or even parallel. Finally, chance is not an alternative form of causality. Rather, at least in the vast majority of stories (as opposed to particle physics), chance is a matter of the description under which an event might or might not be explained naturalistically. As such, it is, so to speak, an opportunity for some form of supernatural causality. If I run into my dean at the grocery store, that is a coincidence in that neither of us planned the meeting. However, my being in the grocery store at that time is open to naturalistic explanation and his being in the grocery store is open to naturalistic explanation. Supernatural causality may supplement naturalistic causality in such a way as to explain those events under an otherwise noncausal description. Thus, if something good comes from the encounter, I might say that it was "providential" that I met the dean, attributing the meeting to divine intervention.

However one might quibble about the precise division of causalities, Richardson does provide a useful framework. Nonetheless, it does not seem to help explain why the preceding sequence of events (my wife finishing her article, someone reading the article, and so on) is not a prototypical story. That sequence involves entirely rigorous naturalistic causality and includes chance only in the degree that chance is always involved in naturalistic causality. We can, of course, imagine the story developing in such a way that it suggests providential guidance as well. For example, suppose the African student eventually discovers a cure for cancer. This certainly comes closer to being a prototypical story. But I suspect it does so more for the emotional interest of the outcome than for the causal "rigor" added by the hint of providence. Indeed, we would have a much more prototypical story if we focused on that African student from beginning to end.

Rather than causality as such, then, the problem with the preceding story appears to be a matter of the people involved. The agents keep changing. We start out with me, then go to my wife, then to the reader of my wife's article, then to the student of this reader. Why is this a problem? Well, in a sense, it is not a problem. To say that this is a less prototypical story is not to say that it is entirely unstorylike. On the other hand, it is not as storylike as a narrative about two people meeting, falling in love, struggling against parental opposition, then finally marrying.

Thus we have another preference rule here. The causal sequence and the emotions of a story should bear primarily on the same agent or small set of agents.

But even this requires refinement. Here we can return to my narrative about my day at school. As we saw, some parts of the narrative were more storylike than others. Even though they were causally continuous and involved the same agent, seeing Smith and checking my e-mail do not seem as fully integrated into the story as the event chain running from the conversation with Jones through the tardiness and the PowerPoint fiasco. Of course, this is not a complete story as it lacks an ending. But it does seem more storylike than the rest of the narrative. To understand why this is the case, we must return to some considerations broached in the preceding chapter, considerations that relate closely to the analyses of appraisal theorists who treat narrative, prominently Keith Oatley. What makes these events cohere more strongly is the fact that we readily understand them as part of a single goal on my part. I have a goal of teaching my class well—or perhaps a cluster of related goals that includes conveying certain information to my students, keeping to a schedule (keyed to the timing of the midterm exam), allowing enough time in class for questions and discussion, earning the respect and appreciation of my students, garnering not-too-awful student evaluations, and so on. Being late for class and delaying things further due to problems with the computer equipment both seem to work against the achievement of these goals. Thus this arc of the narrative seems more storylike in part because it falls within the trajectory of a certain set of goals.

Here as elsewhere, prototypicality judgments might differ. But once again, if my contention is correct, then this should result from differences in elaborative appraisals. For example, perhaps some of my readers find the entire narrative of my day storylike, at least up to the point where it turns to my wife and her article. (Note that finding something storylike is not the same as finding it to be a *good* story.) If so, this is presumably a matter of the relevant sort of elaborative appraisal. Specifically, we might understand my overarching goal as one of maintaining a cheerful mood. In fact, I suspect that something along these lines led me to create just this fictional series of events rather than another, even though I was unaware of it. I begin in a good mood. In connection with this, I go to the coffee shop (which I like). Seeing Smith spoils my mood, so I try to engage in mood repair by talking with Jones. Unfortunately, this inadvertently has negative consequences on my mood when I am late for class. I then try to repair my mood again by checking my e-mail. Our sense of the story prototypicality of this or any other sequence of events may rest on how salient relevant goals are for us.

In any case, we might now rephrase our most recent preference rule in the following way. The causal chain and the emotions of a story should be subsumed within a minimal set of long-term goals. But this too is not enough. Suppose Doe falls ill. As a result, he gets laid off from work. As a result, he loses his house. As a result, he moves in with his parents. As a result, he is able to take care of his father when the father falls ill—and so on. All these events form a causal chain that arguably bears on the single goal of being happy. But they are too diffuse to form a prototypical narrative. Moreover, Doe seems generally a bit too passive in this narrative. Obviously, things of this sort happen. Moreover, we consider them to have high "tellability," primarily due to their emotional content. But our most prototypical stories involve people doing things. Contrast, for example, a story in which Doe thinks about nothing but work, ignoring his parents. Despite health risks, he keeps engaging in a certain sort of work in order to advance himself. He then falls ill, suffers the loss of his job and home, and—to his great distress—has to move in with his parents. He eventually recovers his health and finds a part-time job. Despite his initial attitude, he realizes that there is something valuable in his relations with his parents. When his father falls ill, he is now grateful that he can help. This is, I believe, a fairly prototypical story. In part the difference from the first version is that Doe is active. Moreover, both his actions and experiences are subsumed under a small number of more specific goals—initially, advancing in his career; later, helping his father. Moreover, those goals guide the actions in readily comprehensible ways.

We might, then, try a further reformulation of this preference rule—or, by now, set of preference rules. The causal chain and the emotions of a story should be subsumed within a minimal set of long-term goals; the causal chain should include actions on the part of a minimal number of agents pursuing these goals; and these goals should be specific enough so that the actional choices of the agents define concrete means of achieving those goals. This seems to give us at least a reasonable approximation to what distinguishes stories from mere sequences of episodes.

Character Goals, Prototypicality, and Audience

Up to this point, we have considered only "made to order" anecdotes, mini-stories that I have fabricated in order to illustrate my points. Here, it is important to consider the relations between sequences of events and story structures in actual narratives. There are two sorts of actual narratives we might consider. One sort comprises stories like "how my day went," stories told by ordinary people in ordinary circumstances. Again, that is an extremely valuable research topic. However, it is not the research topic of this book. In the following sections, we look at widely respected narratives, narratives that are not merely idiosyncratic, but have, rather, provoked emotional responses (at least pre-emotional interest) from people in different places and at different historical periods. Before going on to consider actual cases, it is worth dwelling for a moment on just what difference this focus makes to the study of stories.

Some aspects of stories change when we move from individually well-known addressees to a more general audience and when we move from stories that are embedded in unique contexts to stories that are designed to be relatively context-neutral. Put simply, when my wife asks how my day went, she is likely to be interested in aspects of my experience that would make anyone else's eyes glaze over. Indeed, in the preceding discussion, I have simply ignored one aspect of prototypicality—the nature of the goal. Trying to get my class taught is simply not a terribly prototypical narrative goal. This is because it is not a goal for a narrative that is designed to appeal to a wide range of people in a wide range of circumstance at different times. We will focus more specifically on prototypical narrative goals in the next chapter. However, it is worth saying a few things about them here.

When we first consider the difference between narrative goals for "private" and "public" stories, we might think that the issue is something along the following lines. Private stories involve goals that are very personal or idiosyncratic, whereas public stories more often involve goals that are more general. But this is not quite what is going on. Goals come in various degrees of specificity or "proximity." All proximate goals may be related to—indeed derived from—more encompassing emotional propensities. For example, buying food is related to the goals of satisfying hunger and enjoying taste. Getting my class taught is a bit more complex. It is most immediately related to receiving the appreciation or esteem of my students and more distantly related to maintaining my livelihood. Given this, the difference between public and private narratives cannot be a matter of the goals being more general in the former than in the latter. All goals are simultaneously very particular and very general. My goals, no matter how seemingly trivial, are at some level a function of my emotion systems, which are basically identical with those of everyone else (leaving aside pathological cases). In other words, my particular goals can never be entirely particular. Their particularity always instantiates some emotional generality. Conversely, literary narratives may strive to present goals that are broadly accessible, but they must nonetheless be particularized goals. It is of course possible to have a story about a character who simply wants to get married, though he or she does not have anyone particular in mind. But this is not the most prototypical story. Even when a character starts out this way—in keeping with our preceding discussion of the change from temporary normalcy in story beginnings—he or she most often does find some particular person that he or she wishes to marry. Needless to say, that does not adversely affect the prototypicality of the story. Indeed, the shift from generalized nubility to a particular marriage interest actually makes the story *more* prototypical.

What, then, is going on in these cases? Prototypicality of the protagonist's goals appears to be governed by the nature of our empathic responses. Our empathic responses, to real people and to fictional characters, typically involve reduced emotional intensity.[3] The reduction in emotional intensity is probably related to the evolutionary function of empathy—or, rather, of both parallel and complementary responses to the emotions of others. In the case of complementary responses to anger, for example, it is probably beneficial that our response is somewhat inhibited, at least in certain cases. For example, it may be more adaptive to be conciliatory up to a certain point rather than immediately matching someone else's angry aggression with counteraggression, leading to immediate confrontation. A similar point applies to parallel emotions. Parallel emotions are adaptive in that they allow us to bring together the experiences of different members of the group to mutual benefit. When Jones shrieks in fear and begins to run, I feel fear also and thus engage in flight even before I know quite what the danger is. On the other hand, it would not be adaptive for me to experience every emotional whim expressed by everyone around me—hence the value of reduction in intensity.

As we discussed in the previous chapter, there are two importantly distinct components to emotion processing. One is largely subcortical and responds to perceptual information and emotional memories with the activation of emotion systems. The other is neocortical and involves the appraisal-like elaboration of the full perceptual situation, likely outcomes, causes, and so forth. The second system guides the imagination that always supplements direct perception and sometimes substitutes for it entirely; it also affects just which emotional memories are likely to be activated. In this way, it may inhibit, redirect, or enhance emotional responses. Our empathic response to other people has consequences at both levels. At the subcortical level, it is first of all governed by the intensity of the person's expression of emotion. For example, we generally respond more strongly to someone who is weeping than to someone who is simply frowning. On the other hand, insofar as we are prompted to simulate the experiences of a person (say, Jones), we may respond to the eliciting conditions—the situation that gave rise to his or her emotion (e.g., the denial of tenure)—rather than the expressive outcome alone. Indeed, in cases where our simulation suggests very deep feeling, our empathic response may be enhanced by the lowered expectations generated by a relatively unemotional expression (e.g., when we see someone whom we imagine to be in profound grief even though he or she has a relatively neutral facial expression).

So, the first factor governing empathic response is intensity of emotional experience. However, as my reference to simulating the eliciting conditions may already suggest, we do not confine ourselves to the intensity of the emotion. We also evaluate its importance. Indeed, this may be the primary function of self-conscious, elaborative appraisal. It allows us to evaluate the importance of the goal at issue and the bearing of the emotion-provoking incident on that goal.

But what does "importance" mean here? It cannot mean "importance for the person feeling the emotion." Suppose I find that I have run out of cucumbers and cannot put them on my salad tonight. I begin to wail, tear my clothing, and pour dust on my head. Clearly, having cucumbers on my salad is very important *for me*. But most of us would like to say that having cucumbers on one's salad is not *really* that important. On the other hand, it cannot simply mean that cucumbers are not important for the reader or listener—because the reader's or listener's personal preferences may be as weird as mine are. Moreover, at some level of specificity, all our preferences are weird and idiosyncratic. Juliet is in love with Romeo, not Paris. Maybe a given member of the audience actually finds Paris much more attractive than Romeo. But we would not want to say that this means Juliet is being unreasonable about wanting Romeo in the way I am being unreasonable about wanting cucumbers.

The significance of a goal—a specific goal, as instantiated and pursued by the person we are considering—is a function of the degree to which the achievement or nonachievement of that goal will have enduring effects on the person's life. We may think that Juliet is being entirely irrational in preferring Romeo to Paris. However, it is clear that the goal of marrying Romeo is a weighty one, for it is driven by emotions that will have lasting effects on her future if the goal is achieved or if it is not.

Of course, none of us has a crystal ball to view the future. Moreover, at least in the case of fiction, there is no future to look at. So of course we cannot say with certainty just what the future will hold. In many cases we simply rely on automatic, subjective probability assessments. To some extent these will differ from person to person. Some audience members may be inclined to think that young lovers, once separated, will overcome their feelings in a relatively short time. Others may be inclined to expect the feelings of separated lovers to harden into resentment and depression. Others may have no opinion on this issue, considering instead how the intensity of attachment in such relationships may give rise to actions—such as suicide—that themselves have obvious long-term consequences.

On the other hand, despite some differences of this sort, most people are likely to agree that my preference for cucumbers will probably have less bearing on the future of my life than does Juliet's preference for Romeo. Moreover, such probability assessments are not the only issue here. Again, at the right level of generality, all our goals are the same. However, that does not mean that we consider all our goals equally consequential for our happiness. Moreover, it does not mean that we consider all aspects of our particular goals equally crucial for the general goals they instantiate. Thus we all have the goals of having nutrition and of enjoying the taste of food. However, we generally consider the former a far more important goal than the latter, because we know that people will die if they cannot fulfill the first goal, whereas they will probably not die if they cannot fulfill the second goal.

A key variable here is substitutability. At all levels of importance, we consider certain instances of our goals to be open to substitution and others not. A peculiar feature of our goal elaboration is that we tend to consider types substitutable, but not individuals. This suggests the special place of attachment in our emotional lives, for attachment is an emotion that bears on individuals, not on categories or types. The nonsubstitutability of individuals goes beyond positive attachment relations. But one could reasonably argue that its origin lies in attachment nonetheless.

Consider again my love of cucumbers. First, we take the enjoyment of taste to be a less important goal than, say, satisfying hunger. There are obvious reasons for this. Not only is my loss of cucumbers trivial in terms of life consequences, it is readily open to future repair. We eat several times every day. Even granting the importance of tasty food, the worst that can be said is that I will miss out on a preferred taste for one meal on one day. Moreover, it is always possible to substitute something else for cucumbers. Supposing even that there is a cucumber drought or that terrorists have somehow found of a way of destroying all the cucumbers and cucumber seeds in the world—I can always still enjoy pretzels or feta cheese. Now consider Juliet's feelings for Romeo. First, this is a case of a desire for marriage, which we generally accept as a prime goal—indeed, a goal that we expect to develop out of normalcy in both fiction and real life (as children grow to adulthood). In addition, we tend to feel that individuals are not substitutable, particularly in attachment relations. Juliet's preference for Romeo involves an important goal and an individual in an attachment relation. In both respects, it differs crucially from my preference for cucumbers.

Needless to say, not all our daily anecdotes involve goals as trivial as eating cucumbers. The point is simply that we judge different goals appropriate and effective as we move from relatives and friends in intimate discourse conditions to strangers in public discourse conditions. This judgment is at least in part a function of the importance of the general goal and the substitutability of its instantiation.

Now we may turn to some works composed for a broader audience—and indeed, well received by a broader audience. In chapter 1, we focused on *Anna Karenina*, a work that marks a pinnacle of the realist novel in modern Europe. In order to give greater breadth of coverage, in the next section, we turn to one of the earliest narratives available to us—a story composed about four thousand years ago (see William Simpson 3). In addition, this story is not from Europe but from North Africa. Examining this tale allows us to illustrate the aspects of stories that we have isolated thus far—and to isolate some further features of narrative as well.

A Story from Middle Kingdom Egypt

"The Tale of the Eloquent Peasant" concerns a man who sets out from home to get provisions needed by his family. At a certain point, he has to drive past a field of barley. A corrupt, low-level official, Nemtynakhte, blocks the road, then confiscates all the peasant's goods when the peasant's donkey eats some of the barley. The peasant approaches Nemtynakhte's superior, Rensi, in order to petition him regarding the confiscated goods. Rensi receives a report of the events along with some advice from his subordinates, but he does nothing. The peasant then makes a plea directly to Rensi. Impressed by the peasant's eloquence, Rensi discusses the peasant with the ruler of Egypt, Nebkaure the justified. Hearing of the peasant's eloquence, Nebkaure instructs Rensi to support both the peasant and his family (thus temporarily to supply provisions) but to take no action on the suit. Nebkaure is intrigued by the peasant's rhetorical skills and wishes to hear more. He further instructs Rensi to bring him transcripts of the peasant's speeches. The peasant ends up giving nine speeches to Rensi. These alternate between praise for Rensi and vituperation. For example, in one of these speeches, the exasperated peasant refers to Rensi as "a despicable scrubman" who accepts anyone as a brother if that person offers him a bribe (35). After this speech, the peasant is whipped. Eventually, the peasant departs in despair. Two attendants of Rensi go to fetch him back. The peasant expects the worst. But he is in fact rewarded, not only with the return of his own goods but with the receipt of all Nemtynakhte's wealth also.

Despite its early provenance, the main sequence of the story is highly prototypical. It begins in normalcy. The peasant is at home with his wife leading his usual life. However, that opening condition (only suggested in the narrative) is fragile and temporary. Periodically it will happen that the family needs provisions that they cannot supply for themselves. This requires that they trade something that they have for something that they need. Though somewhat vague on the specifics of the need, the story does present an appropriate sort of goal, one that is widely accepted as important (providing the many things needed by one's family). In addition, it has the advantage of being bound up with attachment relations.

Of course, as to the substitutability, one might wonder why this trade is not available locally. There are undoubtedly historical reasons for this. However, for our purposes, perhaps the more interesting reason has to do with the ways in which stories tend to develop cross-culturally. We noted in the first chapter that experienced time and experienced space are both "uneven," and that unevenness is emotional. We structure space first of all into home and away, based in part on neurological processes of place attachment. We organize time into incidents, events, and so on, integrating these structures with longer-term goals. Needless to say, once a protagonist has a goal, the question arises as to how his pursuit of that goal should be developed. Cross-culturally, people generally conceptualize time by mapping it onto space, particularly movement in space, as when we speak of the future as "forward in time" and the past as "back in time." Indeed, the mapping goes in both directions, as Heidegger indicated in discussing temporality. Thus we routinely refer to some location as "five minutes away" or "an hour's distance." It also seems likely that there is an associative connection between our emotional organization of space and our emotional organization of time. Moreover, both forms of unevenness are prominent in stories. Given this, we would expect some storytellers at some point to map the emotional structure of story time onto the emotional structure of story space. In other words, we would expect them to see not only space in general as an analogue for time, but specifically the division between home and away as an analogue for the temporal division between normalcy and "departure" from normalcy (to use a standard spatial metaphor). Indeed, this appears to occur spontaneously across different traditions, thus without the need for contact or influence.

More exactly, we may distinguish between the narrative goal itself and the topological frame in which the goal is located—precisely how it is situated in terms of space and spatiality. Given the cross-cultural propensity to map time onto space, and given the relations between emotional spatiality and emotional temporality, we would expect one prominent topological frame to develop in relation to the division between home and away. As it turns out, this is perhaps the most common topological frame cross-culturally. Its most obvious manifestation is in the widely attested "quest narrative." In quest narratives, the goal is the acquisition of some object (alternatively, some power or knowledge) located in a foreign place, and the unfolding of the story concerns the journey to the place, the acquisition of (or failure to acquire) the object, and the return home. Prominent examples range from sections in the *Epic of Gilgamesh* (e.g., Gilgamesh's journey to Utnapishtim due to his anxiety over death, with his eventual loss of the rejuvenating plant) to Derek Walcott's *Omeros* four thousand years later (e.g., Achilles's journey back in time to Africa in order to acquire self-knowledge).

"The Tale of the Eloquent Peasant" provides us with a clear example of this sort as well. Thus we have temporary, fragile normalcy that reaches its point of (goal-provoking) non-normalcy. This generates an important attachment-related goal, the acquisition of provisions for the protagonist and his family. The temporal structure of pursuing the goal is mapped onto the spatial structure of home and away, producing a journey away from home in order to achieve the goal.

Moving beyond the beginning, we find other cross-cultural patterns as well. Perhaps most importantly, there are two common ways of enhancing the emotional intensity of achieving the goal. The first is through the prior, apparently complete loss of any possibility for achieving the goal. This produces a sharp gradient of emotional change once the goal is finally achieved. The second involves increasing the difficulty of achieving the goal—for our happiness in achieving something is increased if that achievement was difficult. (As Ortony, Clore, and Collins put it, "increases in effort tend to increase the degree to which goals are positively valued" [73]—and, of course, the achievement of a highly valued goal is more rewarding than the achievement of a less-valued goal.) In most stories, these criteria apply to a single sequence. In "The Tale of the Eloquent Peasant," however, they are separated into two distinct episodes or episode sequences. In both cases, there is a conflict between the goal of some antagonist and the goal of the peasant. Making goal inhibition result from such personalized conflict also recurs cross-culturally and evidently serves to enhance the emotional intensity of the story.

In the first of the episodes just mentioned, the peasant encounters Nemtynakhte, who wishes to acquire the peasant's goods. His goal is obviously contradictory with that of the peasant. Thus we say that he is a "blocking" character, for he serves to inhibit the hero's progress toward his goal.[4] In a spatial mapping, such "blocking" might literally involve stopping the hero in his path and requiring that he take a (physical) detour. This is precisely what happens in this tale when Nemtynakhte puts his clothing on the path and forbids the peasant from driving his donkeys over the clothing.

Of course, the conflict between these characters is not simply a matter of incompatible goals. The author of the story clearly expects us to evaluate the characters and their actions through elaborative appraisal and to do so morally. Indeed, we as readers are in a sense parallel to Rensi in making a judgment about the conflict. This gives us a further prototype-enhancing preference rule that appears cross-culturally as well: the conflict between the protagonist and his or her antagonist is not only a conflict of interests but a moral conflict as well. In other words, it is in part a conflict between a hero and a villain. This particular story further maps this moral conflict onto the existential spatiality that partially organizes the plot. Specifically, when Nemtynakhte forbids him from driving over the clothing, the peasant replies that he will avoid the clothing because "my path is good" (27).[5] The suggestion is that the entire quest he is undertaking is just or ethical—in keeping with the story's stress on "Ma'at," both the goddess and concept of order, righteousness, and practical justice, as William Simpson explains (see 25 and 27n.7). Thus we have a clear and highly prototypical case of hero-versus-villain goal conflict, with an enhanced mapping of that conflict onto emotional space, yielding a cross-culturally recurring metaphor of moral action as a path.

What happens next is also consequential, and takes us beyond the preceding analysis. As the peasant and Nemtynakhte are speaking, one of the peasant's donkeys bites off a mouthful of barley. Nemtynakhte takes this as just the excuse he needs to punish the peasant. This is significant because it is not idiosyncratic to this story. Rather, in good Aristotelian fashion, it gives the peasant a flaw. The peasant is presumably responsible for the grazing of his animals and this land and barley are not his, so he has no right to allow his donkey to feed on the barley—something that was likely to happen, given that the peasant had moved "toward the higher ground" where the barley was located (27). In this way, the peasant, though clearly the morally preferable character, is not perfect. Thus his subsequent suffering is not entirely independent of his own action. The recurrence of such a flaw or error is quite common across traditions and suggests that Aristotle was right to isolate it as an important part of a story (even outside tragedy). This is not surprising, perhaps, as a tragic error is one way of satisfying the preference rules involving causal connection and protagonist action. Of course, also in keeping with Aristotle, the fault is slight along two key axes. First, the crime itself is minor, since the amount of barley lost is insignificant. Second, the peasant did not himself commit the crime (though his movement toward the barley did allow it). Moreover, the problem arose only because Nemtynakhte blocked the road. Indeed, many readers may find the fault so slight as to be entirely insignificant. This extensive exculpation of the peasant may be important so that the case before Rensi is unequivocal, since we might expect him to have an initial bias in favor of the official. Indeed, Rensi's consultation with other officials suggests just this, as we will see. Additionally, and in parallel with this, early readers of the tale would not have been peasants. As such, we might expect them to have had an initial bias in favor of the officials as well. Thus a more extreme discrepancy between "guilt" and punishment may have been needed to cultivate their sympathy with the peasant.

In any case, Nemtynakhte beats the peasant and takes his donkeys. The result of this is of course that the peasant can no longer pursue his goal. It is impossible for him to acquire provisions as he has nothing to trade for those provisions. Again, our emotional response to a character (or a real person) is connected with their emotional expression as well as a simulation of their situation. The tale first represents the peasant's emotional expression, explaining that he "lamented exceedingly through grief" (28). Then Nemtynakhte threatens that he will kill the peasant if he does not keep quiet. At this point, the peasant gives a brief summary of his situation that in effect serves to guide us through a simulation, while simultaneously extending the expression of his pain beyond grief to a sort of shock: "You whip me, you take away my property, and you even take the very lament out of my mouth" (28). Our elaborative evaluation of the peasant's situation, both in the short and long term, only enhances the effect. His immediate situation is pathetic (away from home without any goods) and his prospects are only worse. We know from the beginning of the story that his supply of barley is very limited. Far from being able to acquire further provisions, it is not even clear that he and his family will escape starvation.

Thus we find that the middle of the story is formed by the opposite of the overarching goal. Rather than acquiring what his family needs, he has lost what he already had. Again, this is a cross-culturally common pattern, as we would expect given the nature of human emotion systems and the aesthetic goal of intensifying emotional response.

In this particular case, this shift to the opposite of the encompassing goal serves in effect to establish a new goal for the peasant—regaining his confiscated goods. In keeping with the preceding analysis, this remains prototypical (a single, unified story) because the second goal is embedded in the causal sequence and is inseparable from the overarching goal of the entire narrative. (Contrast a case where the peasant is simply sidetracked by some incidental event—for example, a cry for help from a hapless maiden.) In connection with this, we begin a new episode. Unsurprisingly, this episode, with its new goal, is spatially mapped as well, so the peasant leaves the place of the Nemtynakhte episode. Specifically, he travels to the capital in order to make a legal appeal to the chief steward, Rensi. This spatial division is important, for it refers to a third sort of place. This third place is not one's personal home and not an undifferentiated "away from home," but the center of group life. Indeed, it suggests a second axis of spatial relations, one that plays a role in heroic plots particularly. The primary spatial axis is that of personal space, the living place of the home versus whatever is not home. However, there is a secondary spatial axis that is social and that contrasts the space of the in-group (the homeland) with spaces of out-groups (alien lands). Within the homeland, the capital has a particular, orienting function. It may serve as a reference point for social space in the way that the home serves as a reference point for personal space.

In the capital, Rensi brings the peasant's charge to magistrates under him. They see Nemtynakhte's fault as so insignificant as not to require punishment (28). This suggests the bias of the tale's initial readers. Nonetheless, the magistrates do advise that Nemtynakhte be ordered to return the peasant's goods. It is not entirely clear why Rensi does not follow this advice. He laid the charge against Nemtynakhte after reading a transcript of the peasant's complaint. Thus he may wish to punish Nemtynakhte. Alternatively, he may be willing to side with Nemtynakhte. In narrative terms, however, it is clear that the peasant will have to do more. In other words, it is clear that the acquisition of this goal (restoration of the goods), if it comes at all, will not come easily. Rather, it will involve emotion-enhancing difficulty.

We immediately encounter the difficulty faced by the peasant as he has to deliver his first (eloquent) petition. Now Rensi consults with the ruler, Nebkaure. It is still not clear just what Rensi intends to do about the case. As already noted, Nebkaure finds the peasant's eloquence to be entertaining. He therefore instructs Rensi to give temporary provisions to the peasant and his family while keeping him around to deliver more speeches. In this context, we clearly have a conflict in goals, thus a protagonist and an antagonist. Nebkaure's goal of being entertained contradicts the peasant's goal of receiving a favorable legal judgment and thereby retrieving his confiscated goods. On the other hand, the peasant's ultimate goal is to gain provisions for his family. This goal is being furthered (albeit in a limited and temporary manner) by Nebkaure. In this way, Nebkaure is simultaneously a blocking figure and a helping figure. As many writers have noted, it is common for individual stories to combine different character roles into single characters, just as it is common to multiply a single role through different characters (see, for example, Propp 79–83), as we see here in the fact that Nebkaure and Rensi have basically the same role in the story. But it seems fairly unusual to combine helping and blocking roles. This complexity may be one reason why this particular tale remains esteemed millennia after its composition. The point carries over to the moral relation between the peasant and Nebkaure. On the one hand, Nebkaure seems to be preventing justice. On the other hand, he is providing the peasant with the goods he merits.

As already noted, the peasant proceeds through nine petitions. His speeches are noteworthy in many ways. Perhaps most significantly, they manifest a striking ambivalence toward Rensi, both praising and damning him. This is consistent with the reader's sense that Rensi is both a blocking and a helping figure. Since the peasant does not know his provisions are coming from Rensi, he has no reason to believe in Rensi's goodwill. As a result, he comes to see Rensi as a corrupt official in line with Nemtynakhte. This view is apparently confirmed when Rensi has him beaten, recalling the behavior of Nemtynakhte. Indeed, many readers are likely to be uncertain as to just how they should understand and evaluate this development. What is perhaps most striking today is that there is such ambivalence in the story. The peasant is undoubtedly the most accomplished of the characters, due to his eloquence. He is also the character most clearly in the right. While Rensi and Nebkaure are not condemned, one might not have expected such ambiguity in their treatment. One might rather have expected them—particularly Nebkaure—to be elevated above reproach. As we will see in chapter 4, this sort of ambivalence is far more common in canonical stories than one might have anticipated.

In any case, after his fruitless appeals, the peasant despairs. He determines that he has no recourse and sets out to return home. It now seems to him that the achievement of both his goals has become impossible. From the reader's perspective, this appears to be a tragic return to normalcy—a normalcy in which the peasant will never be able to fulfill the needs of his family. When Rensi has him brought back, he reaches an even lower point, anticipating his own execution (43). In simulating his condition at the time, the reader is likely to recognize that the peasant has no reason to expect any other outcome. The emotional impact of the ending, then, is further intensified by making the gradient of change exceedingly sharp. The peasant anticipates death—and perhaps the resulting starvation of his family. However, instead of being executed, he not only receives back his own goods but also the goods of Nemtynakhte. In this way, he achieves both his goals—the subsidiary goal of justice, thus the return of the confiscated goods, and the overarching goal of provisions for his family.

Moreover, the ending achieves idealized aspect normalcy, for the peasant's situation is no longer unstable. The great wealth provided by Rensi's decision will prevent him from ever having to seek provisions again. His family will be provided for from now on. Finally, the one separate narrative sequence—that of Nebkaure—is resolved as well, also in an idealized form. Nebkaure receives the speeches of the peasant "and they were pleasing to his heart more than anything which was in this entire land" (44).

Story, Discourse, and the Place of Culture

In the first section, we distinguished stories from incidents, events, and episodes. In the following sections, we will look at the relation between stories and works. A third axis for the definition of stories involves the conceptual division between story and discourse. This division has come under criticism recently and is sometimes considered theoretically unworkable. I believe that it is in fact an important and consequential distinction. Part of the complexity of the division comes from the fact that it is simultaneously descriptive and normative. In this section, I try to separate out these two components, examining how we can understand them in relation to the theoretical study of story structure, including the study of cross-cultural patterns in that structure. Finally, the story/discourse distinction foregrounds the topic of interpretation and thus the role of cultural particularity in the study of cross-cultural patterns.

A common way of putting the story/discourse division is to say that the story is "what happened" and the discourse is "the presentation of what happened." For example, suppose I hear that Smith has been murdered. My informant then tells me that someone had broken into his house after following him when he left a seedy hotel in the middle of the night. In the discourse, I am first told about the murder, then the break-in, then the stalking, then Smith's departure from the hotel. Clearly, the actual course of events proceeded in the opposite direction. Moreover, the actual course of events included things unmentioned in the discourse (i.e., the discourse is elliptical with respect to the story).

This basic account of the story/discourse distinction is perfectly reasonable and makes the division comprehensible in a practical way. However, if one wishes to develop the division theoretically, it is not really sufficient. If we are talking about a factual discourse, then it is not clear that there is any story at all. There were material conditions, causal relations unfolding in time, and so forth. But no story will give all this. Stories select, segment, and structure. The story is what we take from the facts. Then there is the problem that the discourse may not actually represent the facts anyway. Suppose Smith was not in fact at a seedy hotel but was driving home from working in his office. In that case, would we say that his going to a seedy hotel was part of the story? Maybe or maybe not. Perhaps we should take "story" to refer simply to what is implied by the discourse. But then we have the question of "implied by or for whom"? If real-world events are not the criterion for determining the story sequence, then is it the speaker? A reader? Some community? The same problem arises in fictional discourses. Indeed, once real-world events are rejected as defining the story, we are in effect in the realm of fiction.

One common way of specifying the story/discourse distinction is to say that story is constant across media or versions. But there are obvious problems with this. The story presented in a movie (documentary, fiction film, or something combining the two) gives many physical details that are absent from any verbal account (e.g., an eyewitness account in the case of nonfiction, or a source novel in the case of fiction). Are we to say that the details are not part of the story because they are not part of the verbal account? Is there a difference between fiction and nonfiction here? What about the fact that one can summarize the same work in different ways? Are these different stories, or is the story only what all the summaries have in common?

These and related problems have led some people to reject the story/discourse distinction. In a recent overview of the state of the distinction in narratology, Michael Toolan points to problems of just this sort. As a result of this "skeptical critique," he argues, "the story-discourse binarism is now used" to refer only to "a powerful illusion." In other words, it is seen as illusory but too useful to forego.

This is not, I believe, a very satisfying state of affairs. If the distinction is invalid, then in what sense is it powerful? If the power has something to do with the nature of narrative, then it would seem that the distinction must have some validity, whatever its flaws. This leaves us with the task of formulating the distinction in a way that avoids the preceding problems but preserves what is valid—and thus presumably what is useful. The problems seem to begin with a confusion between normative and descriptive senses of "story." Let us consider a purely descriptive sense first.

What happens when we hear that Smith was murdered, then that someone had broken into his house, then that he had been followed home from a seedy hotel? It is fairly obvious that we change the order of the events and fill in causal connections. We infer that the fellow who followed Smith was the same one who broke into his house and killed him, and we infer that the events occurred in that order. This process has been discussed by a wide range of critics and theorists, perhaps most fully by phenomenological critics such as Roman Ingarden (though he would have phrased the point somewhat differently). The product of a reader's inference or "constitution" (as Phenomenologists would put it) is an "intentional object," a complex mental construction that is, roughly, that reader's understanding of the discourse.

A story, descriptively characterized, is first of all a given reader's intentional object built up from his or her experience of a particular discourse. Note that this definition holds for fiction and nonfiction equally; it holds for written and oral narrative; it holds for formal, continuous narratives and the sort of piecemeal information we get about events in real life. It runs directly counter to the view of story as constant across media because it is entirely individualistic. Each reader will constitute the work in partially idiosyncratic ways. The point holds when the reader is also an author, writing a filmscript from a novel or turning a play into an opera. The constitution of the discourse by the scriptwriter will not be identical with that of the novelist.

In cognitive terms, we all encode experiences differently. That goes for semantic or linguistic experiences no less than perceptual experiences. We select different aspects of a discourse due to different sorts of emotional arousal, different models drawn from memory, fleeting and incidental shifts in attentional focus, and so on. We structure the discourse differently due to slight differences in the scripts, prototypes, and exempla that we draw on spontaneously when reading. Of course, this divergence is not boundless. In fact, among people who are able to make sense of a discourse at all (e.g., those whose competence in the language is not too limited), most will encode much the same things and they will do so in much the same ways. In other words, repeated over a large enough number of cases, we should find a fairly clear central tendency on a wide range of issues. In this way, the stories that result from our discourse encodings and subsequent inferential processes should, in most cases, share the great majority of features. Of course, we are cognitively designed to notice just what does not fit, the small differences that distinguish our understandings. For this reason, we will tend unself-consciously to exaggerate the differences among our various imaginations of the story for any given discourse. But we should not let that tendency mislead us.

On the other hand, to say there is far more overlap than divergence is not to say that the overlap is always the same. Smith may agree with Jones on points A, B, and C, while disagreeing about D. He may agree with Doe on points A, B, and D, while disagreeing on C. There is not necessarily a core of shared story elements. The point is that there will be a wide range of story elements on which most people agree. In some cases, the agreement will be nearly unanimous. In other cases, it will be much lower. Finally, there are likely to be aspects of story imagination on which readers differ quite extensively.

Of course, there are complications here. First, Phenomenological critics have pointed out that we tend to "concretize" our stories. That is, we tend to fill in details that have no basis in the discourse. I might imagine the fellow following Smith as thin and slightly balding. I might have an image of him in an old Chevrolet with the windshield wipers going. In cognitive terms, I am probably drawing on models from episodic memory—in this case, from movies. In and of itself, this is not necessarily a problem. It is just part of the idiosyncrasy of my story construction. However, the complication comes from the fact that I have different degrees of awareness of my imaginations, and these affect my willingness to attribute those imaginations to the story. Thus in at least some cases, I am aware that I am filling things in, adding material to what is given in the discourse. Moreover, I am aware that I am not doing this through rigorous causal inference, but in an idiosyncratic and unjustified way. In keeping with this awareness, I may discount some of my own imaginations. I may distinguish between what I think is really going on in the story and how I am allowing my mind to elaborate on that story material. On the other hand, in many cases I may be unaware that I am filling things in. I may mistake my free concretizations for well-considered inferences.

This complication is of course connected with the normative version of the story/discourse distinction. In this version, the story is not simply what I imagine the story to be, but what the story really is. But how can we tell what the story really is? This is of course a particular case of the question of validity in interpretation. Unfortunately, it would take us too far from our main concerns to treat this issue. For present purposes, we can confine ourselves to individual constitutions of stories and social patterns in such constitutions. In most cases there will be considerable convergence in our constitution of stories at the level where we are discussing them. For instance, I imagine few readers of "The Tale of the Eloquent Peasant" would disagree with my summary of the story even if they happen to disagree with my theoretical account of that story. In this way, the issue of validity will most often not be particularly crucial for the present study.

On the other hand, there are cases of divergence. Occasionally these may be consequential for a general study of narrative and particularly for the isolation of cross-cultural patterns. In connection with this, it is worth outlining some main types of divergence and their implications for narrative study.

Some of the divergence among readers will be idiosyncratic. This is important but will probably vary enough as not to be significant over large enough groups of readers. In contrast, some divergence will be a matter of group attitudes and identities. For example, those who share in-group identifications with the hero are likely to constitute somewhat different stories from those who share in-group identifications with the villain. These are the sorts of difference that advocates of reader-response criticism tend to celebrate, insisting that, for instance, it is right for women to take up a "resistant" attitude toward patriarchal narratives. I broadly agree with this view, and in the following chapters, I address some of the ways in which works may even invite certain forms of such resistance.

On the other hand, some group divergence in story constitution is a matter of cultural or historical particularity and is probably something we do not wish to celebrate. For example, imagine an Indian novel in which a female character appears and we are told that the part in her hair is colored red. European Americans may imagine that this shows the woman is foolish and is incapable of dying her hair properly. Indians, however, will know that this means she is married. There will be divergence in story constitution based on cultural understanding. There are also more subtle forms of such divergence. For example, a European American may know that an Indian widow may be expected to break all her ornaments. However, he or she may not have the sort of emotional memories that give emotional resonance to an episode of this sort. Thus the European

American reader may understand what is happening in a story when a widow's bangles are broken. Nonetheless, he or she may have a response that is, so to speak, emotionally blunted. These types of difference tend not to be celebrated by recent critics and theorists. Rather, these types of difference are commonly viewed as evidence that we need to teach the cultural embedment of narratives. Here, too, I agree.

In cognitive terms it seems clear that our encoding of discourses and our various levels of elaborative thought, inference, imagination, and appraisal will be profoundly affected by cultural knowledge and experience. Such cultural knowledge and experience are crystallized in cognitive elements, ranging from broad schemas to emotional memories. This suggests that one crucial aspect of understanding and responding to stories involves locating them culturally. We have not been concerned with this in treating *Anna Karenina* or "The Eloquent Peasant." There our focus has been entirely on the cross-cultural patterns. However, in considering M. F. Husain's *Meenaxi*, we will address some of the ways in which culturally specific ideas and practices may inflect universal structures. But before turning to Husain, we need to consider one further kind of narrative structure.

From the Story to the Work

In comparison with incidents, events, and stories, there is relatively little to say about works. Nonetheless, it is important to expand our discussion to works. Works form a level of encoding above that of stories. Specifically, they form a level of interpretive and responsive relevance, commonly with some causal relevance as well.

To understand "relevance" in works, we need first to consider the purposes of works. Cross-culturally, all the major traditions of literary and aesthetic theory indicate that there are two primary purposes of verbal art (see Hogan and Pandit on non-European traditions). One is emotional; the other is didactic. Literature entertains, produces catharsis, engages our feelings; literature also communicates ideas, particularly ethical and political ideas. Up through the level of stories, our primary concern has been with emotion and causality. In turning from the story to the work, our focus shifts slightly. Causal concerns are still present, but they are generally less crucial in treating works. Emotions, of course, remain central. In addition to emotions, a great deal of our interest will be in themes, which is to say, the ideas communicated by works.

Specifically, the work is usually the highest level at which we engage in interpretation. We group works together into larger units, such as genres and traditions. However, we do not commonly *interpret* genres or traditions. In terms of theoretical pursuits, the study of genre and tradition are typically generalizing. They address what is common across works. In contrast, the study of works themselves is typically particularizing. It is usually concerned more with what is unique. Thus genre and tradition studies are commonly parts of the "theory of literature" or "poetics," the study of broad trends (across stories or works), whereas the study of individual works is most often a part of the "theory of interpretation."

Interpretation itself has several components. One level of interpretation involves inference to story from discourse and debate over disputed cases of such inference. This is sometimes referred to as "understanding," rather than interpretation per se. Interpretation also involves connecting a work with real-world conditions outside the discourse itself. Scholars of hermeneutics refer to this as "application." That is most obviously central to more directly practical disciplines such as legal study. However, it also bears on literary study in some cases. When we do engage in literary application, we most often draw on our sense of the work's thematic point. This brings us to a final form of interpretation—inference to a work's political, ethical, or other themes. We may refer to this as "interpretation proper." The isolation of thematic concerns need not result in a reduction of the work to a precept. Thematic interpretation may lead to the unfolding of a complex and ambivalent argument, the delimitation of multiple and even mutually incompatible ideas about some difficult issue. Indeed, we are likely to view works with a simple and straightforward moral as not requiring much in the way of interpretation.

A key point about works—one that is crucial for interpretation—is that they are not simply collocations. The most obvious way of defining a work is by reference to a publication unit. But as already noted, we can bind together different plays by different authors and we do not therefore consider the result to be a work. We make a move in the right direction by making the plays all products of one author. But even then we would not consider something a work simply because its components were written by the same person. Thus having a single author is not a sufficient condition for being a work. It is not even a necessary condition. We consider many collaborations to result in works. Among the most extreme cases of this is cinema, which is of course highly collaborative. Of course, prototypically, a work does have a single author. Moreover, even in the case of films, we are likely to expect films to be more unified to the extent that they have someone (usually the director) who makes final decisions on what goes into the product and what stays out. Having a single author is, then, a preference rule. Something is more "worklike" if it has a single author.

In defining a work, then, we wish to isolate some sort of unity or mutual relevance of the component parts. Moreover, that unity must derive from a causal sequence in which the mutually relevant parts have been brought together intentionally. We have a strong preference that this intentional selection be undertaken by a single "selector" who, in making his or her selection, encodes the work as a single interpretive unit. Moreover, in the prototypical case, this is the same person who produced all the parts—thus an author. The preference for a single selector may be violated in certain cases of collaboration, where different selectors have final say over different aspects of the work. However, in cases of this sort, we may end up interpretively dividing the work into those separate aspects, in effect treating it as multiple works rather than one (as when we interpret one aspect of a film in terms of directorial goals and another in terms of the producer's demands or when we tease apart the interests of two coauthors).

But what constitutes unity here? Again, we do not want to count an anthology as a work in this sense—though there may be a single selector and even a single author (if the anthology is an author's compilation of bits from his or her own work). Some hint of what counts as unity is provided in the idea of interpretive coherence, but that remains vague. In part the problem is that we are dealing with a gradient. Some works are more unified than others. A play is commonly more unified than a novel and a novel is commonly more unified than a collection of stories. Indeed, a collection of stories may not constitute a unit in the relevant sense at all.

Given the preceding analysis, we may expect unity to arise in three areas. The simplest area in which unity may arise is causality, thus through "understanding" or interpretation from the discourse to the story. The simplest way for this to occur is when there is only a single causal sequence in a work. Since this case is no different from the case of a story, we may leave it aside. A slightly more complex way of achieving causal unity is through a story frame. A story frame is any causal sequence that encompasses other causal sequences, even when those other causal sequences are otherwise unrelated to one another. An obvious case of this is a journey or quest. In the course of a journey, the hero may have a number of adventures that are causally unrelated to one another—though they are of course causally related to the journey.

Though simple, a story frame does not provide a high degree of unity. Higher degrees of unity are achieved as the author multiplies the number of "intersections" between one causal sequence and another. Specifically, the characters and events from one sequence may or may not play a causal role in another sequence. The more of a causal role they play, the more the work is unified—thus the more "worklike" it is. In *King Lear*, one causal/narrative sequence concerns King Lear and his daughters. Another concerns Gloucester and his sons. All the characters from the latter also appear in the former. (This is one reason why the Gloucester story is considered the subplot while the Lear story constitutes the main plot.) Moreover, many events in one story line are directly causally related to events in the other story line.

The second area of unity is emotion. Again, "unity" here is mutual relevance. Different scenes may be mutually relevant in the emotions they express or convey if those emotions are the same. For example, two narrative sequences in a melodrama may both be sorrowful. However, there are other ways in which sequences may be mutually relevant. For instance, they may bear on similar emotional memories that have different emotional valences. Thus one narrative sequence may prime memories of familial reunion while another primes memories of familial separation. The emotions associated with one are likely to be the opposite of those associated with the other. However, they might serve to intensify one another—or if one is a main plot and the other a subsidiary plot, the subsidiary plot may serve to enhance the main plot emotion by contrast, or to relieve that emotion if it threatens to become aversive for the audience. It is not really possible to give anything like a rule here. For there to be a highly prototypical unity along this axis, the different narratives should serve to enhance the audience's emotional experience. However, there are countless ways in which that emotional experience may be enhanced. Moreover, they will rely on the precise ways in which particular sequences are developed in relation to one another—the timing of different incidents, how and when these incidents evoke emotional memories, and so on. *King Lear* illustrates this point nicely as well. The Lear plot and the Gloucester plot evoke similar emotions for similar reasons. Moreover, they have emotional consequences for one another. For example, the fact that both Lear and Gloucester err in their evaluations of their children may partially mitigate our condemnation of each (since it encourages us to think of the error as less individually idiosyncratic—perhaps more a matter of age or family structure—and thus as less individually blameworthy).

Finally, unity arises through the isolation of themes, which is to say, through interpretation proper. In part this is a simple matter of topic. Different stories in a work may address the same thematic topics or different ones. There is greater unity if they address the same topics. The most obvious way for them to treat a shared topic is simply to make the same thematic points. However, different narrative sequences can present different perspectives on a complex moral or political issue—and that is no less unified in our technical sense of enhancing mutual relevance of the parts. The parts are no more mutually relevant if they say the same thing about a topic than if they present different perspectives on that topic. These different perspectives may involve the exploration of different aspects of a problem (i.e., they may be complementary). Alternatively, they may go so far as to present mutually exclusive positions (i.e., they may be contradictory), perhaps by way of suggesting that standard solutions to a given problem are inadequate or that solutions differ depending on the precise case at hand. (In this way, a work has the same sort of unity as a conversation, which may be highly unified when two people present opposed views of a single topic.)

King Lear proves a highly unified work along this axis as well. For example, both Lear's treatment of Cordelia and Gloucester's treatment of Edgar suggest the difficulty of understanding anyone else's thoughts and feelings, even the thoughts and feelings of one's most intimate relations. They also suggest the importance of doubt and uncertainty regarding those thoughts and feelings. Moreover, they collectively imply that there are no significant gender differences in loyalty (cf. Cordelia and Edgar), promiscuity (cf. Gloucester, Edmund, Goneril, and Regan), cruelty, bravery, and so on. Nor are there any apparent national differences along these lines.

In this section, we considered how works may be unified. In the preceding section, we noted that the interpretations and emotional responses that bear on our understanding and appreciation of narratives are often culturally embedded. The final section of this chapter illustrates these points by considering a postmodern work from outside the European and American tradition. I have chosen a postmodern work because postmodernism is a movement most famously associated with *dis*unity. Successful postmodern works may be disunified in the ordinary language sense. However, they are not disunified in the technical sense of mutual relevance. Indeed, a central technique of postmodernism involves violating our ordinary expectations of unity while maintaining or even enhancing mutual relevance. In order to address the issue of cultural embedment, and to further expand the range of traditions covered in our examples, I have chosen a work from the Arabic-Persian-Urdu tradition, which we have not considered thus far.

Meenaxi and Postmodernism

As just noted, it is a commonplace that postmodern and avant garde literature and art operate to undermine unity. Postmodern and avant garde works do frequently disrupt our expectations of unity, based, for example, on standard uses of causal sequence. This is often a matter of the discourse, the way in which the story is told. But it can be a matter of the story (or stories or substory components) as well. Nonetheless, avant garde works remain works. As such, they may use standard techniques of unification, if in unusual ways. Alternatively, they may draw on other forms of unity that are relatively rare or peripheral in more traditional works.

Consider, for example, avant garde cinema. It often lacks a clear a plot line because it often minimizes causal elaboration. However, it may involve intensifications of thematic and emotional unity or it may draw on alternative aspects of narrative structure to give unity to the work. For example, it may generalize certain techniques of frame definition, drawing on prototypes or standard scripts that have well-defined spatial and temporal beginnings and/or endings. Dziga Vertov's *Man with a Movie Camera* is temporally framed by a film screening in a theater—an event with a clear beginning and ending. It is also temporally framed by the day. It is also framed by filmmaking. The first action in the waking town is that of the cameraman setting out to film. The movie ends with a shot of the camera lens closing. There is topical unity in its representation of common activities of ordinary people in postrevolutionary Soviet society. At the local level, when he sets aside causal relations between shots, Vertov commonly substitutes a form of visual connection, such as a graphic parallelism (e.g., an identifiably similar spatial configuration or type of movement) or a functional parallelism (e.g., different sorts of washing).

What counts as parallelism in avant garde and other works is a function of our cognitive architecture. Our minds operate in such a way as to link certain sorts of property or circumstance. Thus our minds link, for example, objects going up and objects dropping down, a character helping his family and a character harming his family, and so on. In narrative works, this means that one very common sort of relevance is parallelism across stories. We understand various component stories—or, indeed, component episodes, events, incidents—as relevant to one another not only insofar as they intersect but also insofar as they have salient parallels, not only in our emotional response but in the structure itself. As *King Lear* shows, this is an important feature of mainstream narrative works. Parallelism may be intensified in avant garde and postmodern works, either at the level of stories or at some substory level.

M. F. Husain is probably India's most famous contemporary painter. He has made two films. The second, *Meenaxi*, is very much a postmodern work. It concerns a writer, Nawab, who (with some pressure from his publisher) is trying to complete a new novel. He is, however, having some difficulties with his main character. At his sister's mehndi ceremony (part of the extended marriage ritual), he sees a young woman. This woman, Meenaxi, apparently comes to meet him later, asking him to write his novel about her. (I say "apparently" as it is never clear whether or not the woman actually exists.) He agrees. This provides a frame in which Husain embeds two attempts at a novel. The first concerns a young man, Kameshwar, and a young woman, Meenaxi, who meet in Jaisalmer. Just as their relationship seems to be reaching a critical point, the Meenaxi of the frame story burns Nawab's manuscript. Nawab decides to start on a new story. This one concerns a young man, Kameshwar, and a young woman, Maria, who meet in Prague. Nawab himself appears in this story, talking with Maria about her nature as one of his characters. Just as this story seems about to reach a culmination, Nawab dies. He then seems to revive and to be present at his sister's mehndi ceremony, where he meets Meenaxi.

Husain takes up some cross-cultural conventions of postmodernism. But he does so in a culturally particular thematic context. Specifically, Husain is drawing on the mystical tradition of Islam to give thematic unity to his work. Or, rather, he is drawing on postmodernism to give expression to Ṣūfī themes, which provide the thematic point (and thus one element of unity) for his film.

Ṣūfism is a complex religious philosophy and practice which, of course, cannot be adequately summarized in a paragraph. For our purposes, however, its main principles (or the main principles of the most relevant school of Ṣūfism) are that Allāh or God encompasses everything, that our only true happiness comes in being united with Allāh, that our ordinary lives are spent in suffering insofar as we are not united with Allāh, and finally that union with Allāh is a union of love. Ṣūfī mystics have commonly metaphorized Ṣūfī practice in terms of a "path" with specified stages leading to final union. Moreover, they have commonly allegorized the relation between the mystic and God through a standard romantic narrative. In this allegory, the devotee and Allāh are two lovers. The hero pursues the Beloved, who is often hidden. He has perhaps glimpsed her face (thus had a fleeting experience of God) but now finds her inaccessible. Perhaps they communicate by letter, perhaps they occasionally meet. Their union is opposed by forces of religious orthodoxy (since Ṣūfism was considered heretical). In keeping with this, the union of the lovers is often socially inappropriate. One version of this makes the beloved a member of another religious community. Though Ṣūfism is a form of Islam, its tendency toward monism (i.e., its tendency to view everything as a form of Allāh) makes it more open to the validity of other religions. Indeed, its stories often suggest that other religions provide important counterweights to the oppressive legalism of some orthodox forms of Islam. In its most fully monistic forms, Ṣūfism views every individual as God. Thus the final stage of union with God is actually a stage of recognizing one's own identity—seeing one's true self, purified of the false particularity of the material world. In connection with this, Ṣūfī writers often make use of images of mirrors, as in Attar's *Conference of the Birds*, where the final spiritual realization is symbolized by a mirror. In the context of this radical opposition to common sense, it is perhaps unsurprising that Ṣūfī teachers often make use of contradiction and paradox in order to disrupt habitual modes of thought and communicate a sense of true reality. Even from this brief outline,[6] it should be easy to see how someone such as Husain might recruit the practices of postmodernism toward Ṣūfī ends.

Before turning to a detailed consideration of the work, I should briefly outline the story structure in relation to the preceding analysis. We have a frame story in which there is an author trying to write a story. In short, we have a protagonist with a goal. If the pursuit of this goal is going to be resolved, we would expect the protagonist either to write the story (i.e., achieve the goal) or to find it definitively impossible to write the story. The obvious way in which it would be impossible for him to write the story would be if he died. On the other hand, this is a relatively limited goal and it is not clear that it has adequate emotional force to drive a narrative for most viewers. The author, Nawab, therefore has a sort of companion in the writing, a woman who inspires the novel—Meenaxi. The relation between Nawab and Meenaxi has a subdued romantic element. Nawab's sister has recently been married and he is alone in his home. Meenaxi at various points suggests that there could be more to their relationship than that of a muse and a writer, and I suspect that at least many viewers are moved more by Nawab's loneliness than by his difficulty in completing the novel. Indeed, when Nawab first begins to follow Meenaxi at the mehndi ceremony, there is a strong suggestion that he is much more interested in finding a partner than in writing a book. Thus we might hope for some sort of more developed relationship between Nawab and Meenaxi, a romantic story displacing the story about a dilatory writer. Of course, in good postmodern fashion, this is complicated by the fact that we cannot know for sure that Meenaxi even exists. Reinforcing our sense of the relation between Nawab and Meenaxi, the two embedded narratives are both romantic. Thus their resolution is obvious. They both point toward the union of the lovers or the impossibility of their union (e.g., through the death of one or the other).

This is all complicated by the thematic concerns of the work. The film's Ṣūfism suggests that the outcome of all our striving is both death and union with Allāh, a romantic union that follows death.[7] That is in effect what we get (allegorically) when Nawab dies and is then finally joined with Meenaxi at a mehndi celebration. At this celebration, Meenaxi is dressed in white. This suggests a bridal gown, particularly due to the design of the outfit. But it also suggests death, for white is commonly the color of mourning in South Asia.

To get to this conclusion, Husain continually links the three stories (the frame story and the two embedded stories), not only thematically but also through emotion, through narrative intersection, and through parallelism. In short, he makes a postmodern work that is highly unified through precisely the sorts of unification techniques outlined above. We cannot go through the entire work in detail. However, we will consider some of the main points to understand how the stories develop and how the work coheres.

The first scene of the film shows us Nawab riding in a rickshaw. As we will see, each of the three stories has some sort of journey as part of its opening—again, a common technique. This is a journey home, thus the opposite of what one might have expected. As Nawab observes the people around him, he recites a poem in a voice-over. He explains that everyone "walks by," yet the world is at "a standstill." The idea is perfectly comprehensible in Ṣūfī terms—the material world involves constant motion but no progress on the (Ṣūfī) path. However, we do not have any Ṣūfī context yet, so the poem may seem merely paradoxical.

At the level of plot, this recitation introduces the main character as a writer, a poet who observes the world and transforms it into literature. The next scene develops this point, as Nawab leaves home for his publishing house, where there is a press conference. At the publishing house, he explains that he is writing "a story that can never be completed." The point may seem postmodern. But here as elsewhere, it is also Ṣūfī—as is made clear by Nawab's explanation that this is due to his "character." He uses the English word, thus suggesting his own character or ego (the standard impediment on the Ṣūfī path) as well as the character or protagonist he is writing about. He explains that his mind is "cluttered with questions," a comment fitting for both a writer and a mystic. One of the journalists in the audience, mixing Urdu and English, says that this character is "ek [one] mystery." Nawab explains that she is "ek point of reference." Once one is alerted to the Ṣūfī resonances of the story, the double meanings here become almost too obvious to require explication. For example, the use of "ek" rather than the English "a" stresses the singularity of the mystery and the point of reference.

One journalist asks Nawab for the name of his character. We cut back to his home, where a young child is called "Meenaxi." This is clearly set up to suggest a memory. But it turns out that this is later the same day. Before he left, Nawab's sister had told him that today was her prenuptial mehndi celebration. Now the sister and her aunt are discussing that celebration, which is about to occur. Nawab suddenly appears, in noticeably different clothing. This is the first hint we have that space and time are not following their ordinary causal course in this film. It is as if something that should have happened in the past in fact happens in the future (or vice versa); it is also as if Nawab is in two places at once. The discrepancy is not obtrusive at this point, and could in principle be explained naturalistically. But more unequivocally paradoxical cases will turn up later. They fit with both postmodern practices and the Ṣūfī themes.

The next scene is the mehndi celebration. There is Ṣūfī singing accompanied by dances that are either highly sexual or are modeled on Ṣūfī twirling—a form of dance intended to produce a trancelike state related to a sense of oneness with Allāh. The emotional function of this scene is clear, for it is filled with eroticism, joy, and longing. The thematic point is, if anything, even clearer. Indeed, this is the first point where Ṣūfism is more directly suggested, so that we are able to see Husain's development of the story opening as guided by Ṣūfī themes. The point is not confined to the dance. The singers refer to "light divine" and "light in darkness" as Meenaxi, in a white bridal gown, walks among women in black burkas—suggesting the usual Ṣūfī contrast between the free and romantic nature of true devotion on the one hand, and the repressive nature of some forms of official Islamic orthodoxy on the other. Recalling Nawab's earlier statement that his mind was "cluttered with questions," the singers address someone—Meenaxi, Nawab, God?—saying, "Only you know the answer of what is divine." The movement in the scene is often impossible, as when Nawab glides from one spot to another, clearly without moving his legs; the speeds of motion change erratically. All this suggests paradox, unreality.

Nawab glimpses Meenaxi and the singers sing lines such as "I lifted the veil and saw your magnificence" and "I went a step forward to reach your destination." This is a version of a standard scene in romantic stories—the moment when the lover and beloved catch sight of one another. That glimpse is the provoking incident. It may be elaborated into an episode of search. The beloved is seen, but disappears. In keeping with this, Nawab tries to follow Meenaxi. He sees her with some girls. But when he arrives at the place, she is gone. He asks where she went. The girls point in different directions. This is, of course, a Ṣūfī point. The beloved he has glimpsed is one face of the Beloved, and that Beloved is, indeed, in all directions.

At this point, we may expect two stories with Nawab. In one, he is trying to write a novel. In the other, he is trying to marry Meenaxi. We do not yet know how the stories will be related. Quite logically, the next scene takes up this issue. Nawab is alone in his home when suddenly Meenaxi appears. Her appearance is somewhat uncanny. She is suddenly at the door inside his home, almost radiating brilliant white light (in striking contrast with Nawab's black outfit). This is an unusual variation. The lover, in this case, does not have to go in search of the beloved. Rather, the beloved comes to him. The point has some feminist overtones. But the causal elaboration here is largely due to the film's Ṣūfism. God is the one taking the initiative to be united with humans. In any case, Meenaxi explains that she wants him to write about her. This explains just how the two plots will be intertwined—the love plot will be transferred to the tale told by Nawab.

Needless to say, the narrative is guided not only by (Ṣūfī) thematic concerns but also by emotional ones. First of all, Husain has added the separation of Nawab from his only immediate family member, his sister. This is a story element that is outside the main causal sequence, except in providing a context for his first glimpse of Meenaxi. However, it is clearly important to the emotion of the film. Nawab turns to Meenaxi just at the moment when he is about to lose his one close attachment relationship. Indeed, the loneliness of his mansion is palpable when Meenaxi walks through the door. This too has thematic implications. Attachments in the material world are fleeting. Life is necessarily lonely and that loneliness can only be extinguished by an attachment that is not ephemeral.

When Meenaxi and Nawab meet again, he explains that he can write her story only if he has "bilkul āzādī," complete freedom—a common point about religious devotion, and one that fits the Ṣūfī opposition to orthodox legalism. She agrees. He then begins his first story. The beginning is, unsurprisingly, a journey: "Kameshwar is walking down the road. . . ." The name "Kameshwar" refers to the Hindu god Śiva as the god of sexuality and romantic union. The name "Meenaxi" refers to an incarnation of his consort, Pārvatī. The use of these names suggests a mythological model of romantic union as simultaneously divine union. In some mystical versions of Śaivism, the union of the individual soul with God is analogized to the union of Śiva and Pārvatī (see, for example, Feuerstein 31–32; for the larger philosophical point, see B. N. Pandit 15). The use of these (Hindu) names also suggests the Ṣūfī practice of drawing on different religions, even if all these religions are organized and related to one another within a version of Islam.

Heading to Jaisalmer, Kameshwar is walking along a seemingly endless desert road, with some suggestions of loneliness comparable to those of Nawab. He eventually comes to an inhabited spot. This leads to the second song and dance interlude. This one is given far less narrative explanation than the first—understandably, since the first song sequence occurred in the story's frame of "reality," while this one occurs in a fiction embedded within the story's reality. This is a song celebrating color, "Colors of love, colors of union," as the song puts it. This almost certainly alludes to Mohsen Makhmalbaf's film *Gabbeh*,[8] in part a tacit criticism of Islamic fundamentalism in Iran. Indeed, there are verbal echoes between the Urdu verses in the song and some of the Farsi discussion of color in the Makhmalbaf film (see L. Pandit "Emotion"). This scene too includes highly sensual dancing as well as some Ṣūfī-like twirling. It also includes clear discrepancies in time sequence, as when the time of day seems to shift back and forth from one shot to the next. All this is guided by the film's Ṣūfī themes. But at the same time, it has a story function. It presents us with the first glimpse, the moment when the lover sees and falls in love with the beloved—here, another Meenaxi, played by the same actress (Tabu) who is playing the Meenaxi of the frame story. This episode is, then, a direct narrative and emotional parallel to the mehndi scene earlier in the film. This yields a preliminary mutual relevance of the frame and embedded stories, even beyond thematic concerns. Kameshwar, like Nawab in the earlier scene, follows this woman, but without success.

Subsequently, Kameshwar happens upon Meenaxi at a party. Their interaction is a bit peculiar. He tries to impress her with his wit, and apparently succeeds, though nothing he says is terribly witty. This implausibly successful wit does not seem to derive from thematic or emotional concerns. Rather, Husain seems to be engaging in a rather complex form of causal elaboration here. Specifically, he is suggesting that Nawab is not in fact up to the job of representing this love relationship as it should be represented. This is further suggested by the fact that the discourse next shifts back to the frame story, where Meenaxi is criticizing him for what he has written. She goes on to complain that he "doesn't even want to try and understand" her. This elaboration is important for two reasons. First, it is a causal elaboration, and a causal elaboration in the right direction—from the author/frame story to the embedded story. (As we will see in later sequences, the direction of causality is not always the "right" one.) Second, it is consistent with the thematic concerns of the work. Specifically, it seems odd that a highly renowned author such as Nawab would find it difficult to write basic interactions between two potential lovers. The Ṣūfī connections make sense of this, since a famous author may find it difficult to represent the relation between a Ṣūfī aspirant and God. Indeed, a subsequent dialogue between Meenaxi and Nawab indicates this as well. Meenaxi says that Nawab's characters "are still struggling to know the reason for their existence." The point bears more on Ṣūfī allegory than on an ordinary love story. The film now returns us to the embedded story, where Nawab almost immediately reproduces a version of this discussion. Meenaxi asks Kameshwar, "What are you doing here?" He answers, "Exactly my question."

After some further cuts between the frame and the embedded story, we unexpectedly cut from the novel to Husain himself, seated at a table, writing. This clearly points us toward the embedding of the frame narrative in something else—Husain's own life. But it turns out that real life and the frame narrative are not separated. Husain is in a café. He looks over from what he is writing and the camera pans to a nearby table, where Nawab and Meenaxi are sitting.

This scene is followed by a montage sequence in the Jaisalmer story. This serves to represent the period in which the lovers get to know one another. This is a common part of romantic narratives in cultures that allow free intermingling of the sexes. Thus Husain is taking up a standard scene here—just as he did with the "first glimpse" in the two song and dance sequences discussed above. Here again we are repeatedly given contradictory cues about time, space, and motion. The dialogue seems continuous, but the places and clothing change. This sequence leads to another song and dance episode. In this case, the episode uses many standard devices of Hindi cinema to suggest a sexual culmination of the relationship. Thus we have a fairly normal causal development from the love-provoking glimpse, to the first meeting, to the period of getting to know one another, to the sexual union. This development involves extensive narrative parallelism with the frame (leaving aside the sexual culmination), emotional enhancement, and, most importantly, thematic suggestion.

At this point, the prototypical story development requires some sort of inhibition, some blocking to intensify the joy of the lovers' final union (or, if tragic, to make that union impossible). One possibility for this is a rival. Now Meenaxi speaks with her uncle about her feelings, hinting at marriage. Unfortunately, she speaks a bit too vaguely and the uncle seems not to realize that she has someone particular in mind. He announces that he has found just the right boy for her. Here we have the standard interfering parental figure. As a hindrance, this is somewhat implausible, and what follows is awkwardly developed. It recalls Hindi melodrama, but that does not seem to fit the actual conditions of this story. This too is the result of causal elaboration—Nawab's authorial incompetence. But once again this incompetence is presumably not general. It is somehow related to this particular story. That is where the thematic concerns enter.

Back in the frame story, Meenaxi leaves Nawab's home, evidencing disgust with what he has written. In a musical interlude, Nawab follows, holding the manuscript. Out in the street, Meenaxi knocks the manuscript from his hands. The pages scatter and go up in flames, presumably due to a fire burning nearby. The first story will necessarily remain unfinished. Note that this is one way of rendering the achievement of the protagonist's guiding aim impossible. But it is an "external" way. It destroys the story itself rather than, say, killing one of the lovers. Thus it leaves the story unresolved—though it fits the causal development of the frame story perfectly.

This scene is followed by a second meeting with the publisher, parallel to the first and initiating the second half of the film. Instead of returning to the lost story, Nawab decides that he will begin a new story. This new story uses the same actor and actress but is located in Prague. In shifting to Prague, Husain is evidently seeking Christian parallels to the Muslim and Hindu connections set out in the frame story and first embedded story. Thus, in this new story the main character is Maria, her name drawn from the obvious source. She is a waitress and an actress. The religious connections of her character are suggested by the latter, as she is currently playing the role of Joan of Arc. On the other hand, her success in this role is not great.

After we are introduced to Maria, a curious thing happens. Nawab turns up at her restaurant, then in her home. He discusses with her the fact that she is a character and he suggests that she will be "step[ping] out of the book." This has several points of relevance for us (beyond its postmodern self-referentiality). On the one hand, it is guided by thematic concerns. Specifically, it sets up a rough parallel between the mysteriously appearing Nawab in the embedded story and the mysteriously appearing Meenaxi in the frame story. Just as Meenaxi is a sort of stand-in for God in the frame story, the author is a sort of stand-in for God in the embedded story. The author as God is of course a common enough metaphor. However, it is developed in a causally peculiar way here, for the creations of Nawab are presumably not real. Thus he cannot enter into his characters' world, go to their apartments, and talk with them. In having Nawab do this, Husain is, first of all, drawing on one common way of integrating different plots in a work—intersection. But he is developing this intersection in a way that violates the causal principles of the narrative—just as he did by appearing himself in the same café with Nawab and Meenaxi. The point has thematic relevance to the Ṣūfī sense that the material world is itself illusory in comparison with God, just as the world of any story is fictional in comparison with the world of the author. Moreover, it suggests that true spiritual realization is a change of state as profound as that of a character "step[ping] out of the book."

As far as the embedded story goes, however, all this is just character background. The story begins with another journey—Kameshwar's journey to Prague. In this case, Husain opts for counterpoint rather than direct parallelism. He had elaborated the first glance in both the frame story and the Jaisalmer embedded story. In this case, Maria is supposed to meet Kameshwar at the train station. However, they do not know one another and end up not meeting.

Of course, they do meet subsequently. Husain moves to the "getting to know one another" montage, parallel with that of the Jaisalmer story. Here, too, there are many discontinuities in scene and clothing, linking this episode with episodes in both other stories and, once again, with thematic concerns. These discontinuities are very obvious and disorienting. For example, we are prompted to pay attention to clothing by Maria's early remarks on Kameshwar's attire. But the clothing of the two changes from shot to shot even as the dialogue proceeds continuously. For example, in one shot they realize that they have left Maria's bicycle behind. In the next shot, they run up to the bicycle—but their clothing is very clearly different.

In parallel with the Jaisalmer story, we now expect the consummating song sequence—which, in fact, we get not long after this. First, as regards the unity of the work, the sexual culmination sequences in the two embedded stories are closely enough related to lead us to group them together cognitively and thus to see them as parallel. More importantly, here too the episode suggests Ṣūfī themes. Indeed, in this case, religious associations are reinforced by the presence of angels.

Again, in Ṣūfī allegory, sexual union suggests some sort of spiritual realization. In monistic Ṣūfism, it suggests oneness and a realization of the self. Husain develops the following scene directly out of this. In terms of basic narrative development, it is, so to speak, the "morning after," a moment when the relationship of the lovers must be redefined after consummation. The sequence begins with Maria's eyes looking up into a mirror. In a voice-over, she asks, "What are you looking at?" We do not at first know if she is addressing herself in the mirror or addressing him. Though Kameshwar is not in the same room, he answers that he is looking at her colors—alluding to the moment when the other Kameshwar first glimpsed Meenaxi in the song about colors. She replies that this is a recognition. All the time, she is looking in the mirror. The camera pans through a wall. Kameshwar too is looking in a mirror. The pan shows us his mirror, back to back with hers, though we know that they are not even in the same building. They are speaking to one another, but they are also speaking to themselves in the mirror. The monistic Ṣūfī allegory seems clear. Talking to anyone is talking to God, and God is one's own ultimate self. Of course, this true self is not really the image in the mirror, or any other image. As Maria explains, "What you see doesn't exist. What you don't see, does exist."

The next scene places Nawab in Maria's apartment. In one half of the screen, we see his face. In the other half, we see her face, reflected in a mirror. It is as if they too are speaking to one another through a mirror. Maria discusses what she feels, establishing a loose parallel between this scene and the scene where Meenaxi discusses her feelings with her uncle. However, Nawab does not choose her beloved for her, even though he is her author—thus there is a counterpoint between these scenes rather than a direct parallel. This counterpoint fits Nawab's godlike position in this story. Like Meenaxi in the frame, God gives us "bilkul āzādī," absolute freedom. That is, then, what Nawab must do with Maria—though again the causality is inappropriate, since a character cannot be free in the way a human can.

Back in the frame story, Nawab's health begins to decline just as his story seems to be advancing toward the free, enduring union of the lovers. He has developed a serious cough and recites a poem that complains, "Darkness is upon me." Back in Prague, he and Maria are standing on a bridge. She repeats a version of the question that we have heard repeatedly in the course of the film, "You are my creator, why have you brought me here?" Now the story of Nawab and his character (recall the pun from the opening of the film) has become the main narrative concern. Unlike the God found in some rigid orthodoxies, Nawab does not want to impose rules. Rather, like the Ṣūfī God, he wants to "free" her.

This embedded story has led us through a partial realization of the Ṣūfī ideal. Maria and Kameshwar are one, identified in the mirror image, and Maria is both free and identified with Nawab as well. Yet this is not entirely the end. Freedom is not the final delivery. That comes only in death.

This leads us to the conclusion of the film. We are back in the frame story. Sheets of paper fly all over the room, paralleling the flying sheets when the first manuscript burned. Nawab is on his death bed. Meenaxi explains, "Then this pen was no longer yours; it belonged to Meenaxi." The suggestion is that even the frame story, which represents reality, is itself something written. It is written by God—and yet, if God is all, then a separate (authorial) God is one of the characters created or made up by (fictional) people as well. She touches his hand, which relaxes, and the pen slips through his fingers. He has died. Shortly after, his sister returns to the home and finds the corpse. It is a very moving scene, filled with pathos. This pathos only intensifies the joy that follows when he revives. But that too is not the end. Now, suddenly, we hear the Ṣūfī singing and it is as if we were back in the mehndi ceremony. Indeed, his sister, smiling brightly, embraces him and shows him the mehndi painted on her hands. The gradient from sorrow to joy—and particularly the sorrow of loss to the joy of reunion, a joy bound up with attachment—is very steep and effective. But Nawab is distracted, looking still for something or someone he has not found. In a voice-over, he wonders, "Kyā zindigī ek khayāl hai?

Ya khayāl kī talaś?" ("Is life one khayāl? Or the search for/of khayāl?")—
khayāl being both idea or thought and an imaginative, improvisatory
form of classical Hindustānī music. Is life a fiction imagined, presumably,
by God? Or is life, like music, an improvisatory imagination, the sort of
improvisation manifest in the two embedded stories, or perhaps even an
improvisation by which one seeks to realize a further imagination, not of
what is fictional but of what is entirely real? Now we see that the themes
of the film govern not only the relations among the stories but the entire
project of embedding fictional fictions within a fictional ("real") life and
a fictional ("real") death.

However, the resolution has not yet come. Nawab said that he could
never finish his story because of his character. But now his character, in
both senses, seems to have changed. Now we should be able to have our
ending, an ending that is the causal outcome of what went before, if in
the peculiar causality of mysticism.

He sees a woman in a white bridal gown. He goes toward her. She turns.
It is Meenaxi. Each gazes into the other's face with love and recognition.

Conclusion

In sum, stories too are demarcated most significantly by emotion systems.
Specifically, sequences of episodes are increasingly storylike to the degree
that they satisfy a growing number of preference rules. Two sets of preference rules appear to be particularly important. The first set begins with
the rule that the sequence focuses on a small number of protagonists
(usually one or two) seeking the achievement of some goal. That goal is
necessarily defined by reference to emotion systems, specifically expectations of happiness. Moreover, that goal must be effective with respect to
readers' or viewers' empathic response. Thus it should be an important
or strongly motivational type of goal. Moreover, the specification of the
goal should have low substitutability. Attachment goals are very effective
with regard to both criteria. They are strongly motivational and, in taking individuals as their object, they reduce substitutability almost to zero.
(Attachment is also bound up with the usual spatial structure of stories
in which the protagonist begins at home, leaves, then returns.) Finally, in
order to intensify the emotion of achieving the goal, stories preferentially
have a middle in which the goal seems impossible to achieve and/or in
which the achievement of the goal requires considerable effort.

The second key set of preference rules concerns the larger context in which the goal pursuit takes place. The goal should arise out of a normal but partially unstable set of conditions. The beginning of the story is defined by that transition from fragile or temporary normalcy to goal pursuit. The pursuit of the goal should be resolved either by the achievement of the goal or by making that achievement impossible. In either case, the ending involves the reestablishment of normalcy, though without the former instability. If the story is comic (i.e., if the goal is achieved), then the concluding normalcy should be "aspect idealized." In other words, the formerly unstable property, which gave rise to goal pursuit, should not only be stable but to some degree perfected.

All this is also bound up with emotion systems. As to the beginning, our sense of the normal is inseparable from our emotional responses, or at least our pre-emotional response of attentional focus. Specifically, novelty draws our attentional focus and prepares us for emotional arousal. Moreover, as to the ending, our anxious or hopeful imaginative elaboration is likely to continue whenever there is instability in the story situation. Authors may of course make use of that propensity in creating stories that lead us to reflect on unstable outcomes. However, the most prototypical stories involve "resolution." Narrative resolution may be understood as the inhibition of our propensity to spontaneously imagine further episodes in the story. That inhibition occurs most obviously by idealizing goal achievement ("they lived happily ever after") or by rendering further goal pursuit impossible (as when the beloved dies).

There are other preference rules as well, and these too are largely emotion-based. For example, the difficulties associated with the hero's success should be produced by some antagonist. This is related to our general emotional propensity to attribute the causes of inhibition to agents and to the strongly social orientation of our most motivationally important emotions. (Object-related emotions, such as physical disgust, are very important in short-term behavior. But our longer-term goals—thus the sorts of motivation that bear on stories—are far more likely to be bound up with social emotions such as love or hate.) Moreover, that antagonist should be morally inferior to the protagonist. This bears on our emotional response as well. Specifically, it bears on the judgments we make regarding the appropriateness of our support for the protagonist in his or her goal pursuit.[9] If the hero suffers, then it may be preferable that he or she have some sort of moral or other fault. This is for more or less Aristotelian reasons—which are, of course, emotional as well.

This is not to say that no nonemotional processes enter into the definition of stories. Most obviously and most importantly, one preference rule for storiness is that the events be causally connected. On the other hand, even this is not wholly removed from emotion systems. In the real world, the causes of any event are multiple and complex. We select only a small number of those causes. That selection is in part a matter of emotional salience and emotional consequence. (If Jones loses his home, that may be because of changes in mortgage rates, a downturn in his business, and other factors. But suppose his brother refused to loan him the money. When he thinks about losing his home, he will probably think it happened because his brother betrayed him.)

Stories are distinguished not only from incidents, events, and episodes but also from discourses. Though recently challenged, it seems clear that the story/discourse distinction is *descriptively* valid and consequential. As such, *story* refers to the sequences of events, and so on, that one infers from the discourse. On the other hand, we cannot entirely eliminate normative concerns here. These enter most obviously with the cultural embedment of the narratives, which bears importantly on our inferential processes and our emotional responses.

Finally, works too may be understood in terms of preference rules. First, the different stories that comprise works should be causally interrelated. This means that one story (e.g., a frame narrative) should encompass the others or that the different stories should have points of intersection, sharing characters and events. Again, causal connections are emotional connections, for emotions help us to select and organize a small number of particular causes from what in reality would be a multifarious and highly complex causal network. In some cases, distinctive parallelism across stories may also continbute to our sense of a work's unity. This is connected with emotion in that what counts as distinctive parallelism is bound up with expectation, interst, and attention. Emotions are also crucial for the unity of works in that the different elements of a work should be mutually emotionally relevant. In other words, different stories should contribute to the reader's or viewer's ongoing and overall emotional response to the work. This may be a matter of repeating the same emotions or counterpointing emotions. Finally, works are preferentially united by the mutual thematic relevance of their component stories. In other words, the different stories should explore the same thematic topics, whether or not they point us toward the same conclusions. Here emotion enters primarily in leading us to care about those topics—though it is also the case that we will think about themes somewhat differently depending on the emotions evoked in us by the work.[10]

Thus stories and works, like incidents, events, and episodes, are inseparable from the operation of our emotion systems and the structures of stories and works are largely incomprehensible without reference to those systems. As we will see, the same point holds for genre.

Universal Narrative Prototypes
   Sacrifice, Heroism, and Romantic Love

A basic structure for stories begins with fragile or temporary aspect normalcy disrupted by some precipitating event or change in conditions, leading to goal pursuit. The goal pursuit constitutes the bulk of the story. It is obstructed by sometimes severe difficulties, but often still leads to achievement of the goal and a return to normalcy, now with the relevant aspect idealized. Clearly, the goals are crucial here. In discussing these goals, I stressed that they must be empathically effective—thus consequential and nonsubstitutable. The difficulty of identifying effective goals is not terribly acute when we are telling personal anecdotes to family members, who are familiar with our particular circumstances and whose empathy is enhanced by attachment. But that difficulty increases as our audience becomes less familiar, as the stories have to appeal to a range of people in different circumstances and with different sympathies and antipathies. The problem is particularly acute for people who take on the role of social storytellers. Their job is precisely to appeal to a range of people outside their own circle of intimates. They therefore need to set out dissatisfactions and goals that will foster simulation and will appear adequately weighty and nonsubstitutable to an unfamiliar audience.

One part of the solution to this problem is found in prototypes. Prototypes are again the standard cases of given categories. These categories include emotions. Thus we have prototypes for the expressive outcomes of grief and the actional outcomes of anger. We also have prototypes for the eliciting conditions of happiness (i.e., conditions that will make us happy), at least as we imagine those conditions. (We can, after all, be mistaken about what will make us happy.) All our important goals are instances of the eliciting conditions of happiness. This chapter considers the nature and development of happiness prototypes and the operation of these prototypes in generating the major cross-culturally recurring genres of sacrificial, heroic, and romantic tragicomedy. It examines these issues in relation to our emotion systems, then in relation to the social ideologies that invariably alter these prototypes and genres. Finally, it considers examples of each genre in interpretive detail, exploring emotion, narrative structure, and some key ideological issues in each case.

Happiness

Given the basic structure of stories, we could in principle tell tales about anything—for example, my woeful lack of cucumbers. Admittedly, a skilled stylist will be able to turn even this unpromising topic into an engaging narrative. However, most stories do not concern trivialities of this sort. Rather, they concern such matters as the doomed love of Romeo and Juliet or the battle between Lear and his daughters over Britain. It may seem obvious that doomed love and civil war make for more effective narrative goals than cucumbers. But the point of a narrative theory is to make the division precise and explicit (rather than imprecise and intuitive), and to explain it.

We might begin by asking what happens when storytellers want to address uncommitted audiences, that is, audiences that have no prior, personal commitment to the storytellers themselves. In this case, the storyteller must isolate some broadly shared and consequential goals. However, since our engagement with stories is emotional, and emotions concern particulars, these goals cannot simply be general. Rather, they must be particular instances of *types* of goal that are broadly shared. As just indicated, the most general category for goals is "happiness." We seek things that we believe will make us happy. We do not seek things that we believe will make us sad or will leave us indifferent.

But the pursuit of happiness per se is too general. It does not readily foster the imagination of particular goals or ways of pursuing such goals. Thus we need to go a level below happiness proper and discern the varieties of happiness. First, we may make a broad division between types of happiness that bear on physical objects or relations and types of happiness that bear on social objects or relations.[1] Our prototypes for physical happiness and sorrow are, first of all, life and death. Life ideally involves health and all that is needed to sustain oneself, thus plenty of food and drink. The ideal here is, of course, sustained physical happiness or happiness as a *condition*. This is crucial for stories, since the enduring condition of happiness is what defines idealized aspect normalcy. But, of course, there are also happiness *incidents.* Perhaps the most obvious case of a physical happiness incident is sexual union. Thus we might expect that stories bearing on having food and drink, avoiding illness, or achieving sexual union would have some prima facie claim on engaging the interest of uncommitted audiences. Of these, one might expect that the acquisition of food would be particularly likely to develop in a range of societies. First, as already noted, it is a condition—indeed, a life or death condition—rather than an incident or event, which makes it more appropriate than sexual union for idealized aspect normalcy. Second, it is a positive, daily concern for most people, across ages. This differentiates it from the avoidance of disease (a negative goal, oriented solely toward not experiencing pain) and from sexuality (a goal only for people in a certain age range, and then usually not three times every day). Third, societies often have taboos on speaking about sexuality in direct ways; they sometimes have such taboos regarding illness as well. Taboos in speaking about food, however, seem rare. This too would contribute to making food a particularly prominent prototypical happiness goal.

Note that my story about cucumbers does bear on food. But it is not a good happiness goal for a story—and it is not, as we will see, a *prototypical* happiness goal—because it is too narrowly a matter of food preference. It does not bear on a life condition or on a particularly intense pleasure. Thus it does not bear on what we might call the "type universals" of goals. (In this case, the type universals would include, for example, having enough food.)

But again, physical happiness is only one variety. The other variety of happiness concerns, not things, but people—not my body in relation to other objects but my subjective self in relation to other subjective selves. Here, however, we need to make a further subdivision, for we have important happiness relations with both individuals and groups, and these relations are not the same.

What are happiness and sadness with respect to other individuals—"personal" happiness and sadness, as we might call them? These are most obviously a matter of help and antagonism. But our emotional experiences go well beyond such simple instrumental relations to the enduring emotional commitments of mutual bonding or attachment. The most obvious types of such personal bonding are friendship, kinship, and romantic love. Romantic love combines mutual bonding with sexual union. That combination of two type universals should make it particularly appealing as a happiness goal. Moreover, it somewhat mitigates the problems with sexuality. For example, it provides an enduring happiness condition that incorporates sexual union as a recurring event. Moreover, since lovers long for enduring union, not merely fleeting moments of pleasure, the trajectory of the narrative is likely to move toward marriage. This provides a framework in which sexual matters may be suggested without being explicitly treated, thus violating taboos.

When we turn to groups, further issues arise. In order to discuss these, we need to make an initial division between in-groups and out-groups, groups with which we identify and groups against which we identify. Happiness with respect to our in-groups is a matter of individual pride. More exactly, it is a matter of having esteem and authority. Happiness with respect to out-groups is also a matter of pride, but there are two differences. First, our relation to out-groups is not fundamentally individual. It is not a matter of this particular person (me) in relation to the enemy group. Rather, it is collective. It is first of all a matter of us against them (our religion against their religion, our nation against their nation, and so on). The second difference is that the esteem of the out-group is often unimportant. The crucial factor is fundamentally one of dominance. Thus in social relations our happiness prototypes involve individual respect within the in-group and collective superiority over out-groups.[2]

For stories directed at a general audience, we would expect happiness goals to be preferentially type universal. More precisely, we would expect these goals to fall into three clusters, parallel with the three object types or emotion contexts treated above. First, in the physical context, we would expect stories involving food and hunger motivations, specifically motivations relating to abundance and scarcity. (The most emotionally intense version of goal pursuit in this context does not concern having or missing a single meal, but possible starvation.) Second, in a personal context, we would expect attachment and sexuality to be combined in stories bearing on interpersonal relations. Finally, in a larger social context, we would expect the two sorts of pride to be interwoven with one another—and with anger as a response to breaches of authority—in stories bearing on in-group hierarchies and in-group/out-group relations.

Prototypes and Genres

Empirical study of works from a range of different traditions indicates that this is precisely what we do find.[3] Specifically, there are three cross-culturally recurring happiness prototypes, and these happiness prototypes define three cross-culturally predominant narrative prototypes—romantic, heroic, and sacrificial tragicomedy. (I refer to them as "tragicomedies" due to the tragic middle that commonly characterizes them. In some cases, the work may stop in the tragic middle, thus producing a tragedy.) I should stress that these are not the only genres, either within or across traditions of verbal art. However, romantic, heroic, and sacrificial tragicomedy are the genres that appear to govern a majority, or at least a plurality, of stories that achieve widespread and enduring importance in different traditions of verbal art. Indeed, they appear to be well represented in works ranging from elite paradigms to popular tales.

In romantic works, the initial normalcy involves two people who are unmarried and living ordinary, relatively untroubled lives. They meet and fall in love. Some works elaborate the process of falling in love, while others make it almost instantaneous. This is in part dependent on whether or not the encompassing society allows free intermingling of the sexes so that the romance has the possibility of developing over time. Once they are in love, they face conflict with social authority, most often parents. When the blocking figures are the parents, this serves to emotionally intensify the conflict. This conflict commonly involves two components. First, the lovers may be in opposed groups—different classes, castes, ethnicities, nations, or even just feuding families. Second, one or both sets of parents may have chosen someone else for their children. The latter produces one version of a love triangle. Often one of the lovers is exiled (in keeping with the spatial division discussed in previous chapters), while the other lover may be to some degree confined to the home. There is often some imagery of death or a mistaken belief that one or the other lover has died. In tragic versions, of course, one or both of the lovers may die. In the full comic version, the lovers are united, often through the aid of some helper figure. Frequently other attachment relations are repaired as well, with families reunited.

It seems fairly clear that this plot follows directly from the insertion of the romantic happiness goal into the general story structure discussed in chapter 2. The heroic structure is slightly more complex. In the case of the romantic structure, there are two emotions (attachment and sexual desire) but a single object (the beloved). In the case of the heroic structure, there is one basic emotion (pride), sometimes supplemented by a second (anger), but there are two objects (the in-group and the out-group), and correlated with these, two senses of self (as an individual and as a member of the in-group). As a result, the heroic narrative is in many ways two stories that are closely interrelated rather than a single story. Specifically, there is a "usurpation sequence" and a "threat-defense" sequence. The usurpation sequence commonly concerns a national leader (e.g., a king). The reasons for this are, first of all, emotional. Our emotional response to an occurrence is intensified to the degree that the occurrence is consequential. It is unfortunate if Jones is replaced as the coach of the third-grade soccer team, and we may be able to make a good story about it. But it is not nearly as consequential as the monarch being removed from the throne. Similarly, the threat-defense sequence commonly concerns nations and war. It is unfortunate if the mean guys' baseball team seems poised to defeat the nice guys' baseball team, and we may be able to make a good story out of this also. But again, it is not as consequential as the invasion of one country by another.

The usurpation sequence involves just what it sounds like. There is a legitimate social order in the in-group. Someone illegitimately takes over the leadership role. In the usual manner of emotional intensification, this person is often a relative of the legitimate ruler. That legitimate ruler is then exiled or, in some cases, killed. If the ruler is killed and this is not simply a tragedy, then he or she commonly has an heir who is exiled. (Hereafter, I will just assume that the ruler has not been killed. In the variant with the heir, the same points apply to him or her.) The ruler commonly has a helper who is a strong and loyal warrior. In some cases, the warrior may become the hero of the story, overshadowing the ruler. Indeed, in some cases it is the warrior who loses his/her position and is exiled, not the ruler. (For simplicity, I will also leave aside this variant.) An interesting feature of the warrior figure is that he or she is often headstrong. One would expect his or her loyalty to be constant, but there are surprising fluctuations, suggesting perhaps our general ambivalence toward authority. Though the heroic plot generally values strict social hierarchy, many of the greatest heroes (e.g., Achilles, Rostom in the *Shâhnâme*, Fakoli in *The Epic of Son-Jara*) are not as blindly obedient or unswervingly loyal as one might have expected. In any case, the ruler commonly returns to rule with the help of such a warrior.

It is probably clear that the usurpation plot is somewhat truncated.

It establishes a problem, then notes the solution, but it does not out-line any particular way to achieve that solution. The solution frequently comes with the threat-defense sequence. This is the way in which the two sequences become integrated so as to (almost) make them a single plot.

The threat-defense sequence begins with some national enemy. The national enemy is often a mirror image of the home society. There is a ruler. That ruler has a loyal warrior. Indeed, the loyal warrior often questions the wisdom of the conflict, though he or she remains loyal. Often the enemy warrior is a heroic figure admired by the home society (think, for example, of Hector). In some cases, the enemy is at least partially allied with the usurper in the home society. In other cases, the inferior usurper is no match for this enemy in conflict. In any case, the home society is threatened with domination by the enemy. Eventually, the enemy is defeated. Disproportionate credit for the defeat may go to the single great warrior of the home society or to the exiled ruler, who comes out of exile to battle the enemy, and thereby reestablishes his or her right to the throne. In some cases, the hero receives further help from a collaborationist, someone from the enemy side who transfers his or her loyalty to "our" side. This figure parallels the usurper, though of course heroic narratives tend to celebrate traitors to the enemy while execrating traitors to our side. The idealized normalcy that results from this is the restoration of the rightful leader, the subjugation of enemies, and the establishment of peace, security, and prosperity.

The heroic plot is further complicated by a peculiar sequence of events that sometimes follows the achievement of the final goals (i.e., restoration of the rightful leader and defeat of the enemy). I have referred to this as "the epilogue of suffering."[4] It does not by any means occur in every heroic plot. However, it does recur across traditions with surprising frequency. The achievement of the heroic goals would seem to put the hero and his or her society in a state of idealized normalcy. However, this idealization is disturbed by something, commonly a reminder of what was done to achieve that return to normalcy.

In many ways, heroic works operate to occlude the enduring harms of violence, particularly the violence of war. In terms of emotion systems, in establishing the happiness associated with pride and anger, such works commonly seek to suppress the sorrows associated with guilt or shame and with compassion or empathy. But, in part due simply to the ways in which authors elaborate on narratives—for example, in developing characters—some harms become salient. Often we as readers are somewhat ambivalent about the deaths in the story, including deaths on the enemy side, for we are not entirely alienated from all those who die, including all enemies. Indeed, sometimes it happens that "our" side and even the hero him- or herself is responsible for the death of someone whom we see as admirable or innocent or both—someone for whom we feel compassion. Subsequently, we may be reminded of the pain of this loss due to the grief of those who remain behind. In cases such as these, there may be a salient aspect of the situation that is abnormal, even after the establishment of a largely idealized society. This, as usual, gives rise to a goal.

The precise nature of the goal changes depending on what emotion is at issue, or what emotion is predominant. If the primary emotion driving the epilogue of suffering is grief, then the goal will be a matter of mourning. In these cases, the result is likely to be somewhat amorphous and to leave us with a story that is not wholly resolved—as with the ending of the *Iliad* presenting the Trojan laments over Hector. On the other hand, if the primary emotion driving the epilogue is guilt or blame, then the goal is commonly one of reparation or penance. The reparation may be undertaken by the hero or forced on the hero by another party.

More exactly, grief tends to produce a simple or minimal epilogue, which often involves little more than the expression of sorrow, sometimes encompassed by the formal structure of a ritual, such as a funeral. It is, again, relatively unresolved. In contrast, reparation or penance commonly operates through the development of a short but structurally more or less complete story. It commonly begins with the hero leaving home, either voluntarily or through force, in another exile. This exile involves his or her physical suffering and mental anguish. But this time the pain is not produced by a cruel usurper. Rather, it is associated with the judgment of some agency that represents a moral principle higher than the laws governing in-group hierarchy and in-group/out-group relations. That figure may be some sort of divinity or simply the hero's own conscience. This period of exile may involve something along the lines of a test. Success on the test shows that the hero has acquired the moral wisdom he or she needs to rule. That wisdom may involve the cultivation of empathy. However developed, this form of epilogue commonly leads to a humbling of the hero, his or her recognition of limits, of fallibility, and even of the ephemeral and ultimately unsatisfactory nature of goals driven by pride and anger. In any case, the suffering constitutes his or her penance. The hero then returns to the society. Now the truly idealized rule may begin. But that rule is no longer blindly idealized. Part of the idealization is a recognition that power will pass, that even the best of leaders will err, sometimes even that the enemy is no less human than we are.

The epilogue of suffering is peculiar in that it is not really provoked by a positive happiness goal. It is generated, rather, from emotional discomforts that are almost invariably associated with the achievement of certain sorts of happiness goals. Pride and anger are too obviously in conflict with our fundamental empathic sharing of other people's emotions—particularly people we see as individuals (e.g., through particularizing literary imagination) and whose suffering we witness. That conflict leads easily to feelings of remorse and shame.

The sacrificial plot is perhaps the least obviously prototypical. This is in part due to the nature of the happiness goal. The sacrificial plot concerns the absence of food—not simply an empty refrigerator, but famine. This is of course the most consequential and emotionally intense form of the need for food. The difficulty here, however, is twofold. First, prior to the development of relevant modern sciences, it is not clear why famine comes about. Indeed, even after a scientific explanation, famine victims are still likely to feel that their victimhood is unexplained. The second difficulty is that it is not clear how we might respond to famine. For example, what does one do if there is just no rain? In other words, causal elaboration and actional outcomes are stymied in this case. The happiness goal is deeply important. But it is not clear just how we might turn this into a story.

Needless to say, this is not just a problem for stories. It is a problem in real life as well. It turns out that people in different cultures come to pretty much the same conclusions about real life cases of this sort. Natural events are like anything else. There is the normal course of events. Then there are extraordinary events and conditions that provoke "why" questions. When the why questions concern big, sustained, consequential, abnormal events that are not caused by human agents, the first and obvious explanation is some sort of suprahuman agent. Thus, in real life, people tend to treat famine as what insurance companies and airlines refer to as "an act of God." But this only pushes the question back. If God does not normally make such drastic changes in the course of events, why has this occurred now? Here the usual answer is that the suffering people have committed some sin, either collectively or through a leader. This brings us to the other side of the causal elaboration—what can be done to return the situation to normal? Here, the usual solution is that the sinful people must in some way compensate for their sin, commonly through sacrifice.

Thus the sequence of events in the sacrificial story begins with sin. The sin commonly concerns happiness goals, since here too people are motivated to pursue something only if they believe it will make them happy. More exactly, the sin commonly concerns one of the objects of prototypical happiness goals—food, sex, or social power. (The pursuit of attachment usually does not fit here as it seems relatively rare for a society to see this as sinful.) This sinfulness may be general throughout society or it may be confined to a particularly important individual or group, such as a king or court. In addition, there may be one or more tempters who lure the people into sin. (An obvious case is the serpent in the paradigmatic Judeo-Christian-Muslim story of the fall of humankind.) The sinfulness gives rise to collective punishment by a deity, commonly through the withholding of rain and the production of famine, though it may alternatively involve widespread disease or some other form of devastation. The social response is a sacrifice, sometimes mediated by a priest or other religious figure. This sacrifice is often a death, and often the death of someone who is uniquely innocent. The death of the sacrificial victim serves as a sort of social reparation for the sin. It may also be accompanied by the punishment of the actual sinners and/or the tempters. This leads to the restoration of normalcy, perhaps with an actual increase in agricultural production, thus a period of abundance in idealized aspect normalcy.

Audiences and Ideologies

Up to this point, I have been explaining cross-cultural patterns in happiness prototypes and narrative genres by reference to the generalization of audiences, the movement from personal interaction to broad, impersonal appeal. However, things are not that simple. In fact, audiences are not merely personal on the one hand, or general on the other. They are far more differentiated. Different audience members have different material interests, different preferences, different affiliations and commitments. Moreover, not every individual or group has the same degree of authority or impact with respect to the social evaluation and preservation of stories.

In a very simple way, we may draw a broad distinction between elite audiences (often associated with patronage) and popular audiences (often associated with artistic markets). I am not speaking here of intellectually elite audiences but of audiences that represent some stratum of society that has disproportionate power and/or wealth. Indeed, we may divide elite audiences into three groups—the political elite, the religious elite, and the economic elite. The nature of genres and the development of those genres in particular works are necessarily affected by these groups, both in isolation and through their dynamic interactions with one another.

All these groups are likely to take an interest in all three of the major genres. Kings undoubtedly like tales of romance. Priests undoubtedly like heroic tales. The popularity of Christianity suggests that ordinary people take to sacrificial narratives. Nonetheless, there are ways in which different elite groups have different socially consequential relations to different sorts of stories. Specifically, political elites have a particular interest in heroic narratives and religious elites have a particular interest in sacrificial narratives.[5] Given the power of these groups—a power often enhanced through patronage of particular writers—we might reasonably expect these genres to develop most often in ways that are consistent with the interests of elites. In other words, we might expect that the development of stories will proceed not only by reference to emotional elaboration and thematic instruction but also by way of ideology. Given the relation of heroic plots to the experiences, authority, and often patronage of political elites, we might expect these plots to develop in ways consistent with the ideology of governance in a given society and with the associated "national" ideology (i.e., the ideology of devotion to the home society). Similarly, we might expect sacrificial narratives to develop in ways consistent with the religious ideology of the society. In both cases, we do often find this, particularly in works that are considered foundational for a given tradition. On the other hand, throughout most of human history, religious and political authority have been interconnected. Moreover, both genres deal centrally with the definition of an in-group as a unit and with the governing hierarchy of the in-group. For example, sacrificial narratives treat the suffering of an entire group, defined by some sort of identity category. Moreover, that suffering is often connected with the behavior of some leader. In this way, the alignment of these genres with particular elite groups is not entirely straightforward. Heroic plots are widely taken up for religious ideological purposes and sacrificial plots are frequently pressed into the service of national ideology.[6]

There is no particular elite constituency addressed by the romantic narrative. In keeping with this, the romantic narrative appears to be the least ideologically problematic of the three. Indeed, it is fairly consistent in its *opposition* to standard social hierarchies—religious, political, or other. We have already seen a case of this. Husain's use of the romantic plot was religious, but directly opposed to the social hierarchy of religious orthodoxy, in keeping with the standard uses of the romantic plot in Ṣūfism.

Since social elites have tended to be male—and since militarism is almost invariably bound up with gender ideology—we would expect heroic and sacrificial plots to include elements of patriarchal ideology. We do find this, quite clearly in fact. On the other hand, women are present in all elite strata as well. One result of this is a certain complexity in the portrayal of gender relations in many canonical works. As to romantic stories, the use of both a male and a female protagonist, the nature of the relation between the lovers, and the general opposition of romantic plots to social constraint and social hierarchy tend to partially mitigate patriarchal ideology in these works. In cases where the lovers are gay or lesbian, challenges to patriarchal gender ideology are likely to be even more extensive. On the one hand, the focus of romantic narratives is on gender relations. In this way, gender ideology is perhaps most obviously relevant to romantic plots. On the other hand, the general ideological thrust of romantic plots is commonly against hierarchy and in favor of individual freedom. The result of this is often a particularly complex and ambivalent manifestation of patriarchal and antipatriarchal ideology in romantic narratives.[7]

As all this suggests, the development of stories is profoundly related to ideology. This is true of both the standard prototypes and the individual variations. Indeed, when we get to the level of particular stories, perhaps the most important guiding structure that advances beyond emotion and causal attribution is dominant social ideology—national, religious, patriarchal—or alternatively, the resistance to dominant ideology.

Ideology is obviously closely related to theme. Indeed, the two overlap considerably. But it is valuable to distinguish between them, at least as tendencies. First, themes tend to be more effective to the extent that they are perceived self-consciously. I do not mean that they are more effective if they are explicitly formulated in the work. That is usually not true. However, they tend to have their greatest impact only when they are self-consciously inferred by readers or viewers. For example, viewers unaware of the Ṣūfī themes in *Meenaxi* are unlikely to be affected by them—or if they are affected, the effects will be vague and limited.

In contrast, ideology manifests a set of ideas that are most effective when they are not explicitly and systematically formulated, even by the author him- or herself. To a great extent, ideology is unself-conscious.[8] Indeed, it may directly contradict our self-consciously held beliefs. Thus a screenwriter may produce a script manifesting patriarchal ideology even though he or she self-consciously holds feminist views. Similarly, I may understand a work in a patriarchal way or be affected by sexist suggestions in a work despite my self-conscious beliefs. In keeping with this, a self-conscious understanding of the ideological content of a film or novel may lead us to reject that content.

Of course, authors may set out to present particular themes that are, say, patriarchal. For example, a screenplay may be thematically antifeminist. Moreover, readers or viewers may understand that this is the thematic concern of the work. Despite this, the main ideological effects of such a work are still likely to operate below the level of conscious awareness.

Crucially, ideology need not present a single idea or doctrine. More often it sets out a problematic. Thus an antifeminist work may have its most significant impact, not in convincing people that feminists are dangerous or that patriarchy is fine but in simply turning our attention to certain issues—for example, whether feminism harms children by sending mothers out from the home. In this way, it raises some possibilities and occludes others. It sets up the possibility that feminism harms children—a possibility that may be thematized and thus self-conscious. But it occludes the issue of whether sending men out from the home is harmful to children, whether having mothers who are economically dependent harms children, whether any harm done to children of working parents is more the result of bad national childcare policies than of having working parents, and so on.

As this suggests, ideology is also deeply emotional. The most crucial thing about the form of patriarchal ideology just outlined is not that it leads us to think certain things and not think—or even think about—other things, though that is of course important. The most crucial thing is that it makes us feel certain things. For example, we may feel compassion for the child who has been abandoned by his heartless, feminist mother. The sorts of generalization that bear on ideology are first of all emotional generalizations—prominently the association of certain emotional memories with categories of person, event, or action. This contributes to the unconscious operation of ideology, for it does not directly address our self-conscious beliefs. Thus it does not enter directly into rational evaluations. For example, Jones may feel guilty about going to work after having a child, even though she believes that it is important for women to be economically independent and that women's economic subordination is bad not only for the women themselves but also for their children.

A further difference between theme and ideology is that themes operate most importantly at the level of individual works. In contrast, the most important effects of ideology are cumulative. A particular work may have disproportionate ideological impact. Nonetheless, even a highly popular work is likely to have significant ideological consequences only insofar as there is a broader "discourse" in which the work fits. Suppose there is no general discourse of patriarchal ideology. In that case, an individual film may still characterize a particular woman as abandoning her child to pursue a career. But this might suggest only that this particular person behaved wrongly in these particular circumstances. It may not express or provoke generalizations—inferential or emotional—regarding women's proper role in society.

This is not to say that a work must always conform with the dominant ideology of a given time and place. There are "resistant" works, works that offer egalitarian and humane alternatives to dominant ideologies. For example, in my view, Husain's film manifests a largely antipatriarchal and anticommunalist ideology. On the other hand, this does not mean that works are either wholly ideological or wholly resistant. For example, one could argue that there are elements of patriarchal ideology in Husain's film also. Indeed, some form of ambiguity and ambivalence regarding dominant ideology is perhaps the most common case (as a network-based account would suggest).

The point holds not only for individual works. We find this ambiguity and ambivalence even in recurring constituents of the prototypical genres. For example, heroic tragicomedy commonly manifests a nationalist ideology. But the representation of the enemy side is often more equivocal than one might expect from nationalist ideology alone. Again, heroic works often represent some deaths on the enemy side as wrong, as crimes committed by "our" side, crimes that may even require reparation after the conflict is resolved. When fully developed, this gives rise to the epilogue of suffering.

Ideological ambivalence that arises in works of preponderantly dominant ideology often results from the spontaneous development of empathy on the part of the author and, in consequence, on the part of readers. Empathy tends to work against dominant ideology—or more generally, against unjust social stratification—because empathy tends to be equalizing. If I share someone's pain or joy, that tends to put us on the same level. As already indicated, the key feature of ideology, as I am using the concept, is its functionality with respect to social hierarchies. Again, in the case of dominant ideologies, this is a matter of sustaining current hierarchies. In the case of resistant ideologies, it is a matter of opposing those hierarchies—commonly in support of equality along the relevant axis (e.g., sex).

The remainder of this chapter considers four prototypical stories—one sacrificial, two heroic, and one romantic. In discussing these works, I am of course concerned with the ways in which they manifest and specify the genre prototypes outlined above. However, I concentrate on the ideological concerns manifest in these works. In order to continue broadening the scope of our analysis, I have chosen works from traditions that we have not considered thus far.

The first section treats a Chinese play from the late thirteenth or early fourteenth century, *The Injustice Done to Tou Ngo* or *Dou E yuan*. It is the "best-known play" (Idema 811) by "the most outstanding dramatist . . . of the Yuan dynasty" (Wang 7), perhaps the most highly esteemed playwright of China, Kuan Han-ch'ing/Guan Hanqing. Though sacrificial, it takes up a national rather than religious ideology. Moreover, it does this in a complex, historically specific way.

The second section turns to a highly prototypical West African oral epic, the story of Son-Jara, probably the most widely discussed and widely recorded African epic. Indeed, there are many versions of the epic as retold by many *jelilu*, or griots. The version by Djanka Tassey Condé is particularly noteworthy for our purposes, for it is marked by a broad ideological conservatism, particularly with respect to gender relations.

The third section examines the epilogue of suffering. Remaining within African epic traditions, it takes up what is probably the second best known African epic in the English-speaking world, the Nyanga epic of Mwindo as recited by Shé-Kárisi Rureke. As one might expect, the epilogue of suffering in this work addresses the standard ideological concerns of the heroic narrative—reverence for the internal political hierarchy and support of in-group violence against out-groups. But it addresses these concerns in a highly critical way.

Finally, we consider the most celebrated work of Sanskrit drama, *Abhijñānaśākuntalam*. This is a highly prototypical romantic tragicomedy. Moreover, on the surface it appears to be a work with little in the way of thematic development or ideological orientation. However, it is in fact deeply imbued with ideological concerns—complex interests and attitudes that are largely resistant or "counter-ideological" (even more than one would ordinarily expect from a romantic narrative), if also at points partially in keeping with dominant, patriarchal views. We can recognize the work's ideological focus only by placing it in the context of the literary and moral paradigms to which it alludes and which it revises.

Nationalist Ideology and Sacrifice in the *Dou E yuan*

"Nationalist ideology," as I am using the phrase, refers first of all to the sets of beliefs and goals, as well as broader problematics and more diffuse emotional attitudes, that function to sustain the political hierarchy of an existing or possible state and to foster support for that state in conflict with other states. Thus nationalist ideology operates to cultivate loyalty to national leaders or national structures of authority and national offices both within the state and in relation to other states—for example, through obedience to national law and through service during military conflict. It also operates to foster pride in one's country—along with pride in ethnic, religious, or other categories that are seen as isomorphic with the national identity.

National ideology in this sense is central to heroic narratives. Indeed, heroic narratives are bound up with a sort of ethics of pride, both individual and collective. The point is suggested by Kristjánsson when he refers to the "proud, assertive ethical tradition of 'saga morality'" (4; Kristjánsson is presenting a moral defense of pridefulness). During a period of uncertainty and ongoing conflict, heroic narratives are often taken up with particular intensity in order to further enhance feelings of national unity and commitment against the enemy. However, once the nation has suffered decisive defeat, the heroic narrative may no longer seem appropriate and its ideological functions may be taken over by a sacrificial narrative, a narrative that recognizes and seeks to respond to national devastation. This is precisely what we find in China during the period when Guan Hanqing wrote his *Dou E yuan*.

More exactly, the issue of national identity—along with the associated issues of national sovereignty and national pride—arose sharply for many Chinese writers during the period of Mongolian domination, known as the Yüan dynasty. In the thirteenth century, Mongolian armies conquered all of China. This was, first of all, humiliating. As Mote explains, "The Chinese people had experienced alien rule at several points in their history, but never before over their entire nation" (622).

The situation was worsened by the very high mortality rate. Langlois cites figures indicating that by the end of the thirteenth century, the total population of China had declined by roughly a third, a decrease of some 30 million people. Mote's estimates are even more extreme—"the population of China was reduced by one-half during the thirteenth century." Mote explains that accurate population figures are not available, but in any case "one must assume that there was a catastrophic reduction in China's population . . . the most extreme in the history of China" (620). This is just the sort of devastation in social reproduction that tends to foster sacrificial emplotments. Faced with genuine devastation in physical well-being throughout society, people invariably feel the emotional provocation to ask why. Once this occurs, sacrificial emplotments are almost inevitable.

In this case, the devastation was not only physical but cultural. Mote explains that Song society (of southern China) was "an open society in which a new kind of elite of merit was recruited from a broad social base." Indeed, "China before the Mongolian conquest had become a society having no aristocracy by ascription, no legally privileged or legally disfranchised" (627). This system of largely meritocratic hierarchy became part of the national sense of identity, thus part of nationalist ideology and a component of nationalist loyalty and self-esteem.

The Mongolian system altered this radically. Specifically, the social system in the Yüan dynasty involved a division of the populace into four groups, with Mongols on top and Chinese at the bottom (Rossabi 428).

This fourfold class organization bore on almost all aspects of the distribution of goods and services and restrictions on freedom (631). Liu explains that "when a Mongol committed a murder he was exiled, but a Chinese who murdered was executed; when a Mongol beat a Chinese the Chinese was not allowed to return the blow" (8–9). In short, they were not only deprived of sovereignty, they were demeaned and humiliated.

Of course, this is not to say that no one sought sovereignty. Opposition to Mongolian rule, though limited, was often intense. The severity of the punishments served as a practical deterrent to resistance. But the very laws that disprivileged and humiliated the Chinese also served to reinforce their sense of a distinct Chinese national and ethnic identity, and to foster a retrospective loyalty to the displaced political order, now undoubtedly remembered with nostalgia as well as anger toward the current regime. Much of this resistance was overt and military. Indeed, the anti-Mongolian "loyalists" developed a sort of martyrology surrounding those who died for the cause. These martyrs were understood, first of all, as having the virtues of *zhongyi*. Jay explains that "zhong" meant "loyalty," specifically "a subject's allegiance to the ruler." "Yi" meant "righteousness, duty, or obligation" (93–94). The loyalist martyrs were contrasted specifically with the collaborationists, of whom there were many (see Jay 33).

Needless to say, not all resistance was explicit and militant. Much of it was a matter of more quiet noncooperation or other sorts of dissident expression—most obviously through art. Yüan period drama is particularly known for this sort of nationalistic expression. As Liu puts it, "The drama was to be the weapon of the conquered" (10).

Before going on, it is valuable to distinguish several levels or types of representation here. In principle, a playwright might directly depict the situation he or she is criticizing. For example, he or she might portray a scene of life in Yüan China, addressing a case of discrimination resulting from the fourfold class system. This was rare. A common form of indirection continues to treat a problem at a straightforward or relatively literal level. However, it does so by shifting the historical or cultural context, "criticizing the present by pointing to the past," as it is sometimes called. As Jay explains, "Some loyalists used historical analogies to express their thoughts about foreign conquest" (73). Another level is allegorical, where principles or ideas are represented as persons, actions, or things. The meaning of an allegory may not be initially obvious to the viewer. However, once a few of the tacit metaphors or verbal puns are recognized, at least part of an allegory may become clear. This technique of indirection was also common (see Rossabi 469 for an example).

These basically thematic methods of critique are relatively straightforward. However, not all political works—in Yüan China or elsewhere—are so univocal. Put differently, the modes of literary dissent just mentioned are often planned out in detail. They result from a conscious and consistent effort on the part of the author. Though an allegory may have many meanings, at least one of those meanings has probably been developed rigorously by the author. Thus that meaning should be isolable in a more or less systematic way. However, not all works follow such a straightforward thematic path. In fact, literary dissent is often much more loosely structured, much more a matter of shifting allusions and only partially parallel situations. In other words, a work need not develop a detailed argument or analysis, plotting out every point as in an allegory or in a full historical analogy. Rather, an author may rely on an accumulation of suggestions, looser connections with political situations, historical events, and social practices that are not developed in a straightforward, linear manner.

Of course, to say that the political suggestiveness of a work is not reducible to a direct allegorical reading is not to say that the suggestions are random or incoherent. To be a resistant work at all, the hints and allusions must develop toward a consistent set of political ideas. The point is that this development may not involve fixed correspondences or complete narrative continuity. In an allegory, the main character of a work might, for example, primarily represent the Chinese people. Whatever else that character might stand for, he or she will pass through the course of the narrative consistently representing the Chinese people. In the case of a suggestive work, however, this need not be the case. The main character's situation may suggest a particular historical dilemma of the Chinese people at one point, an experience of the emperor's at another point, and so on, without any one of these being developed fully or consistently. On the whole, these various suggestions must contribute to, say, a sense of the injustice of Mongolian rule. But they need not present a single, extended elaboration of one topic or idea. Indeed, the suggestions may operate first of all to cultivate an *emotional attitude* associated with certain political ideas and identifications. They may not necessarily present a conceptually consistent and logically developed thematic analysis.

In my view, a good deal of Yüan drama is resistant in just this way. It is common to read Yüan drama as a drama of dissidence or protest. However, some critics have faulted political analyses of this drama as reductive and even simplistic. For example, Perng is so impatient with political criticism of Yüan drama that he refers to it not as a "school" nor as an "approach" but as a "cult" (10). In part, this is simply a matter of Perng's own critical preferences. But it may also result from the general tendency of political critics to approach works as more straightforward than they are, as analogical or allegorical rather than suggestive. If we approach a suggestive work in the wrong way, our analyses may seem forced and unconvincing, as we fail to recognize the semantic richness and, so to speak, flexibility of the work.

Dou E yuan[9] is an excellent example of a work that is guided by a resistant ideology, manifest through suggestion. The framework for that expression and ideology is the sacrificial structure. The play does not manifest a perfectly prototypical version of that structure. However, that is only a further reason to consider it in this context, for it increases the complexity of the work's relation to the prototype, and thus its interpretive interest.

Liu explains that "little is known of Kuan," though we are "certain" that he was a native of what is now Beijing in northern China (30). Wang estimates that Guan was born "in the twenties or thirties of the thirteenth century and died at the end of it. Most of his plays were written in the later half of the century, especially in the last two decades" (8). This places his birth slightly before or roughly at the time of the Mongolian conquest of the Jin empire (of northern China). It also locates his period of greatest literary activity in the two decades following the Mongolian conquest of the Song empire (of southern China), thus in the period of the most fervent loyalist resistance. It is unsurprising that his work would bear the marks of that historical location. In keeping with this, West quotes a Chinese scholar writing in the mid–fourteenth century that Guan was one of the "*i-lao*," which is to say, "surviving elders of the previous dynasty of Chin" who resisted Yüan rule by withdrawal, refusing "to serve and be advanced" (436). Guan's resistance appears not only in this noncooperation but in his writing as well.

Dou E yuan begins when an impoverished Confucian scholar, Tou T'ien-chang, gives his seven-year-old daughter, Tou Ngo, to the widow, Mother Ts'ai. In exchange, she cancels a debt he owes her and gives him some extra money so that can travel to the capital and take the imperial examination. Thirteen years pass during which Tou Ngo is married to Mother Ts'ai's son, then widowed. Dr. Lu, a physician, is introduced at this point. He owes Mother Ts'ai money and plans to lure her into an obscure place, then strangle her. He follows his plan and almost succeeds when Old Chang and his son, Donkey Chang, enter. In exchange for saving her life, Donkey Chang demands that Mother Ts'ai marry Old Chang and that he be given Tou Ngo himself. She refuses, but then Donkey Chang threatens to strangle her, so she agrees. At home, Tou Ngo refuses this marriage, speaking at length about the importance of loyalty to one's husband. Frustrated, Donkey Chang goes to the pharmacy to buy poison. He happens to find Dr. Lu and threatens to report Lu's attempted murder of Mother Ts'ai if Lu does not give him the poison. Lu complies, then leaves town. Donkey Chang sneaks the poison into Mother Ts'ai's soup, but Old Chang drinks the soup instead. Once Old Chang has died, Donkey Chang accuses Tou Ngo of the murder. They proceed to the court where a corrupt prefect has Tou Ngo beaten. When she will not confess, he decides to have Mother Ts'ai beaten. Fearing that her mother-in-law will not survive the beating, Tou Ngo confesses to the crime. She is condemned to beheading. Before the execution, she makes three predictions. First, her blood will not fall to the ground but will be drawn up into the white banner hung nearby. Second, though it is the middle of summer, the snow will fall until it is so thick that it buries her corpse. Finally, there will be a drought for three years. All three prophecies come true.

In the final act, Tou Ngo's father returns. He has passed the imperial examination and has been made an inspector. He has come to review the records of the different governmental departments in the area. It is three years after Tou Ngo's execution and the drought continues. Tou T'ien-chang is investigating some prison records when the ghost of Tou Ngo appears to him and recounts the events of the first part of the play. Tou T'ien-chang gathers those involved and re-hears the case. He judges that Donkey Chang should be beheaded, the prefect should be beaten and "permanently dismissed from service," and Dr. Lu should be exiled (*Injustice* 157–58; see also *Arousing* 320–23) or that both Donkey Chang and Dr. Lu should be executed, the prefect should be beaten and dismissed, and the court should "offer a great sacrifice / So that [Tou Ngo's] spirit may go to heaven" (*Snow* 47).

The play centrally incorporates a sacrificial structure, but with one noteworthy twist. Specifically, we find the communal violation, the drought, the sacrifice of the innocent representative of the community, and the purging of the violators and the tempters. But the drought follows, rather than precedes, the sacrifice of the innocent victim. Though it may at first seem very odd, this variation is not unique. Sometimes, as here, the sacrifice of the innocent victim is the culmination of the sin and leads to the punishment of the violators. As a first approximation, we might say that in this particular play, the fundamental communal violation is the widespread corruption of the society, corruption that prominently includes sexual misconduct. (I modify this diagnosis somewhat below.) This violation reaches its dramatic pinnacle in the death of Tou Ngo. In this way, it is the corruption that is the underlying cause of the drought. While the execution is the proximate cause of the drought, it is also the event that gives rise to the possibility of purging the violators and ending the drought. In relation to this, it is crucial that the execution is, in a sense, chosen by Tou Ngo herself and that it is explicitly a self-sacrifice for the well-being of others. Moreover, it is a self-sacrifice in keeping with traditional loyalties of just the sort that the larger society is ignoring. The purging of the violators (through death and exile) and the ending of the drought—along with the preservation of Mother Ts'ai—are, in this way, the culminating result of Tou Ngo's death, and of the further "great sacrifice" (*Snow* 47) that finally resolves her death.

The general point is clearer in relation to the play's nationalist themes and ideology. As will become clearer below, Tou Ngo is established as parallel with the loyalist martyrs. It is clear that the death of each such martyr was both a crime committed by the new rulers and also a self-sacrifice that would allow the eventual restoration of the devastated society. In this way, the displacement of the sacrifice marks a point where the particular story not only emplots nationalism through the genre prototype but simultaneously alters that prototype by (tacit) reference to actual historical conditions and events.

For the play's original audience, the nationalist suggestiveness of the story begins with the introduction of the scholar, whose poverty would likely call to mind the situation of Confucian scholars at the time. The Mongolian rulers had abolished the imperial exams. These exams had previously been the means by which scholars could enter into productive careers, careers presumably valuable both to the scholars themselves and to the nation (see, for example, Lao 108 and Mote 639). Tou T'ien-chang's reference to taking the exams would further serve to recall this situation.

The corruption of the court, depicted through the character of the prefect, also pointed to Mongolian rule. Liu explains that corruption was rife in the Yüan legal system. For example, in 1304, "at one inquiry 18,473 corrupt officials were condemned, bribes of 45,865 ingots of silver . . . were discovered, and 5,176 sentences passed on prisoners were proved to be unjust" (9). Wang relates the point directly to Guan's play: "Tou Ngo's struggle with the Changs and the prefect is a penetrating exposure of the corrupt state of local politics and the social disorder during the Yüan dynasty, while her rebellious spirit symbolizes the determined resistance of the common people to their cruel oppressors" (9).

If the prefect recalls the corrupt and incompetent officials of the Yüan administration, what about the other villains? The Changs are, most obviously, uncultured. Along with the prefect, they are in effect the antithesis of the Confucian scholar—indeed, they are what has replaced the scholar in the Yüan system. But the Changs are more than the antithesis of a scholar. Their lack of refinement is almost un-Chinese, despite their name. Tou Ngo characterizes them as a "yokel" and a "ruffian" (*Snow* 28). One has the name of an animal. They have, in short, the characteristics of barbarians, bullying boors who fit the stereotypical portrait of Mongols, to whom some Chinese referred by using animal terms (see Jay 78 for some examples). It is fitting that Donkey Chang tries to force Tou Ngo to kneel before him (*Injustice* 128), in effect what the Mongols did to the Chinese more generally. Both the Changs and the Mongols engaged in humiliating practices. However, showing the pride and bravery of the loyalist militants, Tou Ngo not only refuses but "pushes him and he falls" (128). Finally, the villainous doctor too fits well into the nationalistic purposes of the play. Specifically, the place of physicians was distinctive in China during the Yüan period. As Rossabi explains, "Physicians were one . . . group that benefited from Mongolian rule," as Khubilai "accorded doctors a higher social status" (450–51). To make a doctor one of the villains was, at the time, to attack a group that the Mongols had elevated.

I have been stressing pride and humiliation. Fear and anger obviously figure in the play as well, just as they did in the larger society. But the central emotion, at least in the play, is probably disgust. This fits with the sources of the sacrificial plot. Again, the prototypical happiness goal for the sacrificial narrative is food. Disgust is, first of all, a gustatory response, an aversion to food that may contain contaminants (see Rozin, Haidt, and McCauley "Disgust" [2008], 757). But it is readily extended to disgust at other people, entering into bias against out-group members, including racial bigotry (see Taylor; see also Nussbaum, *Upheavals* 347–49, and Fiske, Harris, and Cuddy 1482–83). Finally, Rozin, Haidt, and McCauley note that moral disgust is continuous with "core" disgust (the disgust response to food) and takes as its object a limited number of moral faults. These include racism and betrayal ("Disgust" [2008], 762). In keeping with this, loyalist Chinese must have felt intense moral disgust at Mongol racism (in addition to feeling their own—racist—disgust at Mongols). This combination of core, interpersonal, and moral disgust is just what we find in the portrayal of the despicable Changs. Indeed, the prominence of disgust contributes to the manner in which Donkey Chang commits his murder, and to the physician's role in that murder. Of the many ways they could have violated the law, Guan chooses one involving food and poison.

Other elements of the play would also have called to mind general features of Yüan rule for an audience at the time. For example, the use of torture is likely to have suggested the use of torture against loyalists (see, for example, Jay 53), at least for some viewers. Here, too, there is emotional continuity. While Guan's representation of torture cultivates empathy for the victim, it seems more fully directed toward fostering disgust with the perpetrators. Following torture, Tou Ngo is to be beheaded. This is historically suggestive, for decapitation was a practice that many viewers at this time would have associated with loyalist martyrs. As Rossabi points out, "there were several uprisings against Mongolian rule" after the conquest of 1279. Thus "in 1281, Khubilai's troops crushed the first of these . . . by beheading . . . twenty thousand rebel soldiers" (476). (Note that by Wang's chronology, 1281 was at the beginning of Guan's most productive period, thus presumably the period in which he wrote *Dou E yuan*.) Here we have another instance of the association between Tou Ngo and the loyalist martyrs. Again, these historical connections more or less forced Guan to alter the sacrificial narrative prototype and make the death precede rather than end the worst devastation.

Though I have been stressing the cultivation of disgust aimed at the Mongols, they cannot be the only target. In terms of the sacrificial emplotment, there has been a social sin that has brought devastation to the Chinese people. On the one side we have the Changs, which is to say, the Mongols. But the sin of the Mongols alone would not bring disaster upon the Chinese, at least not according to the standard sacrificial narrative, just as the sin of the devil alone does not cause the fall of humankind in the Judeo-Christian-Muslim myth. In terms of the sacrificial structure, the home society itself must be at least a partial source of sin as well. The sin here is collaboration, as is regularly the case with sacrificial emplotments of nationalism. Or rather, it is the more general unscrupulous pursuit of individual self-interest that gives rise to both collaboration and corruption. The collaboration is represented first of all by the behavior of the doctor. The related corruption is obviously manifest in the prefect. In addition, there is a more benign acquiescence in the conquest, represented by Mother Ts'ai's acceptance of the Changs and her contemplation of marriage, which Tou Ngo views as a shameful act of betrayal. In keeping with this, Liu points out that "some critics are of the opinion that [Tou Ngo's] rebukes [directed against her mother-in-law] are in fact administered to those Chinese who became willing slaves to their new Mongolian masters, that it was their disloyalty and infidelity the dramatist was attacking here" (29). In all three cases, the blame is bound up with disgust (see Rozin, Haidt, and McCauley "Disgust" [2008], 762, on disgust at betrayal).

A sin of this sort can be expiated—and its devastating consequences can be reversed—only through the sacrifice of the innocent (the loyalist martyrs/Tou Ngo) along with the purgation of the infiltrating tempters (the Mongols/Changs) and the in-group traitors (the Chinese collaborationists/Lu and the prefect). I phrase this in terms of purgation as the metaphor and its emotional resonances are particularly appropriate to the cultivation of disgust.

The sacrificial character of the play culminates, in one version, in a final rite, "a great sacrifice" allowing Tou Ngo's "spirit" to "go to heaven" (*Snow* 47). The statement implies a realignment of heaven and earth, a rejoining of the two that allows the innocent spirit to go up to heaven and, since this rite will end the drought, rain to come down from heaven. Politically, this realignment necessarily includes a return of the mandate of heaven, the divine guarantee of imperial authority. Thus the reference to sacrifice is fitting at a general, symbolic level. However, it is also apt in a more historically particular way. As Jay points out, "the Mongol emperor, by performing the Chinese sacrificial rites to the ancestors and to Heaven . . . also formally brought the Song to an end" (88). A parallel sacrifice would be necessary to reverse this usurpation, ending Mongolian rule, culminating the sacrifice of the loyalist martyrs (releasing them from being "ghost[s] of the Song," as they were sometimes characterized [see Jay 43–44]), and returning rightful sovereignty to China. In the final sacrifice for Tou Ngo, then, we see another accommodation of the sacrificial structure to historical and cultural particulars, an accommodation that serves to support a hopeful nationalist ideology.

In sum, *Dou E yuan* is a sacrificial narrative that expresses but also structures ideas and emotions bearing on Chinese nationalism in the particular historical conditions of Mongolian domination. The emotions include pride and humiliation, anger and fear, but most importantly, disgust—at the persons and policies of the Mongols and at Chinese collaborators. The play manifests both universal principles (the events and roles of the sacrificial narrative) and culturally and historically particular specifications of those principles (e.g., the allusions to the loyalist martyrs with their virtues of zhongyi). It also involves development of the universal and cultural elements by tacit reference to the guiding emotion of disgust. As such, the play integrates thematic, ideological, and motivational concerns into a "structure of feeling" (to borrow a phrase from Raymond Williams) by way of a flexible prototypical emplotment. This presumably in part reflected the inclinations to thought and action felt by audience members (thus the common experiential orientation of many people at the time, what Williams stressed in referring to a "structure of feeling" [see, for example, 63–66 and 84]). It also in part encouraged those inclinations. In short, the historical, cultural, and ideological particularities of the work are inseparable from its prototypical narrative structure, even as those particularities modify parts of that structure. They are also inseparable from the emotional processes that both orient and are oriented by that structure.

Gender Ideology and Heroism in *The Epic of Son-Jara*

As already noted, we have a number of versions of this important West African epic, versions told by different griots in different regions. Though the details vary, sometimes considerably, they mostly share a main story along the following lines. There is a great king of Mali, Fata Magan

Kònatè.[10] His reign is good and thus there is aspect normalcy. However, he does not have a son to inherit his position. This is of course one common motif cross-culturally—unsurprisingly in cultures where leadership is hereditary.[11] A hunter meets the king. This hunter prophesies that the king will have a son who will be the great ruler of a vast kingdom. Thus we have temporary aspect normalcy disturbed, first by a natural and incremental development (the king continues not to have a son), and second, by a provoking event (the prophecy). In other versions, the king does have a son. However, the hunter prophesies that another son will be the great ruler. In these cases, the disruption of normalcy is provoked in opposition to a "developmental normalcy" (since the ordinary course of development has produced an heir).

The hunter explains that in Dò ni Kiri there is a woman who has taken on the form of a buffalo and is killing people there. She is part of the royal family of the place (her precise position varies) but is exacting revenge on the society due to some familial dispute. This is in effect a theme taken over from the sacrificial plot. The leader of society has angered some spiritual power, who is exacting payment by killing members of the larger society. Indeed, there are suggestions of famine in both Sisòkò and Condé. In the former, the Buffalo woman announces that she "brought an end to rice . . . fonio . . . groundnuts" (129), while in the latter the deaths caused by the Buffalo woman are related to "hunger" (24). (This incorporation of elements from one prototype into another is common.) Two hunters will go and kill the buffalo woman. As their reward, they will take back a woman from the place. She should become the king's wife.

These two hunters now appear (how this occurs varies among versions). They go to Dò and treat the buffalo woman with respect. They give her the authority and material goods (e.g., the portion of their hunt) that she merits as a "mother." This treatment mollifies her and she agrees to let them kill her. However, she has a condition. She predicts that the ruler of Dò will offer them a wife as reward for the kill. They must choose a particular woman, a relative of this Buffalo woman, who has been passed over in marriage because of her physical deformities.

The story of the buffalo woman already suggests some of the ideological complexity to be found in Mande society (as in any other society). On the one hand, women are viewed as, in Weil's words, "unstable, unpredictable and mystically very hot . . . innately possessing immense creativity and energy." Thus they are "dangerous to the community as a whole." On the other hand, women could be "placed in positions of public authority and trust." This is not strictly contradictory, as the authoritative women tend to be "postmenopausal." Nonetheless, the social attitudes toward women here are complicated—particularly the male social attitudes (my guess is that women were much less likely to find women dangerous in this mysterious way). Historically, even for people who accepted this standard view (and there were presumably some who did not), there are different ways in which it could be inflected. One could stress the great power of women or the great danger or the potential wisdom. In terms of ideological critique, it is not terribly difficult to conclude that women are perceived as dangerous because they are not the primary political leaders but have nonetheless shown the ability to be political leaders. In every society, women engage in ordinary activities that demonstrate this ability. As to Mande society in particular, Conrad explains that "proverbs reflecting female marginalization on the one hand and epic discourse exalting heroines on the other demonstrate the ambiguous position of women in Mande society." Moreover, there are cases in which men may "appropriate women's abilities for their own use, but women's power must be contained if it is not to overwhelm the men." Indeed, in "matters crucial to political authority . . . female ability can be accorded recognition and even obedience, but once the presence of a woman becomes threatening, she may be destroyed" (193). Despite what the more extreme forms of patriarchal ideology suggest, women always pose a direct and visible threat to male hegemony. The point is clear in Mande society generally and in the Son-Jara epic particularly.

The treatment of the buffalo woman is one of the distinctive features of the Son-Jara epic. It is an enduring element of the story, but unlike most other such elements it is not part of the cross-cultural prototype. In my view, the recurrence of the buffalo woman story is due most importantly to its thematic and ideological function. Needless to say, its precise thematic and ideological elaboration can vary, depending on the ways in which the episode is construed in relation to the main concerns of any particular version of the encompassing work. For example, the film version (Kouyaté) stresses generational differences and modernity/tradition oppositions. Other versions, however, tend to stress the male/female axis of the episode. The latter is probably the main ideological source of the story's durability. In some versions, the fundamental division of emotional geography—between home and away—is broadly associated with a division between what might be called the "domesticated" and "wild" female. The buffalo woman lives apart from the town and thus creates havoc because she is not integrated with society. The magical power, or *dalilu*, of Sogolon, Son-Jara's mother, is evident when she is away from Manden and when she is moving between Dò and Manden. However, her powers seem much curtailed—even at times absent—when she is at home in either Dò or Manden (at least after her initial arrival and defeat by Fata Magan in a contest of magical power). Such representations commonly favor the domesticated women. However, they need not be entirely favorable toward these women nor entirely damning of the "wild" women. In Sisòkò's version particularly, the wild area is linked with powerful sorceresses who hinder and potentially threaten Son-Jara, but who also help him. The suggestion in Sisòkò may be that disruptive female powers need to be domesticated through family life *or* they need to be appeased, as occurs with the sorceresses.

Condé's version is the one most centrally concerned with gender. Condé incorporates most of the gender issues just mentioned. But he also elaborates on the cause of the buffalo woman's disaffection in a relevant way. Specifically, she has not received any inheritance. Her brother had taken it on the grounds that "women do not receive property" (40). She is resentful of this and rebels against a social order in which lines of inheritance are purely male. Her situation is a bit like that of the women in, say, *Pride and Prejudice*. However, her reaction is rather more vigorous. She actually rejects the entire patriarchal structure.

As with many literary works, there are different ways in which one could interpret this episode. For example, one might think that Condé's poem criticizes gender inequality by exposing the buffalo woman's situation. However, I do not believe that the sequence works that way. Specifically, the buffalo woman is not merely forceful in demanding equality. She is not even merely violent. She is murderous and she murders innocent people. She becomes a terror to the entire community. It is difficult not to read this as a forceful condemnation of a woman who has rebelled against patriarchal tradition. In other words, it is difficult not to view this as an ideological characterization designed (at least in part unself-consciously) to orient our feelings toward aversion at such a rebellious woman.

Universal Narrative Prototypes   153

In different versions, the hunters go on to choose Sogolon as their reward for killing the buffalo woman. She is deformed in one or more ways—hunchbacked, lame, covered with boils. In part, the reasons for this have to do with emotional intensification. The deformities pose a difficulty for the hunters in following their agreement. They must show particular nobility in keeping their word. They also pose difficulty for the king, who must beget Son-Jara with this woman.

As the hunters take her home, Sogolon is able to resist their sexual advances with her magical abilities. This suggests a clarification in the account of Mande gender ideology in relation to domesticity. Women's power is not in itself a bad thing. Rather, it is crucial *to protect their chastity*. When used outside that context—or the related context of defending their family—then it is wrong, or at least problematic. In other words, the opposition is not precisely between women's use of powers and their rejection or deprivation of those powers. It is at least in part the much more ordinary opposition between sexual fidelity and familial self-sacrifice on the one hand and sexual freedom and self-interest on the other. Unsurprisingly, in patriarchal ideology, women are expected to subordinate their own interests to that of the men who have a claim on them—primarily husbands and sons. The incorporation of magical power into this ideology serves first to intensify it emotionally by making it more consequential. It also operates to give women even greater obligations. It would not necessarily have been easy for a young woman to resist the sexual advances of two hunters. But if she is endowed with special magical powers, then there is really no excuse for not resisting. Note that an episode of this sort may have emotional consequences by forming emotional memories. Thus it may affect one's attitude to, for example, rape, even if one does not believe literally in magical powers (e.g., it may give one the sense that the victim "could have done *something* to stop him").

At this point the hunters determine that they will turn over Sogolon to Fata Magan. In Condé's version, Sogolon tries to fight Fata Magan as well. Her antagonism toward men seems to be general. Sogolon's generalized resistance may be seen as admirable by readers who value female independence. However, the text itself does little to advance an attitude of that sort. Rather, it suggests that the rightful husband has powers superior to those of his wife and can indeed control her and domesticate her, as Fata Magan does with Sogolon.

After Fata Magan and Sogolon are united, she becomes pregnant. There is elaboration and emotional intensification here as well, with the pregnancy unnaturally extended. Finally, Son-Jara is born. There is wide variation in whether or not Fata Magan has sons before this. But there is agreement that Son-Jara has one rival—his brother, Dankaran Tuman.[12] In some versions, Dankaran Tuman is elder and recognized as such. In others, such as Sisòkò's version, he is elder but falsely perceived as younger. In still others, Son-Jara is elder. There are different emotional, thematic, and ideological reasons why a given griot might choose one option over the other. In all cases, however, the presumption is that Son-Jara ultimately merits the kingship, whatever the birth order.

The birth of Son-Jara begins to introduce us to the main line of the prototypical narrative.[13] However, here another unusual elaboration enters. This concerns Son-Jara's childhood. Specifically, Son-Jara is unable to walk. Thus he inherits a version of his mother's disability. This is not distinctive of any particular version of the story but of the cultural prototype itself. (We may distinguish the "cultural prototype" of the Son-Jara story—manifest differently in different versions—from the "cross-cultural prototype" of the heroic plot.)

Son-Jara's disability fits with emotional intensification in obvious ways. It also fits with a broad, cross-culturally recurring thematic opposition between apparent worth and actual worth. On the other hand, as with so much else in this story, even this recurring element may be put to different ideological uses, in part based on causal elaboration. In Condé's version, all Sogolon's co-wives curse Son-Jara after they have used magic to try to prevent the child's birth. This seems fairly clearly to suggest that women's powers are dangerous and destructive insofar as they are not subordinated to a husband's supervision or a husband's interests.

Of course, Son-Jara does walk eventually. Indeed, he not only walks but shows superhuman strength. The gradient of change from disability to super-ability has the usual emotional function, as well as suggesting some cross-culturally common themes. For example, one such theme is that a person may overcome disability or early failure to achieve great success—a theme with obvious relevance to a new nation, when extrapolated from the individual to the society. (Nationalism is an important concern in some versions, prominently that of Sisòkò.) It may also suggest ideological issues bearing on the place of and judgments about the disabled in Mande society.

In any case, Son-Jara's ability to walk necessarily brings to a head the conflict over inheritance of the throne. Note that the conflict is with members of his own family, which serves the usual function of emotional intensification. At this point, complications arise in those versions where Son-Jara does not actually have the birthright to the kingdom. Specifically, any relatively conservative ideology faces a dilemma here. How can one support tradition but simultaneously support Son-Jara taking a birthright that tradition should deny him? Generally, this problem is solved by having Son-Jara give up inheritance claims. In Condé's version, he reassures Dankaran Tuman that the latter will not lose his birthright. In Suso's version. Son-Jara does have the birthright, but it has been falsely given to Dankaran Tuman. It may seem that he should simply reclaim the birthright. But he also has a traditional duty to obey the wishes of his father, who had pronounced Dankaran Tuman his heir (5). In this version, too, he renounces the throne. All this serves to prepare for our evaluation of Son-Jara as deserving the kingship. Specifically, it establishes a situation in which Dankaran Tuman can demonstrate that he does not merit the throne. This is developed in the prototypical way—through depriving the hero of his rightful position in society and through collaborating with and/or being defeated by the invading enemy.

In some versions, the next event is Son-Jara's exile. In Condé, Dankaran Tuman tries to kill his brother twice before the exile. For reasons of space, I will skip over these episodes.

Son-Jara's exile eventually allows for the invasion of the Manden by the great enemy, Sumamuru. But Sumamuru is not an enemy yet. Indeed, he is commonly spoken of as having been an apprentice of Son-Jara's father. As a result, there is some relation between the families. In Condé's version, there is a particularly striking elaboration of this relationship. Specifically, the first place Sologon and Son-Jara go in their time of exile is Sumamuru's kingdom. Sogolon appeals to Sumamuru as a sort of foster father for Son-Jara. Given the eventual conflict between Sumamuru and Son-Jara, we can recognize this as the same sort of emotional intensification that we find in the usurpation plot. It is a "familialization" of the conflict. Thus it follows the usual elaborative principles, but it does so in an unusual way, for it is more difficult to familialize the threat/defense scenario than the usurpation scenario.

At this point, there is another distinctive development in Condé's version. We have already noted that the group leader often has a helper, frequently a skilled warrior, who is particularly prominent. In some cases, this helper becomes the actual hero of the work. We have also noted that there is commonly a figure from the enemy side who parallels the usurper on "our" side. That figure leaves the enemy and gives crucial help to the hero. Fakoli is Sumamuru's nephew who defects to the side of Son-Jara. However, in Condé's version, he is also the warrior helper, who almost overshadows the ruler. Specifically at this point in Condé's version we encounter a story parallel to that of Son-Jara—a parallel that contributes to our sense of the work's unity even while introducing distinct plot lines. Moreover, this story line allows Condé to treat divided family loyalties, an important thematic issue. Unfortunately, constraints of space prevent me from discussing the Fakoli plot here.

After some development of the Fakoli story, Condé turns to Sumamuru's invasion and devastation of the Manden. Drawing on a cross-cultural motif, Condé explains that Sumamuru is trying to kill Son-Jara, whom prophets have said will defeat him. Son-Jara must now be called back to defend the Manden against this enemy. Here we see the cross-cultural prototype once again—the exiled leader returning to defend the nation.

In keeping with usual patterns of emotion intensification, the early battles do not go well for Son-Jara. In some versions, Son-Jara's sister goes to seduce Sumamuru in order to learn his magical secrets. She may or may not sleep with him, but in either case her use of her sexuality is crucial to Son-Jara's victory. Given the generally conservative gender ideology in Condé's version, it is unsurprising that this episode is absent. Even in cases where Son-Jara's sister does not sleep with Sumamuru, such overt use of female sexuality and such an assertion of sexual freedom by a woman do not seem consistent with the domestic constraint of female sexuality. There are two episodes in Condé's version that may be seen as substitutes for this seduction. In one, Son-Jara gives his sister to another leader, thereby securing an alliance. In another, he has his sister steal magic from Sumamuru, using nonsexual means.[14]

A preparatory scene follows in which Son-Jara meets with Sumamuru before the final battle. Condé stresses the familylike relation between them. This relation has the usual function of emotion intensification.

The final battle is a bit peculiar. Drawing on a motif common in Mande epic (see Conrad 184n.162), Condé has Sumamuru fall into a ravine from which he cannot get out. Son-Jara was going to leave him to die of starvation. Fakoli, however, goes back and strikes him on the head, presumably killing him. He then returns two more times to mutilate the corpse. This violent response to the enemy is unusually extreme among versions of the Son-Jara epic (see Conrad 186n.164). In keeping with the general ideological attitudes of the work, this may suggest a particularly harsh condemnation of the (in effect) familial disloyalty shown by Sumamuru.

There is a final episode in which Son-Jara's army defeats another enemy. This doubling of external enemies is fairly common in heroic plots. It suggests the breadth of the home society's military and political power. For our purposes, there is one particularly interesting thematic detail. Condé connects the ideal of masculinity with group protection—"The time for you to reveal the kind of man you are / Is when somebody challenges your group" (lines 5364–65). This indicates the strong connection between patriarchal gender ideology and heroic emplotment, a connection particularly important in Condé's version.

The epic commonly ends with idealized aspect normalcy, stressing the great benefits of Son-Jara's rule. For example, "the villages knew prosperity again" and due to Son-Jara, "happiness had come into everyone's home" (Niane 81).

In sum, the Son-Jara epic presents us with a highly prototypical case of the cross-cultural heroic structure. It includes the standard elements—familialized usurpation, exile of the rightful ruler, threat by an external enemy, return of the ruler to defeat the enemy with the aid of a warrior helper, restoration of the ruler in idealized aspect normalcy, and so on—along with the usual motivating emotions of pride and anger. There are, in addition, some recurring features of Mande heroic narrative that appear to go beyond the cross-cultural structure, as we would expect. Finally, the elaboration and particularization of the story (or stories) in a specific version of the epic are guided by the usual considerations of narrative explanation (first of all, emotionally oriented causal elaboration), emotional intensification, thematic development, and the central ideological concerns of the work, which are again a matter of both thought and feeling. In the case of Djanka Tassey Condé's version, those ideological concerns center on gender hierarchies and the anxiety of at least some men regarding potential or actual challenges to those hierarchies. We can isolate these concerns most fully and most clearly by examining his poem in relation to the general prototypical structure of heroic tragicomedy and in relation to versions of this particular heroic narrative by other griots.

Pride, Anger, and Suffering in *The Mwindo Epic*

It is difficult if not impossible to determine precisely what the dominant ideologies were in the Nyanga society of *The Mwindo Epic*, either during the poem's historical development or at the time of the telling on which we focus. Indeed, there cannot be a single dominant ideology during that period. For any given society, we can assume that there was some form of "statist" ideology as long as social organization subordinated ordinary people to a ruler. In addition, we can assume that statist ideology was always partially balanced by a more limited "liberal" ideology in which the ordinary people were seen as having some social authority or at least some social value. Moreover, we can assume that it was in the interest of the rulers to stress statist ideology and in the interest of ordinary people to stress a form of liberal ideology (perhaps a selective form that privileged some ordinary people over others). Different societies balance these ideologies in different ways, achieving different compromises between statism and liberalism in different areas of social interaction and authority. Given the interests of rulers and populace, we can assume that some form of statist ideology did have enough of a dominant place in traditional Nyanga society to foster the preservation of chieftaincy and related hierarchies. Nonetheless, due to the difficulty of isolating a precise and enduring balance of ideologies in Nyanga society, I generally avoid the phrase "dominant ideology" in this section. I refer instead to, for example, "statist ideology" or other "component ideologies" that enter into the partial and shifting balances defining "dominant ideology" at any given time. Needless to say, statist and liberal ideologies are not the only important component ideologies. Parallel points apply to what might be called "belligerent militarist" or "expansionist" ideologies and ideologies of intergroup conciliation or cooperation.

The main story of *The Mwindo Epic* involves a relatively common variant of the usurpation plot. We might refer to it as the "prevented accession" story. In this version, the rightful ruler is prevented from taking up his or her place. The usual processes of emotional intensification often make the prevention a matter of attempted murder—in the most extreme case, murder of the heir as a child (for the child is presumably defenseless). We find a version of this story in the biblical account of Herod and Jesus (see Matthew 2). Processes of emotional intensification also make it more likely that the person preventing the accession, thus attempting the murder, is a relative. There is a case of this type in the *Kalevala*. We also find a case of this sort in the story of Kaṁsa's attempted murder of his baby nephew, Kṛṣṇa. *Mwindo* is an instance of this second sort as well.

Specifically, Chief Shemwindo, the father of Mwindo, forbids his wives from having sons. All somehow manage to follow the order, except Mwindo's mother (Nyamwindo). In keeping with common narrative elaborations of the birth of the hero, Nyamwindo's pregnancy is unnaturally long and the child's birth is unusual. Moreover, he has extraordinary powers from birth. Upon learning of Mwindo's birth, Shemwindo tries to kill him. The still tiny Mwindo decides that he should leave home and seek refuge with his paternal aunt, Iyangura. After reaching his aunt, Mwindo decides to return to his home in Tubondo and confront his father. Iyangura comes along and they are eventually joined by Mwindo's maternal uncles. When they reach Tubondo, Mwindo sends his uncles to fight. All but one are killed. Mwindo then calls on Nkuba, or lightning, to destroy the village. The result is that almost everyone in the village is killed. Shemwindo escapes, however. Mwindo revives his dead uncles, then installs them along with Iyangura in the ruins of Tubondo. This massive destruction is of course terrible. But it is in many ways occluded in the main narrative. This might tend to "naturalize" the devastation of war and the dispensability of ordinary people in time of war.

In any case, Mwindo follows Shemwindo. Having captured Shemwindo, Mwindo returns to the village and revives all the people killed in the earlier episode. As a result, this particular war has no casualties. It is possible that this portrayal of war might foster a relatively benevolent view of violent conflict. On the other hand, no member of the audience is likely to believe that a victorious leader can in fact resurrect the dead. As a result, the story may be neutral or ambivalent in its ideological effects regarding military conflict. The poem may also seem to reinforce statist ideology, since Mwindo acts benevolently once he has overcome the threats to his own life. Indeed, he honors his father and they end up dividing the kingdom. On the other hand, Shemwindo himself was the rightful leader before Mwindo. The portrayal of Shemwindo clearly indicates that the socially correct leader is not necessarily admirable in his or her actions.

In sum, the main story involves some degree of ideological ambivalence. But this ideological ambivalence does not result in, so to speak, "narrative ambivalence." We seem to have a clear case, not only of a return to home and a reunion of family members but of an aspect-normalized society. The divinely favored and supernaturally powerful Mwindo is the main ruler. But his father has not been usurped. This should be the end.

On the other hand, there is no clear indication that this resolution is idealized. Indeed, the story continues, suggesting that the resolution of the main plot is not idealized. The second part of the narrative begins innocuously enough. Mwindo wants wild pig meat. He sends his pygmies out to acquire it. They travel a great distance before finding and killing a pig. Dragon is surprised to find anyone else in his territory. He eats all of the pygmies except one, who escapes and reports everything to Mwindo. Mwindo comes and kills Dragon. He then has the corpse transported to Tubondo. Three of the people in the village remark that "he who has killed this one cannot fail to kill one of his relatives" (133). Mwindo responds by killing these three. He does, however, restore many people to life by cutting Dragon open.

Unfortunately for Mwindo, Nkuba had a pact with Dragon. Nkuba therefore punishes Mwindo for killing Dragon. Specifically, he takes Mwindo away from his home and subjects him to a severe, yearlong ordeal in the sky. When Mwindo returns to his people, he is told to "refuse meat" (140). This wiser Mwindo is now able to establish laws and articulate moral precepts. The result is aspect idealization as Mwindo's "great fame went through his country; it spread into other countries, and other people from other countries came to pay allegiance to him" (144).

We have here a clear instance of an epilogue of suffering. The hero kills someone. He is judged guilty for that action and forced to leave his home to wander in punishment. The punishment leads to an enhanced moral understanding, which he is able to employ when he returns to kingship. But the provocation for the epilogue is peculiar.

Here we might consider two things. First, we might compare this sequence with the more standard epilogue. The usual epilogue has the threat/defense sequence as its immediate source. This suggests that the story of Dragon in some way substitutes for the more standard military conflict with an enemy. This substitution is not unheard of. For example, we find it in some Ainu epic narratives. Moreover, it is consistent with other aspects of the story. Groups outside Mwindo's own are commonly associated with animals. Thus Iyangura is married to a serpent and Mwindo's own maternal uncles are bats. In this context, representing a human enemy as a nonhuman dragon is quite fitting. Indeed, it is related to the more general tendency of societies to dehumanize enemies, particularly in periods of violent conflict. The idea is also consistent with Dragon's indication that Mwindo's men have entered his territory. In the context of the more usual epilogue and its precedents in the main heroic plot, we may begin to suspect that the Dragon character points toward a military foe and that the initial conflict results from something along the lines of a territorial dispute. In this suggested dispute, Mwindo's people are claiming rights to game in a territory that Dragon considers to be reserved for his use only.

The second thing to consider in this context is the similarity to an earlier part of the story. Mwindo sending the pygmies to hunt develops in direct parallel with Mwindo sending his uncles into battle. In both cases, all but one are killed. That one returns and tells Mwindo what has happened. This leads to Mwindo going and destroying the village/ Dragon. Moreover, the three pygmies are revived first, then many other people—just as, earlier, Mwindo revived his uncles first, then many others. This parallel itself hints at a relation between warfare and the conflict with Dragon.

Of course, all this is, so to speak, "circumstantial." However, it leads us to what is arguably the crux of the entire story—the judgment of the three Tubondonians. Again they say, "He who has killed this one cannot fail to kill one of his relatives" (133). This necessarily refers the reader or listener back to the point where Mwindo did indeed kill his relatives— when he destroyed the village of Tubondo with the help of Nkuba. So, in the judgment of these characters in the story, Mwindo's killing of Dragon suggests precisely the killings he engaged in during his war with Shemwindo. Indeed, these characters indicate that the killings are not merely superficially similar. They are both objectionable acts, acts that manifest an excessive propensity toward violence. Moreover, the killing and display of Dragon may suggest excessive pride—a key emotion in heroic plots and an emotion that often fosters violence. When Mwindo approaches Dragon initially, he boasts of his heroism and power. He explains his desire to exhibit his accomplishment to the village by saying that he wants

Shemwindo to "see the wonders that I perform" (132). As Biebuyck and Mateene point out, "The Nyanga have a profound dislike for boasting and megalomania" (145n.286).

There is a further connection between the two episodes as well. Nkuba is the means whereby Mwindo killed his relatives. Nkuba is also the means by which Mwindo is punished for killing Dragon. This repetition of Nkuba's presence suggests an extension of the standard thematic concerns of the epilogue of suffering. It suggests, to put it somewhat oversimply, that he who lives by the weapon of lightning, dies by the weapon of lightning. Mwindo's practice of violence eventually almost destroys him.

On the other hand, the point is not moralistic. After all, Mwindo's initial violence was provoked by Shemwindo's initiation of violence. What, then, are we to make of the epilogue, thematically and ideologically?

The mention of Shemwindo reminds us that the entire first narrative was initiated by Shemwindo's project of killing a seemingly helpless child, Mwindo. Mwindo summarily executes the three Tubondonians, who were presumably helpless against him. His violence against them is not entirely unlike Shemwindo's violence at the beginning of the entire work. Given this, it seems clear that the poem is very far from condoning violence simply because it is practiced by a chief. Nor does it appear to support the violent suppression of criticism from ordinary people. But just what is the poet suggesting here?

There are two hints as to the best way of understanding this episode. First, we should consider the emotions underlying the act. They are pride and anger, precisely the emotions underlying the main heroic plot and its associated ideologies. At this point, then, the story seems to be indicating that pride and anger can be excessive, even in a leader. Indeed, it may even imply that simply holding the position of a leader can lead one to an excess of pride and anger, and a proneness to destructive, even self-destructive, violence. The second hint comes in the sequence of precepts spoken by the newly wise Mwindo at the end of the poem, following his punishment. He begins, "Accept the chief; fear him." Had the precept stopped there, it would seem to be affirming the standard heroic, statist ideology. Indeed, it would seem to indicate that Mwindo was right to kill his three critics. But Mwindo continues, "May he also fear you" (144).[15] Clearly, that is not the case with Mwindo when he commits the murders.

Thus the story tacitly criticizes the ideology of absolute loyalty to the internal hierarchy of the in-group, and it does so by tacitly criticizing the results of acting on pride and anger within the in-group. Does it then have nothing to say about the external part of the heroic plot, the part that treats pride and anger in relation to out-groups? This hardly seems likely, given the fact that the explicit reason for Mwindo's punishment is his killing of the out-group Dragon.

To understand the poem's view of warfare and in-group/out-group antagonism, we need to take seriously the place of this particular story in the heroic genre. Nkuba has a pact with Dragon. In other words, they have an alliance. Mwindo had good relations with Nkuba. However, he lost those good relations by attacking Nkuba's ally. Moreover, he did this in the context of what was in effect a form of territorial expansion—for he was claiming certain rights over the land that Dragon saw as his. The story does not indicate that Dragon was justified in his territorial claims. However, Dragon clearly thought himself entitled to the land. He had driven people off the land in the past (130). Moreover, his pact with Nkuba in effect supported his claim. Finally, whatever Dragon's territorial rights might or might not have been, the conflict between Mwindo and Dragon was an unnecessary result of a trivial desire (a hunger for pork). It is not difficult to see the same sort of process operating in other wars.

But again, just what is the suggestion here? This is not a celebration of military might. It is in part a thematic criticism of pride, as a number of readers have recognized.[16] That thematic criticism extends to certain sorts of anger and violence as well. Perhaps more importantly, however, Rureke's poem presents a tacit critique of belligerent militarist and expansionist ideology. Mwindo does not hesitate to fight Dragon, because he knows that he will win. He does win. But he is subsequently defeated by Nkuba. This shows that his pride was excessive. But the story's force—both intellectual and emotional—is not primarily moral. It is, rather, prudential. It is a matter of different possible friends and enemies having different degrees of power. Indeed, it is important that Mwindo does not realize that Nkuba and Dragon have a pact, for this prudential concern is a matter of acts having unrecognized consequences related to power. Mwindo rightly recognized that he could defeat Dragon. He wrongly thought that his killing Dragon would be the end of the story, that it would lead to idealized normalcy. It did not. The point of that result is stressed in the final precept of the narrative: "Even if a man becomes a hero (so as) to surpass the others, he will not fail one day to encounter someone else who could crush him, who could turn against him what he was looking for" (144).

In sum, Rureke's poem is a complexly integrated work that presents slightly atypical variations on the main heroic plot and the epilogue of suffering. The epilogue takes up a version of the war between the in-group and the out-group, establishing close structural parallels with the earlier elaboration of the usurpation plot. This allows Rureke to present a tacit criticism of unswerving loyalty to the in-group hierarchy (thus statist ideology) and of expansionist conflicts with out-groups (thus belligerent militarist ideology). Indeed, the criticism is not entirely tacit, as it is partially manifest in the precepts he presents at the end of the poem. Thus it is partially thematic and partially (counter)ideological.

It is important to point out that these ideas are continuous with social practice among the Nyanga. For example, Biebuyck explains that "there are no elaborate [royal] courts," that "traditions of conquest and large-scale warfare are nonexistent" (6), and that "the Nyanga do not extol warlike traits" (68). In this way, Rureke opposes certain versions of statist and militarist ideology. But it may not be quite correct to say that he opposes dominant ideology.[17]

In any case, Rureke's elaboration of the basic story also foregrounds pride and anger, the fundamental motivating emotions of the heroic plot. That elaboration allows him to suggest that the happiness produced by following the goals of these systems may be highly problematic, indeed self-destructive. Of course, this is not to say that the poem is anarchistic and pacifist. The poem supports political hierarchy to some degree—as Biebuyck points out, "The epics clearly reveal the awe and respect in which the chief is held" (69). Moreover, its critique of militarist ideology is indirect. However, in some ways, that is what makes Rureke's *Mwindo Epic* a particularly illuminating case for this study. Its ideological critique is more subdued, thus more difficult to recognize, without a consideration of its generic relation to the epilogue of suffering.

Local Ideology, Ambivalence, and Romance in
The Recognition of Śakuntalā (Abhijñānaśākuntalam)

The ideologies we have examined in the preceding works are complex. But they are not, I think, equivocal. For example, Condé's epic largely follows a particular patriarchal orientation. Not all stories are so consistent. In fact,

I suspect that strict ideological consistency is more the exception than the rule. I began by speaking of "dominant" and "resistant" ideologies. As indicated above, however, there is a wide range of ideologies present in social discourse in any given society at any given time. Of course, there are broad trends in both social practices and ideologies. Some ideologies are much closer to representing the dominant practices and some are much more committed to changing dominant practices. But few are simply one or the other. Moreover, not all ideologies are equally distributed across the population. Some are far more widely held than others. But there is not always a single, dominant case.

Indeed, there is even a complication here. Individuals do not simply adopt one uniform ideological stance from a social discourse, even for a given topic or area. First, ideologies are not well-developed and well-articulated theories. They are, rather, complexes of conceptual prototypes (e.g., of what men are like and what women are like), emotional memories (e.g., regarding members of different racial groups), in-group affiliations and definitions (e.g., a particular man might only identify with people he considers to be "real men," a group that might exclude many adult human males), and so on. Ideologies are catchalls of ideas, feelings, models, ways of acting. People form these ideas, feelings, and so on, from their own particular experiences, and experiences differ, sometimes very significantly, from person to person. In this way, each person who adopts "patriarchal ideology" or "white supremacy" will actually adopt a somewhat different ideology from everyone else who is patriarchal or white supremacist.

There are of course social practices that partially restrain this diversity. For our purposes, one of the most important is the establishment of ideological paradigms. These are, typically, stories that are widely drawn on for models of admirable individuals, exemplary acts (suitable for imitation), and so on. On the other hand, these paradigms too are not unambiguous. We all understand and experience them somewhat differently. In that way, the constraint provided by paradigms is itself loosened by the multiple interpretability of those paradigms.

Moreover, it is not the case that we choose a single ideology and stick with it. In fact, not only are our ideologies partially idiosyncratic. They are also various *within individual idiosyncrasy*. Even the most vehement patriarch is likely to have been somewhat influenced by feminist ideology today; even the most extreme racist is likely to have some sort of empathic feeling that pushes him or her toward more egalitarian politics. We need not go so far as to say that each of us has internalized versions of every ideology available to us. However, each of us does have quite a few of them. Certainly, we are more inclined to some than to others. But circumstances can alter our hierarchy of ideologies considerably, because circumstances alter just what models, emotional memories, and so on, are prominent for us at any given time.

Drawing on a roughly connectionist model,[18] we could think of each ideology as having a certain degree of "resting activation" in a person's mind and a certain degree of activation from changing circumstances. In addition, ideologies have excitatory and inhibitory relations with one another. For an ideology to have motivational consequences, it has to reach a certain activation level. For purposes of illustration, let us say that this activation level is 1. Suppose Smith is living in apartheid South Africa. Suppose further that he has .8 resting activation for white supremacy and .2 activation for human equality. Suppose he reads that a gold mining company is replacing its white workers with black workers. This may provide enough activation to the (dominant) white supremacist ideology, putting it above the threshold and leading him to denounce the hiring. In contrast, suppose he reads a story about a poor black child who was hit by a car but then turned away from the hospital that was reserved for whites. The empathic emotions aroused by the story may be enough to activate the (resistant) ideology of human equality above threshold. He is clearly far more racist than antiracist, but he is not simply and solely racist.

In this way, we have both *latent* and *currently motivational* ideologies. The currently motivational ideologies reflect not only resting activation but also circumstantial activation. We might say, then, that our motivational ideologies are always *local*, both in the sense that they are idiosyncratic (relying on our unique personal experiences and understandings) and in the sense that they shift with the shifting conditions in which we find ourselves.

A similar point applies to paradigms, at least when these are works of any complexity. Consider the *Rāmāyaṇa*, a paradigm of Hindu gender, family, and national ideology. There are points in this poem that have caused readers considerable discomfort extending back millennia. The basic story of the *Rāmāyaṇa* is as follows. Rāma is to be made ruler in Ayodhyā. However, due to intrigues at court, he and his wife, Sītā, are exiled. Meanwhile, there is a rākṣasa, or demon king, in Laṅkā. This king, Rāvaṇa, poses a general threat to the well-being of the world. He kidnaps Sītā. Rāma finds Sītā and defeats and kills Rāvaṇa. But at the point of reunion, something strange happens. Rāma repudiates Sītā because she has lived with another man. As a result, she has to prove her marital faithfulness by throwing herself in a fire and remaining unharmed, protected from the flames by her chastity. This is already disturbing enough. However, that is not the end. Sītā survives the ordeal and the couple returns to Ayodhyā. At this point, rumors arise about Sītā's chastity. Rāma decides that to protect his reputation, he must exile her. He has his brother take his now pregnant wife out into the wilderness and abandon her. Many years later, he learns of her whereabouts and promises to accept her back if she will once again demonstrate her fidelity. Rather than going through a second fire ordeal, Sītā calls on the earth—her mother—to receive her. (Sītā, an incarnation of the goddess Lakṣmī, is born from the earth, not from a human mother.) The earth opens; a chariot appears; Sītā enters and descends into the darkness below.

Despite Rāma's ideological status as a moral exemplar, his treatment of Sītā after the war has troubled writers for centuries. For example, Bhavabhūti dwells on the exile and completely rewrites the scene of Sītā's death in his play *Uttararāmacaritam*, about the concluding book of the *Rāmāyaṇa*. The disquiet over Rāma's actions began even in the epic itself (e.g., with Rāma's brother's distress in canto 97 and his assertion that "the world will revile me" for taking Sītā into exile [III: 521]).

We have seen how individual works derive from narrative elaborations of prototypes, elaborations often guided by ideological or thematic concerns. But as the case of *Uttararāmacaritam* indicates, narrative elaborations respond not only to narrative prototypes. They respond also to paradigmatic individual works, the most highly esteemed instances of a prototype within a particular tradition. Bhavabhūti did this explicitly with respect to the *Rāmāyaṇa*. There is an extensive tradition of this in South and Southeast Asia (see, for example, Paula Richman's books on this topic). But one need not always take up a paradigm explicitly. There are implicit ideological responses to the *Rāmāyaṇa* as well. *Abhijñānaśākuntalam* is a case of this sort.

More exactly, Kālidāsa draws the main elements of his story from the *Mahābhārata*. This serves, then, as the primary source text for the work, and as such, it is in part an ideological "target" of the work as well. Yet *Abhijñānaśākuntalam* is much more deeply concerned with the ideologically distressing events of the *Rāmāyaṇa* than with those of the *Mahābhārata*. At the same time, Kālidāsa's ideological attention to the *Mahābhārata* is arguably what allows him to address the *Rāmāyaṇa* so effectively.

Specifically, in the *Mahābhārata*, Duṣyanta goes hunting and comes upon a hermitage. He meets Śakuntalā and is taken by her beauty. He proposes that they have sex and that she thereby become his wife. She agrees on the condition that he makes her son the heir to his throne. He concedes. Afterward he leaves, promising to send for her. After about seven years, Śakuntalā and her son go to the capital. The king recognizes her, but abuses her and claims that he has no idea who she is. Śakuntalā responds, but to no avail. Just as she is leaving, a divine voice tells Duṣyanta that he must accept Śakuntalā. Duṣyanta explains that he knew who she was, but he had to pretend ignorance because otherwise people would misunderstand. Thus Duṣyanta claims to have almost exactly the motivation Rāma has in exiling Sītā. However, Duṣyanta does not have the status of an ideological paradigm. Put simply, he is not worshiped as God (unlike Rāma). In consequence, Kālidāsa can approach a critique of Rāma-based ideology—or more simply, work through his discomfort with Rāma's actions—by way of Duṣyanta. Moreover, he can perhaps do this more effectively than if he treated Rāma directly. Indeed, if anything, Duṣyanta in the *Mahābhārata* is someone we can freely repudiate. But if we do repudiate him, that only makes the problems with the parallel actions of Rāma all the more salient. That in turn brings up more general issues, such as the moral obligations of husbands to wives and the degree to which a husband has authority over the life of his wife and children. These are some of the ideological issues Kālidāsa implicitly addresses in developing this source into *Abhijñānaśākuntalam*. Of course, this development not only involves ideological elaboration. It also involves the usual emotional intensifications as well as alterations that make the story a much more prototypical romantic narrative than it is in the source.

Before going on to Kālidāsa's story, I should provide one further piece of background information. An important strand of ancient Indic thought concerns ethics, or dharma. The theory of dharma may be divided into two general types. One stresses social hierarchy and subordination. This includes caste dharma and many treatments of the shared dharma or "sahadharma" of husbands and wives. For example, in some construals of sahadharma, the wife's dharma is a matter of helping the husband follow his dharma, while the husband's dharma is a matter of following his own dharma (period). However, there is also a type of dharma theory that is egalitarian. This is the theory of "universal" dharma, which stresses the sameness of all people in their ethical obligations. Universal dharma includes the duties of ahiṃsā (nonviolence) and truth. A universalist interpretation of sahadharma should grant both husbands and wives duties toward each other's dharmas. Thus there is an ongoing tension within dharma theory itself.[19]

This conflict in theories and types of dharma is sharpened by certain aspects of Hindu metaphysics. A central principle of Vedāntic philosophy is that all individual souls are ultimately identical in brahman, or the absolute, and that individual differences are the result of māyā, or illusion. This obviously does not sit well with the idea of social hierarchy. If differences are all māyā, then surely differences of caste or gender are illusory as well.

Finally, in order to tease out the play's treatment of these ideological and thematic issues, we need to draw one further distinction. It seems fairly clear that the play combines ideological concerns with forms of "pseudo-ideology" or doctrinal conformity. Given the nature of literary production, we would expect authors not only to express ideological ideas that they themselves accept. We would also expect them to express ideological ideas that their patrons accept. In some cases, the patron's ideology and the author's ideology may be in conflict. We could then expect the latter to be presented in more subtle ways, partially contradicting the former. I believe that this too characterizes *Abhijñānaśākuntalam*, particularly in areas relevant to dharma.

The play begins with an invocation of absolute divinity, stressing its manifestation in time, space, matter, and life. Though a prefatory invocation is standard in Sanskrit drama, this particular preface does point toward the metaphysical themes just noted. This hints that Vedāntic concerns may have been present in the mind of the author and may be associatively activated in the minds of readers—as one would expect from Sanskrit intellectual culture generally.

Following the invocation, we have the scene with the stage manager who introduces the play—a convention (or cultural motif) of Sanskrit drama. He speaks of Kālidāsa as tying together (*grathita*) the story (6; here and below, even-numbered pages refer to the Sanskrit, while odd-numbered pages refer to the translation), suggesting the necessarily episodic nature of a story. More importantly, he analogizes the audience to a painting, reversing the usual division into imaginary and real. This is significant because Vedāntic metaphysics would suggest that indeed the audience is in a sense imaginary in much the same way that the play itself is imaginary.

The play begins with Duṣyanta hunting, as in the source. For a king who is not at war, this is culturally "aspect normal" and fits with a standard episodic motif. Since hermitages are also located in remote areas, they may sometimes be continuous with the hunting grounds of the king. Put differently, one may go out into the wilderness of nature to pursue game or to pursue spiritual advancement. The king is doing the former; the "anchorites" (17) or practitioners of "tapas" (16), spiritual discipline, are doing the latter. The king enters the grounds of the hermitage on his hunt. Just when the king announces that he is going to kill the deer, the anchorites enter, forbidding the act. Though it may not be obvious at first, this is a prime example of the opposition between the caste dharma associated with the king (more precisely, the dharma of his own warrior caste) and the universal dharma associated with the hermitage. The doctrine of ahiṃsā forbids not only violence against people but also the killing of animals.

In response to the anchorites' plea, Duṣyanta stops pursuing the deer. He learns that Kaṇva, the "kulapati" (20) or "lord of the family," is absent. Kaṇva has entrusted Śakuntalā with greeting guests. Duṣyanta then goes looking for Śakuntalā. Readers of the play commonly remark on the relation between the deer and Śakuntalā. This is part of Śakuntalā's consistent association with nature. Such an association is ideologically ambivalent. On the one hand, linking women with nature is related to the exclusion of women from learning and affairs of the world. But this does not seem to bear on Śakuntalā, who is literate (she subsequently writes a letter) and who has official duties in the hermitage. In this play, the association tends to suggest metaphysical themes instead, linking Śakuntalā with the absolute (or brahman) as manifest in nature.

Thus far, we have more or less routine events—again, aspect normalcy. However, these events have established the causal conditions for the stan-

dard scene of the lovers' first meeting. Kālidāsa elaborates on this junc-
tural scene. Duṣyanta comes upon Śakuntalā and her friends watering
the plants in the hermitage. He observes them from concealment before
introducing himself. Śakuntalā's identification with nature is emphasized,
as when she is given a "sisterly" connection with some of the plants (25).
In keeping with much romantic literature, her sexual charms are stressed
also. Indeed, her recent sexual development is particularly emphasized.
This suggests the natural development of sexual and romantic needs in
Śakuntalā, preparing for her response to Duṣyanta's subsequent appearance and the shift away from normalcy that is characteristic of story
beginnings. Indeed, her friends tease her with the idea that she is hoping
for "a suitable husband" (29).

The king, on his side, is immediately struck by Śakuntalā's beauty. However, his response is not so narrowly sexual as it is in the *Mahābhārata*
version. Most importantly, he immediately begins to wonder if she is a
possible marriage partner. Since he is thinking this to himself, it suggests his sincerity, in contrast with the *Mahābhārata* source. Specifically,
he wonders if she is of a superior caste and thus inaccessible for marriage. This does introduce caste ideology but in a somewhat attenuated
form, since it involves the king potentially observing a caste restriction
that disprivileges him. This is followed by a peculiar statement. The king
tentatively concludes that he would not feel as he does for Śakuntalā if
she were not "fit to be [his] wife" (31). On the one hand, this is a bit of
pseudo-ideology serving to flatter monarchs. On the other hand, it also
suggests a recurring idea in romantic works—that love should supersede
social hierarchies and oppositions, that the imperatives of love are of a
higher order than the imperatives of social stratification.

Having just flattered monarchs, Kālidāsa proceeds to poke fun at
them. Specifically, Duṣyanta is faced with the opportunity of protecting
Śakuntalā from a threat, a standard manly task that serves to win the
heart of the beloved. But in this case, the threat does not come from a
many-headed demon or a fire-breathing dragon. It comes, rather, from an
annoying bee. Once Duṣyanta enters, initiating conversation, Śakuntalā
succumbs to the same romantic feelings that have already affected
Duṣyanta.[20]

But possible obstacles remain. First, the issue lingers as to whether their
marriage will or will not be socially accepted. Duṣyanta then learns about

Śakuntalā's parentage; the fact that she is not above him in caste makes their marriage possible in principle. After this, he worries that she may be committed to an ascetic, thus unmarried, life. (She is not.) Finally, he wonders about Śakuntalā's feelings toward him. Just at that moment, a crisis arises and Duṣyanta must leave.

The following act dilates on Duṣyanta's longing. Duṣyanta's reflections serve to stress his attachment to Śakuntalā, in contrast with the simple lust of his *Mahābhārata* counterpart. Most of the act involves Duṣyanta contemplating possible obstacles to his love. It is thus in keeping with the development of the love plot, which might be expected to turn to obstacles at this point. The most serious of these is that Duṣyanta has no real excuse to return to the hermitage. The solution to the problem arises when the hermitage is threatened by rākṣasas, or demons, and Duṣyanta must go fight them. This is one of the first links between Duṣyanta and Rāma, for Rāma is the most famous king who defended the world against rākṣasas.

The act ends with the introduction of an ethical dilemma. Duṣyanta's mother calls him home to participate in a ceremony.[21] This in effect takes up the theme of a parent interfering with the union of the lovers. However, it does so in a very peculiar way, for the mother is threatening this union entirely inadvertently. Duṣyanta determines that he should fight the demons and send the vidūṣaka in his place (the vidūṣaka is a comical priest and parasite figure, standard in Sanskrit drama). But, of course, the choice is governed entirely by his interest in Śakuntalā. We know from earlier in this act that Duṣyanta has his general with him. It would make sense for him to entrust this military duty to his general while he returns home to attend to his mother. This violation of a duty toward his mother is subsequently paralleled by Śakuntalā's violation of a duty toward a father-like sage. The latter becomes the explicit reason for the separation of the lovers. However, on its own, it explains only Śakuntalā's suffering. I take it that this violation by Duṣyanta serves to explain why he too suffers.

The following act in effect gives the parallel treatment of Śakuntalā. Duṣyanta had been pining away, to be sure, but Śakuntalā is suffering an actual love*sickness*. Duṣyanta again comes upon the friends and overhears their conversation. In this way, he is able to learn that Śakuntalā shares his feelings. At the same time, he learns that she has been worried about whether he shares her feelings. The king announces himself and declares his love. At this point it seems that we have a very minimal love story.

Two people fall in love. They imagine possible obstacles—prominently those associated with social censure and love triangles. But none of the obstacles materializes. As a result, they are united. But there is a hint of complication at the end of the act. Śakuntalā's adoptive mother, Gautami, enters and speaks of the female cakravāka bird separating from her mate for the night. Mythologically, mated cakravāka birds are condemned to spend their nights separate from one another and to be reunited only in the morning. Gautami's entrance causes Śakuntalā to leave Duṣyanta. It is almost impossible not to view the situation of Śakuntalā and Duṣyanta as parallel to that of the cakravāka birds, suggesting that their separation may be inevitable. In addition, some of the language of the act suggests the thematic and ideological concerns that will become more prominent later in the play. For example, the king compares Śakuntalā to the goddess Lakṣmī. This is an ordinary enough comparison. However, in context, it contributes to the linking of Duṣyanta and Śakuntalā on the one hand, with Rāma and Sītā on the other, since Sītā was an incarnation of Lakṣmī.

The next act finally introduces the obstacle in the first significant plot development after the Duṣyanta and Śakuntalā saw one another and fell in love. Śakuntalā is distracted and fails to greet a visiting sage, Durvāsas. Durvāsas curses her, saying that the person she is dreaming of will forget her. This takes up the standard blocking of the lovers' union by a social authority, commonly a parent or religious figure. In this particular case, the episode has two sources, both from the *Rāmāyaṇa*. One concerns a visit that Durvāsas pays to Rāma (Vālmīki III: 618) where he threatens to curse the entire country if he is not greeted by Rāma immediately. More importantly, the other source concerns the reasons for Rāma's suffering separation from Sītā. As Durvāsas explains, Rāma had deprived a man of his wife in an earlier incarnation. As a result, the man cursed Rāma to suffer the same fate (Vālmīki III: 528). These allusive connections are important for our understanding of the gender ideology of the work. First of all, we see again that Kālidāsa is linking Duṣyanta and Śakuntalā with Rāma and Sītā. However, he is altering the source. Perhaps the most obvious difference would seem to make Kālidāsa's play more, rather than less, patriarchal. Specifically, Kālidāsa explains the separation, not by reference to one of Duṣyanta's actions but rather by reference to one of Śakuntalā's actions. In this way, he apparently shifts the blame from Rāma/Duṣyanta to Sītā/Śakuntalā. However, this is complicated in several ways. First, Kālidāsa is concerned to give an explanation for Śakuntalā's suffering, whereas one could argue that in Vālmīki only Rāma's suffering seems to require explanation. More importantly, as we have already noted, Duṣyanta does in fact commit a parallel "sin" in choosing not to follow his mother's wishes. The parallel between his and Śakuntalā's actions seems straightforward, and given the pseudo-ideological representation of kingship in the play, we might expect Duṣyanta's fault to be downplayed. Finally, it is not necessarily the case that the parallel here is based on sex. We can equally see Śakuntalā as parallel to Rāma (rather than to Sītā) at this point in that she is the one who is connected with Durvāsas and who is the object of a curse. In these ways, the gender ideology of the play appears much more complex and ambivalent.

The curse is a recurring cultural theme in Sanskrit tradition. It is part of a common episode structure in which the person making the curse is subsequently appeased, then qualifies the curse in some way. (Convention dictates that the curse cannot be entirely withdrawn.) In this case, Durvāsas, having been appeased, says that Duṣyanta will remember Śakuntalā as soon as he sees some token of recognition. This appears to solve the problem, for earlier Duṣyanta had given Śakuntalā his ring. Śakuntalā need only produce the ring when she meets Duṣyanta again.

The rest of the act is taken up with Śakuntalā's departure from the hermitage. This separation of the daughter from her parents is an important cultural motif in the Indian tradition. It extends from Sanskrit works through the most recent Bollywood movies. In keeping with his general tendency to extensively elaborate incidents, Kālidāsa develops this separation over many lines. Unsurprisingly, one important function of such elaboration is to intensify the emotion—in this case, sorrow based on attachment. Other important functions of such elaboration are thematic and ideological. In this case, such concerns are developed particularly through the episode's stress on Śakuntalā's identification with nature. The emotional and thematic developments are interrelated, for Śakuntalā's sorrowful departure from nature leads directly to her estrangement from Duṣyanta. As we will see, it is only when Duṣyanta and Śakuntalā meet again in the (sacred) nature of the heavenly hermitage that they can be truly and enduringly united.

In the course of the episode, Kaṇva gives Śakuntalā some advice on how to behave as a wife. The advice is fairly straightforwardly patriarchal in counseling acceptance of ill-treatment by one's husband. When spoken, this appears to be a moment of local patriarchal ideology. However, it is followed very soon after by Śakuntalā's defiant response to her treatment by Duṣyanta and by the male ascetics who accompany her to Duṣyanta's palace. This suggests that Kaṇva's advice is better understood as a moment of pseudo-ideological appeasement to powerful members of the audience—an explicit statement of patriarchal ideology that is soon contradicted by the actions of the heroine.

The fifth act finally leads us to the separation of the lovers—just at the moment of their reunion. Śakuntalā is now pregnant with Duṣyanta's child, like Sītā on her return to Ayodhya with Rāma. The act opens with a discussion of how onerous the dharma of the king is. It continues with such pseudo-ideological flattery as the insistence that the king only suffers, sacrificing "personal comfort" for "daily toil" on behalf of "the people" (147). Some of this seems so obviously backward that it is sometimes difficult to see how anyone could take it seriously. In any case, its pseudo-ideological character is subsequently indicated when Kālidāsa points toward the monetary benefits of kingship. Being bothered, he explains, is the price one pays when one "claims the sixth part" of the land's produce (163).

After this, Duṣyanta meets with Śakuntalā and the ascetics who have brought her to the city. Kālidāsa makes it clear that the king really does not remember Śakuntalā, thus that the curse has worked and he is innocent in his mistreatment of her. Subsequent developments in this act will clearly link Duṣyanta with Rāma and Śakuntalā with Sītā, raising the issue of just what the ideological import of this innocence might be. Does it mean that Rāma too is innocent? Or does it rather suggest that Rāma would be innocent only if he had been subjected to such a curse? The latter seems the more likely interpretation.

In any case, Duṣyanta rejects Śakuntalā. One of the ascetics characterizes this as a rejection of dharma (176), though the doorkeeper has the opposite view (178). Duṣyanta goes on to denounce women as cunning and deceitful. An ascetic replies by pointing toward the conflict between kṣatriya dharma and the universal dharma pursued in the hermitage. This is relevant because truth is a key element in universal dharma, while deceit is a crucial practice among those maneuvering to secure political domination (see 188–89). Duṣyanta is not lying in that he believes what he says. But what he says is also clearly not true. Perhaps most importantly, he gives voice to a misogynistic version of patriarchal ideology. But the audience should find it difficult to take this seriously because it is being applied to Śakuntalā and we know that it is entirely false in her case. Again, the king cannot be blamed for disbelieving Śakuntalā since he is suffering from a curse. However, the entire exchange strongly suggests that kings are the ones who are generally more inclined to lie and that misogynistic ideology is no better than slander. Indeed, Duṣyanta's acceptance of this ideology suggests that his ignorance and delusion (his entrapment in māyā) extend beyond the results of Durvāsas's curse.

The implications of the scene concern not only the misogynistic ideology articulated by Duṣyanta but the patriarchal ideology of the *Rāmāyaṇa* as well. Duṣyanta's rejection of Śakuntalā cannot help but recall the culturally paradigmatic case of a king rejecting his wife—Rāma rejecting Sītā. The point becomes entirely clear when the men decide that Śakuntalā will stay until she delivers and they can determine (through signs supposedly discernible at that time) if the child is indeed an offspring of the king. Clearly rejecting the subservience enjoined on her by Kaṇva's advice, Śakuntalā calls on the earth to open and receive her. Though her speech is more elaborate, this is of course precisely Sītā's call to her mother, the earth, when Rāma says that he will accept her back after a second fire ordeal. Rāma's demand in this case is parallel to the proof suggested by Duṣyanta's priest. Here, once again, the play is ideologically ambiguous. On the one hand, Śakuntalā's son does ultimately show the signs of descent from the king's family. On the other hand, it is fairly clear that, barring genetic testing (unavailable at the time of the play), there is no certain way of establishing paternity by simply looking at the child, as many people at the time must have known. This indicates that Duṣyanta's proposed test of Śakuntalā is unreasonable. That unreasonableness may in turn suggest that Rāma's fire test was untrustworthy as well. Indeed, clichés about vast differences in cultural beliefs notwithstanding, I simply cannot believe all Indians at Kālidāsa's or Vālmīki's time had absolute faith that if you tossed a virgin into a fire she would not be burned. (For example, plenty of young girls must have been burned accidentally in fires—even sacrificial fires—when everyone knew that they were virgins. Moreover, parents must have tried to save their daughters from fires, not assuming that as virgins they would be safe.)

Of course, Sītā in effect put herself to a second test. Her descent into the earth constituted proof of her chastity, since she called on the earth to receive her only if she was entirely chaste. Śakuntalā, in contrast, simply calls out for death. She is not making any claims of chastity. Rather, she is rejecting the entire trial and perhaps thereby indicating the unfairness of having to prove her fidelity. Here, too, Kālidāsa's revision of the source suggests a resistance to at least certain aspects of the patriarchal ideology manifest in the *Rāmāyaṇa*.

If this account of the local ideology is accurate, it explains not only Śakuntalā's call for the earth to receive her but also what happens next. Offstage, Śakuntalā's mother does come to take her. But instead of being taken down into the earth, Śakuntalā is taken up into the heavens, suggesting her superiority to her accusers and judges rather than the inferiority that one might associate with an image of descent. The point is further reinforced by the fact that the ascent occurs in a flash of light, suggesting the relative darkness of those who are left behind.

I have been focusing on the counterideological relation of this episode to the source. However, it is important to note that it involves a very innovative elaboration on a standard romantic plot element as well—the association of the lovers' separation with death. Thus Kālidāsa's alteration of his source in the *Mahābhārata* is guided by both counterideological concerns and the prototypical form of the romantic plot, as well as a commitment to emotion intensification in particularizing that prototypical form.

But, of course, there is an element missing in the story to this point. During this episode, Kālidāsa must explain why Śakuntalā does not revive Duṣyanta's memory with the ring. In fact, she tries to do so. However, when she reaches for the ring, she discovers that it is missing. She reasons that it must have fallen from her finger when bathing. Now Kālidāsa must get the ring from the water back to Duṣyanta, causing the recollection.

The ring is presented to Duṣyanta in the following act. As a result of his revived memory, he suffers great longing and remorse, which are elaborated at length. In the course of his meditations, he identifies his forgetting of Śakuntalā with "māyā" (220). The point not only suggests that the rejection of one's wife is a moment of profound spiritual ignorance, it also hints that there was māyā in Rāma's abandonment of Sītā as well.

Like act 2, which it parallels, this act ends with a demonic threat. In this case, the defeat of the demons will take Duṣyanta to another hermitage, that of Mārīca, as we find at the beginning of the next act. Duṣyanta is in fact victorious. This is in effect Duṣyanta's return from exile, or what would have been exile in the standard plot. But the exile here is peculiar. The city should have been Duṣyanta's home, but it was not. The hermitage—the place of exile in the *Rāmāyaṇa*—is here the place of reunion, the home. Moreover, the final hermitage is in heaven. This suggests a common motif of the lovers being truly united only in death, in a spiritualized version of their love. In keeping with this, the hermitage is in a place "freed from darkness," and it gives Duṣyanta a feeling of tranquility (257).

The opening act of the play presented Duṣyanta's entry into the hermitage, his first glimpses of Śakuntalā, and his uncertainty as to whether or not they could be united. This guides Kālidāsa in his elaboration of this final reunion scene. Since Duṣyanta would now recognize Śakuntalā, Kālidāsa does not have her appear initially. Rather, he has her son appear. Duṣyanta immediately has feelings of attachment to the boy. This is in striking contrast with the attitude of the *Mahābhārata* Duṣyanta, as described by Śakuntalā in that poem: "[W]hy do you reject frowningly a son who of his own accord has come to you and fondly looks at you? [. . .] Neither clothes nor loving women nor water are so good to touch as the infant son you embrace. [. . .] Embrace and touch your handsome son!" (van Buitenen I: 167–68). Kālidāsa's change here is consistent with the gender ideology we have been exploring. It suggests that a father should be as attached to his children as a mother is. Though this particular instance may seem gender-biased (in treating a son), it recalls Kaṇva's attachment to Śakuntalā, suggesting that the ideal is not merely one of attachment to boys. Of course, Duṣyanta cannot be entirely certain that this is his son. Thus he suffers the same sort of doubt that he suffered when observing Śakuntalā. Finally, he receives definitive proof.

When Śakuntalā enters, she briefly does not recognize the king. The point is important because it suggests a sort of symmetry between the two. Not all the authority for recognition is placed in Duṣyanta. Again, we find a plot elaboration that is guided by the (resistant) ideology of the work. There is, however, one important asymmetry in the scene. Duṣyanta throws himself at Śakuntalā's feet (281). One might have expected the dutiful wife to throw herself at the feet of her husband, particularly in a culture where one's husband is commonly analogized to one's god. However, Śakuntalā does not do this. I do not know whether Kālidāsa self-consciously thought through this or not. At least it felt right to him that Duṣyanta should prostrate himself before Śakuntalā. As such, the construction of this incident is guided by a locally intense moment of resistant gender ideology, a moment where the ideology is effectively reversed and the wife is worshiped rather than the husband. Kālidāsa immediately has Śakuntalā call on Duṣyanta to stand. She also blames herself for their separation. This may seem like a reversion to patriarchy. But I believe, rather, that it is guided by the same resistant ideology which, in keeping with Vedāntic thought, is establishing an identity between the lovers rather than a hierarchy (in either direction).

Thus we have a particular version of the prototypical reunion of the lovers. As already mentioned, this reunion is often combined with a larger family reunion. We find an unusual form of that in the meeting of Duṣyanta with his son. No less significantly, there is a sort of reunion with the lovers' parents as well. However, it is not the direct, worldly parents. It is, rather, Mārica and Aditi, "the parents of gods," who look on Duṣyanta and Śakuntalā with "parental affection" (285). This is another peculiar elaboration of the standard structure. However, it too is thematically and ideologically guided. In the context of Vedāntic metaphysics, it makes perfect sense for the reunion to take place, not with particular, mundane parents but with more general, spiritual parents.

Mārica goes on to explain what has happened, since neither Duṣyanta nor Śakuntalā is aware of Durvāsas's curse. In the course of this explanation, he points out that Duṣyanta had rejected the one with whom he should fulfill "sahadharma" (290), explicitly bringing in this thematic concern. He goes on to release Duṣyanta from all blame and to tell Śakuntalā that she "should feel no resentment toward [her] husband" (291). This may seem to lead us back to a patriarchal ideology. However, he goes on to say that "now that he is freed from darkness, yours is the supremacy over him" (291). As with Duṣyanta's prostration at Śakuntalā's feet, this appears to be a sort of balancing statement, guided by the resistant ideology that has become more prominent here. Mārica goes on to suggest the equality, indeed metaphysical identity, of the couple. Specifically, he draws on the common image of a mirror wiped free of dust. When Duṣyanta's mind was in darkness, he could not see in the mirror. Once it was wiped free, however, he could easily recognize the image. But, of course, the image one recognizes in a mirror is one's own. Duṣyanta's recognition of Śakuntalā, and Śakuntalā's recognition of Duṣyanta, are finally recognitions of themselves—a deeply Vedāntic idea. As such, there must be equality.

The play ends with a benediction, parallel to that with which the play began. It has three parts. One concerns giving honor to the learned, including poets. This is a theme that turns up cross-culturally (e.g., we find it in the Son-Jara epics). I take it that the reasons for poets calling on readers to honor poets are too obvious to require explanation. The other parts of the benediction are more significant for our purposes. Both relate to the thematic and ideological concerns of the work. The next calls for the king to benefit his subjects. This is probably as strong a statement questioning political hierarchy as a writer could risk at the time. The final part of the benediction is the most significant. It calls for spiritual liberation through Śiva and Śakti, the female version of Śiva, who is "his energy diffused in all directions" (297). In short, it implicitly connects the reunion of the lovers with an ultimate union in the absolute, such as that of Śiva and Śakti. Here, too, we have a culturally and ideologically specific elaboration of a cross-culturally recurring prototypical element. The unending union of the lovers after death is identified with the absolute—and thus necessarily equal—union of all beings in the unified divine couple, Śiva and Śakti.

Conclusion

Emotion systems provide the fundamental organizing principles for genres—just as they do for story structure generally and for the temporal constituents of stories. The major cross-cultural genres come about through convergent development derived from the need of storytellers to produce narratives of general interest. In other words, storytellers address not only friends and family members but larger, impersonal audiences. Moreover, their stories are largely removed from any shared situation that would give them immediate relevance or contextual force. This affects various aspects of story structure, most importantly the nature of the goals pursued by protagonists. In general, those goals must be instances of eliciting conditions for happiness. For them to be effective across people and contexts, the goals must be widely accepted as important and nonsubstitutable. Prototypical happiness goals provide the most obvious possibilities. By their nature, prototypes are the result of averaging across many instances and thus are likely to be relatively nonidiosyncratic. Put differently, they are likely to travel well across audiences and situations.

Like all prototypes, happiness prototypes vary by situation category. The three key situation categories for happiness prototypes are physical, personal, and social. These recruit different satisfactions from different emotion systems to produce enduring feelings of contentment. In the case of physical happiness, the hunger and thirst systems are primarily in play. In this context, happiness is an enduring satisfaction of hunger and thirst—thus abundance of food and drink. The personal context bears on the attachment system and on the system of sexual desire. The most intense happiness goal in a personal context combines attachment with sexual desire in romantic love. Finally, the social context draws on pride and, to a lesser extent, anger. Pride is of two sorts—individual pride within an in-group and group pride in connection with in-group/out-group relations. Anger enters here when the hierarchies associated with pride are challenged.

Once the happiness prototypes are established, the major genres follow directly. One genre concerns achieving abundance of food. Given the general structure of stories, we expect this abundance to be preceded by the opposite—drought and famine. For reasons bearing on the way people generally understand natural devastation, this drought and famine give rise to the sacrificial narrative of sin, communal punishment, sacrifice, and restoration. The goal of romantic union generates the romantic plot, with the lovers separated in the middle, commonly by social authorities. Finally, the heroic genre is generated by the goal of high position within the in-group and in-group domination over out-groups. Here, too, the narrative middle involves the opposite of both goals—thus the protagonist's loss of position in the in-group (the usurpation plot) and the in-group's temporary defeat by the out-group (the threat/defense plot).

Of course, individual works in these genres involve the elaboration and particularization of the prototypical structures. This elaboration and particularization has many components, three of which seem particularly important. The first is emotional intensification. To some extent, emotional intensification is already built into the prototype, as when the usurper in the heroic plot is commonly a relative of the protagonist. The second component is thematic development, which is the largely indirect presentation of general ideas commonly about politics, social practices, or ethics. The third component is ideology.

Ideology comprises all mental contents and processes (models, attitudes, interests, emotional memories, etc.) that have some functional relation to unjust social hierarchies. Dominant ideology is the set of mental contents and processes that foster the continuation of current hierarchies. Resistant ideology is a set of mental contents and processes that oppose the continuation of those hierarchies. Ideology—at least dominant ideology—is often inconsistent with people's self-consciously held views. As such, it operates most effectively when it is implicit. In contrast, the themes of a work are likely to have effects only to the extent that they are self-consciously isolated by readers in interpretive activity.

The major genres are of course intimately connected with social hierarchies as well as in-group/out-group divisions. Indeed, these hierarchies and divisions are central to the narrative development of all three genres. In consequence, we would expect all three genres to manifest ideological concerns. However, there are differences in the ways the genres typically treat social hierarchies and divisions. Specifically, both the sacrificial and heroic prototypes tend to rely on social hierarchies and in-group/out-group divisions for the emotional force of their plots. As such, we would expect them to incline toward narrative elaborations that express dominant ideology. In contrast, romantic plots tend to oppose social hierarchies and group divisions, for these are precisely what separate the lovers. Thus we would expect romantic plots to be more open to resistant ideologies. This is just what we seem to find.

On the other hand, none of us is entirely consistent in our ideological commitments. Authors present pseudo-ideologies to appease elite (or popular) audiences. They also develop aspects of resistant or dominant ideology locally. Works commonly have a predominant ideological orientation (e.g., patriarchal or feminist). But they rarely (perhaps never) have a single, exceptionless ideology developed throughout the work without variation. This too is a matter of emotion systems. Our shifts in local ideology are not usually a matter of intellectual confusion. They are, rather, a matter of feelings. Social hierarchies are complex and our feelings about them are complex too. In different contexts, different aspects of hierarchies will be salient, as well as different justifications, explanations, and so on. Thus, in different contexts, our emotional responses will change— sometimes conforming with dominant ideology, sometimes taking up a resistant ideology. These local contexts occur in the real world and in literature. As a result, an author's ideological commitments are likely to shift from context to context, just as a reader's ideological responses are likely to shift from moment to moment. In short, we are all to some degree ideologically uncertain, though we may also have more or less strong predominant tendencies.

This shifting of emotional and ideological response is particularly clear in the epilogue to the heroic plot. That epilogue is another place where resistant ideology is likely to arise. This is because it addresses the conflict between group pride and human empathy that is almost inevitable in heroic stories. The epilogue may stress grief or guilt. It if stresses the latter, then it commonly involves some reparative ordeal suffered by the hero, an ordeal that leads to enhanced wisdom.

4 Cross-Cultural Minor Genres
Attachment, Lust, Revenge, and Criminal Justice

Prototypical stories are cross-culturally widespread and generally prominent. They appear to define the dominant genres in the canons of all large written traditions. This is not to say, however, that all individual, canonical stories (not to mention all stories more broadly) fall into these genres—far from it. We can and do have stories with all sorts of plots. First, there are story sequences embedded in prototypical plots—subsidiary plots that parallel, complicate, or provide episodic diversion from the main story. More importantly, there are countless nonprototypical main plots. Both the subsidiary and the main plots may treat any topic.

But this does not mean that plots simply fall into two categories— dominant genres and pure idiosyncrasy with no cross-cultural patterns. In fact, there are intermediate cases.

More exactly, beyond the prototypical genres, some story types do seem to turn up in a range of traditions of verbal art (though not all of them, at least not prominently) and in a range of historical periods (though not all of them, at least not prominently). Others appear to be more localized, and still others do not seem to go beyond a handful of works. My contention is that this gradation reflects the relation of the narrative structure to the emotion-based narrative principles, or preference rules, we have considered thus far. A given story type is more likely to recur cross-culturally and transhistorically insofar as it satisfies more such preference rules.

Why Genres Recur

Given the analysis thus far, we would expect story types to occur more frequently if they have the following characteristics.

First, as discussed in previous chapters, the defining structure of the work should involve broadly shared emotion goals that commonly motivate sustained goal pursuit. In other words, the goals should be important in general and have low substitutability in their particular form. Chapter 3 argues that romantic love, individual and in-group pride, and hunger and thirst define goals of this sort. It further analyzes romantic love as involving the integration of two emotional (or motivational) systems—attachment and sexual desire. This analysis would seem to suggest that at least attachment and sexual desire might each generate goals of the relevant sort. If they define important goals of low substitutability together, they presumably do so separately as well—if with less intensity.[1]

Second, recurring narrative types should be incident-rich. In other words, they should concern the sorts of topics that are likely to involve highly emotionally consequential occurrences. War, famine, and romantic union are clearly topics that are likely to involve such occurrences. In contrast, going to the grocery store to buy cucumbers is not. This is not to say that one cannot write a brilliant story about buying cucumbers. It is merely to say that the relative incident-poverty of the story topic is likely to help make stories about buying cucumbers relatively less common. To take a more complex case, it is obvious that sex is incident-rich in the sense that sexual arousal and sexual congress are intrinsically limited moments of emotional spikes. In contrast, feelings associated with friendship tend generally to be more routine, less intense, less bound up with specific occurrences. Of course, there are situations in which friendship involves spikes of emotional intensity, and thus incidents, but they seem to be less common and, so to speak, less intrinsic to friendship.

Third, frequently recurring story types should involve incidents that are readily expandable into event sequences and episodes. Some emotions are rather punctual. They do not have much in the way of sequelae. Moreover, social practices surrounding some particularizations of emotion do not foster situations in which chains of events and episodes are likely to be developed. As we discuss below, for both men and women, sexual desire readily expands into events and episodes prior to sexual union. Specifically, it expands into sexual pursuit or seduction. However, following sexual union, for men it may not expand at all, only being replaced by a repetition of sexual pursuit or seduction following some interval. For women it is more likely to expand into subsequent events due to physiological consequences (pregnancy) or to socially defined consequences.

Fourth, recurring genres should involve topics and structures that are readily manipulable toward empathically communicable emotion intensification. This seems to be related to the degree to which the emotion systems involved tend to activate parallel emotional memories or to arouse mirror neuron systems in observers. (Mirror neuron systems are systems that are activated when you engage in certain actions or someone you observe engages in those actions. For a recent, detailed, and accessible discussion, see Iacoboni.) Attachment relations seem particularly suited to activate emotional memories and mirroring relations—perhaps particularly at moments of separation and loss. These may be further enhanced when the separation and loss involve a young child. In this way it is relatively easy to intensify emotions—for example, the empathic feeling of separation anxiety—in stories treating attachment. In contrast, it does not seem that sexual desire has these sorts of effects. Bob's desire for Jane may turn my attention to sexual characteristics of Jane, which may in turn provoke desire on my part. However, that will not be empathic desire. Thus sexual pursuit narratives may intensify our emotions. But they are most likely to do so by intensifying our own sexual feelings, thus by changing from sexual pursuit stories to erotica or pornography.

Fifth, the topic should be readily integrated into the standard narrative structure of aspect normalcy, change from aspect normalcy, the establishment of goals, the pursuit of goals by an agent, the temporary occurrence of the opposite of the goal, the achievement of the goal, and the establishment of enduring, idealized aspect normalcy. For example, parent-child attachment relations may easily be integrated into most of this structure. Aspect normalcy would be the initial union of the parents and children, the change comes with their separation, leading to the establishment of reunion as a goal to be pursued by one or both parties, and so on. In fact, the same point holds for my buying cucumbers, if at a lower level of emotional intensity. Normalcy is having cucumbers. I run out, and so on. The one point where getting cucumbers does not fit is with idealized aspect normalcy. When I buy cucumbers at the store, I have only returned to a sort of banal normalcy. Perhaps surprisingly, we will see below that there is a problem with idealized aspect normalcy in parent-child attachment stories as well.

Sixth, the concerns of the narrative should be open to either dominant or resistant ideological development—or rather, to both. This is really two ideological criteria. First, a genre is likely to be more prominent to the degree that it bears on recurring, ideologically consequential issues (e.g., gender hierarchies). Second, it is likely to be more prominent to the degree that it allows the expression not only of dominant views but of resistant views. It seems clear that societies will generally favor works that express dominant ideology. Indeed, that is part of what makes a given ideology dominant. However, it is also the case that literary works are widely used to express opposition to dominant ideology. There are complex reasons for this—the enhancement of empathic response that tends to go along with the elaboration of stories, an enhancement that does not readily leave aside socially dehumanized enemies; the ways fiction allows one to imagine nonstandard social relations; the ways fiction allows one to express criticisms of society indirectly, and so on. Moreover, there are always different groups in societies with partially contradictory interests, interests that inflect their response to narrative. Thus the ideological flexibility of a plot type is likely to increase its appeal to a broader range of readers.

Furthermore, we might expect genres to recur more readily insofar as they are open to a geographical organization into home and away and insofar as this is related to normalcy, emotion goals, ideology, and so on. The idea of "home" here is variable depending on the emotion system involved. In the case of attachment, "home" is a place of continuing personal contact and immediate accessibility. In the case of in-group pride, "home" is the broader area of in-group dominance.

Finally, we might expect a genre to be more prominent depending on the degree to which it depicts changes from aspect normalcy that are widespread, thus part of the audience's experience and emotional memory. The change from the normalcy of living as a child to pursuing a marriage partner is almost universal. In contrast, the experience of being separated from one's parents in early childhood is not nearly as common.

How Genres Develop and Which Genres Develop

As we have seen, the personal happiness prototype is romantic union, which derives from the integration of emotion systems for sexuality and desire. The social happiness prototype is social dominance, both individual within the in-group and collective for the in-group over out-groups. This prototype derives from pride, with some element of anger. Finally, the physical happiness goal involves enduring physical well-being and bears on the emotional (or motivational) systems of hunger and thirst. Sacrificial tragicomedy also may involve guilt, both in the sense that the sinner may feel remorse and, more commonly and more importantly, in the sense that the community will attribute guilt to the sinner and respond to him or her as guilty. Guilt attribution is not simply an intellectual attribution of fault. It is, rather, a complex emotional response to the guilty person, incorporating elements of disgust and anger. Both remorse and blame are important in the epilogue of suffering also.

Again, the first and fundamental way in which genres develop involves emotion systems generating happiness goals, which in turn generate narrative structures. One thing that is noteworthy about these particular genres is that they are complex. This is most obviously true of the romantic narrative, in which sexual desire and attachment are both crucial. (No matter how much Jane likes Joe, it is not romantic love if she just wants to be friends.) As noted above, this suggests something. If sexual desire plus attachment defines a happiness goal, it would seem that sexual desire and attachment should separately define happiness goals as well. Their combination may make for a particularly strong happiness goal. Thus their motivational force, when considered separately, may be weaker. But it should not be insignificant. Thus we might expect genres to develop based on goals defined by the lust and attachment systems—and indeed, we do find such genres.

The situation with respect to the sacrificial and heroic plots is less clear. In the case of the heroic plot, pride is already central, though we might expect anger to point toward a separate genre definition. In the case of the sacrificial plot, hunger and thirst are already central, though we might expect guilt to point toward a genre definition. Indeed, the relevance of guilt is reinforced by its importance in the epilogue of suffering. One apparent difficulty with these emotion systems is that they are a bit too diffuse in their objects. I can be angry at anything—for example, the front door that keeps getting stuck when I try to open it. Moreover, most experiences of anger tend to be ephemeral. In consequence, our most common experiences of anger may not withstand the attenuation of intensity that is part of empathic response.

On the other hand, we are dealing with prototypes here, and prototypes are not simply the most common or most average case of a category. Rather, prototypes are weighted averages. They highlight the distinctive characteristics of the category. The prototypical man is more masculine than the statistical average, and the prototypical woman is more feminine. In some cases, the prototype represents an actual extreme. Lettuce is widely seen as a prototypical diet food since it has no calories (see Kahneman and Miller 143), but clearly, zero calories is the extreme of diet foods, not their mean. Perhaps it is worth distinguishing between prototypes that actually present average or close to average cases (call them "mean prototypes") and prototypes that present the most distinctive cases (call them "limit prototypes"). Our prototype formation probably depends at least in part on the practical contexts in which we make use of the relevant categories. In the case of "diet food," for example, we want to judge the degree to which a particular food fits with a program of slimming. As a result, the limit prototype is more relevant. Due to the importance of emotion intensification in stories, limit prototypes are likely to be particularly significant in the generation of narratives as well.

The most distinctive and extreme forms of both guilt and anger—thus the limit prototypes for their eliciting conditions—should bear on actions that have strongly negative emotional consequences, prominently consequences for the pursuit of important goals. Death is of course the most extreme form of harming the pursuit of goals, for it makes such pursuit impossible. This suggests that the limit prototype, at least for guilt, would be murder.

The case of anger is a little more complicated. Here we need to say something about both eliciting conditions and actional outcomes. I become angry when I have suffered harm. But if I am killed, then I am no longer around to be angry. Someone else's death may constitute a harm for me. But obviously we do not react to all deaths equally. Our emotional response to someone's death is intensified particularly when the victim is an attachment figure. As a result, the extreme case of personal harm that generates anger would seem to be the death of a loved one. Moreover, an extreme actional outcome for anger is itself murder. In this way, a good candidate for the limit prototype of anger is a person who has suffered the death of a loved one and is set to kill in response to that death.

If the preceding inferences are valid, they suggest that we should find a second level of genres below that of the main prototypical narratives. This level of "minor genres," as we might call them, would include stories treating attachment, sexuality, anger, and guilt. But the precise structure of these genres is still somewhat unclear, which brings us to the second way in which genres develop.

Once we have individual stories, we begin to form cognitive structures from our experience of those stories, and not just from our happiness prototypes. Just as we form the prototype for a "bird" by seeing many birds, we form story prototypes by reading or hearing many stories. Note that we do not simply have a single prototype for "bird." We have prototypes for different sorts of bird—robins, seagulls, and so on. The same point holds for stories. I form a prototype for a story generally, then other prototypes for different types of story—for example, horror stories. Thus we produce story genres in two ways, one by happiness prototypes, the other by grouping actual stories into subcategories. We may refer to the genres produced by happiness prototypes as "generative" and the genres produced by the clustering of individual stories in our experience as "empirical." It should happen that the empirical genres include the generative genres in some form. But the empirical genres will invariably exceed the generative genres.

Note that having a genre prototype, generative or empirical, does not entail having a word for it. Sometimes we have a genre prototype without any exactly corresponding name. Conversely, sometimes we have a genre name without any exactly corresponding prototype. Genre names are part of self-conscious theorization regarding genres, not our tacit, spontaneous formation of categories. Here as elsewhere our theorizations can diverge quite significantly from our tacit conceptual formations.

If we are talking about cultural variation in genres, then we obviously want to look carefully at the development of empirical genres. Indeed, even with the cross-culturally recurring, major, prototypical genres (romantic, heroic, and sacrificial), there will be cultural peculiarities that result from readers' empirical formation of romantic, heroic, and sacrificial prototypes. But not all empirical prototype formation necessarily produces cultural divergence. Indeed, some patterns in empirical prototype formation are likely to recur cross-culturally.

More exactly, the development of empirical prototypes for stories, like the development of empirical prototypes for anything else, will involve multiple, overlapping forms of categorization. In other words, it will not be confined to categorization in terms of the protagonist's general happiness goals. It may proceed through, say, variable structural features that are initially generated by the happiness prototypes but that are not confined to one of the major genres. When we spontaneously group works together by reference to the presence of such features, they in effect come to define their own genres. For example, due to its effectiveness in emotion intensification, the parent-child separation and reunion structure may be found in romantic, heroic, and sacrificial plots. Readers may spontaneously class these separations and reunions together, unself-consciously abstracting a genre prototype, thus a genre. Ascertaining and punishing the source of a social violation occurs in both heroic and sacrificial plots, as well as an occasional romantic plot. Stories with this feature may be categorized together, leading to a genre prototype. More exactly, there is a common version of the sacrificial narrative in which the sacrificial victim is the guilty party. That version supplies a parallel with some versions of the usurpation sequence in the heroic plot. These parallels allow readers to abstract a minor genre based on guilt and punishment. Of course, that guilt and punishment may occur in different ways. In sacrificial plots, investigation may be required to determine who is guilty. Moreover, the punishment may be undertaken by an established social authority. In heroic plots, in contrast, the usurper is usually known. Moreover, the punishment may be undertaken by the usurped ruler him- or herself— initially alone and outside the (newly) established social authority (of the usurper). This may foster the abstraction of two subprototypes and thus two subgenres.

In combination with the emotion systems mentioned above, such empirical categorizations would seem likely to foster four recurring minor genres. The first and probably most widespread of the four is the story of the separation and reunion of parents and children. The second takes up the other emotional component of romantic plots—sexual desire—but in this case sexual desire dissociated from attachment. The third combines anger with the individual response to social violation, particularly murder. This yields revenge plots. Finally, there is the combination of guilt with socially supervised investigation and punishment. This yields crime investigation and court narratives. (Obviously, the "court" stories need not involve a law court in the contemporary European sense. They need only involve systematic processes leading to a socially official determination of guilt and punishment. I am using the word "court" to give a general sense of the genre by reference to a familiar specification.) Needless to say, different elements of these genres may be combined in different ways. However, these four genres do tend to recur—if, again, not as frequently as the three major genres.

The remainder of this chapter considers these minor genres in turn. In each case, it outlines some common features of the genre. I should stress that my outlines for these genres are not so elaborate as those of the major prototypes, set out in chapter 3. This is for two reasons. Both result from the sparser distribution of the minor genres. Again, they are less continuous across traditions and historical periods and they are less dense or prominent in the traditions and periods where they do occur. The first reason for the reduced elaboration, then, is that we simply have much less data on these genres than we have for the major genres. The second reason is that the data themselves are somewhat more diffuse.

It might seem that having a more limited data set would lead to greater uniformity. In fact, the opposite is the case. For example, romantic plots are prominent within the canonical literature and have a clear presence among paradigmatic works. Consequently, many instances of such works are widely known. The tacit averaging of these instances across readers will therefore have a certain degree of uniformity. As people come to share an increasing number of works within a certain category, their prototypes for those works will tend to converge as idiosyncratic differences tend to be averaged out. Conversely, as more people produce romantic plots, their productive idiosyncrasies will tend to balance one another as well, again resulting in the convergent development of a standard prototype. However, with relatively fewer and more widely distributed instances, opportunities decrease for balancing idiosyncratic patterns in reading and production. In other words, the instances that go to make up individuals' reading experiences of, say, parent-child reunion stories may be more likely to diverge; thus their resulting prototypes may be more likely to diverge. Moreover, the more limited production in this narrative category may also make it less likely that particular idiosyncratic productions will be balanced by other works. Put differently, individual (thus potentially idiosyncratic) instances will tend to have more weight in a small population. Note that this is true both for general readers and for authors in particular. In the second case, idiosyncrasies of reading have direct consequences for the production of new works.

This multiplicity and uneven distribution also mean that the minor genres often divide more into subtypes. In other words, the convergence that does occur within minor genres tends to be more partial than what occurs in the major genres. As a result, it often makes sense to outline the subcategories rather than, or in addition to, the encompassing categories (e.g., stories of accidental parent-child separation versus stories of parental self-sacrifice in the case of parent-child attachment plots). Put differently, we may think of the major genres as having a "central" or "governing" prototype along with various "subprototypes." For example, there is a prototypical form for romantic narratives generally, and there are subprototypes for different clusters of romantic narratives (e.g., Hollywood romances of the 1950s probably have features in common that are not shared by, say, Sanskrit romances). In the case of minor genres, however, we are more likely to find a complex of related "subprototypes" without the governing prototype above them—or with a larger higher-level prototype that is less well-defined and apparently less cognitively consequential.

After outlining the main plot features of the minor genres and their subgeneric variants, I turn to the degree to which minor genres do or do not fulfill the narrative desiderata outlined above. My concern here is to indicate how, in light of the preceding analyses, we might explain the intermediate status of these genres. On the one hand, they do seem to recur cross-culturally and transhistorically.[2] Moreover, there are times when they become quite significant. For example, "Revenge Tragedy . . . flourished in the late Elizabethan and Jacobean period" (Drabble 821). "Crime and its eventual punishment" formed a "major topic of early *tsa-chü*" (Idema 808; *tsa-chü* was "a major theatrical genre . . . in northern China" from the thirteenth to the fifteenth centuries). In contemporary America, "many episodic dramatic programs" follow "the process by which a self-contained narrative enigma is solved through detective work" or "legal maneuvers" (Mittell 163). On the other hand, despite their prominence at different times and places, these genres are not continuously prominent nor do they seem to make their way into canonical literature at anything approaching the rate of the three major genres. I hope to explain this, at least partially.

Before discussing the minor genres individually, however, it is perhaps worth noting one way in which all four of the minor genres tend to fall short in relation to the preceding list. All four have some problems with the idealized aspect normalcy that marks the ending of the most highly prototypical narrative structures. This does not merely contribute to their reduced frequency. It also tends to make these stories more "troubled."

They tend to be more emotionally ambivalent and more thematically uncertain. Of course, ambivalent, non-idealized resolutions are not absent from the major prototypes. They occur with particular frequency and prominence in heroic plots, as seen in the epilogue of suffering. The problematization of revenge and crime stories is not unrelated to that epilogue. In the case of minor genres, the ambivalence extends to stories of attachment and sexual desire, though it is rare in romantic stories.

The troubled nature of the minor genres is perhaps most obvious—but perhaps also the most complex—in the case of revenge plots. These prototypically begin with the death of some attachment figure—a spouse, a parent. The revenge surrounds the hero's harming of the villain who caused that death. Clearly, there cannot be a return even to nonidealized normalcy in cases of this sort. Nonidealized normalcy would involve the resurrection of the dead person. The accomplishment of the revenge only leaves the hero back in the situation of being unable to do anything to be reunited with the lost relative or friend. Of course, revenge stories may treat topics other than murder. In those cases, there may be idealized aspect normalcy at the end (e.g., the hero, unfairly deprived of his job at Super-Corp, may end up becoming chief executive officer and demoting his antagonist to the mail room). But in cases of death, thus in the most emotionally intense cases, this is usually not possible. Moreover, there is the further problem that revenge easily gives rise to cycles of retribution from different sides in a conflict. Such cycles simply multiply the tragic losses in the story. Finally, as this suggests, there is a problem parallel to that faced in the epilogue of suffering in heroic plots. Revenge typically involves repeating the initial crime, prototypically a murder.[3] But for murder to be entirely unambivalent, the victim and his or her family and friends must inspire no empathy. As soon as any one of these figures is humanized, we are likely to begin to feel ambivalence about, or even revulsion at, the revenge.[4]

It may seem that criminal investigation and judgment stories have this problem as well—and they do. As Kerrigan notes, "revenge and retributive justice are hard to disentangle" (23). However, there are some mitigating factors in this case. The result is that crime investigations are often less "troubled" or problematic than other minor genres. Of course, here as elsewhere, in the prototypical case of murder, the mere fact of the crime prevents idealized aspect normalcy at the end. However, the investigation tends to turn our attention away from the victim to an investigator and a legal process. The tragic outcome of the initial crime may remain unchanged. Nonetheless, our emotional response to the narrative is often not focused on the initial loss or the victim of the loss. Rather, it may be focused on the investigative system. Indeed, in some cases, the unfolding of the investigation signals the return to or even inauguration of just principles of legal procedure after a period of injustice or chaos. In this way, the just decision itself constitutes the establishment of idealized aspect normalcy for society generally. For example, in the case of *The Injustice Done to Tou Ngo*—which integrates sacrificial and criminal investigation plots—the death of Tou Ngo remains real. However, the concluding investigation and prosecution represent a return to systemic justice in legal proceedings. The focus of this ending is not on the impossibility of restoring the dead (sacrificial) victim. It is, rather, on the actual restoration of processes that should assure justice throughout the foreseeable future. Put differently, there is a sense in which such criminal investigation stories could end with the summary phrase "and they all lived justly ever after."

On the other hand, I should not exaggerate this. While stories of criminal investigation and punishment are less often troubled than stories in other minor genres, they are far from being entirely untroubled. Instances from *Oedipus the King* to Kieslowski's *Decalogue V* (based on the commandment "Thou shalt not kill") suggest that problems may come at both ends of the process. Again, there is the initial death, which is not overcome, even if it is often deemphasized. Second, there is the legal punishment, which to some extent repeats the initial crime even when that is done by the state after a fair legal process. Indeed, as we discuss below, this point is suggested even in work such as the *Oresteia*, which has as one main purpose the celebration of the Athenian legal system.[5]

The cases of sex and attachment are, perhaps somewhat surprisingly, no less problematic. A key element of idealized aspect normalcy is, obviously, the idealization. What does it mean for aspect normalcy to be idealized? First, there is some narratively crucial feature of normalcy. The alteration of this feature in non-normalcy triggers the protagonist's emotions and generates his or her goals. This feature is idealized when the situation has not only stopped giving rise to those emotions and goals but has fulfilled the goals in a way that is intensified and that is no longer fragile or temporary. More simply, the hero has not only returned to what is ordinary.

Rather, with respect to the goal-relevant feature, he or she has achieved a condition that is markedly superior—perhaps even flawlessly superior—in both quality and durability. Duşyanta was perfectly content with his wives at the beginning of the play. But he did not have the profound relation to any of them that he finds with Śakuntalā, a relation suggested by the spiritual context of their union at the end—a context that also suggests eternity. Son-Jara's father was a fine ruler, "a good king loved by all the people" (Niane 4). But it is only with Son-Jara that the society reaches heights of glory and prosperity: "From Ghana in the north to Mali in the south and from Mema in the East to the Fouta in the west, all the lands . . . recognized Sundiata's [Son-Jara's] authority" (72). Moreover, "the villages knew prosperity again, for with Sundiata happiness had come into everyone's home" (81). Indeed, "during the reign of Sundiata the world knew happiness" (82). Put differently, idealized aspect normalcy is the development of a condition that maximizes the satisfaction of the goal by the establishment of an intensified and enduring condition.

The goal of purely sexual desire is, of course, sexual satisfaction. There are several problems with the idealization of sexual satisfaction. The first is that idealized sexual satisfaction tends to involve mutual attachment. Or put more crudely, the ideal sexual relation either involves wanting to be with one's partner afterward or not having to be with one's partner afterward. The idealized condition of wanting to be with one's partner afterward involves mutual attachment, thus romantic love. Once romantic love rears its head, however, we are in the realm of romantic narrative rather than sexual narrative. Thus the idealization of nonromantic sexual desire would seem to involve not having to be with one's partner. But this is a peculiar sort of idealization, for it is no different from the opening situation, which precipitated the entire plot—the protagonist is alone without a partner. It is as if the sexual relation never occurred.

A second problem is related to this. This idealization of complete removal from a continuing relationship with one's sexual partner is a possible "idealization" only if the sexual relations have no consequences. Here, of course, there is a discrepancy between men and women. In societies that prize virginity prior to marriage, the mere deflowering of the woman is highly consequential. Thus, from the woman's point of view, the preferred idealization will almost always be mutual attachment. The chance of impregnation only increases this discrepancy. Of course, a narrative may be written in a highly patriarchal society and aimed at an audience of men. This is likely to make the positions of the man and the woman unequal in the assessment of the writer and the readers. In other words, male readers may have considerable empathy with a man who seduces a woman and then abandons her, whereas women probably would not. However, empathy is never entirely simple. Our empathic capacities do not stop with people of our own sex (or race or nation). Moreover, even if we are disinclined to simulate the point of view of strangers (thus elaborating on our spontaneous empathic responses to them), men are likely to have some inclination to adopt the point of view of female relatives (e.g., daughters or sisters). Moreover, men are likely to have actually done this in some cases and are likely to have emotional memories resulting from that empathic engagement—emotional memories that will affect their response to literary works. Thus very few men are likely to have unqualified and absolute male sympathies in such cases. In this way, discrepancies between the man's interests and the woman's are likely to be troublesome, not only for women readers but for men as well.[6]

Finally, things are not even that simple for the male protagonists. Sexual desire is not a single event in one's life. It recurs. As such, the male protagonist is likely to want to have sexual relations again. If his experience was very good the first time, then he is likely to want to be joined with that woman again—which points toward an enduring relationship. On the other hand, if the experience did not inspire a desire for such an enduring relationship, then it was presumably not ideal to begin with. Either way, we do not have goal achievement producing idealized aspect normalcy. The very best possible outcome is simply a repetition of the opening situation—thus temporary normalcy that is not idealized.

In the case of parent-child attachment, it is easier to imagine what would constitute idealization in the sense just discussed. Parents and children often have opposed interests and thus real, material conflicts, as well as various sorts of discrepancies in taste and attitude. At the same time, attachment leads them to care about one another's well-being, to experience increased empathy with one another, to act toward one another in altruistic ways, and to trust one another. An idealized relationship between parents and children would minimize the first set of relations and maximize the second—something that is, of course, particularly easy to do when the child is very young and also, if to a lesser extent, when the parent is very old.

This reference to age suggests the problem with establishing idealized aspect normalcy in these cases. Parent-child reunion stories simply cannot be stories in which the reunited family lives "happily ever after." If there is no outside causal interference, no catastrophic intervention of disease or accident, parents die before their children. Moreover, other things being equal, they do not die hours or days or weeks before their children, but at least a dozen or fifteen years, perhaps twice that or even more. It is simply the natural course of internal causal developments that parents and children will be separated. Obviously, in real life this occurs with spouses as well, particularly when there is a significant age difference between the husband and the wife. But in literature it is possible to vaguely suggest an idealization in which spouses will live on together to some hazy point in the distant future when they will both pass into the next life. But there is actually something wrong with imagining this across generations. It is simply not an idealization to imagine that the children die with their parents—for that means that the children's lives are significantly shorter than they should be. Of course, we do not think out these issues when reading a story. Moreover, there are ways in which this discrepancy may be partially occluded. But it remains a concern that may tacitly make problematic even the most seemingly optimistic and idealized family reunions.

Having treated this shared property of the minor genres, we may now consider those genres individually in greater detail.

Attachment

Attachment is the emotion that leads us to want to be near someone else, to share a home with them, to have physical contact and cooperative interaction with them—particularly cooperative interaction that has no further purpose beyond the interaction itself, thus play. In attachment relations, the mere presence of the other person brings joy and his or her absence brings sadness. Moreover, attachment entails a particular interest in the physical and emotional well-being of the other person. Its most intense form appears in early parent-child bonding, though it makes a less intense appearance in friendship, particularly in "companionate love" (the phrase commonly used to refer to, for example, the form of affection experienced by older couples who no longer feel intense romantic love).[7]

In short, the main concerns of attachment relations are the proximity and well-being of the other person. In consequence, the main story lines bearing on attachment concern separation and reunion along with the well-being of the "attachment objects" (e.g., children). Parent-child plots appear to be by far the most common narratives of this sort. Friends appear importantly in many works. Moreover, they may be separated and reunited. However, it seems relatively rare for the separation and reunion of friends to give rise to the main plot line of a work. We may therefore concentrate on the parent-child variety.

As already discussed, parent-child separation and reunion stories cannot readily achieve aspect idealization. In part for this reason, the development and resolution of these stories is often tragic. Even when apparently "comic," the conclusion may be particularly uneasy, problematic in a way that makes the story tragicomic, not only in its developmental trajectory but in its final outcome as well.

More exactly, the shared structure of these plots is roughly the following. Parents and children are together and familial life is normal. Some event causes their separation. This leads eventually to one party seeking the other. An interesting aspect of the parent-child separation plot is that the separation can be very long—years or decades. Indeed, it often stretches from the child's infancy to adulthood. I suspect that this has something to do with the ways in which human relations actually develop, and the reasons why attachment plots are so resistant to idealized aspect normalcy. We are deeply attached to our parents when we are very young. We gradually come to be concerned with separating from them. For a long time, our relation to our parents is colored by this need to be someone other than our parents. Many years after this is accomplished, however, we realize that our parents will not live forever, that we will have to spend perhaps decades of our lives without them. We see this starkly and poignantly as they age. Whatever has happened in the interim, our bodies are still pervaded by the emotional memories of those early attachments. There is nothing more painful for those feelings of attachment than the realization that the parents' loss of well-being will be absolute and that our separation from them will be irreversible. In this way, many, perhaps most of us, experience something like a story of parental separation and troubled reunion. The separation is not literal and physical but emotional—the result of our necessary struggle to be distinct. The search for reunion results from a nostalgic and painful feeling that in that struggle, something precious and irrecoverable has been left behind. Sometimes the search begins only after one's parents have passed away.

One result of this prolonged separation in attachment narratives is that parents often do not know what their children look like, and children too do not know their parents. They often make some mistake in the middle of the story—failing to recognize one another or erroneously "recognizing" someone else. (This point is developed to mirthful excess in some works, such as Shakespeare's *Comedy of Errors*.) This too has psychological correlates. It is the sort of thing psychoanalysts refer to as "transference," the response to someone in our contemporary environment as if he or she stood to us in the relation of our father or mother in early childhood. In cognitive terms, it is the activation of emotional memories of attachment in the wrong contexts and in association with the wrong people.[8]

The "comic" conclusion of this story structure is of course the reunion of parents and children. However, as emphasized above, there is often a problem here. Again, the standard structure of stories would lead us to expect the reunion to be idealized, the parent-child interaction and well-being to be perfect, or nearly so. However, it often is not. Indeed, the imperfection is often the thematic point of the reunion. Even when the reunion seems to be idealized, the perfection is sometimes so clearly artificial, so clearly the result of authorial manipulation, that it suggests problems even when it overtly denies them. There are, of course, exceptions to this. However, among relatively nonephemeral works, the exceptions are often mixed stories involving not only parent-child reunion but also the union of lovers or spouses. Shakespeare's *Comedy of Errors* is an instance of this sort, as are the early Chinese dramas *A Playboy from a Noble House Opts for the Wrong Career* and *Wind and Moon in the Courtyard of Purple Clouds* (both in Idema and West). In these cases, the aspect idealization seems inseparable from the romantic story line—or put differently, the enduring happiness of the conclusion is not solely reliant on the parent-child reunion.

Writers on attachment have stressed that there are different sorts of attachment relation. Specifically, early childhood attachments fall into one or another of a limited number of patterns. These patterns commonly persist into later life, not only biasing our relation to our own parents but coloring our relations to others (including lovers). One key axis along which attachment relations vary is that of security. Roughly, a child may feel secure in his or her attachment relations or insecure (see Shaver and Mikulincer). (Obviously, there are gradations in between. But there does appear to be a tendency toward a broad bifurcation of this sort.) These different sorts of attachment relation bear on the ways in which attachment narratives are developed.

First, one fundamental division in separation narratives is between stories in which the parent's action has produced the separation and stories in which something else has produced the separation—thus stories in which the child is abandoned by the parent (a sort of internal development in the parent-child relationship) and stories in which some external force causes the separation. It may seem that this is the same as the division between insecure attachment (the parent abandons the child) and secure attachment (something else causes the separation). However, it is not. In fact, the sense of security or insecurity cuts across this division, producing four sorts of parent-child separation stories. First, the separation was wholly out of the parent's control. Second, the separation, though effected by someone else, might have been prevented by the parent. Third, the separation was produced indifferently or malevolently by the actions of the parent. Finally, the separation was produced by the actions of the parent, but for benevolent reasons and at the cost of great pain to the parent. One might reasonably expect different outcomes from these different scenarios. Specifically, one might expect that reunion in the final, sacrificial case would be idealized; that it would be partially idealized in the first case, where the parent is innocent; that the second case (where the parent might have prevented the separation) would be mildly disturbed; and that the third, malevolent or indifferent case would be the most problematic. There is some tendency of this sort, but it is less than one might have expected. There is, however, one further feature of the plots where the parent is responsible for the separation. It is often the case that the rejected child achieves great success and the reunion is motivated by some need of the parent. This produces the ironic situation where the parent did not aid the helpless, needy child, but now expects the child to help when the parent is in need.

The parent-child plot shows many of the characteristics that should make works of this sort fairly common. It is incident-rich, at least potentially, due to the possibility of separation and reunion sequences. It is readily expandable into events and episodes. The fit with the standard narrative structure is good, except for the relative lack of idealized aspect normalcy, as already noted. It is closely linked with a geographical organization into home and away. The results are mixed with respect to experiential commonality. Again, everyone or almost everyone goes through a period of differentiation from parents. This gives each of us an experience that is metaphorically parallel to the separation and reunion story. However, few of us have literally experienced abandonment, abduction, and so forth. Moreover, experience of deep separation commonly occurs only with death. Thus it is associated with the impossibility of reunion, which may make the problems with idealized aspect normalcy more salient.

Two more complicated aspects of the parent-child story are its relation to ideological concerns and emotional intensification. Ideologically, it is simply not clear what dominant and resistant ideologies are regarding parent-child reunion. My sense is that no particular position is dominant; thus it is unclear what might count as resistant. Indeed, it is not evident that there are social hierarchies bound up with this issue. There are, of course, ideologies relating to filial piety, parental authority, and so on. But it is not clear what consequences these have for, say, the parental self-sacrifice version of this story. It is always a good thing to sacrifice oneself to save the life of another person, so it is good when parents do this for children—or when children do this for parents. But it is not obvious that depriving a child of a parental attachment relation is a good thing, just because it will give the child material well-being (a standard development in melodramas of this sort). Conversely, however, it is also not obvious that prolonging an attachment relation is right when it deprives the child of material well-being—particularly when the child will eventually need to live after the parent has died. Of course, there may always be ideological complications in particular stories, no matter what the genre. But it is difficult to identify a common baseline from which such complications may proceed in the case of this genre.

Finally, there is an emotional peculiarity in attachment stories. Everyone's emotional memories and emotional formation for attachment extend back to early childhood, thus a period of particular vulnerability. Moreover, our attachment relations are necessarily ephemeral, particularly with respect to parents. In addition, they are almost always ambivalent, complex, and conflicted. I had a particular relation with my parents when I was an infant and they were in their thirties. I have a very different relation with them now that I am fifty and they are in their eighties. In effect, it is a relation between different people. But unlike relations among genuinely different people, I still carry with me all the emotional memories that bound me to them fifty years ago. Put differently, I retain at least some of the lability that I had as a small child, even if the resulting feelings and behaviors are relatively controlled. For this reason, it is unusually easy to intensify the emotional impact of attachment relations, particularly in relation to parents.

Yet the consequences of this are not straightforward. Most of us do not like to feel vulnerable. Suppose Jones sees a Hallmark card commercial about a dutiful son who shows up unexpectedly at his father's home on Father's Day (bearing a Hallmark card). The father is sitting morosely until the son arrives. Now his wrinkled face grows radiant with affection and joy on seeing his beloved boy. Jones can hardly fight back the tears as he thinks of his own father, living a thousand miles away. But in fact Jones's father is not alone on Father's Day. Moreover, when Jones visits, they invariably quarrel about whether George W. Bush is or is not the savior of the nation, leading the forces of righteousness under the direction of a stern but righteous God. The commercial has activated emotional memories that have no real bearing on Jones's current life. When we have experiences of this sort, we say that a narrative is "emotionally manipulative," that it has not earned or justified the emotional response it provokes. I suspect it is for this reason that narratives bearing on attachment seem to occur with great frequency in popular ephemera but then tend not to be preserved as canonical works. If, indeed, attachment vulnerability is easy to provoke but much more difficult to justify, then we would expect many attachment-based works to have immediate success but to suffer in light of our cooler, retrospective judgments. We might also expect the most enduring attachment-based works to be the ones that challenge rather than reproduce the nostalgic idealization that is so commonly a part of emotional manipulation (as in Hallmark card commercials).

Particular canonical cases of this genre would include the story of Joseph as recounted in Genesis and in the twelfth surah of the *Qur'ān*. Though affecting, it is neither sentimental and idealized nor tragic. Indeed, in this case, reunion is at least relatively successful, consistent with the fact that the separation was not the father's fault.

Parental rejection tends to lead to more problematic conclusions. A case expressing bitterness on the part of the child, thus the impossibility of emotional reconciliation, may be found in the story of Karṇa from the great Sanskrit epic, *Mahābhārata*. Having been abandoned as a child, Karṇa as an adult rejects his mother's offer of reunion.

However, explicit rejection does not necessarily lead to greater acrimony or less attachment between parent and child. For example, in Motomasa's Nō drama, *Yoroboshi*, a father has rejected his son due to slander. They are eventually reunited and apparently reconciled. However, the ending is far from idealized, for the son's suffering has led to blindness.

The difference between *Yoroboshi* and the Karṇa story suggests another variable—the child's age when the separation took place. Stories of parental rejection may begin long after the initial bonding occurs. These too tend to end badly. But they may be less likely to involve bitterness on the part of the child. An obvious canonical case from the European tradition is *King Lear*. On the one hand, this is a straightforward heroic tragedy, complete with usurpation and invasion. But that tragedy is intertwined with an attachment plot—the story of Lear and Cordelia. Just prior to the ending, Shakespeare elaborates on a sort of perversely pseudo-idealized normalcy of reunion. Specifically, he has Lear say that he and Cordelia will treat prison as a place where they can, in effect, play—like a young father and a tiny daughter—though in this case their play will be one of confession and absolution: "Come, let's away to prison," Lear says. "We two alone will sing like birds i' the cage. / When thou dost ask me blessing I'll kneel down / And ask of thee forgiveness" (V.iii.8–11). These aspects of the ending clearly derive more from the problematic plot of parent-child separation and reunion than from the encompassing heroic tragedy in which they are embedded.

On the other hand, even an early loss of attachment need not produce resentment. The well-known Nō drama *Kagekiyo* concerns a father who simply ignored his daughter when she was born. At the time, he was a warrior and had no interest in a little girl. She grows up and goes to find him. Here (as in the stories of Karṇa and Joseph—and, briefly, Lear) we have the usual nonrecognition. When father and child do finally recognize one another and are reunited, Kagekiyo rejects his daughter, telling her to go back—not out of disdain for her but out of shame at his own decline (see lines 115–19, 127–30). In this way, the story thematizes the problem with all parent-child reunions—the inevitability of aging and death.

As already noted, the parental self-sacrifice version—in which a parent abandons the child for its own good—may seem less likely to have a troubled ending. The most famous instance of this is perhaps the biblical story of the harlots who come to Solomon disputing who is the mother of a particular child. A similar but more plausible story may be found in the well-known Chinese Yüan drama *The Story of the Circle of Chalk*. On the other hand, in these two stories the parent-child separation and reunion is not developed. Indeed, the separation is really only threatened. Moreover, in the case of the Chinese play, this episode is part of a larger story of crime and punishment. In contrast, melodramas—which typically eschew happy reunions—often elaborate on this self-sacrificial separation. Indeed, that self-sacrifice is often a crucial part of melodrama, as Noël Carroll has discussed (36). In film studies, perhaps the most commonly cited example of melodrama is *Stella Dallas*.[9] This is not to say the developed self-sacrificial subtype is confined to melodramas or to the modern period.[10] It is not. For example, we see a version of this structure in the story of the Lady of Akashi and her daughter from the eleventh-century *Tale of Genji*, a virtual compendium of parent-child separation stories.[11]

There are, of course, cases where the reunion is, at least apparently, entirely untroubled. One case of this sort may be found in one of the paradigmatic narratives of the European tradition, the *Odyssey*. The *Odyssey* is in many ways a highly elaborated story of familial separation and reunion. Odysseus is separated from his own parents and his son, as well as his wife and his motherlike nurse. While he is gone, his mother dies, illustrating the theme of parental loss. For our purposes, however, the most interesting instance is the seemingly smooth reunion of Odysseus with his son, Telemachus. In keeping with the usual structure, Odysseus had been separated from Telemachus from early on, though in this case the separation was neither a repudiation nor a self-sacrifice. Telemachus and Odysseus need one another at this point because the suitors of Penelope are a threat to both. When they meet, there is the usual nonrecognition. However, after recognition, they join together harmoniously to defeat the suitors. Despite the time of separation, everything seems to go well. In short, we seem to have a successful reunion here.

But as it turns out, things are not that simple. There is a strange hint of something else in this story. When he arrives in Ithaca, Odysseus needs a disguise. Athena makes him into an old man (see 13.429–38). When

Telemachus does not recognize him, he is still in this disguise. However, when he reveals himself to Telemachus, he is young again. The transformation is explained literally in the plot by Athena's power (see 16.166–215). But the entire sequence suggests something else, a sort of wish fulfillment that the effects of parental aging—the effects illustrated so poignantly in, for example, *Kagekiyo*—can simply be dissipated with the wave of a hand. The reunion of Odysseus and Telemachus is apparently untroubled precisely because the aging of Odysseus is explicitly denied—though at the same time, that explicit denial may create a sense of unease in at least some readers, returning us, covertly, to the problem.

The *Aeneid* is less coy in treating this story. A part of this epic too concerns parent-child separation and reunion. But here the separation is due to the parent's death, and the reunion is a reunion in the underworld. Moreover, the reunion is flawed not only by being temporary and literally involved with death but also because it is almost nothing but a dream. When Aeneas tries to embrace his father, he cannot. His arms merely pass through the substanceless spirit (see 3:807–11).

Perhaps unsurprisingly, this image may be found in other stories of failed attachment reunions. For example, we find it in the meeting of Gilgamesh and Enkidu (friends rather than family members) and, more relevant to our purposes, the mother and child in Motomasa's *Sumidaga-wa*. The physical presence and "touchability" of the attachment figure are clearly a crucial part of attachment goals. The loss of that physical presence and bodily contact in effect reduces the reunion to one of mere imagination.

The general structure we have been considering extends even to postmodern literature. Consider, for instance, one of the paradigms of the postmodern novel, Alain Robbe-Grillet's *Dans le Labyrinthe*. As with many postmodern works, the precise plot line of this novel is not entirely clear. It is difficult to tell just what part of the novel is "real," what part is a dream, what part is a true or false memory, what part is a historically accurate flashback, what part is fever-induced confusion. I give one possible interpretation. However, for our purposes it is not crucial whether I have gotten the real part right relative to the fantasy and so on—or even if there is a right answer here. All that is crucial is that part of the sequence is structured by a parent-child separation-and-reunion scenario, whether that part is "real" or not. Indeed, whatever is true or false in the story world, this is the primary narrative structure in the work, despite its apparent embedment in a heroic narrative.

The French army has recently been badly defeated at Reichenfels. Everyone in the nearby town anticipates the arrival of the occupying German troops. One French soldier trudges through the snow in this town trying to deliver a package. But he has forgotten the name of the street where he is to meet his contact. Moreover, he is suffering from a fever, which further confuses him and leads him to mix up fantasies, dreams, and memories from different times. He circles through the deserted streets, lost and disoriented. I imagine that most readers initially imagine that the box contains something of military importance and that the soldier intends to meet some military operative. In the course of the novel, we gradually piece together a rather different story along the following lines. The soldier helped a wounded comrade off the field at the time of the battle. Eventually, the man died. The "hero" of the novel is told that the dying man entrusted him with this box. He takes a telephone call from the dead soldier's father and arranges to bring the box to the father. However, the man has a different surname from the soldier, suggesting that perhaps the dead soldier was raised by his mother or was otherwise separated from his father. Indeed, in keeping with the motif of nonrecognition, the hero is not even entirely sure that the man actually is the soldier's father. (He also at one point mistakes someone for his contact [see 152] in another form of nonrecognition.) This is, then, an extremely attenuated version of the separation and reunion sequence. Perhaps the father and son have been separated since the son's youth. In any case, they are somehow now in separate families. The son would go to the father himself, but the son dies. Thus the reunion can only be by proxy—and even then it does not take place. Trying to save a boy, the protagonist is shot by the advance guard of the German troops. When he dies, nothing is done with the package—the contents of which are trivial anyway.[12]

In the usual manner of postmodern novels, *Dans le Labyrinthe* is, one might say, radically deflationary. First, the father-son relation is uncertain. Second, the son never reaches the father but merely sends a proxy with a box. Third, even the proxy does not reach the father. Finally, even if the box had arrived at its destination, it was filled primarily with letters from the soldier's fiancée—not anything that would seem to have a place with the father.

What is perhaps most interesting about this, however, is the way that recognizing the genre of the novel affects one's understanding of just what the novel is about. For example, it no longer seems to be solely or primarily a self-referential novel about novels. This is a very common reading of the work. Thus Leki states that this novel "is a study of the creation of a fiction," not only "the story of the soldier's wanderings through a city" but also "the trajectory of each element of the fiction through the text" (78–79). Rightly stressing the emotional force of the novel, Morrissette writes that "we feel simultaneously the anguish of the soldier lost in the labyrinth and that of his creator in the act of fashioning him" (184). But in a new generic context, *Dans le Labyrinthe* begins to take on a different shape as a novel about attachment, separation, and the always frustrated desire for reunion. The hero's experience of the city as all the same, as incomprehensible, is simply the experience of its complete alienness. The city is, first and foremost, not home. His sense of being lost and disoriented is precisely a sense of having no clear relation to home, thus no clear point of orientation. The repeated references to his being alone and to abandonment (see 28, 54, 160) all resonate with attachment separation. It makes sense in this context that his final act should involve him with a young boy who is separated from his own father due to the war.

Further, the constant repetition of the protagonist's feeling of being lost and alone (the first line of the book is "I am alone here"), and his wandering in the inscrutable, lonely streets, creates a sort of normalcy out of this extremely abnormal situation. It creates a sense that at least in the world of the novel, this is just the way things are. The brief moments of comfort—of being taken into a home, for example—are fleeting, familylike incidents in what is otherwise an enduring (or repeating) condition of isolation and alienation. The point suggests the absolute normalcy of our separation from everyone—parents, children, spouses—and the random, ephemeral character of our apparent unions or reunions with them. In short, the novel inverts our sense of what is normal and what is abnormal in attachment, going directly against the patterns of the attachment genre—or perhaps simply working out the implications of the genre's troubled conclusion.

Sexual Desire

Again, just as attachment may be isolated from romantic love, so too may sexual desire. This gives us stories in which the main motivating emotion for the protagonist is lust and at least one part of the main story line involves the pursuit of sexual congress.

The first thing I should emphasize here is that I am not referring to pornography. Certainly, some narratives of sexual desire may be pornographic. However, pornography is work that elaborates the representation of arousal triggers in such a way as to produce sexual excitement on the part of readers or viewers. Pornographic development is only one possible, local elaboration of the sexual narrative and is by no means intrinsic to it. Indeed, in canonical literature, the thematic and ideological orientations of sexual narratives tend to be virtually the opposite of pornography.

Like the other minor genres, sexual narratives seem to be somewhat limited in their frequency. Moreover, they are almost certainly less common than attachment narratives. This is unsurprising, given the preceding analysis of what makes a particular genre likely.

A pure sexual narrative may seem incident-rich, since sexual congress is a highly emotionally intense moment. However, sexual union constitutes a single incident or a single type of incident. It may be repeated. But it is not clear that there is much scope for other types of incident in sexual narratives. Thus it is not clear that they truly count as incident-rich. There is one obvious way of adding (nonsexual) incidents and expanding the main, recurring (sexual) incident into events and episodes—the elaboration of pursuit and seduction. This, however, remains limited in its emotional and narrative scope. It also tends to be ideologically problematic, even in highly patriarchal societies with straightforward male privilege. It is problematic because societies organize sexual relations in such a way as to make them stable, particularly with respect to reproduction and childrearing. It is not always easy to reconcile this with serial seduction. On the other hand, the expansion of the narrative in the other direction—to consequences of sexual union—does allow for the fuller development of further incidents, events, and episodes. Moreover, this elaboration is compatible with both dominant (e.g., sexually conservative) and resistant (e.g., antipatriarchal) ideological elaborations.

As to our other criteria, the most obvious way in which emotion intensification can occur in sexual narratives is through the enhancement of the desirability of the person pursued by the protagonist. This is clearly important and will appeal to at least certain sets of readers. However, it is also very limited. Intensification may also be developed through the consequences of the act.

Sexual stories do bear on commonly shared feelings. However, in their dissociation of desire from attachment, they do not necessarily reflect common emotion goals, since for many people the pursuit of sexual congress is bound up with the pursuit of attachment relations. On the other hand, the expansion of the narrative beyond coitus—the elaboration of events and episodes to consequences of sexual union—allows for a number of other emotions to enter.

The relevance of geographical organization is limited in purely sexual plots. However, when narratives are expanded to include reproduction, this may enter in more important ways.

Finally, as already discussed, there is a difficulty with idealized aspect normalcy. Sexual desire recurs, so no single sex act can define an enduring condition. Moreover, a single, lasting relationship seems to require attachment as well as desire. In this way, there is no clear point at which a sexual narrative will establish stable aspect normalcy even of a nonidealized variety.

Given these properties, it is not surprising that the sexual plot recurs in the canonical literature of various traditions, but it apparently does so only sporadically. This obviously increases the problem of data acquisition and synthesis for the investigator. It also decreases the likelihood that the production of sexual narratives will reach the critical point necessary to yield central or governing prototypes. Nonetheless, the cases I have been able to find do seem to share a remarkable number of features.

We might begin by distinguishing two different sorts of goal within the sexual plot. One involves the pursuit of sexual pleasure. We may refer to this as the sexual hedonism plot. The other involves the pursuit of offspring. We may refer to this as the fertility plot. In both cases, the non-normalcy motivating the protagonist leads him or her to pursue sexual congress. However, the precise emotion involved is different in the two cases. The motivating emotion in the first case is lust. In the second case, however, the motivating emotion is often a desire for power (through the social position of the child). In this way, the second type of sexual plot is frequently not precisely a sexual plot. Indeed, material gain may be the goal of sexual congress outside conception as well. For these reasons, in sexual narratives the fertility plot and related structures tend to be dependent on a hedonism plot (e.g., when the woman sees the man's lust as an opportunity for having children and/or gaining advancement).[13]

The hedonism plot has two obvious variants—that in which the sexual relations are consensual and that in which they are not. Both pose problems. If the relation is consensual, then the woman may be acting on sexual impulses, which may devalue her in patriarchal societies. If the relation is not consensual, then it is difficult not to view the man as behaving criminally. Even in societies that do not recognize a woman's right to her own body, no ordinary human being with intact empathic capacities can view sexual violence with indifference. (Admittedly, there seem to be shockingly many people whose empathic capacities are not intact. However, literary examples suggest that these are matched by people whose capacities are indeed functioning.) Even when everything seems to work out in the end, nonconsensual plots give us what Shakespeareans refer to as "problem comedies," stories in which we cannot be fully satisfied with the "happy" ending.

In order to isolate a general structure for the sexual plot, it is useful to begin by looking at examples. The story of Kullervo in the *Kalevala* presents a clear instance of some recurring patterns in sexual narratives. First, the man seduces the woman for purely hedonistic reasons. The woman succumbs for reasons that may include sexual desire but also involve worldly concerns. The seduction is almost entirely anonymous, proceeding without either party having a clear and accurate sense of the other's identity. This is consistent with the intercourse being almost purely a bodily encounter, a physical engagement without attachment. The result of this encounter is despair and death when they learn that they are brother and sister. The final point is obviously in keeping with the ideological operation of such narratives. Sexual narratives often solve the ideological problem of unregulated sexuality by the simple device of punishing the couple, frequently by death.

We find a very different case in the *Mahābhārata* story of Śakuntalā (in contrast with Kālidāsa's play), considered very briefly in chapter 3. In this case, again the man's interest is solely a matter of sexual pleasure. The woman's interest is simultaneously one of having a child and achieving worldly power. Thus the *Mahābhārata* story combines the hedonistic and fertility versions, assigning the former to the man and the latter to the woman. After sexual union, the man abandons the woman, who is suffering the consequences of the seduction in the form of pregnancy. She is thus forced to pursue her errant lover. When they meet again, the man tries to escape from any commitment to the woman and claims not to recognize her—thus we have the motif of not knowing the other person's identity (though the lack of knowledge is a pretense in this case). A spiritual event transforms the relation between the man and the woman so that it either becomes or at least imitates an attachment relation. A form of aspect normalcy that is typical of romantic plots—marriage—follows.

These stories begin to suggest a prototype along the following lines. A man experiences sexual desire, perhaps linked to a particular woman (specifically, a particular woman's body)—thus a particular trigger that shifts him out of aspect normalcy and motivates him to engage in the pursuit of a (sexual) goal. He approaches the woman and tries to seduce her, in part by exhibiting his own wealth or position. The woman sees this as an opportunity to have a child and/or to gain some of the man's power. They have sexual relations. The man then leaves. The woman experiences some consequences of this relation—either pregnancy or the humiliation of having had nonmarital sexual relations. She pursues the man. At one or more points in this sequence—either before the sexual relations or after or both before and after—there is some uncertainty regarding identity. There are three possible results of the woman's pursuit of the man. In the purely comic version, the lovers are united, often due to some spiritual or otherwise nonphysical event that shifts the relationship from a purely physical one to something that at least might involve attachment. This is particularly common when the woman is pregnant. In the tragic version, all the parties, innocent and guilty, die—the man, the woman, perhaps even a child. In what might be called the "justice" version, the guilty person dies (e.g., the man who deceived the woman or women), while the others live on in a new form of normalcy that may be more or less comic or more or less tragic.

In many instances of this genre, the man uses deceit to seduce the woman (e.g., by pretending to be her husband) or to avoid commitment afterward. Moreover, the man commonly initiates the seduction and the woman alone is interested in offspring. However, some versions vary in this. A fascinating example may be found in ancient Sumerian literature in the story of Enlil and Ninlil (see Jacobsen 167–68). In this case, Ninlil (the woman) clearly initiates the seduction. Moreover, the story involves mistaken identity and deceit. But these too are transformed. Specifically, Enlil deceives Ninlil into thinking that he is *not* her husband. (After they have intercourse initially, she clearly considers herself to be his wife.) Moreover, he appears to do this, not for hedonistic reasons but to produce further offspring. This sort of deception seems more likely to occur in the opposite direction, with the wife pretending to be some fascinating new conquest in order to seduce the husband. For instance, Shakespeare uses tricks of this general sort in the problem comedies *All's Well that Ends Well* and *Measure for Measure*.

We find some particularly emotionally complex and ideologically nuanced instances of the sexual plot in *The Tale of Genji*. Despite Murasaki's clear concern with attachment, it is undeniable that many stories in this work are simply sexual. Over and over, Genji or others become sexually fascinated with some woman—often due to such an unlikely event as the glimpse of a sleeve. As this suggests, Murasaki highlights the degree to which physical attraction itself is a sort of mistaken identity. It is not merely a matter of filling in unperceived aspects of the object. In at least some cases, it is a matter of creating the object entirely in one's imagination. Several aspects of Murasaki's development of the sexual plot are worth mentioning.

First, in many stories of this genre, "seduction" serves to rationalize rape—as when the woman says "no" but is represented as "really meaning yes." Murasaki does not rationalize the seductions in her book. Sometimes the women are willing—commonly for reasons of sexual desire and attachment. Sometimes, however, they are unwilling and are clearly forced or coerced. Readers today are often disturbed by this aspect of the work, feeling that Murasaki is condoning rape. However, these episodes are open to a feminist reading as well. In this interpretation, Murasaki is simply refusing to justify the ill-treatment of women. As Earl Miner put it, there are many points at which Murasaki's portrayal of Genji's action "implies an adverse judgment" that is "perhaps not so explicit as moralists might wish" but also is "less remote than Genji's wholehearted admirers think" (72).

Murasaki also tends not to have the women pursue the men who abandon them. Moreover, Genji himself does not flee the women with whom he has sexual relations. In this aspect particularly, it seems that Murasaki is working against a tacit prototype of male abandonment. This is clearest in cases where Genji discovers that he does not find the woman particularly attractive. But the point holds even for women whom Genji does find attractive. Consider, for example, Genji's collection of various women in his home. Many readers are likely to view this as simple harem building. But in fact men did not bring multiple wives into their home during this time. As William McCullough explains, there is actually no historical precedent for the situation in Genji's household. Moreover, it was seen as very "romantic" for the man to bring a woman into his home at all, since wives commonly lived in their family homes. The "most romantic" unions occurred when "the husband supplied the residence for an orphaned girl or a woman of inferior rank or circumstances" (138), as we find with Genji. Haruo Shirane isolates a literary pattern of the "amorous hero" who "moves from one woman to another." Shirane notes that Genji fits this pattern, but he is different from the amorous hero in works such as the *Ise Monogatari*. Specifically, "Genji compensates, at least in part, for the iniquities and suffering caused his women: he provides patronage and support, and finally builds for them the palatial Rokujō-in" (118). It is difficult to understand Murasaki's apparent admiration for Genji if we do not appreciate the contrast between Genji's behavior and common social practices of the period, as well as the genre pattern of the sexual story with its irresponsible "amorous hero."

Finally, one could think of *The Tale of Genji* as radically critiquing— analyzing and evaluating—both romantic and sexual narratives. In this book, Murasaki systematically examines the consequences of both lust and attachment, the relations they may have to one another, and the conflict between reality and imagination—including literary imagination—on these topics. Put in a different way, she tacitly revises common, patriarchal narratives—or narrative prototypes—of desire and seduction, friendship and romantic longing, suggesting the ideological problems with such views and narratives.

In the European tradition, the sexual plot is developed most obviously in Don Juan stories, prominently Tirso de Molina's *The Trickster of Seville and the Stone Guest* and the Lorenzo da Ponte's libretto of Mozart's *Don Giovanni*. In these cases, the presence of the preceding structure, in an elaborated form, is clear.

The culminating development of the sexual genre in the European tradition is undoubtedly Goethe's *Faust*. Like the variations on the story of Don Juan, the versions of the Faust story have a set of distinctive features, relating them to one another. These include the relatively unusual feature of Faust seeking knowledge as an initial goal. In Goethe's version, the frustration of a desire for ultimate knowledge leads Faust to suicidal despair, which is fortunately reversed by the reminder of Jesus's resurrection. This foiled self-destruction does, however, suggest that some spiritual realization will prevent Faust's ultimate destruction, even when he takes up the Lothario role in a sexual narrative. The point is reinforced by Mephistopheles's self-identification as a force or power (*Kraft*) that sets out to do evil but produces good (due to God's providence; see lines 1335–36). Faust does of course succumb to Mephistopheles's enticements. But we can expect that this will ultimately produce good.

Initially, Faust resists Mephistopheles, naming the devil's temptations as "food," "gold," a "girl," and "honor" (lines 1678–85)—thus the three primary happiness goals (with wealth [gold] and honor combined in the happiness goal of high social position or authority). But again he does ultimately enter into an agreement with the devil, and the pursuit of the "girl" quickly becomes his primary preoccupation. This is particularly important for our purposes for, as Jane Brown explains, "the love affair with Margarete" is "Goethe's original and most influential addition to the Faust legend" (92).[14] One may even see this addition as a crossing of the Faust legend with the Don Juan story. As Hawkes writes, "The Faust myth formally incorporates the parallel myth of Don Juan through the figure of Gretchen" (129).[15] Indeed, the incorporation of the sexual plot is in effect manifest structurally. Specifically, the first three sections after the prologue take up knowledge, despair, and salvation. Then there is a radical change with section 4. Hamlin notes that "Faust's drastic change of mood to pessimism and despair is unmotivated as the drama now stands. Goethe intended to write a disputation scene . . . that would have explained the change" (42n.2). It is not clear that such a scene would be effective. We are not faced simply with an alteration in Faust's attitude here. The change between these sections rather marks the shift from the so to speak "epistemic" (Faust) plot to the sexual (Don Juan) plot. The point is suggested by Faust's first speech in the scene, where he explains, "I am too old to be content with play, / Too young to be without desire" (lines 1546–47). This reference to his age is an elaboration that requires the restoration of his youth. That restoration, then, becomes a narrative prologue to the main sexual story.

In the scene immediately following Faust's transformation, we find Faust approaching Gretchen. He will soon appeal to Mephistopheles, a version of the usual helper figure, for assistance. In keeping with the general spiritual context of the Faust story, the emotional cost—thus emotional force—of the seduction is intensified by making Gretchen "so dutiful and pure" that she has "mere nothings to confess" to her priest (lines 2611, 2625). In the usual manner, Faust uses flattery, false promises, and wealth to seduce Gretchen. Initially, in keeping with a recurring pattern, Gretchen is protected by the prudent advice of her mother. However, she finds a helper in Marthe. This eventually allows for her union with Faust. Again, in a standard scenario, Faust leaves and engages in other pursuits (e.g., a temporary attraction to "The Fair One" or "The Beauty" [*Die Schöne*] during the Walpurgis Night festivities). Gretchen is, as we might expect, left behind with the consequences of the liaison.

Goethe seems to draw on the justice version of the sexual plot when he compounds Faust's sexual crimes with apparent murder. Specifically, Faust kills Gretchen's mother and her brother. This prepares us for Faust's eventual condemnation and death (in the manner of Don Juan). But this also appears to contradict the initial characterization of Mephistopheles as an unwitting agent of providence, with its implication of Faust's eventual salvation. The same point holds for Gretchen. Rather than pursuing Faust, she drowns her child, thus evidently condemning herself. On the other hand, there is complexity in all these events. Faust may be unaware that the sleeping potion he gives to Gretchen will kill her mother. He is challenged by Gretchen's brother and follows Mephistopheles's instructions, possibly not realizing that he will kill his opponent in doing so. Finally, Gretchen seems to have killed her child when not entirely sane. In each case, the crime seems to have been committed with limited awareness, thus with only partial responsibility. The events are not wholly accidental nor entirely outside the understanding of Faust and Gretchen (e.g., both Faust and Gretchen know that there is something amiss about giving her mother a potent drug). But at the same time, Goethe emphasizes the limits of that responsibility. The same point holds for the feelings of both Faust and Gretchen. Faust is seeking sexual pleasure. But at the same time, he seems to have genuine affection for Gretchen, if affection that waxes and wanes with his particular circumstances. Similarly, Gretchen is attracted by Faust's wealth. But her relation with him is not simply a matter of self-interested calculation (in contrast with, say, the *Mahābhārata*'s Śakuntalā).

This complexity of motivation is bound up with a certain complexity of knowledge. Indeed, the play suggests that our knowledge of other people and even of ourselves is always incomplete and often misdirected in its incompleteness. This gives the work greater unity than it might initially have seemed. The initial focus on the impossibility of achieving absolute knowledge is not simply a separate story somehow tacked onto a sexual plot. It is closely related to the themes of the sexual plot, as developed by Goethe.

Ambivalence and epistemological uncertainty extend to the ending of part 1. Faust tries to aid Gretchen by helping her escape from prison—an act of compassion and even love, but not entirely unproblematic, given that she has evidently committed a crime. Gretchen acknowledges the murder sufficiently to suggest that it was not entirely unconscious, though at the same time she evidences clear signs of madness, particularly with regard to the child. Recognizing her at least partial guilt, she refuses to escape. Instead, she calls on God to be her judge. In the famous final lines, she is accepted by God, while Faust is borne away by Mephistopheles. Particularly given the legal context of Gretchen's condemnation, this suggests the justice version of the plot, where the wronged woman is saved and the exploitative man is damned (cf. Hamlin 133n.5). However, Gretchen's salvation is the result of a simple appeal to God and a divine act of forgiveness. That divine intervention also recalls the comic version of the plot. But in this case, it does not lead to a romantic elevation of the couple in marriage (as we find in the *Mahābhārata* story of Śakuntalā). Rather, here the divine intervention in effect shifts us out of sexual and romantic narratives entirely to a story of salvation. Perhaps what is most interesting for our purposes is that this shift crucially involves forgiveness. In this way, the ending reverses the justice version of the sexual plot, substituting forgiveness for punishment. On the other hand, Faust remains with Mephistopheles. At this point, then, Goethe's version remains ambivalent and uncertain, pending the developments of part 2.

Faust and the Don Juan stories present some connection between serial seduction and criminality, along with instances of revenge or attempted revenge. Thus they provide an apt transition to crime and revenge plots.

However, before going on to these we should briefly consider another aspect of narrative production raised by *Faust*'s differences from the sexual story prototype. Up to this point, I have treated prototypes as if they are solely positive models for the development of new stories. In this account, a given author's prototype of the sexual plot combines with various other mental structures, processes, and contents to generate a particular story. The same point holds for prototypes generally. When asked to imagine a bird, I rely on my prototype for a bird, imagining something roughly robinlike. Where my prototype has wings, I imagine wings; where my prototype has a little beak, I imagine a little beak. If I am drawing a picture, I may vary the prototype—change the size of the beak, vary the colors of the wings, and so on. Nonetheless I am still generating the basic imagination "positively" from the prototype. That is, I am repeating the properties and relations from the prototype in the imagined bird, even as I vary them.

But I may also treat the prototype in another way. Take a very simple example. Suppose I am writing a story and creating the character of a politically engaged female English professor. I may draw on my prototype positively. Indeed, I almost certainly will draw on it positively. However, in order make the character more distinctive, I may feel it is not enough simply to specify standard traits, fill in gaps, or vary the prototypical properties within common limits. I may instead choose to go entirely outside the prototype. Given the semantic organization of our minds, one obvious way of doing this is by using the prototype or certain aspects of the prototype negatively. In other words, I might invert or negate properties and relations given in the prototype. For example, suppose my prototypical female English professor is a Democrat. In this prototype, the Democratic commitments of this prototypical person are centrally a matter of women's rights, somewhat less centrally a matter of other social policies, and most distantly a matter of certain sorts of fiscal policy. Unreflectively, I might be inclined to create a woman character who supports abortion rights but is relatively indifferent to capital gains taxes. However, I might draw on this prototype negatively, making the woman an opponent of abortion rights.

For our purposes, the crucial point here is that we have many story prototypes, major and minor. These may interact in various ways and particular authors may develop them positively or negatively. When the author draws on a prototype negatively, he or she may create a work that relies on the reader drawing some (usually implicit) connection with that prototype. In this case we may say that the negative prototype is not only a source but a *subtext* for the story. Note that this does not require any self-consciousness about the prototypes. It requires only an unreflective sense of expectation. We have already seen some likely examples of this. Genji's nonabandonment of the women he seduces appears as an admirable characteristic only if we have the implicit expectation that he would abandon them. This expectation is part of a tacit narrative prototype. Another example of this sort may be found in *Faust*. In that case, the ambiguous responsibility for various crimes and the complexity of Faust's feelings for Gretchen are significant primarily by contrast with the subtext of the sexual plot prototype (manifest, for example, in *The Trickster of Seville*, where the seduction and abandonment are more unequivocal and uncomplicated).

In sum, prototypes can serve as positive or negative models for the creation and reception of new stories. The negative models particularly may serve as subtexts as well. Finally, given the structure of the human mind, we would expect certain conjunctions of prototypes to occur with particular frequency. We would then expect subtextual uses, not only within one prototype category but across some related categories as well. For example, we might expect the romantic and sexual narratives to be connected in this way—and this is what we find. For example, in the sexual plot the perfidy of the seducer is enhanced by a tacit contrast with the romantic hero, whose vows are a sincere expression of attachment. We see the reverse as well, with the sexual plot serving as a subtext for the romantic plot. Though perhaps less common, this use of a subtext is arguably the more interesting and interpretively consequential. *Abhijñānaśākuntalam* provides an excellent example, with its subtext cued by the *Mahābhārata*. Terence's *Hecyra* is in some ways an even more striking instance. It includes both the romantic and the sexual plot. The two works form a nice, contrasting pair as well. Kālidāsa's play draws on the sexual plot to celebrate romantic love and contrast it with mere seduction. In contrast, Terence's play makes it difficult for us to take seriously the romantic story of Pamphilus and Philumena after Pamphilus's scurrilous behavior in the sexual plot with Bacchis.

Crime, Revenge, and the Law

In its most basic form, the revenge story begins with some grievous personal offense against a protagonist, prototypically the murder of an attachment figure. This offense leads a protagonist to pursue the goal of punishing the perpetrator of that offense. The legal investigation genre begins with some grievous offense against society (which is commonly a grievous offense against an individual as well). In this case, however, it is not the individually offended party but the state or some representative of society that undertakes a (presumably) unbiased inquiry into the case, determining the nature of the crime, the perpetrators of the crime, the degrees of responsibility, and the appropriate punishment.

The two genres are distinct. They have different protagonists and different animating goals. However, they are also closely related in an obvious way. For that reason, we may treat them together. The relation between the genres is brought out with particular force in Aeschylus's *Eumenides*. In that play, Aeschylus famously celebrates the establishment of a legal system replacing personal retribution. Indeed, the two genres are in effect brought together in the *Oresteia*, such that criminal investigation and judgment are seen to develop out of revenge. Moreover, this development involves a resolution of conflicts in the revenge narrative and the establishment of an idealized aspect normalcy (of social stability and justice) through the criminal investigation narrative. At least this is the obvious way of interpreting Aeschylus's trilogy. In fact, I modify this reading considerably below. However, it does serve to suggest why it makes sense to treat these two genres together. Indeed, I follow Aeschylus, not only in combining these two genres but also in beginning with revenge. However, perhaps unlike Aeschylus, I seek to draw conclusions that apply across both prototypes.

As already noted, murder is the primary provoking incident in both genres. However, the revenge plot comes in two varieties. Or, rather, like all genres, it comes in many varieties. However, these varieties are all not equally significant. Two varieties seem to achieve particular prominence. The most prominent is the murder plot. However, there is a plot of sexual violation as well. As Griswold explains, referring to English Renaissance cases, "Usually the initiating action is the murder of a kinsman or lover [note the attachment relation], although sometimes rape, incest, or adultery sets a revenger in motion" (59). This sexual revenge plot is important on its own. But it is also important because it often enters into the murder plot as well, providing additional narrative sequences, further specifying details of character and story, and so on. (As Griswold notes, "Sex and death are linked explicitly and repeatedly" in English Renaissance revenge tragedies [61].) I therefore outline the sexual violation version before turning to the murder version.

Again, the murder and revenge plot prototypically concerns an attachment relation. Unsurprisingly, the sexual violation and revenge plot concerns a sexual relation, but that sexual relation appears typically to have attachment elements as well. This is a result of the usual processes of emotion intensification. When a provoking incident involves harm to the protagonist, our response to that harm is intensified when the harm involves a sense of betrayal. Readers are likely to be more intensely affected by a case of adultery when the wronged spouse is attached to his or her erring partner than when he or she simply feels entitled to sexual ownership of that partner.

Very briefly, we might outline a sexual revenge plot along the following lines. Aspect normalcy begins with a couple, commonly a husband and wife. This normalcy is interrupted by sexual infidelity. The infidelity is discovered, often due to the woman's pregnancy if she is the adulterous partner. This obviously requires some prior sexual separation of the married couple so that it is clear the child is the result of adultery. The discovery leads to the victimized spouse feeling humiliated. In response, the spouse may respond with violence, killing one or both adulterers. This revenge is almost always in some way excessive and often encompasses innocents. The point is obvious in cases where there has not been any adultery—as in *Othello*, which follows this format closely. However, it may be the case even when there has been adultery.

Consider, for example, *The Drum of the Waves of Horikawa*, by the great Japanese playwright, Chikamatsu Monzaemon. Hikokurō's wife, Otane, has been unfaithful with a drum teacher. Hikokurō kills her and her lover. Though both acts of revenge are successful, the ending is obviously problematic. Chikamatsu makes clear that the sexual infidelity was a minor crime, the result of diminished capacity for decision and peculiar circumstances. Whatever one thinks of the act, it is difficult to believe that either the drum teacher or Otane merited death for this transgression. Moreover, it is difficult to understand just what benefit is gained from these acts. Indeed, Hikokurō would clearly have welcomed any excuse not to kill Otane, and surely Hikokurō's family will be deeply distressed by his death. Finally, there is one clear criminal in this story and he is the one character who does not suffer at all. Indeed, he is largely responsible for both the initial transgression and the subsequent revenge. This actually introduces a plot element found in both revenge and criminal investigation narratives—the punishment of those who are proximally responsible for committing a crime, but the nonpunishment of those who are ultimately responsible for it.

Again, sexual violations occur not only on their own but in murder narratives as well. Often they are simply an addition to the crimes of the villain. However, there are cases where the murder revenge plot—or indeed the criminal investigation plot—incorporates a fuller version of the sexual revenge plot as well, as for example in Middleton and Rowley's *The Changeling*.

These two plays together begin to suggest the main elements of the revenge prototype—or, rather, a prototype that we may construct from the somewhat uneven appearances of revenge plots cross-culturally. Again, we will focus on the far more prominent murder version.

The main characters of the revenge plot are, of course, the victim, the villain, and the hero. The villain may be divided into the person who plans and initiates the murder or is otherwise ultimately responsible for it and the person who performs it. One or both may be involved in sexual transgressions as well. The victim and the hero stand in some sort of attachment relation, often that of parent and child. The victim may appear after his or her murder as a restless ghost or may be referred to as such without actually appearing in disembodied form. The plot commonly begins with the motivation for and plotting of the murder. The murder initiates the hero's quest for revenge. This quest involves an investigation that may lead temporarily to a false attribution of blame. Though temporary, the false attribution may have dire consequences. For example, it may result in another murder. Moreover, there may be additional, incidental murders that occur on the way to the achievement of revenge. The revenger does eventually find and kill the person who committed the murder. However, the person ultimately responsible for the murder may go unpunished and/or the hero may himself die, sometimes through suicide. (Griswold summarizes this final trend in English Renaissance works, explaining that "revengers succeed, but then are killed" [64].) The result is an ending that is often deeply unhappy.

Probably the most famous revenge plot in world literature is *Hamlet*.

Though of course not every element is present, the play follows the pro-totypical structure closely, while varying it in significant ways as well. *Hamlet* is a heroic tragedy as well as a revenge tragedy. However, our concerns here are only with the latter. The story treated in the play begins with Claudius killing his brother and marrying his sister-in-law, Ger-trude. Thus we have a murder and associated sexual violation. The murder deprives Hamlet of his father (an attachment relation) and to some extent impedes his relation to his mother as well. Indeed, Claudius's marriage to Gertrude is in some ways a part of a sexual revenge plot, where Hamlet feels betrayed by his mother's sexual behavior rather than by a spouse's. (The connection is suggested particularly by his subsequent treatment of Ophelia, most obviously through his insistence on women's sexual incon-stancy [III.ii.137–38].)

One interesting twist in *Hamlet* is that our hero does not know for certain that a murder has actually occurred. He learns of the murder only through the testimony of the ghost. Of course, one difficulty of the play is that it is not entirely clear how the ghost knows about the murder. After all, he was asleep when Claudius poured the poison in his ears. But in any case, Hamlet has no other means of determining that this was a murder. (For example, the elder Hamlet was not discovered hacked to death with a sword.) This gives the restless ghost a larger part in the play than is com-mon and it yields some of the subsequent complications.

A version of the usual mistaken identification occurs when Polonius hides in Gertrude's room. Hamlet kills him, erroneously believing that he is Claudius. Among other things, this sets in motion a second revenge plot involving Polonius's son, Laertes. Subsequently, there are other incidental murders as well—the killings of Rosenkrantz and Guildenstern and, at the end, the poisoning of Gertrude (though the outcome of this poisoning may be seen as consistent with the sexual revenge plot). The culmination of the play does involve Hamlet killing Claudius. But he dies in the course of the revenge—killed by Laertes, as the result of Laertes' own quest for revenge, which itself results in Laertes's death. To put it mildly, these events do not lead to idealized aspect normalcy.

Before considering further examples, we should outline the criminal investigation narrative. This is, again, closely related to the revenge nar-rative. However, there is one crucial difference. In place of the personal revenger, we have a representative of society in the judge or other investigator. This judge comes in two common varieties—upright and corrupt. Other than that, the sequence is in many ways the same. There is a murder, enacted by one character perhaps due to the instigation of another character. The investigator sets out to find and punish the culprit, who is often guilty of some sort of sexual deviance as well. There may be a mistaken identification. If the "mistake" is the result of corruption, then it may have dire consequences—specifically, a second murder. If it is an honest mistake by the upright judge, it probably will not have such consequences. There may be incidental killings along the way, but these are likely to be further killings by the villain or the result of corruption, not acts by the upright judge or hero. In the end, the criminal is found and convicted—however, the punishment may be confined to the agent of the crime, missing the initial instigator. (Needless to say, in the investigation plot, the hero does not usually die at the end with the villain.)

We have already seen a good example of this structure in *The Injustice Done to Tou Ngo*, in this case embedded in a sacrificial narrative. (Minor genres are often embedded in works partially organized by one of the major genres. Generally, minor genres seem to be less autonomous, that is, less likely than major genres to appear as the sole organizing structure of a story.) Like other criminal justice stories, *The Injustice Done to Tou Ngo* works out rather better than most revenge plays. The criminals are punished and the just judge is not responsible for any deaths other than those of one or two of the criminals.

The superiority of legal investigation over individual vengeance is of course just what one would expect for ideological reasons. One would expect societies to develop representations of justice that favored official modes of criminal investigation and punishment and disfavored individual initiatives outside the control of the state. As Simkin put it, referring to Elizabethan England in particular, "Anyone who felt compelled to enact private revenge was expressing, implicitly or explicitly, dissatisfaction with the state's ability to intervene in an effective manner" (2). Obviously, the degree to which revenge is allowed will vary among societies. Moreover, authors will differ in their precise attitude toward both revenge and criminal justice. (For example, Molly Smith's valuable work on *The Spanish Tragedy* indicates that Thomas Kyd's critical representation of revenge simultaneously suggests an implicit critique of criminal justice.) However, over a broad enough range of cases, one would expect dominant ideology to result in a general preference for social justice when there is a conflict between social and individual punitive action.

On the other hand, this division is not at all as absolute as one might expect. Just as the epilogue of suffering and the romantic genre challenge standard social hierarchies and divisions, the development of social investigation often includes at least some degree of ambivalence. Indeed, such ambivalence is not entirely absent from *The Injustice Done to Tou Ngo*. In this play, we see two instances of criminal investigation. One is corrupt; one is not. That does mean that we have a more or less untainted hero, Tou T'ien-Chang,[16] which may occur less frequently in revenge plots. However, it also means that social investigations are corrupt and destructive half the time in this play. The final result, then, is not that different from a standard revenge narrative. The number of people killed may be smaller. But in both cases the process of punishment serves to increase rather than decrease deaths.

Before going on to consider some further cases, we should quickly review the degree to which these genres satisfy the criteria presented above for likely universality. We have already noted that idealized aspect normalcy is often impossible in these genres. This is because the initiating incident, in cases of murder, is an irreversible loss. Punishment of the guilty parties cannot revive the dead. At best, it reduces the anger of those left behind while leaving the grief unaffected. Moreover, the usual development of these narratives suggests that violence invariably produces further violence, thus further degradation of people's lives. Once violence begins, it is likely to be repeated. When it is repeated, it is likely to cause further irreparable harm, thus making a return to normalcy of any sort (not to mention the achievement of idealized normalcy) impossible for increasing numbers of people. Finally, even (perhaps especially) in the criminal investigation plot, only the proximate agents of the murder are likely to be punished. In this sense, not only are innocents harmed but some of the guilty almost invariably remain unpunished. Indeed, these works sometimes suggest that there is not a sharp line between the innocent and the guilty. (A good example of this point may be found in the Mayan drama, *Rabinal Achi*.)

Though weak in terms of aspect idealization, both genres do pretty well by most of the other criteria. They are incident rich in treating the murder of loved ones, and often adulterous betrayal as well. They are readily expandable into events and episodes involving plans for the murder, examination of the clues as to who committed the murder, and so on. They are open to emotional intensification through treatment of attachment, shame, and other emotions. They clearly involve a change from normalcy, the pursuit of a goal, the possible interruption through the opposite of a goal (e.g., accusing the wrong person), and achievement of the final goal (revenge or social punishment). The goals also seem to be broadly shared. With respect to the revenge genre, we all commonly feel the impulse to punish anyone who has harmed us. With respect to the criminal investigation genre, no one seems to want crime to escape systematic social consequences.

Ideology is particularly interesting here. Both genres seem open to a variety of dominant and resistant ideological uses. Thus the criminal investigation drama may be used to support the view that the state operates fairly and in the interest of the people or that it does not. If it does not, it may operate too violently or not violently enough. Parallel points hold for revenge, particularly when it is paired with state-based criminal investigation. A particular story may suggest that revenge is always deleterious, is a necessary supplement to a weak judicial system, and so on. (Of course, this is not to say that all ideological uses are equally common. They are not.)

There is some limitation on the degree to which either or both types of experience are common. This obviously varies socially. Some societies seem to have more overt or familiar cases of revenge than others. Some have more highly developed legal systems than others. On the other hand, all societies are likely to have some instances of revenge and all people are likely to have engaged in acts of small-scale revenge. Societies differ a great deal in the frequency of murder. But all are likely to have murder, and most people have some familiarity with the unexpected loss of a loved one as well as some personal harm done by someone else. These two experiences are enough to give all of us a rough (and admittedly very diminished) sense of what it is like to have a loved one murdered. On the other hand, relatively few people are likely to have had that specific experience outside war—and in cases of war the emplotment of the events is different. As to legal processes, these are common enough in most societies that many people may be broadly familiar with them and have adequate interest in the way they operate, even if they have never been directly involved themselves. Thus the emotional consequences of the genres in these areas are somewhat mixed. (There is also little that fosters geographical organization in these genres.)

Beyond the usual criteria, I should mention that these genres seem to lend themselves particularly well to problem-solving activity on the part of readers or viewers. Problem-solving is a pleasurable activity for most people. It is not specific to literature, but it does seem that we are particularly interested in problem-solving when it is "off-line" (i.e., when it does not have real world consequences for us) and when it involves people (rather than, say, mathematical objects or physical forces). This contributes to the recurrence of these genres in popular literature. However, the very nature of problem-solving is likely to make these genres less likely to be the objects of repeated reading and sustained study. Insofar as our primary pleasure in reading a particular work is figuring out the ending, our pleasure is almost certain to decrease appreciably once we have read that ending.[17] Thus we might expect these genres to be more prominent in popular, ephemeral works than in enduring canonical works.

We may now return to instances of our two genres. We have already seen some revenge stories with troubled endings (e.g., *The Drum of the Waves of Horikawa* and *Hamlet*). There is a revenge component to the Kullervo story from the *Kalevala* that illustrates these points nicely as well. Kullervo vows vengeance against his uncle for the slaughter of his family. He later discovers that his family is alive, but he undertakes the revenge anyway. Here, it is as if the living family substitutes for the appearance of the ghost. Indeed, like a ghost, they are finally and truly dead after Kullervo enacts his (now pointless) revenge. Specifically, he returns from his revenge to find his family gone forever. He ultimately kills himself.

The revenge tragedy was particularly popular in the English Renaissance. In addition to the plays cited above, one could include here, for example, Kyd's *Spanish Tragedy*, one of the seminal texts of English Renaissance drama. This is a very intricately plotted play that includes most of the elements we have been discussing.

Revenge drama also flourished in Japan. We have already discussed a case from Chikamatsu. Historically, perhaps the most popular drama in Japan has been a revenge story, *Chūshingura*. The links between this story and the general revenge structure, including the difficulties of the final "resolution"—a mass suicide of the revengers—are straightforward to anyone familiar with the work.

As already noted, criminal investigation narratives commonly have a very similar organization and similarly problematic endings. Just as revenge plots were developed with particular intensity and skill in Japan and England, court dramas were particularly characteristic of Chinese writing. Many of these works centered on the legendary Judge Pao, a figure of near perfect judgment and unswerving rectitude. Yet even in these cases, the endings are often uneasy.

Consider, for example, *The Flower of the Back Courtyard* by Cheng T'ing-yü. Though this plot is particularly convoluted, it manifests the usual structure. In the end, most of the guilty parties are punished. However, the person who instigated the initial crime achieves her purpose and is unharmed. Due to this and due to the irreversible deaths that occur in the play, the ending still remains ambivalent.

Though particularly prominent in certain times and places, the criminal investigation genre is far from absent elsewhere. I mentioned a Native American case (*Rabinal Achi*). Western examples of the genre—if usually with less ambivalent endings—are ubiquitous in popular literature. But they also appear in paradigmatic works. Perhaps the most famous example is *Oedipus the King*. Here we have a murder and a sexual transgression. We also have the common revenge plot motif of the son being charged with finding the murderer of his father. Of course, the son does not realize this and acts as an impartial official investigator. Moreover, we have a particular emotional intensification since the son is also the murderer—and of course the sexual violation is incestuous. Oedipus proceeds through an investigation where, in keeping with the mistaken attribution element of the plot, he makes accusations against Creon and Teiresias. He eventually discovers his own guilt, leading to Jocasta's suicide and his own blinding and exile.

The sacrificial plot in which Oedipus's criminal investigation narrative is embedded does suggest that this punishment will end the plague and famine, as announced at the beginning of the play. But the play does not dwell on this. Rather, the ending focuses on the suffering of the two figures who acted wrongly, but did so without knowledge of what they were doing, thus with limited responsibility (a recurring motif in these stories). Moreover, the revelation of Oedipus's crime is connected with the revelation that he was abandoned as a child. This points generally toward the personal history of people who have committed crimes, a history that at least partially explains the crimes, even if it does not excuse them. It also, and perhaps more importantly, suggests that responsibility is more general than criminal investigations allow. In a way, those ultimately responsible can never be found and punished, for there are simply too many of them. Finally, the conclusion of the play stresses the separation of Oedipus from his children and the helplessness of the girls who will now in effect be orphaned. This makes salient the harm to innocents that follows even when a malefactor is justly punished, for his or her family and friends suffer too, particularly when the punishment is harsh.

Criminal investigation narratives are found in modernist and post-modernist work as well. Kafka's *The Trial* is a paradigmatic modernist work, and one that draws prominently on the criminal investigation plot. It is particularly noteworthy for our purposes since not only its conclusion but its entire development indicates the fallibility of the criminal justice system. The entire prosecution of K. suggests mistaken identity. There are repeated references to corruption as well as instances of sexual misconduct. In this case, the main problem with the legal structure, however, appears to be a matter of bureaucracy. This layering of authority ultimately serves to prevent rather than systematize the acquisition of information; it serves to perpetuate errors rather than eradicate them. It has the advantage that it slows the entire process, perhaps reducing the destructive consequences of individual judicial corruption. But it also makes the process more or less impervious to correction. In the end, "the trial" produces nothing more than an act of murder by the state.[18]

But not all canonical revenge and criminal investigation narratives are as strongly ambivalent or tragic in their conclusions. If these genres incline toward at least partially negative endings, what deflects that tendency, what shifts the conclusion to something that is relatively (though, most often, still not entirely) unproblematic? Here we might consider some narratives of this sort.

The first is a story we mentioned earlier. Tirso's *Trickster* (and da Ponte's *Don Giovanni*) obviously follow the structure we have been considering. There is a villain who commits murder, separating loved ones, and who is guilty of sexual transgressions. There is mistaken identity and false punishment. There is a restless ghost. The ending of this story is not really uplifting, since so much suffering has gone before. However, we hardly regret the final condemnation and death of Don Juan—even though the latter is, in effect, a form of revenge carried out by an individual agent. Why is this? I think here we should take our cue from Tolstoy, recalling his epigraph to *Anna Karenina*: "Vengeance is mine; I will repay, saith the Lord" (xv). The revenge is put in the hands of the ghost. For religious viewers, this means that retribution is put ultimately in the hands of God (since a demonic ghost would presumably not have the power to kill). For nonreligious viewers, it means that retribution is, in any case, removed from fallible human agency. Put more simply, there is no act of human revenge here that might give rise to ambivalence.

A second example we might consider is from the *Popol Vuh*. Indeed, it is a section of the book to which *Rabinal Achi* alludes in its own (ambivalent) ending. Here, Hunahpu and Xbalanque descend into the underworld to revenge the murder of their father and uncle, One Hunahpu and Seven Hunahpu. They achieve this end by engaging in multiple murders and resurrections. This is in part a very unusual use of the mistaken punishment motif. Note that, since the victims are revived, the misdirection of the revenge has no lasting consequences. Eventually, the murderers of One Hunahpu and Seven Hunahpu ask that they be killed and resurrected. These murderers are One Death and Seven Death. Hunahpu and Xbalanque kill them, but do not revive them. I take it that this is relatively unambivalent in part because the victims of revenge are not human and in part because death is presented as reversible.

These works represent one set of cases in which ambivalence may be lost—when there is some supernatural involvement such that (a) the agents of the revenge are viewed as superhuman, thus divine or associated with the divine; (b) the objects of the punishment are dehumanized though still understood as threatening (thus typically having greater than human powers); and/or (c) the irreversibility of death is mitigated by supernatural power. These conditions are not innocuous. As the history of racism shows, representing enemies as inhuman is a common strategy for undermining empathy and thus facilitating atrocities. Similarly, social violence is often justified by an appeal to divine will. In this way, these qualifications to ambivalence are not confined to literary response.

Of course, even if these stories do not have "protagonist ambivalence," as we might call it, they do lack idealized aspect normalcy. In other words, even if they are relatively unambivalent about the punitive actions taken at the end, they remain troubled.[19]

There are, however, some cases of these genres in which the ending is idealized. These too seem to be Tolstoyan, but in a different way. These cases suggest that the only genuine resolution comes with forgiveness. In the case of the renowned Nō drama, Zeami's *Atsumori*—a sort of revenge story—that forgiveness comes from the victim. Forgiveness may also come from society. One might expect that this is what one would find when aspect normalcy appears in criminal investigation narratives. In connection with this, it is fitting to conclude with what is perhaps the most important paradigmatic work of court narrative in the European tradition, Aeschylus's *Eumenides*.

The *Eumenides* concludes Aeschylus's *Oresteia*. In the first play, Clytemnestra killed Agamemnon, at least in part as revenge for his murder of their daughter, Iphigeneia. In the second play, Orestes revenged his father's murder by the highly ambivalent act of killing his mother. Now he is pursued by the furies seeking vengeance for the murder of Clytemnestra. The *Eumenides* concerns the replacement of this cycle of personal revenge with the objective pursuit of justice by a disinterested court representing the society generally. It is widely—and no doubt correctly—read as a play celebrating a system of social justice over a system of personal retribution (see, for example, Goldhill 49 and Spatz 90). Given the horrible sequence of crimes that have occurred in the preceding plays, it hardly seems possible that the conclusion would involve idealized aspect normalcy. However, to some extent, it does. We have witnessed a seemingly endless cycle of murder and retribution. The judgment of the court puts an end to this. It promises that the cycle will not continue. In this sense, aspect normalcy is idealized relative to the self-generating mutual destruction of revenge.

But is this curtailing of violence only a matter of substituting public processes for private ones? I have no doubt most of us would agree with Aeschylus that courts are better than vendettas. But there is another key feature of the *Eumenides* that makes the cycle of retribution end and that contributes crucially to the idealized aspect normalcy at the conclusion of the play. Orestes is not condemned. He is forgiven by the court. Moreover, he is forgiven in a decision that suggests courts should generally favor leniency or forgiveness—for in a split vote on Orestes's guilt, the goddess Athena herself casts the tie-breaking ballot for acquittal.

These two minor genres, then, indicate that judgment and punishment are problematic whatever their source. In literature—and more importantly, in real human life—the troubles of guilt and anger are often resolvable only by forgiveness.

Conclusion

The analyses in chapter 3 suggested that, beyond the major cross-cultural genres, there should be other recurring literary genres connected with other goals and associated emotion systems. Those analyses also suggested that these genres may not be as constant and widespread in literary canons as the major genres. Specifically, given the account of romantic tragicomedy, we would expect distinct genres for attachment and sexuality. In addition, given the goals and structure of the heroic and sacrificial plots, we would expect both guilt and anger to give rise to genres or at least literary tendencies that might develop into genres.

As this reference to "developing into" genres suggests, there are two ways in which genres arise. The first or "generative" origin of genres is through happiness goals. This is the source of the major prototypical genres treated in chapter 3. The other way genres develop is "empirical." This formation of genres results from our spontaneous, unself-conscious categorization of works and our implicit averaging of properties of those works. Many localized and transient genres (e.g., the Hollywood "gross-out" comedy) develop in this way. The "minor" genres are the result of both processes in combination. For example, the attachment system is important in generating goals for protagonists. However, those goals may manifest themselves most frequently as subsidiary elements in major genre narratives. Readers may spontaneously group together stories that share nonsexual attachment goals. They may then implicitly abstract a separate prototype from these works, yielding the empirically derived attachment genre.

There are many variables governing the likelihood of a given genre being widespread cross-culturally and transhistorically. Beyond their recruitment of highly motivational emotion systems into shared emotion goals, more widespread genres will tend to have the following characteristics. They are potentially incident-rich, with incidents readily expandable into events and episodes. They are easy to elaborate in such a way as to produce empathically communicable emotional intensification. Their plot elements may be readily integrated into the ordinary story structure of normalcy, deviation from normalcy, and so on. They are open to recruitment by both dominant and resistant ideologies. They easily incorporate the emotional division of space. Finally, they treat a type of deviation from normalcy that is widely shared by readers or viewers.

As predicted, there are at least four genres that occur cross-culturally and transhistorically, but not with the same frequency as the major genres. These are narratives of attachment, sexual desire, revenge, and criminal investigation. (There probably are other recurring genres as well. The preceding analyses suggest that these genres should occur in different times and places. They do not suggest that no other genres will do so.)

The attachment genre treats the separation and reunion of parents and children. The main story typically involves a lengthy separation caused by one of the parents or by some outside force. This is commonly followed by one party seeking the other and finding him or her after some errors or misrecognitions. The reunion, however, is often not fully successful and the parents and children may end up separated again. One main difference in subtypes concerns whether or not the parent abandoned the child and, if so, whether it was for selfish or selfless reasons.

The sexual desire genre usually treats a man's sexual pursuit and abandonment of a woman, often with deliberate deceit or other misrecognition at some point. The woman is left with the consequences of the affair—for example, a child. She pursues the man in turn. The couple may end up united, particularly if there is some supernatural agency involved. However, one or both may end up punished for the transgression. Moreover, even when the couple is united, it is not always clear that this is an entirely beneficial outcome—particularly in cases where the initial sexual encounter was not consensual.

The most emotionally intense form of the revenge narrative is initiated by the murder of some attachment figure. The murderer often commits a sexual transgression as well. In some cases, there is a difference between the person who commits the crime and the person who is ultimately responsible for it. The protagonist pursues the murderer, commonly making some mistake in identification on the way to exacting his or her revenge. That mistake may lead to the loss of innocent lives. In the end, the protagonist kills the person who committed the initial murder, often dying in the process. The person ultimately responsible for the initial murder may go unpunished.

The criminal investigation plot is very similar to the revenge plot. However, there is one key difference—the protagonist is not the injured party. Rather, he or she is a representative of the larger society. One variation in the story concerns whether the judge is corrupt or honest.

As these brief summaries make clear, the endings of these four genres are often problematic. It is very uncommon to achieve idealized aspect normalcy in any of these genres. In the case of attachment narratives, this may have to do with the parent's guilt in abandoning the child or the indelible harm that resulted from the separation. More generally, however, it is because the generational difference between parents and children necessarily makes their reunion unstable, specifically temporary (in the terminology of chap. 2). Sexual pursuit narratives may be connected with the initial perfidy of the seducer or the impossibility of completely isolating sexual union from its consequences, which are often onerous for the woman. Moreover, even in the best cases, sexual satisfaction is necessarily of very limited duration and cannot in itself give rise to an enduring condition. In the case of the revenge genre, it is because the initial death is irreversible; the quest for retribution has commonly led to the deaths of further innocents; the successful revenge does not in fact ameliorate the situation; and the person ultimately responsible for the initial death often escapes punishment anyway. The criminal investigation genre is much the same, except that there is less of a tendency for innocents to be killed—unless of course the judge is corrupt. There is a partial mitigation of ambivalence when the punishment is divine, those punished are dehumanized, and/or the death is reversible (thus not really death). The revenge and criminal investigation genres suggest the possibility of an aspect-idealized conclusion in one condition—the simultaneously emotional and practical condition of forgiveness.

Finally, genre prototypes may be used either positively or negatively to guide the composition of new works. In other words, an author may develop his or her story on the basis of, say, a sexual prototype or in tacit opposition to that prototype. Moreover, the new text may rely for its thematic implications or its emotional or ideological impact on its relation to that prototype and the reader's or audience member's (self-conscious or unself-conscious) experience of that relation. When this occurs, we may say that the use of the prototype is "subtextual."

Afterword

Stories and the Training of Sensibility

In the previous chapters, we considered the ways in which emotions (or emotion systems) make stories. We examined the ways in which incidents, events, episodes, general story structures, works, and genres are a function of emotional processes. But if stories and emotions are so closely interrelated, one might ask, are all the effects in one direction only? In other words, do emotion processes only affect stories, or can stories affect emotion processes as well?

It is, of course, obvious that stories can affect emotion episodes. Everyone knows that stories can make us cry or laugh, get us angry or frighten us. Indeed, there would be no point in emotion intensification if the results had no consequences for readers' feelings. The question is whether operations of our emotion systems can be affected by stories outside the narrow context of emotion episodes.

Here, too, there are some obvious ways in which the answer is yes. If I watch a sad movie, it can affect my mood for hours or, off and on, for days. This is not entirely insignificant. But it is still a matter of relatively short-term consequences. Are there longer-term consequences, consequences that are significant for our lives more generally or for society?

This is, of course, really the topic for another book. However, before concluding this examination of narrative and emotion, it may be valuable to at least suggest some ways in which we might begin to think about this topic. After all, it has potentially significant implications for a range of things, from what we read to how we teach, and even to how we explain the value of literary study generally.

But before considering this issue, we need to have some sense of the longer-term implications of emotion itself, whether in relation to narrative or not. Antonio Damasio has influentially argued that the European tradition has wrongly denigrated emotion. Emotion, according to Damasio, is not the antithesis of reason, something to be denied and suppressed.

Rather, Damasio tells us, it is a crucial part of reason. Without emotion, we are hopelessly irrational, condemned to make terrible decisions, to engage in imprudent and immoral actions.

Fundamentally, emotions are evolved mechanisms that approximate survival functions. For example, fear allows us to respond quickly to threatening situations, when more elaborate processing would mean death. As Damasio explains, coming to a decision via "rationality" alone may take "an inordinately long time." We may even "get lost the byways of . . . calculation" and be unable to come to a decision (*Descartes' Error* 172). Emotion solves this problem. But, as with all other adaptive mechanisms, emotions do not fit their functions exactly. For example, fear leads us to flee some situations that are not dangerous and does not lead us to flee some situations that are dangerous. (Of course, Damasio acknowledges that emotion has both beneficial and deleterious effects on decisions and actions; see *Descartes' Error* 191–95.)

More generally, it would not be right to say that emotions are part of reason and lead us to make good decisions. Rather, emotions motivate us. In doing this, they are honed by evolution. Therefore, in a wide range of situations—particularly situations parallel to those in the ancestral environment where the adaptations evolved—emotions will incline us to avoid threats and pursue opportunities. Crucially, emotions do not operate only on actual experiences. They operate on simulations or imaginations also. Indeed, among humans, one major adaptive function of emotions is that they contribute to our decisions about what to do in the future. In other words, our emotions crucially motivate our action regarding situations that are not present. Obviously, if I see a lion on the street, I will feel afraid and will act on that fear. But in my real life, I am perhaps just as likely to base my actions on imagination as on actual perception—whether I am deciding about a vacation safari (do I feel frightened by the prospect of seeing lions that are not in cages?) or about asking my boss for a raise (do I feel too much anxiety in imagining myself standing before my boss's door?). Emotion is bound up with our decision-making processes. Indeed, it seems that our decisions are primarily not a matter of strict cost-benefit calculation, but of imagination and emotional response.

Suppose I am trying to decide whether or not to ask my boss for a raise. I could try to gather statistics on the frequency with which he or she grants raises based on requests, the subsequent career paths of people who ask for raises, and so on. For example, it may be that, statistically, the boss primarily gives raises to people who ask for them—or it may be that the boss primarily gives raises based on productivity reports and not on requests. I could do this sort of statistical analysis. But I probably will not. Rather, I will probably imagine different scenarios—asking and being refused, asking and being rewarded, and so on. Insofar as there is a cost-benefit calculation here, it will be a tacit and emotional cost-benefit calculation in which I have an overall emotional response to the imagined scenarios. That overall emotional response, inflected by particular events at work that day, will (or will not) motivate me to ask for the raise. Indeed, this is true even if I do the statistical analyses. Those analyses simply serve to guide my imagination, which produces the emotional response in the usual, perceptual manner.

In short, Damasio is certainly right that emotion is crucial for the decisions we make and the actions we undertake. But it is important not to overstate the benefits of emotion. My (emotion-based) decision to ask the boss for a raise may be just the wrong decision. Moreover, even if it is the right decision, my emotional attitude when asking (too cocky?, too nervous?) may bias the boss against my request. If the boss says no, my irritated response may harm our relationship.

Both the positive and negative points are crucial for thinking about the relation between narrative and emotion. If emotion is profoundly consequential for the way we make decisions, including important life decisions—indeed, if it is at the very center of those decisions and our subsequent behavior—then whatever affects our emotion systems is itself profoundly consequential. Second, if our emotions are not already preset to result in ideal decisions—if they are fallible—then whatever affects our emotion systems has the potential to improve our decisions and behaviors. In other words, these points together suggest that there may be some validity to the Romantic view that literature can humanize us, that art can "train the sensibility" (see, for example, Schiller on "aesthetic education"). More exactly, literature bears on our emotions, and emotions are—fallibly but inevitably—bound up with our thought and action in the world. At least in principle it seems possible that, if art can affect our emotions, it can thereby benefit the way we live our lives. Of course, it could also harm the way we live our lives. But either way, art has potential for affecting the real world beyond the satisfaction and enjoyment it provides during the time we are experiencing it.[1]

But, of course, this is true only to the degree that our emotional processes are plastic. If our emotions are simply fixed genetically, then we just have to make do with what we have. It would be nice to improve our partially functional mechanisms—but we are stuck. It is only if there is leeway in the operation of our emotion systems, some possibility for alteration, that narrative (or anything else) can have effects, positive or negative.

Given the model of emotion presented earlier, we may isolate several sorts of plasticity in human emotion. Again, according to that model, there are innate sensitivities (e.g., to facial expressions). These are probably not open to a great deal of modification. Moreover, any alteration would presumably have to proceed by surgical, chemical, or related processes, not storytelling. In addition to innate sensitivities, there are critical-period experiences that orient our subsequent emotional lives. These are undoubtedly most affected by social interactions and bodily experiences—thus such things as the degree to which one's caregiver is around (e.g., when one is hurt). On the other hand, once the child learns language, there may be critical-period experiences that are affected by narratives. This is an empirical question for early childhood research.

The other two sources of plasticity are more obviously relevant to our concerns. The first of these is emotional memories. Again, emotional memories are formed throughout life and they may affect our emotional responses to new situations. Narrative may have consequences here because stories produce emotion episodes. Any strong emotion episode is likely to be stored as an emotional memory. As such, it may have effects on one's emotional behavior. This is perhaps the less interesting way in which stories can have consequences for our emotional lives. The effects here are, roughly, the effects of propaganda. On the other hand, there is sometimes something to be said for propaganda. My almost puritanical opposition to alcohol is due primarily to personal experiences (e.g., of alcoholic relatives). But my comparable opposition to illegal drugs is based almost entirely on aversive responses to movies. I suspect that if I ever saw someone injecting heroin, I would have a disgust (gag) reaction of the sort that I experience mildly when I think back on the film *Requiem for a Dream*.

One difficulty with the cultivation of emotional memory, however, is that it is not always easy to calculate the precise emotional effect of a work. For example, I do not have the same strong emotional aversion to anyone using marijuana. In part, this is a rational realization that marijuana and heroin are not the same in their effects, even if they both fall under the category of "illegal drugs." But it is also in part due to the fact that antimarijuana films tend to be highly implausible, thus to have the emotional effect of satire. Indeed, my emotional memories of marijuana in films seem to be largely mirthful, which would give marijuana precisely the opposite valence. (Obviously, there are further complicating factors here, relating to friends, more general cultural tendencies, etc. But that only reinforces the point.)

Perhaps more importantly, the operation of emotional memories is quite mechanical. It is, in effect, a form of conditioning. As such, it is open to "extinction." In other words, it is relatively easy to overcome the effects of emotional memories produced by films. After seeing *Requiem for a Dream*, Jones may initially have a strongly aversive response to seeing someone inject heroin. However, even a few exposures to such injections will almost certainly habituate him to the sight. Moreover, emotional memories do not always operate with the same force. At times, they are very powerful; at other times, they are relatively weak. One's other attitudes and interests also fluctuate. If Jones is around people injecting heroin, there are likely to be moments when he finds it repulsive, but other moments when he finds it attractive. If it happens that he is offered heroin at one of the moments when he finds it attractive, there is a decent chance that Jones will try the drug. From that point on, emotional memories of the direct experience (along with changes in the endogenous reward system) are likely to overwhelm any effects derived from emotional memories produced by Jones's empathic experiences of stories.

In short, stories may have effects through emotional memories. Moreover, these may not be inconsequential. However, these effects are sometimes difficult to determine beforehand. Moreover, the material circumstances of one's life are likely to be a far more important factor in guiding one's emotional responses and decisions—not simply in the case of drug use, but generally.

Nonetheless, the real if limited impact of emotional memories is not without consequences for the study of literature. Insofar as strong emotional experiences in literature affect behavior, just what films we show or what books we read may have consequences for our students. I am not speaking of some sort of censorship here. But we do not show our students every movie ever made and we do not have them read every book ever published. We always select. In general, then, it seems reasonable to select works that tend to discourage imprudent or inhumane behavior and not to select works that encourage imprudent or inhumane behavior—for example, works that develop strongly aversive emotional responses (typically disgust and/or fear) to members of racial or ethnic groups that are subject to social discrimination.

The point about social out-groups is worth expanding on briefly. If we wish to oppose, say, racism, there are different ways we might go about it in our selection of stories. For example, one common approach is to cultivate compassion for the disabilities that go along with out-group status. This is important and should not be dismissed. But it can result in a patronizing attitude which, though better than race hatred, is hardly ideal. Another common option is to show the strength and ability of out-group members, even when faced with discrimination. This too is valuable. However, it may foster voluntarism, the view that even the largest social impediments may be overcome with enough effort.

Of course both these possibilities return us to the issue of effect. Indeed, even my earlier reference to racist works raises this issue. The effects of literary works are not set once and for all. Our emotional responses to novels, poems, stories, and films may be affected by analysis, reflection, or breadth of reading. In this way, completely ignoring racist, sexist, or other discriminatory works in our classes may not really be politically or ethically desirable. (Given the influence and technical or other significance of some discriminatory works, it may also not be historically or intellectually desirable.) Rather, it is sometimes important to read works that present ideologies that we find repugnant, in part so that we can discuss those ideologies with students. In other words, it is valuable for students to develop reading strategies that allow them to read critically—thus questioning aversive portrayals of blacks, Jews, Arabs, women, and even aversive portrayals that many of us might favor (e.g., of Christian fundamentalists). There are ways in which our emotional responses—including our empathic responses—may be attenuated or enhanced. In part, such modulations result from interpretive processes—just the sort of processes we cultivate in literary study. In this way, our emotional responses to stories—thus our emotional memories—are not only a matter of what is in the stories but also of how we think about what is in the stories.

This brings us to the final component of my emotion model, which is appraisal or imaginative elaboration. This is, again, a complex process that expands our direct experiences into causal sequences, including possible outcomes. Indeed, even the recruitment of emotional memories to a current experience is in part a matter of just how we imaginatively unfold the precedents and consequences of that experience. This is the area of our emotional response that is perhaps the most plastic. It is plastic in part because it relies on changeable cognitive contents to organize those inferential processes. Those cognitive contents include smaller units, such as situation prototypes (e.g., going to a restaurant). But they also include larger units, such as story prototypes. Again, our emotional responses seem to be particularly affected by very short-term expectations, thus expectations that are much more temporally limited than a story. However, we select and organize those current perceptions, memories, and working anticipations within larger units, including story prototypes. In this way too, the Romantics seem to have been right. One important part of the way we relate to the world is a function of the way we imagine the world—or, more technically, the way our imaginative elaboration of incidents and events selects, segments, and structures perceptions, memories, and possible trajectories of action and experience.

However, this leaves us with the question of just how these narrative structures operate and how they might be understood as improving (or worsening) our thought and action. Again, empathy is a key part of our emotional response to stories. Empathy is also deeply important for ethical judgment and response, as a number of theorists have pointed out (see, for example, Prinz). Empathy is, then, the obvious point of connection here. More exactly, stories seem particularly well suited to affecting our emotional responses to other people, thus our social and personal interactions. One crucial aspect of our emotional responses to other people, both prudential and ethical, involves our willingness and ability to simulate other people's situations and thereby to some degree experience the emotions they are likely to be feeling. Because literature can foster or inhibit our willingness and ability to simulate the thoughts and feelings of fictional people, it might in principle have the same general sorts of effect on our responses to real people. In fact, to a great extent our experience of real people is simply an impoverished version of our experience of fictional people. We get glimpses of real people in various activities, hear them say certain things, receive reports about them—but we do not have a reliable narrator who can tell us just what they are thinking or how they are feeling.

There are obviously many complex issues surrounding ethics and empathy. One cannot possibly discuss those in a brief afterword. I will therefore simply assume that, in general, empathy is ethically desirable. There is, however, one problem with empathy. It tends to be limited. One way in which it is limited is in being channeled to what we see, know about, are aware of—"those who are close," as Suzanne Keen puts it (19). If Jones, an American, thinks about the war in Iraq, he is likely to think about American soldiers and their suffering—because he knows people who have gone there or who have children who have gone there, because he was an American soldier himself, and so on. He is unlikely to think about the suffering of Iraqis.

This is in some ways related to Coleridge's distinction between mechanical fancy and creative, organic imagination. Jones's thoughts about Iraq are, in Coleridge's terms, a matter of fancy. They proceed along the lines of well-established, highly salient connections. One function of narrative in this case would simply be to broaden associations beyond the familiar, the immediate—to change and expand what is salient. In another idiom, it is to make cognition creative, to move it outside the confines of ordinary connections among ideas, concepts, memories (on creative cognition, see Smith, Ward, and Finke; see also Sternberg).

Like the development of emotional memories, the broadening (or narrowing) of empathic associations results from our experience of individual, particular works. As such, it is related to the development of emotional memories and some of the same points apply to both. For example, here too we would generally wish to deemphasize works that cultivate disgust or fear with respect to particular racial or ethnic groups. However, the main implication of the empathic narrowness problem is that the types and objects of empathy portrayed in the works we read should be as diverse as possible. In other words, this problem points us toward precisely the sort of global study of literature that underlies the present volume. On the other hand, literary and cultural traditions are not the only axes of diversity that are important here. Nor would the list be complete if we added sex, race, and ability. The axes of possible diversity are countless. Indeed, it is important that they not be confined to particular identity categories, such as race and nation, for that will tend to make those categories more salient and consequential. Rather, the crucial thing here is that the contexts, agents, tasks, impediments, and so on, change in different ways in different works.

In keeping with the preceding observations, writers such as Martha Nussbaum have stressed the value of novel reading for the cultivation of empathy. Keen has recently argued against this optimistic view of the impact of novel reading. Both make valuable points. But there seem to be several problems with this debate. First, the discussion is somewhat too focused on reading literature as such rather than on the particular works that might be read by particular groups. When writers such as Nussbaum refer to books they find particularly valuable, this tends to be a matter of celebrating individual novels, not a matter of systematically distinguishing types of novel and types of reader. To take an extremely simple case, one imagines, for example, that Northern Irish works that feature good Catholics and bad Protestants are rather more valuable for Protestants to read than for Catholics to read, and vice versa.

Of course, even this is overly simple. Reading literary works with "good" representatives of out-groups can contribute to stereotyping, which in fact inhibits effortful simulation of individual experience. Moreover, "good" representatives of out-groups are, in practice, all too often represented as victims of other, "bad" out-group members. For instance, with respect to India, Europeans and Americans seem to be particularly fond of literary works and films that show just how awful Indian men are to Indian women, how upper castes brutalize lower castes, or how Hindus hate Muslims. These works present us with victims that we pity along with (commonly stereotypical) villains that we despise. Often, while appearing to challenge identity categories (e.g., the traditional opposition of European or American versus Indian), they in fact reinforce identity categories (e.g., good moderns vs. bad traditionalists, or even good culturally American people [including Indians] vs. bad culturally traditionalist/ Indian people).

But this is not to say that there are no benefits that result from reading literary narratives generally. Recent studies by Keith Oatley and others show that reading narratives has both short-term and long-term benefits for emotional intelligence, which is to say, our skills at interpreting, simulating, and responding to emotions (see Oatley "Communications").

Thus such reading should make us better at empathizing, at least once we engage in effortful simulation.

Finally, there is the issue of possible actional outcomes. Keen worries that, despite all her reading of stories, she did not do more for the victims of Hutu massacres beyond writing checks (xxi). She later considers whether people who helped Holocaust victims read more novels (23). These are good points for those who are starry-eyed about the utterly transformative value of art. However, this assumes a sort of heroic model for ethical action.[2] There are three problems with such an assumption. First, when heroic action is warranted, it requires extraordinary devotion, skill, highly unusual conditions, and so on. It requires a rare confluence of circumstances, experiences, talents, and propensities that have multiple sources. Second, heroic action is not always warranted. Suppose more people had felt more strongly about reports of Hutu barbarism. I assume the result would have been some sort of U.S. air strikes against Hutus. It is far from obvious that this was a better option than writing checks—or than doing nothing. The famous case of this is Yugoslavia, where NATO bombing clearly increased the slaughter (see Chomsky, and Herman and Peterson). Finally, heroism is the wrong model anyway. Cultivating skills in empathy and encouraging the effortful simulation that promotes empathy are first of all valuable in ordinary acts of daily life. These range from simple matters of consideration regarding other people's interests and emotional responses, through decisions about hiring, through electoral politics. Judging the benefits of emotional skills by heroism is like judging the benefits of jogging by reference to escaping unharmed from muggers.

Put differently, societies afford different opportunities for humane and for inhumane action. The most we can reasonably expect from the cultivation of empathy through literature is that it will foster a greater inclination to choose the humane options and refrain from the inhumane options. Both are very broad and diffused throughout our personal, social, professional, and political lives.

Of course, this does not mean that inhibitions on empathy are not a serious problem. They are. Nor does it mean that they can be easily overcome simply by reading literature. They cannot. Indeed, literature can operate to enhance one's commitment to particular identity categories (e.g., those of nation, race, or gender) and the in-group/out-group divisions they codify. These divisions appear to inhibit empathy more severely and fixedly than mere familiarity or saliency. Jones's lack of empathy with Iraqis is probably not due solely to their unfamiliarity and relatively lower saliency in his experience. There is undoubtedly a more active, if unself-conscious, suppression of empathy due to a fundamental identity division between Americans and Iraqis or Europeans and Arabs or Christians and Muslims (or all three).

Research indicates how common this sort of intergroup response is. For example, Caucasian subjects showed greater amygdala activation when seeing Caucasian subjects showing fear in comparison with African American faces showing fear (see Ambady et al. 213). This suggests that test subjects responded more strongly with parallel emotion, thus empathy, to in-group members. The point extends from feeling to action. Preston and de Waal note that "in experiments with adults, human subjects who witness" other people receiving shocks "offer to take the shocks . . . if their similarity is manipulated with demographic descriptions," thus in-group categorization (16). Indeed, things are worse than this suggests. Kunda reports research that "the mere exposure to an African American face can suffice for other Americans to activate the construct of hostility, which, in turn, can lead them to behave in a more hostile manner" (321). In video simulation research discussed by Ito and colleagues, "behavioral results showed a consistent bias against blacks relative to whites. Participants were faster and more accurate in 'shooting' armed blacks compared with armed whites. By contrast, they were faster and more accurate in 'not shooting' unarmed whites than unarmed blacks" (198, though this concerns target categorization, not intergroup relations).

As Suzanne Keen puts it, actually understating the problem, "Empathy intersects with identities in problematic ways. Do we respond because we belong to an in-group, or can narrative empathy call to us across boundaries of difference?" (142). Here, Keen is referring to an issue raised earlier in her book. "Patrick Colm Hogan," she writes, "regards categorical empathy (with characters matching a reader's group identity) as the more prevalent form, while situational empathy, the more ethically desirable role taking, depends upon a reader's having a memory of a comparable experience, which is never guaranteed. If situational empathy alone, as Hogan argues, leads to the ethics of compassion, the quick-match categorical empathy looks weaker and more vulnerable to bias through ethnocentrism or exclusionary thinking" (96).

I would now formulate the division slightly differently. In keeping with the preceding discussion of emotion, I would say that emotion contagion is triggered by spontaneous mirror-neuron responses to another person's emotion expressions. Empathy is made possible by imaginative simulation of another person's experience and results from the usual innate, critical-period, and emotional memory triggers that are part of that simulation. Emotion contagion is distinct from empathy but commonly contributes to it (and to helping behavior).[3] I would no longer consider categorial identification as being a form of empathy per se. (Categorial identification is an individual's definition of himself or herself in terms of an in-group based on a category such as race, nation, or religion.) Rather, I would say that categorial identification enhances the likelihood of emotion contagion with the in-group and diminishes that likelihood with the out-group. This is due to a mental set that biases our emotional response toward being parallel with that of in-group members and complementary to that of out-group members. (If Jones is angry at Smith, then Doe has a parallel emotion if he becomes angry at Smith, but a complementary emotion if he becomes afraid of or angry at Jones.) Moreover, such identification fosters effortful simulation of the experience of in-group members while inhibiting that simulation with respect to out-group members. Such effortful simulation is crucial, because as Davis points out, citing experimental research, "instructions to imagine the affective state of a target frequently trigger a process which ends in the offering of help to that target" (145) or in "inhibit[ing] aggressiveness" (162). Thus I would now see only one sort of empathy, with a number of variables governing its initiation, development, and final intensity. In-group/out-group division or categorial identification is one of the most important variables.

As already noted, individual literary works may foster categorial identifications. But they may also weaken those identifications by cultivating empathy across group boundaries. Again, that is why diversity in reading and in literary discussion is important—particularly reading that genuinely cultivates empathy across group boundaries (rather than simply concealing those boundaries by presenting us with, say, good Americanized Indians and bad traditional Indians).

At the same time, the issue of identity categories brings us to a topic of more direct relevance to the preceding chapters—genre. It seems clear that, in general, some genres are more likely to cultivate categorial iden-

tifications than others. Indeed, such cultivation is perhaps the main ideological function of heroic plots. As such, heroic narratives are likely to be
particularly politically problematic. Sacrificial narratives too can cultivate
categorial identification. In any case, they certainly tend to encourage
harmful forms of blame assignment in cases of communal distress. In
contrast with heroic plots, romantic narratives commonly work directly
against identity categories. Again, identity categories—class, caste, race,
nation, ethnicity, family—are among the primary obstacles to the union
of the lovers, and romantic plots almost invariably incline us to empathize
with the lovers. Moreover, while there is sometimes divine intervention
in romantic narratives, the lovers commonly face human problems and
they respond to them in human ways. This sets them apart from sacrificial
narratives by making the causality generally comprehensible and control-
lable, not a mysterious and frightening matter of divine wrath. Moreover,
in romantic narratives, the blocking characters are commonly members
of the lovers' families and thus are unlikely to be dehumanized—or if they
are dehumanized, their relation to the lovers prevents a generalization of
this to a racial, ethnic, or other category. This suggests that a pedagogical
variant of the 1960s slogan might be a good rule of thumb: Teach love,
not war!

Of course, here as elsewhere, things are not as simple as this suggests.
The problem with romantic plots is that their concerns are perhaps too
purely personal, and they tend to focus on characters whose material
circumstances are rather good. There are romantic plots that treat lovers'
inability to wed due to financial burdens. But even then the focus often
remains on inhibited attachment and desire. These are important, certainly. But they are not everything. For example, romantic plots tend simply to
ignore the crucial social issues raised by the heroic and sacrificial plots—
war and hunger. In this way, romantic plots are ill-suited to cultivating
our empathic elaborative imagination with regard to these experiences.
In contrast, the epilogue of suffering may function to challenge the value
of even a war that "our side" has just won. In this way, a work such as
Euripides's *Trojan Women* would seem to have a greater value in cultivating empathic imagination than countless romantic plots. Indeed, when
we are dealing with out-groups, it is not clear that even main heroic plots
are problematic. For example, it is not clear that European Americans will
be more inclined to support U.S. invasions of foreign countries because

they have read *The Epic of Son-Jara*. In addition, despite problems with standard identity categories, we may not wish to entirely condemn all identity categories. In particular, we may feel much less troubled by some elective identity definitions (i.e., identity definitions that one can choose), such as antifascist versus fascist.[4] As to the sacrificial plot, it is possible to have secular versions of this narrative that serve to cultivate empathy with out-groups and that do not rely on fearful and incomprehensible causal principles. For example, Kamala Markandaya's *Nectar in a Sieve* is in many ways a sacrificial narrative—but it is a secularized version of that narrative, pointing toward economic policies, not deity-appeasing sacrifice, as a solution to hunger.

I am still inclined to stress the special value of romantic narratives. However, it is clear that the major prototypical genres all may have value in cultivating empathy. Moreover, once again, that cultivation is inseparable from diversity of reading and from the development of critical reading practices.

What, then, about the minor genres? Obviously, they can have significant emotional effects. Those effects may be beneficial or deleterious in various ways as well—depending, as always, on how we interpret and concretize their individual stories. Indeed, though I have referred to them as "minor," the genres treated in chapter 4 may, at least in certain respects, manifest greater wisdom than the dominant genres, particularly the heroic and sacrificial plots. Specifically, the minor genres—at least in their canonical and paradigmatic forms—recurrently suggest something about human feeling, human knowledge, and human morality. They point us toward the emotional centrality of attachment, not the group pride of heroic plots. They indicate the inferential centrality of fallibility (manifest in recurring mistakes about identification and blame), not the mystical knowledge of sacrificial narratives. They imply the ethical centrality of forgiveness, not the blind loyalty to king and country of the heroic plot nor the divine demand for harsh punishment found in the sacrificial plot.

Perhaps the difference is the result of, so to speak, a greater ideological coercion affecting heroic and sacrificial plots. Of course, the minor genres are not free from dominant ideological uses, as many popular instances show us today. Indeed, in recent years it may be that criminal investigation narratives are the primary repositories of dominant ideology, at least in the United States, where they have contributed significantly to, for example, the acceptance of torture. Nonetheless, historically, these genres do not appear to have been so directly bound up with the institutional authority of state and church. The result may be that the minor genres have more accurately expressed human aspiration and experience as they really are—ambivalent and uneasy, except in the act of forgiveness—rather than expressing the ways in which human aspiration and experience might best be channeled into the service of social elites.

In the preceding chapter, we saw reasons why the endings of works in minor genres are more likely to be problematic. But these reasons appear to apply almost equally well to heroic and sacrificial plots. Indeed, the epilogue of suffering suggests that there is always a tendency for heroic plots to manifest just the sort of ambivalence we see in the minor genres. This leads me to question my previous assumption that the default mode for narrative is comic. It is, of course, the case that agents seek happiness. Thus stories are about the pursuit of happiness and aim toward comedy. But I wonder now if the heroic and sacrificial plots do not equally tend toward outcomes that are ambivalent. Put differently, the development of the minor genres leads me to ask if the epilogue of suffering is not the default ending for the heroic plot. Perhaps this epilogue is present only sporadically, not for emotional, inferential, or ethical reasons, but due to its relative inconsistency with dominant ideologies—and thus, to put the point somewhat crudely, its incompatibility with the interests of those who are paying for the story.

If this is true, it suggests a view of life that may at first appear somewhat grim, for it indicates that ambivalence, not happiness, is the outcome of most human endeavors. But on reflection, the situation may not be so grim at all. Happiness can be achieved. But it is not achieved through violence—war, sacrifice, revenge, the subordination of the individual to the leader or to the group. It is not even achieved by just legal proceedings. In some cases, one or all of these may be necessary. But the results will at best be mixed, emotionally conflicted. Thus we are well advised to avoid them whenever possible. In contrast, happiness comes from love, from forgiveness, and from a recognition of our common human fallibility.

Notes

Introduction

1. Note that a story based on sexual goal pursuit is not necessarily or even usually pornographic. Pornography involves the depiction of sexual relations, which may occur in any genre.

2. This idea extends back at least to William James's seminal "What Is an Emotion?"

3. The latter simply require that the relevant gene expression not be blocked by abnormal experiences (e.g., brain trauma) or unusual interference from other genetic instructions (e.g., due to mutation). Technically, neuronal pathways formed in this way may or may not be "activity dependent," which is to say, dependent on activation from experience. However, they are not constrained or specified by *particular and variable* activity patterns.

4. This possibility of convergent development is one of the things that opposes my approach to that of Franco Moretti. Moretti sees the literatures of separate cultures producing "diversification . . . from their origins" (116). He claims that "sameness appears . . . sometime around the eighteenth century" (116). I agree with Moretti that the sameness that has developed since the eighteenth century is the result of economic forces in an international, highly unequal market. However, my contention throughout this book is that there is an enormous degree of sameness in stories across cultures. Much of this sameness is due to cross-cultural emotional patterns. They are in part innate. But their commonalities are also due in part to convergent social developments (e.g., in childrearing techniques) leading to common critical-period experiences or emotional memories.

5. Kay Young's *Ordinary Pleasures* presents an unusual case here. Young combines different theoretical orientations to focus on the pleasures of marriage. In doing this, she does draw attention to an important recurring, functional component of stories—the lovers' dialogue. This is, in fact, a consequential part of romantic plots cross-culturally.

6. Appraisal theories see emotion as resulting from the evaluation of experiences in relation to goals. Perception theories stress direct perceptual triggers along

with emotional memories. As should be clear from the preceding outline, my approach is basically perceptual. One task of chapter 1 is to reconcile this account with appraisal theory.

7. The study of universal narrative patterns has grown into a significant research program in recent years. For an accessible overview of some current trends, see Hsu.

8. I usually use the word "ideology" in the pejorative sense. If I use it in the neutral sense, I signal that usage—for example, by referring to "resistant ideology," which is to say a guiding set of ideas that opposes the dominant ideology of a given society in a given area.

9. I have devoted another book to this topic, *The Culture of Conformism*.

10. The idea of networks has recently been taken up in a roughly Marxist context by Hardt and Negri. They use the concept in a nontechnical, indeed highly metaphorical way (much as Jameson uses the concept of a Freudian unconscious). Moreover, they use it to refer to a contemporary development, a "new form" (*Multitude* xii). In contrast, I use the term in the sense that it is used in network theory. (For an accessible introduction to network theory, see Buchanan; for a briefer summary, see Ferrer i Cancho.) It is a complex of unequally distributed connections, such that any given state of the system is the result of the precise nature of the connections at any given moment. Since the connections are unequally distributed, any given aspect of the resulting state will depend more on some "vertices" (or connection points) than others. This makes it possible to refer loosely to class domination, class hegemony, etc. But by this account, classes are not ontologically fundamental explanatory categories. They are abstractions from shifting network states. Moreover, in keeping with network theory generally, I see this as a transhistorical and cross-cultural principle of social interaction. Indeed, given the technical use of the term, it is difficult to see how it could characterize one period and not others, how it could arise as a "new form."

1. Before Stories

1. In this chapter, I consider several passages from *Anna Karenina* in detail, exploring the ways in which emotions organize time and space in this novel. There has of course been an enormous amount of extremely valuable criticism written on *Anna Karenina*. It has covered such issues as class, the embedment of the novel in the Russian political economy of the time, the relation of the events and discussions in the novel to philosophical debates, the operation of formal techniques such as defamiliarization, the development of character, realism, moral themes, and so on. (For an overview, see chapter 7 of Turner.) However, relatively little has focused on emotion, and none (as far as I can tell)

has treated the specific issue of emotion systems organizing narrative space and time. The critical works treating emotion have tended to focus on love and/or sexual desire. For example, Adelman discusses both topics lucidly, addressing Tolstoy's concern with separating love from sex. In connection with this, Adelman discusses some scenes that I consider below (e.g., the opening of the novel) and he brings out aspects of these scenes that I do not touch on. However, Adelman's account of emotion is formulated in terms of ideas that preceded the enormous growth in our understanding of emotion over the last two decades. Moreover, it does not address such issues as the formation of minimal narrative units. Similar points could be made about Tapp's analysis of "the desirous sexuality which drives the plot" (341). Tapp makes a convincing case that motion in the novel is bound up with emotional arousal or agitation, often of a sexual sort. Her discussion is illuminating, but obviously on a different (if not entirely unrelated) topic.

2. This and subsequent citations of the text refer to the Carmichael translation unless otherwise noted.

3. Clearly, space is important in our stories, even for spatiality (e.g., a beloved's distance in space is commonly correlated with the lover's sense of isolation or exile). For a very illuminating discussion of the reader's construction of space, in some respects complementary to the present discussion, see Ryan's "Cognitive Maps."

4. Alternatively, we may feel that we would be the target of aversion if our shameful act were revealed—hence the possibility of private shame, discussed by Lewis ("Self-Conscious").

5. As Alexandrov remarks, "Dolly acts as though she cannot fully understand [the letter] and turns to Stiva to ask what it means. In other words, in her distraught state she is willing to rely on Stiva's mediating reaction, on whatever context or code (or lies) he may bring to an utterance that she hopes does not have the fixed meaning it appears to have" (75).

6. Admittedly, there are complex interpretive issues surrounding precisely how we are to understand and apply the epigraph. These are brilliantly explored by Alexandrov (see 67–70 and 120–22). However, as Alexandrov concludes, "All of these alternatives remain plausible, and it is doubtful that there is any way to decide among them. But perhaps it is not necessary to choose, for the simple reason that all the possibilities evoke the same ethical norm, which thus continues to hover over the novel" (123).

7. In addition, perception theorists sometimes refer to appraisal. Thus they may appear to follow an appraisal account. However, that is because the term "appraisal" is often used to refer to any sort of neurocognitive processing, and is thus opposed to some simple, behavioristic stimulus-response model. I pro-

vide fuller characterizations of these two theories of emotion below. Neither is behaviorist in this sense.

8. On the activation of memories in emotional response, see Oatley, "Why" and "Emotions."

9. One reader pointed out to me that the work of Kawabata and Zeki may have relevance here. Specifically, Kawabata and Zeki examined brain response to beautiful and ugly stimuli. They found that in "the motor cortex, stimuli judged to be ugly produced the greatest activity and the beautiful ones the least" (1702). Moreover, there was activation "in the parietal cortex, in a region associated with spatial attention" (1703). Clearly, narrative emotions are not solely, nor even primarily, a matter of beauty or ugliness. Nonetheless, our evaluation of a story as verbal art is often connected with such aesthetic judgments. In this way, Kawabata and Zeki's research may have bearing in the present context.

10. One reader of this book suggested that the idea is similar to Bruner's conception of narrative as making "comprehensible a deviation from a canonical cultural pattern" (49–50). In fact, it seems to me very different. First, existential explanation need not be narrative. For example, medical explanations may be quite existentially satisfying. Second, I do not believe that narratives in general treat deviations from canonical cultural patterns. I return to the second point in the chapter 2.

2. Stories and Works

1. Preference rules, introduced into semantic theory by Ray Jackendoff, are not strict necessary and sufficient conditions. Rather they are principles that additively make for a better instance of some category. Take a simple example. We may understand the concept "bird" in terms of preference rules. These rules would include the following. Birds fly. Birds have feathers. Birds have beaks. Birds are small. Something that flies, has feathers, and has a beak (e.g., an eagle) is a pretty good example of a bird. It is better than something that only has feathers and a beak (e.g., a penguin). But it is not as good an example as something that flies, has feathers and a beak, and is small (e.g., a robin). As this case suggests, preference rules may be used to explain or define prototypes. (The more prototypical a bird, the more preference rules it satisfies.) They may also be used to treat complex relations that we would not ordinarily think of as being prototype-based. These complex relations include proximity in story space. (For a brief account of preference rules, see Jackendoff.)

2. Ryan gives a series of eight hierarchized "conditions of narrativity." These include causal connection (number 6) and emotional response of agents (number 4). Some of Ryan's conditions, though correct and significant for Ryan's own

analysis, are so basic that I will be leaving them aside. For example, the most fundamental of her conditions is that there be "individuated existents" (29). This is really a condition for any sort of representation.

3. The point is related to the fact that "the firing rate of mirror neurons is not the same for actions of the self and actions of others"; rather, "there is a much stronger discharge for actions of the self than for actions of others" (Iacoboni 133). As this suggests, mirror neurons are activated by our own action or by observing the action of others. There is evidence that they are at "the foundation of empathy" (Iacoboni 5).

4. Needless to say, many theorists have pointed out the importance of helping and blocking characters. I have in mind Frye's work here. But perhaps the most systematic treatment may be found in Greimas (see 112 on helpers and opponents).

5. This and subsequent quotations refer to the Tobin translation ("The Tale of the Eloquent Peasant). Readers may also wish to consult "The Eloquent Peasant."

6. For a further overview of Ṣūfism, see chapter 5 of Waines.

7. Note that our uncertainty about Meenaxi's existence is fitting here because it parallels a common uncertainty about the existence of God—an uncertainty suggested by the stage of feeling lost in nothingness on the Ṣūfī path (see Attar 221–22 and Waines 142).

8. Along with other sources, such as Mani Ratnam's *Dil Se . . .*

9. This becomes interesting in cases where an author uses our strong propensity to support the protagonist in order to challenge standard moral hierarchies or to raise moral questions.

10. On the ways different emotions lead to different forms of cognitive processing, see Fiedler, Bless, and Forgas "Affect."

3. Universal Narrative Prototypes

1. In this section and the next, I am largely summarizing arguments developed in *The Mind and Its Stories*. In making these arguments, I drew on experimental and survey-based research treating happiness goals. That research is difficult to overview quickly, due to the different ways researchers have organized their data. I therefore refer the interested reader to the discussion of this material in chapter 3 of that work.

2. For a useful overview of the extensive research on in-group/out-group relations, see Duckitt.

3. In *The Mind and Its Stories*, I presented both experimental and literary evidence that our happiness prototypes are of these general sorts (see particularly chapters 3 and 6) and that cross-cultural narrative patterns follow these happiness prototypes. The literary evidence ranged across three millennia and was drawn

from European, Chinese, Japanese, Middle Eastern, African, Indian, Native American, and other traditions. As I explain in *Understanding Nationalism*:

Some of the works that I considered include the following. From the European tradition: *The Iliad*, Aeschylus' *Oresteia*, Sophocles' Oedipus plays, Euripidēs' *Trojan Women*, *The Bacchae*, and *Phoenissae*, poetry by Pindar, Sapphō, Tyrtaios, and Kallīnos, Virgil's *Aeneid*, Chariton's *Chaereās and Kallirrhŏē*, works of Roman New Comedy (e.g., Terence's *The Mother-in-Law*), *The Song of Roland*, *Beowulf*, *Jerusalem Delivered*, the *Niebelungenlied*, various plays by Shakespeare, Goethe's *Faust*, novels by Jane Austen, poetry by St. John of the Cross, Sidney, Spenser, Browning, Yeats's *The Countess Cathleen*, works by Kafka, Joyce's *Ulysses*, *Gone With the Wind*, Alain Robbe-Grillet's postmodern *La Jalousie*, and the *Star Wars* movies. From South and Southeast Asia: the *Mahābhārata*, various versions of the *Rāmāyaṇa*, Bhāsa's *Vision of Vāsavadattā*, Kālidāsa's *Abhijñānaśākuntalam*, Śūdraka's *Little Clay Cart*, Harṣadeva's *Ratnāvalī*, Bhavabhūti's *Uttararāmacaritam*, Śaktibhadra's *Āścaryacūḍamaṇi*, Ilangô Adigal's *Shilappadikaram* (*Cilappatikāram*), poems from Tamil and Sanskrit anthologies, Bilhaṇa's *Fantasies of a Love Thief*, Bihārī's *Satasaī*, Jayadeva's *Gītagovinda*, stories from the history of Kashmir, Kondh poetry, the Thai folk drama *Manohra*, Kamala Markandaya's *Nectar in a Sieve*, Santosh Sivan's *The Terrorist*. From China: the *Book of Songs*, Chêng's *The Soul of Ch'ien-Nü Leaves Her Body*, Ma Chih-yüan's *Autumn in Han Palace*, poetry by Wang Wei, Li Bo, Li Ch'ing-chao, and Du Fu, Kuan Han-ch'ing's *The Injustice Done to Tou Ngo*, Cao Xueqin and Gao E's *The Story of the Stone*, *Conversations from the States*, and *Three Kingdoms*. From the Middle East: the epic of *Gilgamesh*, *Genesis*, the *Song of Songs*, ancient Egyptian lyric poetry, works in the ghazal tradition, various psalms, Ferdowsi's *Shâhnâme*, Iranian *ta'ziyeh* dramas, Gurgānī's *Vīs and Rāmīn*, the *Sīrat 'Antar*, narratives from Muslim history, the *Book of Dede Korkut*, Niẓāmī's *Laylā and Majnūn*, various stories from *The Thousand and One Nights*, some Bedouin love poetry. From Japan: *The Tale of the Heike*, Lady Murasaki's *Tale of Genji*, several Nō dramas by Kan'ami and Zeami, several plays by Chikamatsu, Izaemon and Yūgiri's *Love Letter from the Licensed Quarter*, Namiki Sōsuke's *Chronicle of the Battle of Ichinotani*, the *Tale of Ise*, the *Tosa Diary*, works by Bashō, the *Kokinshū*, and a range of Ainu epics. From the Americas: Bororo and Arawak tales, poetry from the Abanaki, Sia, Pueblo, Hopi, Navajo, and Chippewa, the Mayan *Cuceb*, the Nahuatl/Aztec *Quetzalcoatl*, Luis Puenzo's *The Plague*. From sub-Saharan Africa: the *Mwindo* epic, various versions of the *Epic of Son-Jara*, the epic of Oziki, the epic of Da Monzon of Segou, poetry from the Bambara and Dinka, Amos Tutuola's *The Palm-Wine Drinkard*, plays by Wole Soyinka. Elsewhere: Trobriand Island poetry, Tikopia poetry, New Guinea poetry of the Kurelu, Aboriginal poetry of Australia. (198–99n18)

4. See chapter 4 of *The Mind*.
5. The purely economic elites of capitalist societies may have either political or religious interests, but they are often most interested in return on investment. Thus their narrative commitments are first of all a matter of the extent and speed of sales. This no doubt has effects on genre structure and development. However, these effects are complex and indirect. In addition, the major genres were established before the advent of modern capitalism. I will therefore leave aside the purely economic elite of capitalism.
6. Note that this partial alignment, but also intermingling of dominant groups, is what we would expect from a distributed network of the sort discussed in the introduction.
7. Again, this sort of complexity is what one would anticipate from a distributed network.
8. In other words, ideologically consequential ideas are part of a set of presuppositions about and implicit attitudes toward social relations, work, political economy, and so forth. This is different from saying that they are "unconscious" in the psychoanalytic sense. Indeed, these ideas are not even *analogous* to the contents of psychoanalytic unconscious in the way that, say, Jameson may suggest. Rather, they are ordinary cognitive and affective propensities that one has not considered and thus evaluated self-reflectively.
9. The play is readily available in several English translations, one under the title *The Injustice Done to Tou Ngo*, a second called *Snow in Midsummer*, a third entitled *Arousing Heaven Stirring Earth Is Tou O's Injustice*. They present slightly different versions of the play. (On the different Chinese texts of the play, see Chung-Wen Shih xiv.) I will refer to all three, distinguishing between them by reference to their different English titles. As indicated earlier, "Guan Hanqing" and "Kuan Han-ch'ing" are alternative transliterations of the same name. I will use the two transliterations interchangeably.
10. The precise names of the characters vary somewhat from version to version. In order to minimize confusion, I will use the names from the Johnson transcription even when discussing Condé and others—except, of course, in direct quotations, where I will supply Johnson's version of the name in brackets.
11. Motifs are separable narrative units that may be inserted into different encompassing narratives and particularized to fit those narratives.
12. Mande culture distinguishes between two key types of sibling relations, *fadenya* and *badenya*. The former refers the relation among children of one father and different mothers, such as Son-Jara and Dankaran Tuman. The latter refers to

children of one mother. However, *fadenya* also refers to rivalry, while *badenya* refers to harmony. Criticism of the Son-Jara epic often stresses the relevance of these concepts to the work (on *fadenya* and *badenya*, see chapter 2 of Jansen; for a discussion of the poem in relation to these concepts, and for a broader treatment of power in Mande society, see Johnson "Dichotomy").

13. Though the heroic plot need not extend back to the hero's birth, such a framing elaboration is not uncommon—due to the recurrence of the "human life" frame for stories, due to the bearing of the birth on succession and usurpation, and other factors.

14. David Conrad kindly sent me a copy of his translation of the second episode, which is not included in his published version of the poem.

15. It is worth noting that the fear here is not simply metaphorical. Nyanga tradition allowed for certain conditions in which the chief could be ritually killed (see Biebuyck 59, 60).

16. Biebuyck presents a particularly nuanced version of this analysis.

17. On the other hand, Biebuyck may be somewhat overstating the case here. For example, Shekwabo's version of the Mwindo story manifests a much more militaristic orientation.

18. Connectionism is a theoretical account of mental functioning that models the human mind on a simplified version of neural architecture. In a connectionist model, different mental contents are represented by nodes that have input and output links. These links may be excitatory or inhibitory. A connectionist network produces a result by cycling through sequences of excitation and inhibition to produce a steady state in which one configuration of nodes is excited while alternatives are not. That configuration represents some mental state (e.g., an emotional state, such as anger). For an overview of connectionism, see McLeod, Plunkett, and Rolls.

19. For discussions of dharma theory, see O'Flaherty, Parekh, and *Laws*.

20. Such conversations recur in the course of the play. On the importance of such conversations in romantic stories, see Young.

21. Some interpretations of the ceremony suggest that the son's presence was crucial. For discussion, see Kale 64 of "Notes."

4. Cross-Cultural Minor Genres

1. The point could be put in terms of Todorov's well-known distinction between genres and types. I derived principles of explanation in part from three empirically isolated *genres*. Those principles allow me to generate a broader range of possible *types* that include, but are not confined to, the already-discovered genres (see his "Literary Genres"). On the other hand, it is important to distinguish between Todorov's conception of genres as rule-governed (see *Les Genres*

46 on rules) and the preference-rule, thus prototype-based, account presented here.

2. For example, as Simkin notes, revenge plots have been of great importance in the West from the ancient Greeks through contemporary Hollywood films (2–3). The point is particularly clear from the range of works treated by Kerrigan.

3. For example, speaking of English Renaissance works, Griswold writes that "most revenger-protagonists begin with the sympathy of the audience, for they have been grievously wronged, but they forfeit much of the sympathy during the course of the play by becoming sadistic killers who enjoy their revenge far too much, slaughtering totally innocent people along the way" (60).

4. The ambivalence extends to theme and even ideology. In keeping with this, there is often critical disagreement on the moral attitude of individual revenge narratives, or in some cases on the moral attitude of a body of such narratives (see, for example, chapter 5 of Camoin as well as Lever 35–36 on Jacobean revenge plots). In connection with this, Burnett rightly warns against projecting our own moral preferences onto works from other periods and cultures. She even goes so far as to claim, for example, that for "early Greeks revenge was not a problem but a solution" (xvi). This is undoubtedly the case for particular works and particular readers. But Burnett seems to be overcompensating here. For example, *Medea* would hardly count as a tragedy at all if contemporary Greek audiences saw killing one's children as perfectly fine (or if audiences today could have no sympathy with Medea). More generally, revenge narratives are likely to give rise to a range of moral assessments in part because, even when revenge is presented as a solution, it is commonly not a cognitively or emotionally unproblematic solution. Kerrigan is, I believe, closer to the mark when he suggests that "ethical ambiguity and emotional turbulence" are almost intrinsic to revenge (vii).

5. The problems with legal evaluation are even clearer in works that are directly critical of criminal investigation, such as Kafka's *The Trial*.

6. Some readers have wondered about the relation of these comments to Keen's typology of empathy. Drawing in part on my own earlier distinction between "categorial empathy," based on group identity, and "situational empathy," based on emotional memories (see *The Mind* 140–50), Keen distinguishes three types of empathy. The first is "bounded strategic empathy" that "occurs within an in-group, stemming from experiences of mutuality, and leading to feeling with familiar others." It is not clear that this is a single type. On the one hand, it refers to empathy based on group membership; on the other hand, it refers to shared experiences and familiarity. In fact, categorial empathy often overrides familiarity—as when Smith, who identifies as white, empathizes with a white

stranger in some conflict with her (familiar) black coworker. Moreover, familiarity—or rather, attachment (as in the case of a man empathizing with his sister)—does not give rise to a distinct type of empathy. Rather, it gives a motive
for sustaining the effort of simulating another person's experience.

Keen's second category is "ambassadorial strategic empathy," which
"addresses chosen others with the aim of cultivating their empathy for the
in-group." I have no doubt that many authors do have a purpose of this sort.
But this is a way of using situational empathy. It is not a separate sort of
empathy. Finally, she distinguishes "broadcast strategic empathy," which "calls
upon every reader to feel with members of a group, by emphasizing our common vulnerabilities and hopes" (142). This too is a form of situational empathy. Indeed, the difference from the second category appears to be that it is
addressed to more people. The extent to which one appeals for empathy (e.g.,
whether in a private letter or a public testimony) is not in itself a distinction
in types of empathy, though it may contribute to our sense of a work's implied
reader. In short, Keen and I are both concerned with the ways in which identity
categorization relates to empathy. However, though Keen's book is extremely
valuable and insightful, her conclusions about types of empathy do not seem to
have consequences for the present discussion. (We consider the issues of empathy and identity categorization more fully in the afterword.)

7. On attachment, particularly in relation to romantic love, see Shaver and Mikulincer; Leckman et al.; and Fisher. On companionate love, see Berscheid 177–78.
On all three topics, see Hatfield and Rapson.

8. It is worth noting that both the long period of separation and the difficulty of
recognition can develop into motifs, which may then be used elsewhere. Thus
we have long periods of separation in such basically romantic works as *The
Winter's Tale* and Bhavabhūti's *Uttararāmacaritam* (on the relation between
these plays, see Pandit, "Patriarchy") and we have the motif of nonrecognition
in *Abhijñānaśākuntalam*.

9. The criticism of this film shows once again the peculiar absence of serious emotion study in most discussions of narrative. As Greg Smith explains, the film
"provoked one of psychoanalytic feminist film criticism's most extensive dialogues. Considering how strong an emotional appeal this melodrama makes, it
is remarkable that emotions are rarely mentioned in the two key articles in this
exchange" (*Film* 85). Smith's chapter on *Stella Dallas* (85–107) is an exception to
this trend.

10. There are also separations that are benevolent, but not self-sacrificial. A love-
ly—and still ambivalent—case of this sort is *Autumn Moon* by the Hong Kong
director Clara Law.

11. Sometimes an author will focus on one genre structure, developing variations

within or across works. A remarkable case of this is the Japanese filmmaker Yasojiro Ozu. Many of Ozu's films develop subtly differentiated particularizations of the attachment prototype, in whole or in part. Indeed, Ozu may be the greatest master of the genre, given the range, creativity, and complexity of these particularizations.

12. After the protagonist's death, a doctor takes the box. He decides that it is "impossible" to find the father (215) and that it would be inappropriate to mail it to the fiancée. He considers bringing it to the fiancée in person. However, the final reference to the box locates it in a drawer of the house where the soldier died (219).

13. The two plots may be intertwined, with the hedonism plot subordinated, as in Jean-Luc Godard's *Une Femme est une Femme*. But this seems less common.

14. I hope it goes without saying that my emphasis on the transhistorical and cross-cultural aspects of Goethe's play by no means contradicts analyses stressing the particular historical conjuncture that produced this work—a conjuncture explored by a number of critics and brought out nicely by Brown.

15. In addition to his comments on Goethe, Hawkes presents a valuable overview of some other works that integrate Faust and Don Juan stories (see his chapter 5).

16. One might raise questions about his treatment of his daughter at the beginning of the play. But that is distinct from his behavior and accomplishments as a judge.

17. I should stress that I am not at all claiming that our primary pleasure is *in general* a matter of figuring out the ending. There are different components to our pleasure in any particular work. One component is solving problems, such as inferring how a story will turn out. Revenge and legal investigation narratives are particularly well designed to provide this sort of pleasure. Because of this, our primary enjoyment of such works often is a problem-solving sort of enjoyment. This, in turn, would tend to make works in these genres less appealing for repeated reading. In contrast, I take it that our enjoyment of romantic, attachment, heroic, and other genres is most often *not* primarily a matter of figuring out the ending. Indeed, we often know that ending before our first reading (e.g., when we know a work is a romantic comedy or a historical, heroic tragedy).

18. In keeping with this, according to one influential interpretation of Kafka's book, "any claims to a 'higher' truth, religious or ethical, which the Court may appear to have are actually exposed during the novel as the psychological and ideological tools of a secular power" (Dodd 136, referring to Deleuze and Guattari).

19. Moreover, it remains possible for readers to differ in their response to these endings. However, here again, I would argue that such differences reflect some difference with respect to the generalizations articulated above. For example, a

reader who is ambivalent about the *Popol Vuh* story may not experience One Death and Seven Death as dehumanized.

Afterword

1. I should perhaps note that, unlike some critics, I believe that such satisfaction and enjoyment are good in themselves. More generally, the experience of beauty is a crucial part of a decent human existence. Thus I do not think that art needs to be justified by some practical value beyond aesthetics. It just happens that I think it does potentially have that practical value—paired, unfortunately, with possible practical harm.

2. Keen does allow for more limited forms of empathic responsiveness (see 26).

3. In certain cases, though, emotion contagion may produce a degree of personal distress that inhibits simulation and thus empathy, as Eisenberg has discussed. The point about helping behavior is consequential for discussions of whether or not empathy may lead to genuine altruism (see Batson and Shaw, and Hoffman "Is Empathy Altruistic?"). In fact, I cannot make much sense of this debate, since it seems that empathy can only work if it engages some motivational system, and the way "altruism" is framed in this discussion, it seems that it can occur only in the absence of emotion. Personally, I would count an action as altruistic if the agent's emotional gain is contingent only on the immediate well-being of the other person. Suppose Jones cannot bear to see Smith, a stranger, run over by a car. Jones therefore saves Smith. I consider this altruistic if Jones is motivated by personal distress over Smith's likely pain. After all, if Smith saved himself from the car, that would be his motivation. It seems odd to have more stringent emotional criteria for altruism (Jones saving Smith) than for egocentrism (Smith saving Smith).

4. In fact, I see identity categories as generally problematic, even in a case such as this. However, my point is simply that few of us would object to a work cultivating an antifascist categorial identity in the same way that we would object to a work cultivating, say, a racial categorial identity.

Works Cited

Adelman, Gary. *Anna Karenina: The Bitterness of Ecstasy*. Boston: Twayne, 1990.

Aeschylus. *Aeschylus II: Agamemnon, Libation-Bearers, Eumenides, Fragments*, translated by H. Weir Smyth and H. Lloyd-Jones. Cambridge MA: Harvard University Press, 1926.

Alexandrov, Vladimir. *Limits to Interpretation: The Meanings of "Anna Karenina"*. Madison: University of Wisconsin Press, 2004.

Ali, Maulana Mohammad, ed. and trans. *The Holy Qur'ān*. 2nd ed. Columbus OH: Ahmadiyyah Anjuman Isha'at Islam, 1995.

Althusser, Louis. "Ideology and Ideological State Apparatuses (Notes towards an Investigation)." In *Lenin and Philosophy and Other Essays*, by Louis Althusser, translated by Ben Brewster, 127–86. New York: Monthly Review Press, 1971.

Ambady, Nalini, Joan Y. Chiao, Pearl Chiu, and Patricia Deldin. "Race and Emotion: Insights from a Social Neuroscience Perspective." In Cacioppo, Visser, and Pickett, *Social Neuroscience*, 209–27.

Aristotle. *Poetics*. In *Aristotle's Theory of Poetry and Fine Art*, edited by S. H. Butcher. 4th ed. New York: Dover, 1951.

Attar, Farid Ud-Din. *The Conference of the Birds*, translated by Afkham Darbandi and Dick Davis. New York: Penguin, 1984.

Austen, Ralph A. *In Search of Sunjata: The Mande Oral Epic as History, Literature, and Performance*. Bloomington: Indiana University Press, 1999.

Baker, Mark. *The Atoms of Language*. New York: Basic Books, 2001.

Batson, C. Daniel, and Laura Shaw. "Evidence for Altruism: Toward a Pluralism of Prosocial Motives." *Psychological Inquiry* 2.2 (1991): 107–22.

Berscheid, Ellen. "Searching for the Meaning of 'Love.'" In Sternberg and Weis, *New Psychology of Love*, 171–83.

Biebuyck, Daniel P. *Hero and Chief: Epic Literature from the Banyanga Zaire Republic*. Berkeley: University of California Press, 1978.

Biebuyck, Daniel P., and Kahombo C. Mateene, ed. and trans. *The Mwindo Epic*, by Shé-Kárisi Rureke. Berkeley: University of California Press, 1969.

Bless, Herbert. "The Interplay of Affect and Cognition: The Mediating Role of General Knowledge Structures." In Forgas, *Feeling and Thinking*, 201–22.

Bordwell, David. *Narration in the Fiction Film*. Madison: University of Wisconsin Press, 1985.

Bortolussi, Marisa, and Peter Dixon. *Psychonarratology: Foundations for the Empirical Study of Literary Response.* Cambridge: Cambridge University Press, 2003.

Bremond, Claude. *Logique du Récit.* Paris: Editions du Seuil, 1973.

Brody, Leslie R., and Judith A. Hall. "Gender, Emotion, and Expression." In Lewis and Haviland-Jones, *Handbook of Emotions,* 338–49.

Brooks, Peter. *Reading for the Plot: Design and Intention in Narrative.* New York: Vintage Books, 1984.

Brown, Jane K. "Faust." In *The Cambridge Companion to Goethe,* edited by Lesley Sharpe, 84–100. Cambridge: Cambridge University Press, 2002.

Bruner, Jerome. *Acts of Meaning.* Cambridge MA: Harvard University Press, 1990.

Bruzzo, Angela, Benno Gesierich, and Andreas Wohlschläger. "Simulating Biological and Non-Biological Motion." *Brain and Cognition* 66.2 (March 2008): 145–49.

Buchanan, Mark. *Nexus: Small Worlds and the Groundbreaking Theory of Networks.* New York: W. W. Norton, 2002.

Burnett, Anne Pippin. *Revenge in Attic and Later Tragedy.* Berkeley: University of California Press, 1998.

Cacioppo, John T., Penny S. Visser, and Cynthia L. Pickett, eds. *Social Neuroscience: People Thinking about Thinking People.* Cambridge MA: MIT Press, 2006.

Camoin, Francois Andre. *The Revenge Convention in Tourneur, Webster, and Middleton.* Salzburg: Institut für Englische Sprache und Literatur, Universität Salzburg, 1972.

Carroll, Noël. "Film, Emotion, and Genre." In Plantinga and Smith, *Passionate Views,* 21–47.

Cheng T'ing-yü. "The Flower of the Back Courtyard." In *Crime and Punishment in Medieval Chinese Drama: Three Judge Pao Plays,* edited and translated by George A. Hayden, 129–75. Cambridge MA: Harvard University Press, 1978.

Chikamatsu Monzaemon. "The Drum of the Waves of Horikawa." In *Major Plays of Chikamatsu,* edited and translated by Donald Keene, 57–90. New York: Columbia University Press, 1990.

Chomsky, Noam. *The New Military Humanism: Lessons from Kosovo.* Monroe ME: Common Courage Press, 1999.

Clark, David L., Nashaat N. Boutros, and Mario F. Mendez. *The Brain and Behavior: An Introduction to Behavioral Neuroanatomy.* 2nd ed. Cambridge: Cambridge University Press, 2005.

Clore, Gerald L., and Andrew Ortony. "Cognition in Emotion: Always, Sometimes, or Never?" *Cognitive Neuroscience of Emotion,* edited by Richard D. Land and Lynn Nadel with Geoffrey L. Ahern, John J. B. Allen, Alfred W. Kaszniak, Steven Z. Rapcsak, and Gary E. Schwartz, 24–61. Oxford: Oxford University Press, 2000.

Condé, Djanka Tassey. *Sunjata: A West African Epic of the Mande Peoples,* edited and translated by David Conrad. Indianapolis: Hackett Publishing, 2004.

Conrad, David C. "Mooning Armies and Mothering Heroes: Female Power in Mande Epic Tradition." In Austen, *In Search of Sunjata*, 189–229.

Currie, Gregory. *Image and Mind: Film, Philosophy, and Cognitive Science*. Cambridge: Cambridge University Press, 1995.

Damasio, Antonio. *Descartes' Error: Emotion, Reason, and the Human Brain*. New York: G. P. Putnam's Sons, 1994.

———. *Looking for Spinoza: Joy, Sorrow, and the Feeling Brain*. Orlando FL: Harcourt, 2003.

Da Ponte, Lorenzo. Libretto. *Don Giovanni (Don Juan): A Grand Opera in Two Acts*. Music by Wolfgang Amadeus Mozart. New York: Fred Rullman, n.d.

Davis, Mark. *Empathy: A Social Psychological Approach*. Madison WI: Brown and Benchmark, 1994.

Deleuze, Gilles, and Felix Guattari. *Kafka: Toward a Minor Literature*, translated by Dana Polan. Minneapolis: University of Minnesota Press, 1986.

Dhanaṃjaya. *The Daśarūpa: A Treatise on Hindu Dramaturgy*, translated by George Haas. New York: AMS Press, 1965.

Dodd, Bill. "The Case for a Political Reading." In *The Cambridge Companion to Kafka*, edited by Julian Preece, 131–49. Cambridge: Cambridge University Press, 2002.

Drabble, Margaret, ed. *The Oxford Companion to English Literature*. 5th ed. Oxford: Oxford University Press, 1985.

Duckitt, John H. *The Social Psychology of Prejudice*. New York: Praeger, 1992.

Eder, Jens. *Die Figur im Film: Grundlagen der Figurenanalyse*. Marburg, Germany: Schüren, 2008.

Eisenberg, Nancy. "Distinctions among Various Modes of Empathy-Related Reactions: A Matter of Importance in Humans." *Behavioral and Brain Sciences* 25 (2002): 33–34.

"The Eloquent Peasant." In *Ancient Egyptian Literature*, vol. 1: *The Old and Middle Kingdoms*, edited and translated by Miriam Lichtheim, 170–82. Berkeley: University of California Press, 1973.

Ferrer i Cancho, Ramon. "Network Theory." In Hogan, *Cambridge Encyclopedia of the Language Sciences*, 555–57.

Feuerstein, Georg. *The Shambhala Encyclopedia of Yoga*. Boston: Shambhala, 2000.

Fiedler, Klaus. "Toward an Integrative Account of Affect and Cognition Phenomena Using the BIAS Computer Algorithm." In Forgas, *Feeling and Thinking*, 223–52.

Fisher, Helen. "The Drive to Love: The Neural Mechanism for Mate Selection." In Sternberg and Weis, *New Psychology of Love*, 87–115.

Fiske, Susan T., Lasana T. Harris, and Amy J. C. Cuddy. "Why Ordinary People Torture Enemy Prisoners." *Science* 306.5701 (November 26, 2004): 1482–83.

Fludernik, Monika. "Natural Narratology and Cognitive Parameters." In Herman, *Narrative Theory*, 243–67.

Forgas, Joseph P. "Affect and Information Processing Strategies: An Interactive Relationship." In Forgas, *Feeling and Thinking*, 253–80.

———, ed. *Feeling and Thinking: The Role of Affect in Social Cognition*. Cambridge: Cambridge University Press, 2000.

Franke, Herbert, and Denis Twitchett, eds. *The Cambridge History of China*, vol. 6: *Alien Regimes and Border States, 907–1368*. Cambridge: Cambridge University Press, 1994.

Frijda, Nico H. *The Emotions*. Cambridge and Paris: Cambridge University Press and Editions de la Maison des Sciences de l'Homme, 1986.

Frye, Northrop. *Anatomy of Criticism: Four Essays*. Princeton NJ: Princeton University Press, 1957.

Gathercole, Susan. "Models of Verbal Short-Term Memory." In *Cognitive Models of Memory*, edited by Martin Conway, 13–45. Cambridge MA: MIT Press, 1997.

Gaut, Berys. 1999. "Identification and Emotion in Narrative Film." In Plantinga and Smith, *Passionate Views*, 200–216.

Gilbert, Charles. "Neural Plasticity." In *The MIT Encyclopedia of the Cognitive Sciences*, edited by Robert Wilson and Frank Keil, 598–601. Cambridge: MIT Press, 1999.

Godel, Armen, and Koichi Kano, eds. and trans. *La Lande des Mortifications: Vint-Cinq Pièces de Nô*. Paris: Gallimard, 1994.

Goethe, Johann Wolfgang von. *Faust: A Tragedy*. See Hamlin.

———. *Faust: Eine Tragödie*. In *Goethes Werke*, 3:9–364. Hamburg: Christian Wegner Verlag, n.d.

Goldhill, Simon. *Reading Greek Tragedy*. Cambridge: Cambridge University Press, 1986.

Greimas, A. J. *On Meaning: Selected Writings in Semiotic Theory*, translated by Paul Perron and Frank Collins. Minneapolis: University of Minnesota Press, 1987.

Griswold, Wendy. *Renaissance Revivals: City Comedy and Revenge Tragedy in the London Theatre, 1576–1980*. Chicago: University of Chicago Press, 1986.

Geuss, Raymond. *The Idea of a Critical Theory: Habermas and the Frankfurt School*. Cambridge: Cambridge University Press, 1981.

Hamlin, Cyrus, ed. *Faust: A Tragedy*, by Johann Wolfgang von Goethe, translated by Walter Arndt. 2nd ed. New York: Norton, 2001.

Hardt, Michael, and Antonio Negri. *Multitude: War and Democracy in the Age of Empire*. New York: Penguin, 2004.

Hatfield, Elaine, and Richard L. Rapson. "Love and Attachment Processes." In Lewis and Haviland-Jones, *Handbook of Emotions*, 654–62.

Hawkes, David. *The Faust Myth: Religion and the Rise of Representation*. New York: Palgrave, 2007.

Heidegger, Martin. *Being and Time*, translated by John Macquarrie and Edward Robinson. New York: Harper and Row, 1962.

Herman, David, ed. *The Cambridge Companion to Narrative*. Cambridge: Cambridge University Press, 2007.

———. "Cognition, Emotion, and Consciousness." In Herman, *Cambridge Companion to Narrative*, 245–59.

———, ed. *Narrative Theory and the Cognitive Sciences*. Stanford CA: CSLI Publications, 2003.

———. "Storytelling and the Sciences of Mind: Cognitive Narratology, Discursive Psychology, and Narratives in Face-to-Face Interaction." *Narrative* 15 (2007): 306–34.

Herman, Edward S., and David Peterson. "The Dismantling of Yugoslavia: A Study in *In*humanitarian Intervention—and a Western Liberal-Left Intellectual and Moral Collapse." *Monthly Review* 59.5 (October 2007): 1–62.

Hoffman, Martin. "Empathy and Prosocial Behavior." In Lewis, Haviland-Jones, and Barrett, *Handbook of Emotions*, 440–55.

———. "Is Empathy Altruistic?" *Psychological Inquiry* 2.2 (1991): 131–33.

Hogan, Patrick Colm, ed. *The Cambridge Encyclopedia of the Language Sciences*. Cambridge: Cambridge University Press, 2011.

———. *The Culture of Conformism: Understanding Social Consent*. Durham NC Duke University Press, 2001.

———. *The Mind and Its Stories: Narrative Universals and Human Emotion*. Cambridge: Cambridge University Press, 2003.

———. *Understanding Nationalism: On Narrative, Cognitive Science, and Identity*. Columbus: Ohio State University Press, 2009.

Hogan, Patrick Colm, and Lalita Pandit. "Ancient Theories of Narrative (Non-Western)." In *The Routledge Encyclopedia of Narrative Theory*, edited by David Herman, Manfred Jahn, and Marie-Laure Ryan, 14–19. London: Routledge, 2005.

Holland, Norman N. "Where Is a Text: A Neurological View." *New Literary History* 33 (2002): 21–38.

———. "The Willing Suspension of Disbelief: A Neuro-Psychoanalytic View." *PsyArt: An Online Journal for the Psychological Study of the Arts*, January 22, 2003. http://www.clas.ufl.edu/ipsa/journal/2003_holland06.shtml. Accessed February 16, 2006.

Hsu, Jeremy. "The Secrets of Storytelling: Our Love for Telling Tales Reveals the Workings of the Mind." *Scientific American Mind*, August/September 2008, 46–51.

Husain, M. F., dir. *Meenaxi: Tale of Three Cities*. Story and dialogues by M. F. Husain and Owais Husain. Screenplay by Owais Husain. Art direction by Sharmishta Roy. Edited by Sreekar Prasad. Director of photography, Santosh Sivan. Music by A. R. Rahman. Producer, Reima-Faiza Husain. Culture of the Street Films, 2004.

Iacoboni, Marco. *Mirroring People: The New Science of How We Connect with Others*. New York: Farrar, Straus, and Giroux, 2008.

Idema, Wilt L. "Traditional Dramatic Literature." In *The Columbia History of Chinese Literature*, edited by Victor H. Mair, 785–847. New York: Columbia University Press, 2001.

Idema, Wilt, and Stephen H. West. *Chinese Theater, 1100–1450: A Source Book.* Wiesbaden: Franz Steiner Verlag, 1982.

Ito, Tiffany A., Geoffrey R. Urland, Eve Willadsen-Jensen, and Joshua Correll. "The Social Neuroscience of Stereotyping and Prejudice: Using Event-Related Brain Potentials to Study Social Perception." In Cacioppo, Visser, and Pickett, *Social Neuroscience*, 189–208.

Izard, Carroll E., and Brian P. Ackerman. "Motivational, Organizational, and Regulatory Functions of Discrete Emotions." In Lewis and Haviland-Jones, *Handbook of Emotions*, 253–64.

Jackendoff, Ray. "Preference Rules." In Hogan, *Cambridge Encyclopedia of the Language Sciences*, 659–60.

Jacobsen, Thorkild. *The Harps that Once . . . : Sumerian Poetry in Translation.* New Haven CT: Yale University Press, 1987.

James, William. "What Is an Emotion?" *Mind* 9 (1884): 188–205.

Jameson, Fredric. *The Political Unconscious: Narrative as a Socially Symbolic Act.* Ithaca NY: Cornell University Press, 1981.

Jansen, Jan. *Épopée, Histoire, Société: Le Cas de Soundjata, Mali et Guinée.* Paris: Éditions Karthala, 2001.

Jay, Jennifer. *A Change in Dynasties: Loyalism in Thirteenth-Century China.* Bellingham: Western Washington University Center for East Asian Studies, 1991.

Jenkins, Lyle. *Biolinguistics: Exploring the Biology of Language.* Cambridge: Cambridge University Press, 2000.

Johnson, John William. "The Dichotomy of Power and Authority in Mande Society and in the Epic of *Sunjata*." In Austen, *In Search of Sunjata*, 9–23.

———, ed. and trans. *Son-Jara, the Mande Epic: Mandekan/English Edition with Notes and Commentary.* 3rd ed. Bloomington: Indiana University Press, 2003.

Jourdain, Robert. *Music, the Brain, and Ecstasy: How Music Captures Our Imagination.* New York: Quill, 2002.

Kafalenos, Emma. *Narrative Causalities.* Columbus: Ohio State University Press, 2006.

Kagekiyo. In Godel and Kano, *La Lande des Mortifications*, 457–71.

———. In *Troubled Souls from Japanese Noh Plays of the Fourth Group.* Original Japanese, with facing translation by Chifumi Shimazaki, 257–87. Ithaca NY: East Asia Program, Cornell University, 1998.

Kahneman, Daniel, and Dale T. Miller. "Norm Theory: Comparing Reality to Its Alternatives." *Psychological Review* 93.2 (1986): 136–53.

Kale, M. R. *The Abhijñānaśākuntalam of Kālidāsa.* 10th ed. Delhi: Motilal Banarsidass, 1969.

The Kalevala, or Poems of the Kaleva District, compiled by Elias Lönnrot, translated and edited by F. Magoun. Cambridge MA: Harvard University Press, 1963.

Kālidāsa. *Abhijñānaśākuntalam*. In Kale.

Kawabata, Hideaki, and Semir Zeki. "Neural Correlates of Beauty." *Journal of Neurophysiology* 91 (2004): 1699–1705.

Keen, Suzanne. *Empathy and the Novel*. Oxford: Oxford University Press, 2007.

Kerrigan, John. *Revenge Tragedy: Aeschylus to Armageddon*. Oxford: Clarendon Press, 1996.

Kosslyn, Stephen. *Image and Brain: The Resolution of the Imagery Debate*. Cambridge MA: MIT Press, 1994.

Kouyaté, Dani, dir. and writer. *Keïta! The Heritage of the Griot*. AFIX Productions, 1994.

Kristjánsson, Kristján. *Justifying Emotions: Pride and Jealousy*. London: Routledge, 2002.

Kuan Han-ch'ing. *Arousing Heaven Stirring Earth Is Tou O's Injustice*. In Shih, *Injustice to Tou O*, 37–325.

———. *Snow in Midsummer*. In *Selected Plays of Kuan Han-ch'ing*, translated by Yang Hsien-yi and Gladys Yang, 21–47. Peking: Foreign Languages Press, 1958.

———. *The Injustice Done to Tou Ngo*. In *Six Yuan Plays*, translated and edited by Liu Jung-en, 115–58. New York: Penguin, 1972.

Kunda, Ziva. *Social Cognition: Making Sense of People*. Cambridge MA: MIT Press. 1999.

Kyd, Thomas. *The Spanish Tragedy*, edited by Charles T. Prouty. Northbrook IL: AHM Publishing, 1951.

Labov, William. "Narratives of Personal Experience." In Hogan, *Cambridge Encyclopedia of the Language Sciences*, 546–48.

Langlois, J., and L. Roggman. "Attractive Faces Are Only Average." *Psychological Science* 1 (1990): 115–21.

Langlois, John D., ed. *China under Mongol Rule*. Princeton NJ: Princeton University Press, 1981.

———. Introduction to Langlois, *China under Mongol Rule*, 3–22.

Lao, Yan-shuan. "Southern Chinese Scholars and Educational Institutions in Early Yuan: Some Preliminary Remarks." In Langlois, *China under Mongol Rule*, 107–33.

Laws of Manu. Edited and translated by Wendy Doniger with Brian K. Smith. New York: Penguin, 1991.

Lazarus, R. S. "Thoughts on the Relations between Emotion and Cognition." *American Psychologist* 37 (1982): 1019–24.

Leckman, James F., Sarah B. Hrdy, Eric B. Keverne, and C. Sue Carter. "A Biobehavioral Model of Attachment and Bonding." In Sternberg and Weis, *New Psychology of Love*, 116–45.

LeDoux, Joseph. *The Emotional Brain: The Mysterious Underpinnings of Emotional Life*. New York: Touchstone, 1996.

Leki, Ilona. *Alain Robbe-Grillet*. Boston: Twayne, 1983.

Lever, J. W. "Tragedy and State." In Simkin, *Revenge Tragedy*, 24–40.

Lewis, Michael. "The Emergence of Human Emotions." In Lewis and Haviland-Jones, *Handbook of Emotions*, 265–80.

———. "Self-Conscious Emotions: Embarrassment, Pride, Shame, and Guilt." In Lewis, Haviland-Jones, and Barrett, *Handbook of Emotions*, 742–56.

Lewis, Michael, and Jeannette M. Haviland-Jones, eds. *Handbook of Emotions*. 2nd ed. New York: Guilford Press, 2000.

Lewis, Michael, Jeannette Haviland-Jones, and Lisa Barrett, eds. *Handbook of Emotions*. 3rd ed. New York: Guilford Press, 2008.

Lichtheim, Miriam. See "The Eloquent Peasant."

Liu Jung-en. Introduction to *Six Yüan Plays*, translated and edited by Liu Jung-en, 7–35. New York: Penguin, 1972.

Macherey, Pierre. *A Theory of Literary Production*, translated by Geoffrey Wall. London: Routledge, 2006.

McCullough, William H. "The Capital and Its Society." In *The Cambridge History of Japan*, vol. 2: *Heian Japan*, edited by Donald H. Shively and William H. McCullough, 97–182. Cambridge: Cambridge University Press, 1999.

McLeod, Peter, Kim Plunkett, and Edmund T. Rolls. *Introduction to Connectionist Modelling of Cognitive Processes*. Oxford: Oxford University Press, 1998.

Miall, David. *Literary Reading: Empirical and Theoretical Studies*. New York: Peter Lang, 2006.

Middleton, Thomas, and William Rowley. *The Changeling*. In *Three Revenge Tragedies*, edited by Gāmini Sālgado. New York: Penguin, 2004.

Miner, Earl. "The Heroine: Identity, Recurrence, Destiny." In *Ukifune: Love in The Tale of Genji*, edited by Andrew Pekarik, 63–81. New York: Columbia University Press, 1982.

Mittell, Jason. "Film and Television Narrative." In Herman, *Cambridge Companion to Narrative*, 156–71.

Moretti, Franco. "Evolution, World-Systems, *Weltliteratur*." In *Studying Transcultural Literary History*, edited by Gunilla Lindberg-Wada, 113–21. Berlin: Walter de Gruyter, 2006.

Morrissette, Bruce. *The Novels of Robbe-Grillet*. Ithaca NY: Cornell University Press, 1975.

Mote, Frederick W. "Chinese Society under Mongol Rule, 1215–1368." In Franke and Twitchett, *Cambridge History of China*, 6:616–64.

Motomasa. *Sumidagawa (La Rivière Sumida)*. In Godel and Kano, *La Lande des Mortifications*, 305–25.

———. *Yoroboshi (Le Frêle Moine)*. In Godel and Kano, *La Lande des Mortifications*, 327–47.

Murasaki Shikibu. *The Tale of Genji*. 2 vols. Translated by Edward G. Seidensticker. New York: Knopf, 1977.

Niane, D. T. *Sundiata: An Epic of Old Mali*. From Djeli Mamoudou Kouyaté. Translated by G. D. Pickett. New York: Longman, 1965.

Nussbaum, Martha C. *Hiding from Humanity: Disgust, Shame, and the Law*. Princeton NJ: Princeton University Press, 2004.

———. *Upheavals of Thought: The Intelligence of Emotions*. Cambridge: Cambridge University Press, 2001.

Oatley, Keith. *Best Laid Schemes: The Psychology of Emotions*. New York: Cambridge University Press, 1992.

———. "Communications to Self and Others: Emotional Experience and Its Skills." *Emotion Review* 1.3 (2009): 206–13.

———. "Emotions and the Story Worlds of Fiction." In *Narrative Impact*, edited by Melanie Green, Jeffrey Strange, and Timothy Brock, 39–69. Mahwah NJ: Lawrence Erlbaum, 2002.

———. "Why Fiction May Be Twice as True as Fact: Fiction as Cognitive and Emotional Simulation." *Review of General Psychology* 3.2 (1999): 101–17.

O'Flaherty, Wendy Doniger. "The Clash between Relative and Absolute Duty: The Dharma of Demons." In *The Concept of Duty in South Asia*, edited by Wendy Doniger O'Flaherty and J. Duncan M. Derrett, 96–106. N.p.: South Asia Books, 1978.

O'Leary, Dennis, Naomi Ruff, and Richard Dyck, "Development, Critical Period Plasticity, and Adult Reorganizations of Mammalian Somatosensory Systems." In *Findings and Current Opinion in Cognitive Neuroscience*, edited by Larry R. Squire and Stephen M. Kosslyn, 307–16. Cambridge MA: MIT Press, 2000.

Ortony, Andrew, Gerald Clore, and Allan Collins. *The Cognitive Structure of Emotions*. Cambridge: Cambridge University Press, 1988.

Palmer, Alan. *Fictional Minds*. Lincoln: University of Nebraska Press, 2004.

Pandit, B. N. *Essence of the Exact Reality or Paramārthasāra of Abhinavagupta*. New Delhi: Munshiram Manoharlal, 1991.

Pandit, Lalita. "Color and Artefact Emotion in Alternative Cinema: A Comparative Analysis of *Gabbeh*, *Mirch Masala*, and *Meenaxi: A Tale of Three Cities*." *Projections: The Journal for Movies and Mind* 3.9 (2009): 105–23.

———. "Patriarchy and Paranoia: Imaginary Infidelity in *Uttararāmacarita* and *The Winter's Tale*." In *Literary India: Comparative Studies in Aesthetics, Colonialism, and Culture*, edited by Patrick Colm Hogan and Lalita Pandit, 103–33. Albany: State University of New York Press.

Panksepp, Jaak. *Affective Neuroscience: The Foundations of Human and Animal Emotions*. New York: Oxford University Press, 1998.

———. "Emotions as Natural Kinds within the Mammalian Brain." In Lewis and Haviland-Jones, *Handbook of Emotions*, 137–56.

Parekh, Bhikhu. *Colonialism, Tradition, and Reform: An Analysis of Gandhi's Political Discourse.* New Delhi: Sage, 1989.

Pavel, Thomas. *The Poetics of Plot: The Case of English Renaissance Drama.* Minneapolis: University of Minnesota Press, 1985.

Perng, Ching-Hsi. *Double Jeopardy: A Critique of Seven Yuan Courtroom Dramas.* Michigan Papers in Chinese Studies, vol. 35. Ann Arbor MI: Center for Chinese Studies, 1978.

Phelan, James. "Rhetoric/Ethics." In Herman, *Cambridge Companion to Narrative,* 203–16.

Plantinga, Carl, and Greg Smith, eds. *Passionate Views: Film, Cognition, and Emotion.* Baltimore: Johns Hopkins University Press, 1999.

Preston, Stephanie D., and Frans B. M. de Waal. "Empathy: Its Ultimate and Proximate Bases." *Behavioral and Brain Sciences* 25 (2002): 1–72.

Prinz, Jesse J. "Imitation and Moral Development." In *Perspectives on Imitation: From Neuroscience to Social Science,* vol. 2: *Imitation, Human Development, and Culture,* edited by Susan Hurley and Nick Chater, 267–82. Cambridge MA: MIT Press, 2005.

Propp, Vladimir. *The Morphology of the Folktale,* translated by Laurence Scott. Austin: University of Texas Press, 1968.

Qur'ān, Holy. See Ali.

Rabinal Achi: A Mayan Drama of War and Sacrifice, edited and translated by Dennis Tedlock. Oxford: Oxford University Press, 2003.

Richardson, Brian. "Drama and Narrative." In Herman, *Cambridge Companion to Narrative,* 142–55.

———. *Unlikely Stories: Causality and the Nature of Modern Narrative.* Newark: University of Delaware Press, 1997.

Richman, Paula, ed. *Many Rāmāyaṇas: The Diversity of a Narrative Tradition in South Asia.* Berkeley: University of California Press, 1991.

Robbe-Grillet, Alain. *Dans le Labyrinthe.* Paris: Editions de Minuit, 1959.

Rossabi, Morris. "The Reign of Khubilai Khan." In Franke and Twitchett, *Cambridge History of China,* 6:414–89.

Rozin, Paul, Jonathan Haidt, and Clark McCauley. "Disgust." [2000.] In Lewis and Haviland-Jones, *Handbook of Emotions,* 637–53.

———. "Disgust." [2008.] In Lewis, Haviland-Jones, and Barrett, *Handbook of Emotions,* 757–776.

Rubin, David C. *Memory in Oral Traditions: The Cognitive Psychology of Epic, Ballads, and Counting-Out Rhymes.* New York: Oxford University Press, 1995.

Rureke, Shé-Kárisi. See Biebuyck and Mateene.

Ryan, Marie-Laure. "Cognitive Maps and the Construction of Narrative Space." In Herman, *Narrative Theory,* 214–42.

———. "Toward a Definition of Narrative." In Herman, *Cambridge Companion to Narrative,* 22–35.

Sartre, Jean-Paul. *Being and Nothingness*, translated by Hazel Barnes. New York: Washington Square, 1966.

Scarry, Elaine. *Dreaming By the Book*. New York: Farrar, Straus, and Giroux, 1999.

Schiller, Friedrich. *On the Aesthetic Education of Man in a Series of Letters*, translated by Reginald Snell. London: Routledge and Kegan Paul, 1954.

Scholes, Robert, and Robert Kellogg. *The Nature of Narrative*. Oxford: Oxford University Press, 1966.

Schore, Allan. "Attachment and the Regulation of the Right Brain." *Attachment and Human Development* 2.1 (2000): 23–47.

Shaver, Phillip R., and Mario Mikulincer. "A Behavioral Systems Approach to Romantic Love Relationships: Attachment, Caregiving, and Sex." In Sternberg and Weis, *New Psychology of Love*, 35–64.

Shekwabo. *The Mwindo Epic*. In Biebuyck, *Hero and Chief*, 134–73.

Shih, Chung-Wen. *Injustice to Tou O (Tou O Yüan): A Study and Translation*. Cambridge: Cambridge University Press, 1972.

Shirane, Haruo. "The Uji Chapters and the Denial of Romance." In *Ukifune: Love in the Tale of Genji*, edited by Andrew Pekarik, 113–38. New York: Columbia University Press, 1982.

Simkin, Stevie. Introduction to *Revenge Tragedy*, edited by Stevie Simkin, 1–23. New York: Palgrave, 2001.

Simpson, Joseph R. Jr., Wayne C. Drevets, Abraham Z. Snyder, Debra A. Gusnard, and Marcus E. Raichle. "Emotion-Induced Changes in Human Medial Prefrontal Cortex: II. During Anticipatory Anxiety." *PNAS* 98.2 (January 16, 2001): 688–93.

Simpson, William Kelly, ed. *The Literature of Ancient Egypt: An Anthology of Stories, Instructions, Stelae, Autobiographies, and Poetry*, with translations by Robert K. Ritner, William Kelly Simpson, Vincent A. Tobin, and Edward F. Wente Jr. 3rd ed. New Haven CT: Yale University Press, 2003.

Sisòkò, Fa-Digi. *Son-Jara*. In Johnson, *Son-Jara, the Mande Epic*, 98–259.

Smith, Greg M. *Film Structure and the Emotion System*. Cambridge: Cambridge University Press, 2003.

———. "Local Emotions, Global Moods, and Film Structure." In Plantinga and Smith, *Passionate Views*, 103–26.

Smith, Molly Easo. "The Theatre and the Scaffold: Death as Spectacle in *The Spanish Tragedy*." In *Revenge Tragedy*, edited by Stevie Simkin, 71–87. New York: Palgrave, 2001.

Smith, Murray. "Gangsters, Cannibals, Aesthetes, or Apparently Perverse Allegiances." In Plantinga and Smith, *Passionate Views*, 217–38.

Smith, Steven M., Thomas B. Ward, and Ronald A. Finke, eds. *The Creative Cognition Approach*. Cambridge MA: MIT Press, 1995.

Spatz, Lois. *Aeschylus*. Boston: Twayne, 1982.

Stella Dallas. Directed by King Vidor. From the novel by Olive Higgins Prouty. Dramatization by Harry Wagstaff Gribble and Gertrude Purcell. Screenplay by Sarah Y. Mason and Victor Heeman. Cinematography by Rudolph Maté. Produced by Samuel Goldwyn. Samuel Goldwyn Company, 1937.

Sternberg, Robert J., ed. *Handbook of Creativity*. Cambridge: Cambridge University Press, 1999.

Sternberg, Robert J., and Karin Weis, eds. *The New Psychology of Love*. New Haven CT: Yale University Press, 2006.

Stockwell, Peter. "Texture and Identification." *European Journal of English Studies* 9.2 (2005): 143–53.

The Story of the Circle of Chalk: A Drama from the Old Chinese, translated by Frances Hume. London: Rodale Press, n.d.

Suso, Bamba. *Sunjata: Gambian Versions of the Mande Epic by Bamba Suso and Banna Kanute*. Edited by Lucy Durán and Graham Furniss. Translated by Gordon Innes with the assistance of Bakari Sidibe. New York: Penguin, 1991.

Takeda Izumo, Miyoshi Shōraku, and Namiki Senryū. *Chūshingura (The Treasury of Loyal Retainers): A Puppet Play*, edited and translated by Donald Keene. New York: Columbia University Press, 1971.

"The Tale of the Eloquent Peasant." In William Simpson, *Literature of Ancient Egypt*, 26–44.

Tales from the Thousand and One Nights, edited and translated by N. J. Dawood. New York: Penguin, 1973.

Tan, Ed S. *Emotion and the Structure of Narrative Film: Film as an Emotion Machine*, translated by Barbara Fasting. Mahwah NJ: Lawrence Erlbaum, 1996.

Tan, Ed, and Nico Frijda. "Sentiment in Film Viewing." In Plantinga and Smith, *Passionate Views*, 48–64.

Tapp, Alyson. "Moving Stories: (E)motion and Narrative in *Anna Karenina*." *Russian Literature* 51 (2007): 341–61.

Taylor, Kathleen. "Disgust Is a Factor in Extreme Prejudice." *British Journal of Social Psychology* 46 (2007): 597–617.

Terence. *Hecyra/The Mother-in-Law*. In *Terence*, translated by John Sargeaunt. Cambridge MA: Harvard University Press, 1965.

Tirso de Molina. *The Trickster of Seville and the Stone Guest*, edited and translated by Gwynne Edwards. Warminster UK: Aris and Phillips, 1995.

Todorov, Tzvetan. *The Fantastic: A Structural Approach to a Literary Genre*, translated by Richard Howard. Cleveland OH: Press of Case Western Reserve University, 1973.

———. *Les Genres du Discours*. Paris: Editions du Seuil, 1978.

———. "Literary Genres." In *Encyclopedic Dictionary of the Sciences of Language*, by Oswald Ducrot and Tzvetan Todorov, translated by Catherine Porter. Baltimore: Johns Hopkins University Press, 1979.

———. *The Poetics of Prose*, translated by Richard Howard. Ithaca NY: Cornell University Press, 1977.

Tolstoy, Leo. *Anna Karenina*, translated by Joel Carmichael. New York: Bantam, 2006.

Toolan, Michael. "Story and Discourse." In Hogan, *Cambridge Encyclopedia of the Language Sciences*, 805–6.

Turner, C. J. G. *A Karenina Companion*. Waterloo ON: Wilfrid Laurier University Press, 1993.

Vālmīki. *Srimad Vālmīki Rāmāyaṇa*, trans. N. Raghunathan. 3 vols. Madras [India]: Vighneswara Publishing, 1981.

van Buitenen, J. A. B., ed. and trans. *The Mahābhārata 1: The Book of the Beginning*. Chicago: University of Chicago Press, 1973.

van Leeuwen, Cees. "Perception." In *A Companion to Cognitive Science*, edited by William Bechtel and George Graham, 265–81. Malden MA: Blackwell, 1999.

Waines, David. *An Introduction to Islam*. Cambridge: Cambridge University Press, 1995.

Walter, Henrik. *Neurophilosophy of Free Will: From Libertarian Illusions to a Concept of Natural Autonomy*, translated by Cynthia Klohr. Cambridge MA: MIT Press, 2001.

Walton, Kendall. *Mimesis as Make-Believe: On the Foundations of the Representational Arts*. Cambridge MA: Harvard University Press, 1990.

Wang Chi-ssu. Foreword to *Selected Plays of Kuan Han-ch'ing*, 5–17. Peking: Foreign Languages Press, 1958.

Weil, Peter M. "Women's Masks and the Power of Gender in Mande History." *African Arts* 31.2 (1998): 89–91, 95–96.

Weis, René, ed. *King Lear: A Parallel Text Edition*, by William Shakespeare. London: Longman, 1993.

West, Stephen H. "Mongol Influence on the Development of Northern Drama." In Langlois, *China under Mongol Rule*, 434–65.

Williams, Raymond. *The Long Revolution*. 1961. Orchard Park NY: Broadview Press, 2001.

Young, Kay. *Ordinary Pleasures: Couples, Conversation, and Comedy*. Columbus: Ohio State University Press, 2001.

Zajonc, Robert B. "Feeling and Thinking: Closing the Debate over the Independence of Affect." In Forgas, *Feeling and Thinking*, 31–58.

Zeami Motokiyo. *Atsumori*. In *The Noh*, vol. 2: *Battle Noh*, edited and translated by Chifumi Shimazaki, 60–87. Tokyo: Hinoki Shoten, 1987.

———. *Yūgao*. In *The Noh*, vol. 3: *Woman Noh*, edited and translated by Chifumi Shimazaki, 69–87. Tokyo: Hinoki Shoten, 1976.

Index

Abhijñānaśākuntālam (Kālidāsa), 23, 168–81; ideology in, 140; subtext in, 220

abstraction, and narratology, 80

Ackerman, Brian P., 38

actional outcome, 40, 42, 47, 57–61, 67; alternative responses to, 37–38; and anger, 190

actional responses, 3, 5–6, 13, 67

Aeneid (Virgil), 207

Aeschylus: *Eumenides*, 221, 232; *Oresteia*, 196, 232

aesthetic judgment, and emotional responses, 256n9

affective science, 9; and narratology, 10, 12

ahiṃsā (nonviolence), 170–71

Alexandrov, Vladimir, 21

alienation, in postmodern fiction, 209

allegory, and resistant themes, 142–43

All's Well that Ends Well (Shakespeare), 214

ambiguity: between innocent and guilty, 226; in works, 138–39

ambivalence: in criminal investigation and court narratives, 195–96, 226, 261n5; in *Faust*, 218; in genres, 20; in minor genres, 195, 251; in *The Mwindo Epic*, 161; and supernatural causality, 231; in "Tale of the Eloquent Peasant," 97; in works, 138–39

anger, 39–40, 189–90

Anna Karenina (Tolstoy), 21, 29–30, 32–40, 62–65, 254–55n1; and appraisal theory, 43–45; expectations in, 50–54; revenge in, 231

antagonists, 122; dehumanization of, 249. *See also* blocking characters

anticipation, 49, 61–62, 66. *See also* working anticipation

appeasement response, 38–39, 41, 255n5

application, 104

appraisal, 42–43, 66–67, 255–56n7; in *Anna Karenina*, 51–54; and culture, 103; and elaboration, 73–74; and perceptual emotion, 47–48; and plasticity, 243

appraisal theory, 19, 42–45, 49–52, 57, 253–54n6, 255–56n7; and belief, 56; and storiness, 83

Aristotle, 16, 79–80; on story structure, 75–77; and tragic fault/error, 94

Aristotle (*Poetics*), 10

art and literature, transformative value of, 242–46

aspect idealization, 122, 161

aspect normalcy: in *Abhijñānaśākuntālam*, 171; in attachment plots, 200; and criminal investigation and court narratives, 195–96; in minor genres, 194; and recurring narrative types, 187; and recurring story patterns, 188. *See also* idealized aspect normalcy aspect realization, endings as, 81

Atsumori (Zeami), 232

attachment: as happiness goal, 189; and
minor genres, 233; and sex, 192, 196–
97; and substitutability, 89–90

attachment genre, summary of, 234

attachment patterns, 33–34, 120–21;
in *Abhijñānaśākuntālam*, 179; and
aspect normalcy, 200; and elaboration, 175; and failed reunions, 207; in
minor genres, 227; place attachment,
30–31, 188; and social factors, 7; in
"Tale of the Eloquent Peasant," 91–92

attachment relations, 200–204; and
death, 190; and empathy, 187; in
minor genres, 222–24

attachment theory, 5

Attar, Farid Ud-Din (*Conference of the
Birds*), 110

attentional focus, 6, 66, 122; and incidents, 61; and inhibition, 57–58

audience experience, 235; and recurring
story patterns, 188; and universality
of genre, 227

audience response, and simulation, 95

audience-response criticism, 102

audiences, 100–103, 135–36; appeas-
ing with pseudo-ideology, 176;
elite, 183, 259nn5–7; and emotional
memories, 14–15, 55–56; heroic
action influenced by narratives, 246;
identification with narrative content,
14; large and impersonal, 181; narrative's effects on behavior of, 241–42;
problem solving activities for, 228,
263n17; and significant consequences
of exposure to narrative, 237–38

author as God, 118

Autumn Moon (film), 262n10

avant-garde cinema, 108–9

Barthes, Roland, 15–16

beauty, 264n1

beginnings, 75–78, 80, 122; as destabilizing events, 79, 122, 151; as goal pursuit, 78–79; journeys as, 112, 114; and
normalcy, 171, 172

behavior, narrative's effects on, 241–42

Being and Time (Heidegger), 29

belief, 56, 60–61, 138

Best Laid Schemes (Oatley), 78

Bharatamuni, 10

Bhavabhūti (*Uttararāmacaritam*), 168

Biebuyck, Daniel P., 22, 165

birth of the hero, 155, 160, 260n13

blocking characters, 257n4; in
Abhijñānaśākuntālam, 174; families as, 173, 249; in *Meenaxi*, 117; in
romantic narrative, 129, 173, 249; in
"Tale of the Eloquent Peasant," 93,
94, 96–97. *See also* helping characters

Bordwell, David: (*Making Meaning*), 11;
(*Narration in the Fiction Film*), 11

Bortolussi, Marisa, 11

brain, and spatial organization, 57–58

Bremond, Claude, 77, 79

Brody, Judith A., 38

Brooks, Peter, 17

Brown, Jane, 216

Bruner, Jerome, 77–78

Cambridge Companion to Narrative
(Herman, ed.), 12

caste: and dharma, 170–71; ideology
of, 172

categorizing, 191–92, 233, 248–50, 264n4

causal attribution, 40, 42, 66; for emotional outcomes, 34–36; and episode,
62

causal connections, 123

causal elaboration, 71, 74–75, 82; and
avant garde cinema, 108; in *Meenaxi*,
115–16

causality, 82–83

causal laws, 82

causal sequences, 76–77, 105–7, 122

chance, as causality, 82–83

The Changeling (Middleton and Rowley), 223

character emotions, 12

character emotions, audience response to, 95

characters, representative, 143

Cheng T'ing-yü, 229

Chikamatsu Monzaemon, 222, 228

childhood experiences, 5

China, 140–42

Chinese drama, 194, 201, 205–6, 229; resistant themes in, 142–50

Chomsky, Noam, theories of, 5

Chūshingura (Japanese drama), 228

Clore, Gerald, 93

coercion, 25

cognition, and emotion, 48

"Cognition, Emotion, and Consciousness" (Herman), 12–13

cognitive science, 1; and narratology, 11, 70

cognitive structure, 190–91

Coleridge, Samuel Taylor, 244

collaborations, 104–5

Collins, Allan, 93

Comedy of Errors (Shakespeare), 201

comic, as narrative default mode, 251

commonality, across works, 8–9

companionate love, 199

conceptual prototypes, 166

Condé, Djanka Tassey, 139, 153, 156–58

Conference of the Birds (Attar), 110

connectionist theory, 167, 260n18

Conrad, David C., 152

consequential occurrences, 186

conventional reaction, 13. *See also* stylistic devises

criminal investigation and court narratives, 192, 195–96, 224–31; ambivalence in, 261n5; and dominant ideology, 250–51; judges in, 263n16; as minor genre, 221; summary of, 234–35; troubled endings of, 263–64n19

critical period experience, and plasticity, 240

critical period triggers, 4–5, 253n4; and expectations, 50; and ideology, 26; and perception theory, 48; and social factors, 7

critical reading, 242

cross-cultural patterns, 9, 19–21, 91–95, 181, 191–94, 254n7; and culture, 98; and happiness prototypes, 128–29, 257–58n3; in minor genres, 194, 234; and preference rules, 185; of themes, 155

culture, 13, 103; and cross-cultural patterns, 98; and genres, 191; and narrative, 123; of Nyanga society, 260n15

Currie, Gregory, 55, 56

curses, as recurring cultural theme, 175–77

Damasio, Antonio, 237–39; *Descartes' Error*, 238; and perception theory, 43

Dans le Labyrinthe (Robbe-Grillet), 207–9, 263n12

da Ponte, Lorenzo, *Don Giovanni* libretto, 215, 230–31

Daśarūpa (Dhanaṃjaya), 78

death: and goal pursuit, 190; and lovers, 178, 181; in sexual narrative, 213

Decalogue V (film), 196

decision making, and emotion, 238–39

dehumanization: of antagonists, 249; and racism, 231

Descartes' Error (Damasio), 238

desire: and plot, 17. *See also* sexual desire

despair, alternative responses to, 38

de Waal, Frans B. M., 247

Dhanaṃjaya (*Daśarūpa*), 10, 78

dharma, 169–71, 176

dialectic, 27

Die Figur im Film (Eder), 12

discourse, 11; and audience, 100–102; definition, 108; and encoded experience, 100; and story, 98

disgust, 147–49, 150

display rules, 59

diversity: and empathy, 248–50; importance of, 244–45

Dixon, Peter, 11

dominant ideology, 188; and criminal investigation and court narratives, 250–51; and social hierarchies, 183

Don Giovanni libretto (da Ponte), 215, 230–31

Don Juan stories, 215–16, 218, 263n15

Dou E yuan (Guan), 22, 139, 141–50, 259n9

The Drum of the Waves of Horikawa (Chikamatsu), 222, 228

Eder, Jens (*Die Figur im Film*), 12

egocentric parietal system, 59

elaboration, 66, 76; in *Abhijñānaśākuntālam*, 179; and attachment patterns, 175; and culture, 103; and empathy, 188; in *The Epic of Son-Jara*, 155; and episodes, 63; in minor genres, 233; of prototypical structure, 182. *See also* causal elaboration

elaborative appraisal: and goal pursuit, 88; and storiness, 84; in "Tale of the Eloquent Peasant," 93, 95

eliciting conditions, 2–4, 61

emotion, 1, 237–40; and belief, 60–61; and cognition, 48; complementary, 3; components of, 57; and ideology, 137; and prototypes, 125

emotional experience, 2–3; and appraisal theory, 51, 54

emotional geography, 31, 41–42; and women, 153

emotional history, 41–42

emotional intelligence, and reading, 245–46

emotional intensification: in *Abhijñānaśākuntālam*, 169; effect on audience, 237; in *The Epic of Son-Jara*, 155; and families, 156–58, 160, 182; in minor genres, 227; in *Oedipus the King*, 229; in parent-child plots, 203; in sexual narrative, 210–11

emotional manipulation, 204

emotional memories, 48, 54, 154–55, 241, 253n4; and attachment relations, 200–201, 203–4; and audience response, 14–15, 55–56; and culture, 103; and emotional responses, 240; and emotion processing, 87, 150; and empathy, 187, 243–44; and episodic triggers, 5; and event, 61; and expectations, 50; and habituation, 241; and ideology, 26, 138, 166; and incidents, 61; and long-term implications of narrative, 242; and perception theory, 48

emotional object, 58

emotional outcomes, 34–36

emotional responses, 238–40; and aesthetic judgment, 256n9; and inhibition, 59; innate, 3–4; smiles as, 38–39; and works, 123

emotional risk, 30–31

emotion contagion, 248, 264n3

emotion elicitors, 48

emotion processing, 87

"Emotions" (Oatley), 14–15

emotions of approach, 6

emotion systems, 4, 5–7, 18, 45–46, 66, 121–24, 181–83; and goal pursuit, 86; isolated, 19–20; mutually enhancing or inhibiting, 6; and recurring story patterns, 11; and story structure, 1–2

emotion triggers, 5–6, 33–34, 48, 54

empathy, 87–88, 186–87, 198–99, 243–50, 257n3; in *Anna Karenina*, 62; and emotional model, 56; and ideology, 140; and revenge plots, 195, 261nn3–64; in stories, 121

empirical genres, 191, 233

empirical prototypes, 191–92

empirical research, and narratology, 14–15

emplotment, 71

encoding, 31–32, 41–42, 66; of experiences, 100; perceptual, 45–46

endings, 75–80, 122, 232; in heroic narratives, 251; in minor genres, 230–31, 235; in problem comedies, 212

English Renaissance revenge tragedies, 221–22, 228

Epic of Gilgamesh, 92

The Epic of Son-Jara, 22, 139, 150–58, 259n10; idealized aspect normalcy in, 197; patriarchal ideology in, 165

epilogue of suffering, 22, 140, 184, 260n15; and guilt, 189; in heroic narratives, 131–33; heroic plot default ending, 251; in *The Mwindo Epic*, 161, 163, 165

episodes, 33–34, 40, 42, 61–62, 65–67; in *Anna Karenina*, 63; and appraisal theory, 43; and causal attribution, 62; and parallelism, 109; in parent-child plots, 202; in recurring story types,

186–87; sequences of, 121; and story structure, 71–72; in "Tale of the Eloquent Peasant," 95; units of, 15

episodic triggers, 4–5

equality, 180–81

Eros, 17–18

ethics, and empathy, 244

Eumenides (Aeschylus), 221; as paradigmatic work, 232

Euripides, *Trojan Women*, 249

event, 33, 36, 40–43, 61, 66; in *Anna Karenina*, 63; and parallelism, 109; in parent-child plots, 202; and recurring story types, 186; in space, 57; and story structure, 71–74

evolution, and emotion, 238

exiled leader, 157, 179

existential explanation, 64–66, 256n10

expandability: of minor genres, 227, 233; of recurring story types, 186

expectations, 50–51, 60

experience enabled systems, 5

experiential triggers, 4–5, 253n3, 352n3

explanation, existential, 64–66, 256n10

expression-triggered emotions, 35–36

expressive outcomes, 3, 5, 13, 33–34, 40; and display rules, 59; and incidents, 61; and inhibition, 47, 57–58

facial expression, 39

facts, and story/discourse distinction, 99

false attributions, 223

familial conflict, 156–58, 160

families: as blocking characters, 173, 249; and emotional intensification, 182. *See also* parent-child plots

family reunions, as prototypical plot element, 180

famine: in *The Epic of Son-Jara*, 151; and genres, 182; and incident-richness, 186; in sacrificial works, 133. *See also* food

Father-son acceptance theme, 14

Faust (Goethe), 216–19; negative prototypes in, 220

fear, 37–38, 45; in *Anna Karenina*, 62; in *The Mwindo Epic*, 163, 260n15

feature sensitivities, 4

feeling, structure of, 150

fertility plot, 211–13, 263n13

fiction, 99; social criticisms in, 188

fictional consciousness, 12

film studies, 206, 262–63nn9–11. *See also* avant-garde cinema

The Flower of the Back Courtyard (Chang), 229

Fludernik, Monika, 70

folktales, 79

food: and genres, 182; as happiness prototype, 126–27; and sacrificial narrative, 148. *See also* famine

forgiveness, 232; as emotional response, 41; and minor genres, 250

Freud, Sigmund, 17–18

friendship, and incident-richness, 186

Frijda, Nico, 14, 35, 43

Frye, Northrop, 16–17

Gabbeh (Makhmalbaf), 115

Gaut, Berys, 14

gender ideology: in *Abhijñānaśākuntālam*, 169–70, 174–75; in *The Epic of Son-Jara*, 151–54, 158

gender relations, 136, 139

genetic instruction, 4–5

Genette, Gérard, 15–16

genre names, 191

genres, 181–83; ambivalence in, 20; audiences for, 135–36; and categorial identification, 248–49; development of, 189–91, 233; as distinct from types, 260–61n1; and ideology, 187;

minor, 23; and preference rules, 185, 260–61n1; and prototypes, 128–29; recurrence of, 185–86. *See also* minor genres

genre structure, in films, 262–63nn11

geographical organization, 188, 203; in minor genres, 228; in sexual narrative, 211

Geuss, Raymond, 24

Gilgamesh. See Epic of Gilgamesh

goal pursuit, 10, 67, 86–88; and beginnings/endings, 78–79, 122; and death, 190; and goal changes, 132; and happiness, 126–27, 134, 181, 189, 251; in *Meenaxi*, 111; in minor genres, 227; and narrative, 83–84; and prototypes, 125; sexual, 2, 253n1; in stories, 121; in "Tale of the Eloquent Peasant," 91–93, 96–97

goals, 42–44; achievement of, 55; in *Anna Karenina*, 52; changing, 132; difficulty increases value of, 93, 96; knowledge as, 216; overarching, 95; and probability assessment, 88–89; and substitutability, 185–86

Goethe, Johann Wolfgang von (*Faust*), 216

Greimas, A. J., 15–16, 77, 79

Griswold, Wendy, 221

group antagonism, 164

groups: and heroic structure, 129–30; membership in, 128, 261–62n6; and story structure, 135–36

Guan Hanqing (*Dou E yuan*), 22, 139, 141–42, 144

guilt, 192; and epilogue of suffering, 189; and limit prototypes, 190; and sacrificial narrative, 188–89, 192

habituation, 56–57, 78; and actional outcome, 59; and emotional memories, 241

Haidt, Jonathan, 148

Hall, Leslie R., 38

Hamlet (Shakespeare), 8, 223–24; troubled ending of, 228

Hamlin, Cyrus, 216

Hawkes, David, 216, 263n15

Hecyra (Terence), 220

hedonism plot, and sexual narrative, 211–13, 263n13

Heidegger, Martin, 91; (Being and Time), 29

helping behavior, 248. *See also* blocking characters

helping characters, 257n4; in *The Epic of Son-Jara*, 157; in *Faust*, 217; in heroic works, 130–31; in romantic works, 129

Herman, David: "Cognition, Emotion, and Consciousness," 12–13; ed., *Cambridge Companion to Narrative*, 12; "Storytelling and the Sciences of the Mind," 13

hermeneutics, 8, 104

heroic action, by audiences influenced by narratives, 246

heroic genre, 182

heroic narratives, 139; audiences for, 135–36; and categorial identification, 249; and endings, 251; and epilogue of suffering, 184; helping characters in, 130–31; *The Mwindo Epic* as, 165; and nationalist ideology, 140–41; normalcy in, 131; and pride, 163; as tragedy, 224

heroic plots: exiled leader, 179; and genre development, 189; and patriarchal ideology, 158

heroic structure, 129–32

historical analogies, 142–43

Hoffman, Martin, 56

Hogan, Patrick Colm, 247; *The Mind and Its Stories*, 19–20

Holland, Norman, 57

home, 30–31; and attachment patterns, 188; and geographical organization, 203. *See also* place attachment

honoring the learned, 181

Husain, M. F., 116, 118–19; *Meenaxi*, 103, 109–13; and resistant themes, 138; use of romantic plot, 136

hypotheticals, 14

idealized aspect normalcy, 197–202; In *Eumenides*, 232; in minor genres, 226, 231, 235. *See also* aspect normalcy

identity categories, 250, 264n4

ideological criticism, 165

ideological elaboration, 169

ideological flexibility, 188

ideology, 24–28, 136–38, 158–60, 165–67, 182–84, 254n8; of authors and patrons, 170; in *Dou E yuan*, 144; and empathy, 140; and minor genres, 227, 234; nationalist, 140–41; in parent-child plots, 203; patriarchal, 152–54, 174–78; and recurring narrative types, 187; and sexual narrative, 210; and stories, 259n8. *See also* pseudo-ideology

idiosyncratic narratives, 193

"If" (Kipling), 14

Iliad (Homer), 132

imagination, 48–49, 67; in *Anna Karenina*, 62; in *Anna Karenina*, 52–54; of the audience, 101; and audience response, 56; and culture, 103; and emotional responses, 238–39; and spatial organization, 58

implicit memories, 5

incident, 18–19, 32–33, 40, 42, 61; in *Anna Karenina*, 62–63; incident-richness, 186; and parallelism, 109; and story structure, 71–72. *See also* incident richness incidental killings, 223–26

incident richness, 186; in minor genres, 226, 233; and parent-child plots, 202; and sexual narrative, 210

inference, 103–4

Ingarden, Roman, 100

in-group/out-group divisions, 165–66, 182–83, 249–50; and empathy, 246–47; and genres, 183; out-group associated with animals, 162; and pride, 188; and racism, 242, 247. *See also* groups

inhibition, 45–47, 49, 57–59, 67; and empathy, 87; and goal pursuit, 93; in *Meenaxi*, 117

The Injustice Done to Tou Ngo, 196, 225–26

innate sensitivities: and perception theory, 48; and plasticity, 240

interpretation, 98, 104, 242

interpretation theory, 104. *See also* hermeneutics

Ise Monogatari (Japanese poetry and narrative collection), 215

Ito, Tiffany, 247

Izard, Carroll E., 38

Jacobson, Thorkild, 214

James, William ("What Is an Emotion?"), 253n2

Japanese drama, 228

Jenkins, Lyle, 5

Joseph, story of, 204

Jourdain, Robert, 48–49

journeys, as beginnings, 112, 114

Kafalenos, Emma, *Narrative Causalities*, 79–80

Kafka, Franz, 261n5; *The Trial*, 230, 263n18

Kagekiyo (Japanese play), 205, 207

Kahneman, Daniel, 63

Kalevala (Finnish epic poem), 160, 212; troubled endings in, 228

Kālidāsa, 168–69, 179–80; *Abhijñānaśākuntālam*, 23, 174–75, 220

Kawabata, Hideaki, 256n9

Keen, Suzanne, 14, 244, 247

Kellogg, Robert, 16–17

Kieslowski, Krzysztof, *Decalogue V*, 196

King Lear (Shakespeare), 106–7, 205; parallelism in, 109

Kipling, Rudyard ("If"), 14

knowledge: as a goal, 216; problematics of, 218

Kristjánsson, Krisján, 140

Kunda, Ziva, 247

Kyd, Thomas, *The Spanish Tragedy*, 225, 228

Labov, William, 10, 76

Lacanian theory, 18

Langlois, John D., 141

language, and narratology, 11

Law, Clara, 262n10

LeDoux, Joseph, 6, 31, 43, 45

Leki, Ilona, 209

limbic system, 6

limit prototypes, 190

linguistic models, 15–16

literary dissent, 143. *See also* resistant works

literary emotion, 54–55

literary ephemera, 204

literary structure, 16–17

literature: and effects on behavior of audience, 241; postmodern, 207–9; providing satisfaction and enjoyment, 239, 264n1; purposes of, 103; and working anticipation, 49

Liu, Jung-en, 142, 144, 147

local contexts, 183
localized genres, 233
love: companionate, 199; and preference rules, 172
lovers, 178, 180–81
lover's dialogue, 253n5

Mahābhārata, 168–69, 178, 205, 212–13
Makhmalbaf, Mohsen, *Gabbeh*, 115
Making Meaning (Bordwell), 11
Mande society, 151–52
Man with a Movie Camera (film), 108–9
Marxist theory, 25, 26–27
māyā (illusion in Vedāntic philosophy), 178
Mayan drama, 229
McCauley, Clark, 148
McCullough, William, 215
mean prototypes, 190
Measure for Measure(Shakespeare), 214
mechanical fancy, 244
Meenaxi (film), 109–20; resistant theme in, 138
melodramas, 203, 206
memory systems, 49–50
mental systems, 44
Mephistopheles as helping character, 217
Miall, David, 15, 65–66
Middleton, Thomas, 223
Miller, Dale, 63
The Mind and Its Stories (Hogan), 19–20
Miner, Earl, 214
minor genres, 23, 192–99, 261n2; characteristics of, 233–34; development of, 190–91; embedded in major genre works, 225; and significant emotional effects, 250–51. *See also* individual minor genres
misogynistic ideology, 177
mistaken identity, 214, 224, 230

mistaken punishment motif, 231
modernist works, 230
moral conflict, 93–94, 122, 257n9
Moretti, Franco, 253n4
Morphology of the Folktale (Propp), 79
Morrissette, Bruce, 209
Mote, Frederick, 141
motif, 151, 175, 231, 259n11. *See also* non-recognition motif
Motomasa, 207, *Yoroboshi*, 205
Murasaki Shikibu, 214, 262nn9–10
murder revenge plot, 221, 223
The Mwindo Epic, 22, 159–65, 260n15; and ideology, 140

narration, sustaining interest in, 10–11
Narration in the Fiction Film (Bordwell), 11
narrative, 7–11, 86; audience response to, 14; comic mode default for, 251; and culture, 103, 123; and empathy, 247; and goals, 2, 86; influence on behavior, 241–42; long-term implications of, 242–44; and neurocognitive systems, 1–2; prototypical, 83–84; public, 86; sacrificial, 22; significant consequences caused by, 237–38
Narrative Causalities (Kafalenos), 79
narrative content, audience identification with, 14
narrative theory: *See* narratology
narratology, 1, 10–12, 14–16; and abstraction, 80; classical and post-classical, 15–16; natural, 70
national identity, 140–41
nationalist themes, 144–45, 155
naturalist approach to emotion, 12–13
naturalistic causality, 82–83
nature, 171–72
networks/network theory, 27, 254n10
neurobiology, 7–8

neurocognitive systems, 1–2
nonrecognition motif, 201, 205–6, 213, 262n8, 263n12
nonviolence, 170–71
normalcy, 30–31, 40–41, 67; in *Abhijñānaśākuntālam*, 171; alienation as, 209; in *Anna Karenina*, 63–65; and beginnings/endings, 76–78, 122, 149–51, 171–72; developmental, 151; in heroic works, 131; in minor genres, 233; in sacrificial works, 134; in sexual narrative, 211, 213; and story structure, 33, 80–81; in "Tale of the Eloquent Peasant," 91–92, 97; temporary, 198
nothingness, 29–30
novels, and empathy, 245
Nussbaum, Martha, 245
Nyanga society, 159, 165, 260n15

Oatley, Keith, 21, 42, 58, 83; and appraisal theory, 43–44; and audience response, 55; *Best Laid Schemes*, 78; "Emotions," 14–15
Odyssey (Homer), 206–7
Oedipus the King (Sophocles), 80, 196, 229–30
Omeros (Walcott), 92
oral narrative, 22; emotion in performance, 13; structural elements of, 10
Oresteia (Aeschylus), 196, 221, 232
Ortony, Andrew, 93
Othello (Shakespeare), 222
Ozu, Yasujiro, 262–63n11

Palmer, Alan, 12
Panksepp, Jaak, 6
Pao, Judge, 229–30
paradigmatic works, 229, 232
paradigms, 166–67
parallel emotion, 3, 87

parallelism, 109, 112, 117–18, 162, 173–74
parental aging, 207
parent-child plots, 198–99; parental abandonment in, 229; parental rejection in, 204; separation and reunion in, 192, 199, 200–203, 206–8, 262n8
particularity, 8–9, 182
passion, and story structure, 1
The Passion of the Christ (film), 60
Pavel, Thomas, 78–79
perception, 48
perception process, 51–54
perception theory, 19, 42–43, 48–52, 57, 253–54n6, 255–56n7; and belief, 56
perceptual emotion, 47–48
perceptual experiences, 45–46; and emotion processing, 87; and inhibition, 59
perceptual system, 49
Perng, Ching-Hsi, 144
Phelan, James, 10–11
phenomenological criticism, 100, 101
phenomenological tone, 3, 6, 253n2; and incident, 61; and inhibition, 57–58
physiological outcome, 61
physiological reactions, 13
physiological response, 60
place attachment, 30–31
plasticity: and appraisal, 243; in emotion, 240
play, 199
A Playboy from a Noble House Opts for the Wrong Career, 201
plots, 1, 17; ideological flexibility in, 188; nonprototypical plots, 185. *See also* individual types of plots
poetics, 104
Poetics (Aristotle), 10
political criticism, 142–43
political hierarchies, and ideology, 140
Popol Vuh, 231

pornography, 187, 210, 253n1

postmodernism, 22, 108–10, 207–9; and criminal investigation and court narratives, 230

power, in sexual narrative, 211–13

preference rules, 72–73, 121–23, 185, 256n1, 260–61n1; goal pursuit as, 83; love supersedes other concerns, 172; and moral conflict, 93–94; and number of primary characters, 83, 85; single author as, 105

Preston, Stephanie, 247

pride, 189; in heroic works, 162–63, 165; and in-group/out-group divisions, 188; as tragic fault/error, 164

private narratives, 86

probability assessment, 88–89

problematic endings: *See* troubled endings

problematics, 24–25; and ideology, 137; of knowledge, 218; in minor genres, 195

problem comedies, 212, 214

problem solving activities for audiences, 228, 263n17

propaganda, 240

Propp, Vladimir, *Morphology of the Folktale*, 79

prosody, 13

prototypes, 25–27, 125, 180–83, 256n1; central and subprototypes, 194; and culture, 155, 157, 193; elaboration of, 168; and exaggerated characteristics, 189–90; and happiness, 126–29, 188, 257–58n3; negative development of, 218–19, 235; romantic, 19; and stories, 19–20, 73, 76, 79–80; of subtexts, 219–20, 235. *See also* limit prototypes; mean prototypes

prototypical narrative: birth of the hero as, 155, 260n13; *Dou E yuan* as, 150; and goal pursuit, 86–87

proximate cause, 36

pseudo-ideology, 170, 175–76, 183

psychoanalysis, 17; influence on literary theory, 15

psychonarratology, 11

punishment, 226–28; inappropriately applied, 222–23; in minor genres, 227; mistaken punishment motif, 231

queer theory, 7–8

quest narrative, 92

Rabinal Achi (Mayan drama), 226, 229, 231

racism: and dehumanizing enemies, 231; and in-group/out-group divisions, 242, 247

Rāmāyana (Vālmīki), 23, 169; gender ideology in, 167–68, 177

readers: *See* audiences

reading literature, 245–46

reason, 16–17, 237–38

recognition, as story element, 10

recurring genres, 185–87

recurring narrative types, 187, 211

recurring story patterns, 11, 12, 16, 186, 188; in sexual narrative, 212

recurring themes, curses as, 175–77

relatability, 72–73

relevance, 103

representational memories, 61

Requiem for a Dream (film), 240, 241

resistant ideologies, 138–39, 183–84, 188; and gender, 180; in *The Trial*, 230, 263n18

resistant themes: in Chinese drama, 142–50; in *Meenaxi*, 138; and patriarchal ideology, 178

resistant works, 138, 144–50

resolution, 161

resolution, in stories, 122

revenge, 222

revenge genres, 226–28, 231; troubled endings of, 263–64n19

revenge narrative, summary of, 234

revenge plots, 8, 220–23, 261n2; and empathy, 195, 261nn3–64; as minor genre, 192; problematics of, 195

revenge tragedy: and English Renaissance, 221–22, 228; *Hamlet* as, 194, 224, 261n2

reversal, as story element, 10

Richardson, Brian, 16, 82

risk, emotional, 30–31

rituals, 17

Robbe-Grillet, Alain (*Dans le Labyrinthe*), 207–9, 263n12

romantic love, 7–8, 182; idealized aspect normalcy in, 197–98; and incidentrichness, 186; as prototype, 127–28

romantic narrative, 249; and sex, 172; and Sufism, 110

romantic plots, 22–23, 182, 183, 253n5; blocking and helping characters in, 129, 173, 249; elements of, 178; and story structure, 80–81

romantic works: audiences for, 135–36; as tragicomedy, 129, 140

Romeo and Juliet (Shakespeare), 55

Rossabi, Morris, 147, 148

Rowley, William, 223

Rozin, Paul, 148

Rureke, Shé-Kárisi, 22, 140, 164–65, 260n17

Ryan, Marie-Laure, 73, 78, 256–57n2

sacrificial emplotments, 141, 151

sacrificial narrative, 22, 133–36, 182; and categorial identification, 249; *Dou E yuan* as, 148–50; and guilt, 192; and sinfulness, 134

sacrificial plots: and film studies, 206;

investigation narrative embedded in, 229; as tragicomedy, 188–89

sacrificial prototypes, 183

sacrificial structure, 133–34, 144

sacrificial tragicomedy, 188–89

sahadharma (husband-wife dharma), 170

salvation story, *Faust* as, 218

Sanskrit drama, 170–71

Sanskrit theorists, 10, 78

Sartre, Jean-Paul, 29

Scarry, Elaine, 49, 56

Scholes, Robert, 16–17

security, and attachment relations, 201–2

self-consciousness, 39

self-sacrifice, 206, 262n9

sensorimotor projections, 49–50, 54, 61, 66; and audience response, 56; and inhibition, 59

sensory experience, and encoding, 31–32

sequences, 69–70; and stories, 72–74, 81–82; and story structure, 85

sex: and attachment, 196–97; and incident-richness, 186; and minor genres, 233; and plot, 17, 221, 222–24; and romantic narrative, 172

sexual desire: dissociated from attachment, 192; and empathy, 187; as happiness goal, 189; and temporary normalcy, 198

sexual desire genre, summary of, 234

sexual genre, 216

sexual motivation system, 18

sexual narrative, 210–19

shame, 36–37, 39, 255n4; in minor genres, 227

Shirane, Haruo, 215

sibling relations, 155, 259–60n12

Simkin, Stevie, 225

Simpson, William, 93–94
simulation, and audience response, 95
sinfulness, 134
Sisòkò, Fa-digi, 151
situation, interpretations of, 45
situational response, 36
smiles, 38–39
Smith, Greg, 262n9
Smith, Molly, 225
Smith, Murray, 14
social constructionist approach to emotion, 12–13
social criticisms, 188
social development, 13, 253n4
social emotions, and event, 61–62
social factors, and emotion, 7
social hierarchies, 188; and ideology, 183; and Vedāntic philosophy, 170
social ideologies, and official justice, 225–26
social issues, and romantic plots, 249
social justice, 232
social sin, 149
Solomon, 206
space/spatiality, 95–96, 255n3; as emotional experience, 29–30; encoding of, 41; and minor genres, 234; and space-time mapping, 91–92, 116; spatial proximity, 72–73; spatial organization, 57–59; and time, 113
space-time mapping, 91–92, 116
The Spanish Tragedy (Kyd), 225, 228
spatial organization, 57–59, 116
spiritual liberation, 181
spiritual parents, 180
startle reflex, 58–59
Stella Dallas (film), 206, 262n9
stereotyping, and reading literature, 245
Stockwell, Peter "Texture and Identification," 14
stories, 42–43, 69, 121–22; components

of, 253n5; constituents of, 1; elements of, 10; and emotional memories, 241; and ideology, 136–37, 259n8; and parallelism, 109; as part of works, 70; prototypical, 84–85, 91, 185; and rituals, 17; and sequences, 72–74, 81–82
storiness, 73, 75, 83–84, 123
story/discourse distinction, 98–102, 123
story frame, 106
story function, 115
The Story of the Circle of Chalk (Li Xingfu), 206
story structure, 125, 181–82; and cross-cultural patterns, 95; and emotion, 8, 10, 15, 70–77, 79–81; and emotion systems, 1–2, 5–6; heroic narratives, 135–36; and recurring narrative types, 187; and sequence, 85
"Storytelling and the Sciences of the Mind" (Herman), 13
structuralism, 16–17
stylistic devises, 12–13
subsidiary plots, 185
substitutability, 89–90, 121, 185–86
subtexts, 219–20, 235
subworlds, 14
Sufism, 110–20, 136–37, 257n7
suggestive work, 143, 146–49
Sumerian literature, 214
Sumidagawa (Motomasa), 207
supernatural causality, 82, 231
system development, 4–5

taboos, 127
tacit anticipation, 33–34
tacit expectations, 39–40
The Tale of Genji (Murasaki), 206, 214–15, 220
"Tale of the Eloquent Peasant," 90–97
Tan, Ed, 11–12, 14
target of emotion, 36, 40

temporality, 36, 61; temporal proximity, 72–73. *See also* time

temporal organization: and imagination, 48–49; and story structure, 70

Terence, 220

"Texture and Identification" (Stockwell), 14

thematic development, 182

themes, 136–39, 155–56; in *Meenaxi*, 114, 117–18; and unity, 107; in works, 103–4, 123

threat-defense plot, 182

threat-defense sequence, 131, 161

time, 66; encoding of, 41; hierarchical structure of, 54; in narratology, 16; and space/spatiality, 113; and space-time mapping, 91–92, 116. *See also* temporality

time sequence, 115

Tirso de Molina, 230–31; *The Trickster of Seville and the Stone Guest*, 215

Todorov, Tzvetan, 15–17, 77, 79–80, 260–61n1

Tolstoy, Leo (*Anna Karenina*), 21, 34, 37, 40, 42, 46, 47, 231

Toolan, Michael, 99

topological frame, 92

tragedy, 79–80; revenge plots in, 194, 224, 261n2

tragic fault/error, 79, 94, 123, 161–64; in *Abhijñānaśākuntalam*, 175

tragicomedy, 80, 129, 140, 188–89, 200

transformative value of art and literature, 242–47

transhistorical patterns, 9, 20–21; in minor genres, 194, 234; and preference rules, 185

The Trial (Kafka), 230, 261n5, 263n18

The Trickster of Seville and the Stone Guest (Tirso de Molina), 215, 220, 230–31

Trojan Women (Euripides), 249

troubled endings, 231, 251; in minor genres, 228–29, 231, 235, 263–64n19

truth, 176–77

tsa-chü: *See* Chinese drama

types, as distinct from genres, 260–61n1

type universals, 127

unity, 105–9, 123; in *Meenaxi*, 112, 119

universal genres, 2

universality, in minor genres, 226–27

usurpation plots, 159, 165, 182; Hamlet as, 223

usurpation sequence, 130–31, 156; and guilt, 192

Uttararāmacaritam (Bhavabhūti), 168

Vālmīki (*Rāmāyana*), 23

Vedāntic philosophy, 170, 171, 180. *See also* māyā

Vertov, Dziga, 108

violence, 163

visual system, 45–46

Walcott, Derek, *Omeros*, 92

Walton, Kendall, 60

Wang Chi-ssu, 144, 147, 149

war, and incident-richness, 186

Weil, Peter M., 151

"What Is an Emotion?" (James), 253n2

Williams, Raymond, 150

Wind and Moon in the Courtyard of Purple Clouds (Chinese play), 201

women, 151–54; associated with nature, 171–72

working anticipation, 49–50, 54; and audience response, 56. *See also* anticipation

working memory, 49–50, 59–61, 66

works, 69–70, 103–7, 123–24, 138–39; discriminatory, 242; heroic, 131–33;

particularity of, 8–9; resistant, 144–50

Yoroboshi (Motomasa), 205
Yüan dynasty, 141–44

Zeami Motokiyo, 232
Zeki, Semir, 256n9
zhongyi, 142

IN THE FRONTIERS OF NARRATIVE SERIES

To order or obtain more information
on these or other University
of Nebraska Press titles, visit
www.nebraskapress.unl.edu.